Parker's Will Precedents

Parker's Will Precedents

8th edition

by

Richard Dew LLB TEP

Kevin Shannon BCL (Int.) Dublin

Bloomsbury Professional

Published by
Bloomsbury Professional Ltd, Maxwelton House, 41–43 Boltro Road, Haywards Heath, West Sussex, RH16 1BJ

British Library Cataloguing-in-Publication Data.
A catalogue record for this book is available from the British Library.

ISBN 978 1 78043 494 0

Typeset by Phoenix Photosetting, Chatham, Kent
Printed and bound in Great Britain by CPI Group (UK) Ltd, Croydon, CR0 4YY

Preface

This work is now into its eighth edition. As new editors to such an established work we approached its revision with some trepidation. We did not wish, in making our revisions, to spoil what had come before us, either in the quality of the text or the elegance and simplicity of the precedents. In the end we have chosen to focus on bringing the work up to date, both in its content (the last edition was in 2011) and in its style.

The title of this new edition has discarded the word 'modern'. Nevertheless, we very much intend this to be an edition with a modern feel and made for the modern world. A feature of that modernity is the ever increasing quantity of regulation which professionals are faced with and its constantly changing nature. So one of the changes we have made is to refer to the requirements of the various regulators or associations, particularly those of the Law Society and of the Society of Trusts and Estate Practitioners (STEP), when taking instructions for, making and then supervising the execution of Wills. We have also been conscious of the requirements made of professionals by the courts in the context of professional negligence and probate disputes.

Another feature of our modern world is the increasing prevalence of digital communication and, accordingly, digital assets. There is some way to go before there are clear and unified means to bequeath digital assets; indeed there is some way to go before even the ownership of such assets is dealt with other than on an ad hoc basis. We have added an additional chapter to this work to assist the Will writer with the issues that present themselves from such assets.

We have not forgotten to address those changes that have occurred recently in this area. So this work is written with the assumption that the Inheritance and Trustee Powers Act 2014 is in force, including its changes to the statutory provisions on maintenance and advancement. We have also revised the work to take into account those areas that currently provide most challenge for the Will writer, by expanding the discussion of inheritance tax and inheritance tax mitigation, flexible life interest trusts, charitable giving and business assets. Given the increasing reach of the Court of Protection we have also added a chapter regarding the principles and practice of obtaining the authority for a 'Statutory Will'.

We owe a great debt to the authors who came before us. The previous editor, Michael Waterworth, is a friend and colleague. Sadly he has not been able to take on this latest edition after suffering a serious accident resulting in a catastrophic injury. His life before the accident was an example to us all as to how to live and work; his extraordinary resilience and character afterwards has been an example to us all when faced with hardships.

Many others have contributed to this work in many other ways. Vincent Oakley has provided many comments and suggestions that have proved invaluable. The staff at Bloomsbury and the editor, Vickie Tomlinson, have been unfailingly helpful in the face of ever moving deadlines. We must also thank our colleagues in chambers, particularly our clerks Keith Plowman, Marc Schofield and Fay Bennett; without their patience this work would not have been possible. Finally, we must thank our families for their continuing love and support.

This book is dedicated to Michael and his family who are always in our thoughts.

The law is stated as at October 2014.

Richard Dew and Kevin Shannon

Ten Old Square, Lincoln's Inn WC2A 3SU

clerks@tenoldsquare.com

Contents

Preface		*v*
Table of Statutes		*xiii*
Table of Statutory Instruments		*xix*
Table of Cases		*xxi*
Chapter 1	**Introduction**	**1**
1.4	Drafting	1
1.10	Precedents	3
Chapter 2	**General Considerations**	**4**
2.2	The intestacy rules	4
2.8	Joint property	5
2.14	Contentious probate claims	7
2.31	Claims under the Inheritance (Provision for Family and Dependants) Act 1975	10
2.45	Foreign issues	14
2.46	Changing circumstances	14
2.56	Binding of wills	16
Chapter 3	**Taking Instructions**	**17**
3.2	Protocols and codes of practice	17
3.5	Arrangements for taking instructions	18
3.14	Taking instructions	19
3.23	Other matters	21
3.25	Checklist	22
Chapter 4	**Opening and Revocation**	**41**
4.2	Identity of the testator	41
4.11	Precedents	44
Chapter 5	**Joint, Mutual and Reciprocal ('Mirror') Wills**	**46**
5.2	Joint Wills	46
5.3	Reciprocal/mirror Wills	46
5.4	Mutual Wills	47
5.11	Precedents	49
Chapter 6	**Foreign Issues and Declarations as to Jurisdiction**	**51**
6.2	Formal validity	51

6.6	Essential validity	52
6.12	English private international law of succession	53
6.18	EU Regulation No 650/2012	54
6.23	Location of declarations as to jurisdiction	55
6.24	Precedents	56
Chapter 7	**Funeral Wishes**	**57**
7.1	Declarations concerning funeral arrangements and disposal of the testator's body	57
7.5	Expenses	58
7.6	Cremation	58
7.7	Donation of the body and organs	58
7.9	Precedents	59
Chapter 8	**Appointment of Executors and Trustees**	**61**
8.1	Definitions	61
8.2	Advice to testator	61
8.5	Executors and trustees	62
8.10	Common appointments	63
8.11	Appointment of a beneficiary	63
8.14	Appointment of a friend or business acquaintance	64
8.16	Appointment of solicitors	64
8.23	Appointment of accountants	65
8.24	Appointment of a trust corporation	65
8.26	Appointment of the public trustee	66
8.27	Power to charge fees	66
8.32	Final points	67
8.33	Precedents	68
Chapter 9	**Appointment of Guardians**	**75**
9.4	Appointment	76
9.9	Revocation	77
9.12	Other points	77
9.14	Precedents	78
Chapter 10	**Legacies**	**80**
10.1	The use and type of legacies	80
10.5	Gifts free of inheritance tax	80
10.8	The priority and timing of legacies	81
10.11	The satisfaction of debts and the presumption against 'double portions'	81
10.13	Nil rate band legacies	82
10.14	Legacies to the draftsman	82
10.15	Precedents	83
Chapter 11	**Specific Gifts of Real Property and Rights of Occupation**	**88**
11.1	Simple gifts of land	88
11.8	Gifts of land on trust	89
11.25	Precedents	95
Chapter 12	**Specific Gifts of Chattels and Other Personal Property**	**100**
12.1	Need for a gift of chattels	100

12.3	Inheritance tax and gifts of chattels	100
12.4	Gifts of personal chattels	100
12.8	Collections	101
12.9	Rights of selection of chattels	101
12.12	Chattels subject to a charge	102
12.14	Releases and gifts of debts	103
12.15	Gifts of shares	103
12.17	Gifts of bank accounts	103
12.18	Precedents	104
Chapter 13	**Business Interests**	**112**
13.2	Tax reliefs	112
13.16	Gift of a business interest	115
13.33	Trustees' powers	119
13.35	Business executors	119
13.37	Precedents	120
Chapter 14	**Charities and Charitable Giving**	**127**
14.1	Introduction	127
14.3	Whether a gift is charitable	127
14.6	Reduced rate of inheritance tax	128
14.12	Gifts to charity	129
14.22	Precedents	132
Chapter 15	**Digital Assets**	**138**
15.1	Digital assets	138
15.5	Current rules	139
15.7	Practical problems concerning digital assets	139
15.12	Digital asset list	140
15.13	Gifts of digital assets	140
15.16	Caveat	141
15.17	Precedents	142
Chapter 16	**Residuary Gifts**	**149**
16.4	Survivorship clause	149
16.30	Precedents	156
Chapter 17	**Minors**	**165**
17.2	Receipt clauses	165
17.3	Trustee powers	165
17.6	Inheritance tax	166
17.13	Income and capital gains tax	167
17.17	Summary of options	168
17.20	Precedents	170
Chapter 18	**Disabled and Vulnerable Beneficiaries**	**172**
18.2	Flexibility	172
18.6	Inheritance tax	173
18.12	Income and capital gains tax	174
18.16	Means tested benefits	174
18.21	Drafting considerations and options	175
18.24	Precedents	177

Chapter 19 Powers of Trustees **181**
19.9 Investment and management powers and duties 183
19.13 Power to insure 184
19.14 Power to borrow 184
19.15 Powers and duties in relation to delegation 185
19.30 Duty of care 188
19.31 Powers and duties in relation to trusts of land 189
19.39 Miscellaneous additional powers 190
19.43 STEP provisions 191
19.45 Precedents 193

Chapter 20 Declarations **198**
20.2 Intermediate income 198
20.3 Legitimated, illegitimate, adopted and step-children 198
20.5 Survivorship, lapse and accrual 199
20.9 Satisfaction and ademption 200
20.12 Precedents 201

Chapter 21 Attestation **204**
21.8 Witnesses 206
21.12 Draftsman's duty in relation to attestation 206
21.20 Precedents 209

Chapter 22 Inheritance Tax **212**
22.3 An outline of inheritance tax 212
22.5 Inheritance tax on death 213
22.9 Inheritance tax on lifetime transfers 213
22.12 Settlements 214
22.17 Age contingent gifts 215
22.22 The spouse exemption 216
22.23 Transferable nil rate bands 217
22.26 Charities 217
22.28 The burden and allocation of inheritance tax 218
22.31 The foreign aspect 218
22.34 Anti avoidance 219
22.37 Precedents 220

Chapter 23 Inheritance Tax Mitigation in Wills **221**
23.4 Agricultural and business property 221
23.8 Avoiding grossing up 222
23.9 Transferable nil rate bands 223
23.14 Nil rate band gifts 224
23.17 Life interests and exempt beneficiaries 224
23.20 Gifts to charities 225
23.21 Short term discretionary trusts 225
23.24 Precedents 227

Chapter 24 Complete Wills **232**
24.6 Precedents 234

Chapter 25 Single Adults **239**
25.2 Precedents 240

Chapter 26 Wills for Married Couples or Civil Partners with no Children **247**
26.2 Precedents 248

Chapter 27 Wills for Married Couples or Civil Partners with Children **253**
27.1 Married couples or civil partners with children 253
27.12 Precedents 257

Chapter 28 Unmarried Couples with Children **280**
28.2 Precedents 281

Chapter 29 Second Marriages or Civil Partnerships **287**
29.3 Precedents 288

Chapter 30 Wills in the Court of Protection **296**
30.1 Introduction 296
30.2 The jurisdiction 296
30.8 Statutory Wills and codicils 298
30.11 Best interests in statutory Wills and codicils 298
30.18 Procedure 300
30.26 Executing the Will or codicil 302
30.28 Precedents 303

Chapter 31 Variations after Death **304**
31.8 Disclaimer 305
31.10 Deed of variation 306
31.19 Precedents 308

Chapter 32 Letters and Other Support Materials **318**
32.3 Letter enclosing Wills for completion 318
32.4 Letter about a life interest trust 319
32.5 Letter about a discretionary trust 320
32.6 Notice of severance 321
32.7 Promisssory note 322
32.8 Appointment ending a short term discretionary trust within two years of death 323

Appendix Part 1: Attestation, Construction and Interpretation **329**

Appendix Part 2: Powers **348**

Appendix Part 3: Intestacy Rules **378**

Appendix Part 4: Inheritance Tax and Capital Gains Tax **383**

Index *393*

Table of Statutes

[*All references are to paragraph number*]

Administration of Estates Act 1925 . . 12.16; 31.19
s 3(4) 2.8
33A 31.8
34 . . . . 8.30
(3) 10.10
35 . . . . 11.4; 33.16
41 . . . . 19.42, 19.45; 24.6; 25.2; 26.2; 27.12; 28.2; 29.3
44 . . . . 10.8
46 . . . . 2.4; 16.10; 35.1
(3) 16.10
46A 31.8
47 . . . . 2.4; 35.2
47A 2.4; 35.3
49 . . . . 2.3
55 . . . . 12.6; 33.17
(1)(x) 12.6, 12.16; 13.29, 13.37; 25.2; 26.2; 27.12; 28.2; 29.3
Sch 1
Pt II (paras 1–8) 10.10
Administration of Justice Act 1977
s 28(1)(b) 35.1
Administration of Justice Act 1982
s 17 . . . . 33.3
18(1) 33.5
(2) 4.7; 33.6
19 . . . . 33.14
20 . . . . 33.19
21 . . . . 33.20
27 . . . . 6.5
28 . . . . 6.4, 6.5
Administration of Justice Act 1985
s 9 . . . . 19.24
Adoption and Children Act 2002
s 66 . . . . 33.27
67 . . . . 20.3; 23.24; 33.28
68 . . . . 33.29
69 . . . . 33.30
Adoption and Children Act 2002 – *contd*
s 70 . . . . 33.31
72 . . . . 33.32
73 . . . . 33.33
139(1) 33.24, 33.25
Sch 3
para 50 . . . . 33.24, 33.25
51 . . . . 33.24
52 . . . . 33.25
Charities Act 2006
s 75(1) 34.19, 34.46
Sch 8
para 197 . . . . 34.46
Sch 9
para 182 . . . . 34.19
Charities Act 2011 . . . . 14.4, 14.22
s 1, 2 . . . . 14.4
3(1) 14.4
37 . . . . 14.3
311 . . . . 14.6
354(1) 34.60
Sch 7
para 90 . . . . 34.60
Children Act 1989 . . . . 9.4
s 2(1) 9.3
3(1) 9.1
(2) 17.2
(3) 19.6
4(1) 9.3
4A, 4ZA 9.3
5(4) 9.7
6(2), (3) 9.9
(3A) 9.11
(4) 9.4, 9.9
(5) 9.12
108(5) 33.1
Sch 1
para 1 . . . . 33.1
Civil Partnership Act 2004 . . . . 1.6
s 71 . . . . 4.7; 33.4, 33.7, 33.17, 33.18; 35.1, 35.2

Civil Partnership Act 2004 – *contd*
s 261(1) 34.2, 34.4
Sch 4
para 1 . . . . 33.7
2 . . . . 4.7; 33.7
3 . . . . 33.4, 33.18
7 . . . . 35.1
8 . . . . 35.2
12 . . . . 33.17
Sch 27
para 5(1) 34.2
(2)(a), (b) 34.2
(3), (5) 34.2
6 . . . . 34.4
Commonhold and Leasehold Reform Act 2002
s 68 . . . . 34.20
Sch 5
para 8 . . . . 34.20
Consumer Credit Act 1974 . . . . 12.12
Corporation Tax Act 2010
s 1124 . . . . 19.24
1177 . . . . 34.46
Sch 1
para 319 . . . . 34.46
County Courts Act 1984
s 148(1) 33.17
Sch 2
para 15 . . . . 33.17
Courts Act 1971
s 56(4) 33.17
Sch 11
Pt II 33.17
Equality Act 2010 . . . . 14.5
s 4 . . . . 14.5
193 . . . . 14.5
(4) 14.5
Estates of Deceased Persons (Forfeiture Rule and Law of Succession) Act 2011 . . . . 31.8
s 1(1), (3), (4) 35.2
2(1), (3) 33.14
3 . . . . 35.2
Family Law Act 1986
s 53(a), (b) 33.6
Family Law Reform Act 1969
s 1(3) 34.2
3(1)(a) 33.2
(2) 35.2
Sch 1
Pt I 34.2
Family Law Reform Act 1987
s 1 . . . . 20.3, 20.12; 23.24; 33.24
19 . . . . 20.3, 20.12; 23.24; 33.25
33(1) 34.4
Sch 2
para 2 . . . . 34.4
Family Law Provision Act 1966
s 1(2)(b) 35.1
s 9, 10 . . . . 35.2
Sch 2 . . . . 35.2
Finance Act 1978
s 68(1)–(5) 36.5
Finance Act 1980
s 93(3) 36.5
Finance Act 1986
s 101 . . . . 36.5
102 . . . . 22.10, 22.34
(1) 22.10
102A–102C, 102ZA 22.10, 22.34
103 . . . . 22.36
Sch 19
para 24 . . . . 36.5
Sch 20
para 6 . . . . 22.11
Finance Act 1998
s 121(3) 36.10
Sch 21
para 1, 5 . . . . 36.10
Finance Act 2002
s 52(1) 36.10
120(1) 36.5
Finance Act 2003
s 49 . . . . 31.16
Sch 3
para 4 . . . . 31.16
Finance Act 2005 . . . . 17.13; 22.10
Sch 1A 18.8
Finance Act 2006 . . . . 16.14, 16.30; 27.6, 27.12
s 156 . . . . 36.7
Sch 20
para 7 . . . . 36.7
27(1)–(5) 36.7
Finance Act 2008
s 8(2) 36.10
10 . . . . 36.1, 36.2, 36.3
Sch 2
para 23 . . . . 36.10
29(1)–(3) 36.10
Sch 4 . . . . 36.4
para 1, 2 . . . . 36.1, 36.2, 36.3
Finance Act 2010
s 30 . . . . 22.26
Sch 6
Pt I (paras 1–7) 22.26
Finance Act 2011
s 65 . . . . 36.4
Sch 16
para 84(d)(i) 36.4
Finance Act 2012
s 209 . . . . 36.4
Sch 33
para 9 . . . . 36.4

Finance Act 2013 . . . . 17.15; 18.8
s 219(1) 36.10
Sch 46
para 74, 79 . . . . .36.10
Finance Act 2014
s 290. . . . . .36.7
Sch 37
para 9, 16 . . . . .36.7
Financial Services Act 2012
s 114(1) 34.55
Sch 18
para 90(1)–(3) 34.55
Gender Recognition Act 2004 . . . . 1.7
Human Fertilisation and Embryology Act 2008
s 56. . . . . .33.24
Sch 6
para 24(1)–(3) 33.24
Human Tissue Act 2004. . . . . 7.7, 7.8
s 3(5) 7.7
56. . . . . .33.1
Sch 6
para 1 . . . . .33.1
Income Tax (Trading and Other Income) Act 2005
s 624, 625, 629. . . . . .31.7
Inheritance and Trustees' Powers Act 2014 . . . . 1.9; 2.4, 2.5; 12.6; 17.4, 17.5; 19.4, 19.7; 22.18
s 1(1)–(4) 35.1
3(1) 33.17
4(1)(a), (b). 33.30
7. . . . . .33.19
8. . . . . .17.4
(a), (b) 34.2
9. . . . . .17.4
(1), (2) 34.3
(3)(a), (b). 34.3
(4) 34.3
(5)(a), (b). 34.3
(6) 34.3
11. . . . . 35.1, 35.3
Sch 3
para 3 . . . . .33.19
Sch 4
para 1(1), (2) 35.1, 35.3
Inheritance (Provision for Family and Dependants) Act 1975 . . . . .2.31, 2.33, 2.34, 2.36, 2.40, 2.41; 5.8, 5.9; 16.30; 20.12; 26.2; 27.9, 27.12; 29.1
s 3. . . . . 2.38; 5.9
(2), (2A), (3), (4) 2.39
4. . . . . .2.32
Inheritance Tax Act 1984. . . . . .16.7
s 1. . . . . .22.3
3. . . . . 22.3, 22.9
Inheritance Tax Act 1984 – *contd*
s 3A 22.3
(2), (4). .22.9
4. . . . . .22.3, 22.5; 23.10
5. . . . . .22.5
6. . . . . .22.32
7. . . . . 22.3, 22.13
(4) 22.9
8A 22.24; 36.1, 36.4
(7) 23.10
8B 22.24; 36.2, 36.4
8C 22.24; 36.3, 36.4
18. . . . . .22.7
23. . . . . 14.2, 14.22; 22.7, 22.26
43. . . . . .22.12
(2) 22.18
Pt III Ch II (ss 49–57A). 11.15
s 49. . . . . .22.13
(1A). 22.15
49A 22.15; 26.2; 27.12
49B 22.15
64, 65. . . . . 22.3, 22.13
71. . . . . .16.18
71A 17.7,17.12, 17.13, 17.16, 17.19; 22.15, 22.18; 23.24
71D 16.18; 17.9, 17.12, 17.18, 17.21; 22.15; 23.24; 27.6, 27.12
89. . . . . .18.6, 18.7, 18.9, 18.10, 18.11, 18.13, 18.15, 18.23, 18.24
(4)–(6) 27.12
89A 18.6
89B 18.6; 22.14
(1) 27.12
92. . . . . .16.7
Pt V Ch I (ss103–114) 13.4
s 103. . . . . .22.6
(3) 13.4
104. . . . . 22.6; 23.4
(1)(b) 23.4
105. . . . . 13.4, 13.5; 22.6; 23.4
(1) 13.37; 23.24
(cc), (d), (e). 23.4
(3) 23.4
106. . . . . 13.7, 13.37; 22.6; 23.4
107–109. . . . . .13.7; 22.6; 23.4
109A 23.4
110–114. . . . . .22.6
Pt V Ch II (ss 114–124C). 13.12
s 114. . . . . .13.15
115. . . . . 22.6; 23.5
(2) 13.37; 23.5, 23.24
(3) 23.5
116. . . . . .13.12; 22.6; 23.5
(2) 23.5
117–121. . . . . 22.6; 23.5

Inheritance Tax Act 1984 – *contd*
s 122–124B 22.6
141 . . . . 16.4
142 . . . . 31.7, 31.17; 36.5
(1) . . . 31.3, 31.6, 31.9, 31.11, 31.19
(2) 31.19
(3) 31.6
(4) 23.19
143 . . . . 12.11, 12.16; 36.6
144 . . . . 12.11, 12.16; 23.21; 36.7
(1) 23.19
160, 168 . . . . 13.37
211 . . . . 22.28
218A 31.12
267 . . . . 6.10; 22.6, 22.31
Sch 1 . . . . 22.4
Table row 1 . . . . 23.10
Sch 1A 14.6, 14.8, 14.22
para 7, 8 . . . . 14.22
Interpretation Act 1978 . . . . 11.11
Intestates' Estates Act 1952
s 1(1) 35.1, 35.2
(3)(a) 35.1
(b)(i), (ii) 35.1
(c) 35.2
(4) 35.1
Law of Property Act 1925
s 36(2) 2.12
164–166 . . . . 16.19
184 . . . . 16.10; 33.15
196(4) 32.6
Law of Property (Miscellaneous Provisions) Act 1994
s 21(2) 33.17
Sch 2 . . . . 33.17
Law Reform (Succession) Act 1995
s 1(1) 35.1
(2)(a) 35.2
3 . . . . 4.7
(1) 33.6
5 . . . . 33.6; 35.2
Schedule 35.2
Legitimacy Act 1976
s 5 . . . . 20.3, 20.12; 33.26
Mental Capacity Act 2005 . . . . 3.20; 21.19; 30.2, 30.11, 30.12, 30.14, 30.28
s 1 . . . . 30.3
(5) 30.6, 30.11
2(1)–(3) 30.4
3(1)–(4) 30.5
4 . . . . 30.13
(1) 30.6, 30.13
(2)–(7) 30.6
16 . . . . 33.21
(1), (2) 30.8
18 . . . . 33.22
(1)(i) 30.8

Mental Capacity Act 2005 – *contd*
s 42 . . . . 30.7
67(1) 33.17; 34.22
(2) 33.17
Sch 2
para 1–4 . . . . 33.23
Sch 6
para 5(1), (3) 33.17
42(1), (2) 34.22
Sch 7 . . . . 33.17
Mental Health Act 1983 . . . . 30.12
Pt VII (ss 93–113) 30.2
Partnership Act 1890 . . . . 13.24
s 33 . . . . 13.25
Perpetuities and Accumulations Act 1964 . . . . 16.16
s 1 . . . . 34.5
4 . . . . 16.19
Perpetuities and Accumulations Act 2009 . . . . 1.8; 16.15, 16.16, 16.19, 16.30; 25.2; 27.11, 27.12
s 1 . . . . 34.6
5 . . . . 34.7
(1) 16.15
6 . . . . 34.8
7 . . . . 16.16; 34.9
8 . . . . 34.10
11 . . . . 34.11
13 . . . . 16.19; 19.5
15 . . . . 34.12
20 . . . . 34.13
Prescription Act 1832 . . . . 33.4, 33.18
Senior Courts Act 1981
s 114(1) 8.4
116 . . . . 8.4
152(4) 33.17
Sch 7 . . . . 33.17
Statute Law (Repeals) Act 1969
s 1 . . . . 33.1
Schedule
Pt III 33.1
Statute Law Revision Act 1893 . . . . 33.1
Statute Law Revision (No 2) Act 1888 . . . . 33.2, 33.4, 33.12
Taxation of Chargeable Gains Act 1992
s 62 . . . . 36.10
(6) 31.3, 31.9, 31.11, 31.19
(7) 31.19
92, 225 . . . . 16.21
Trustee Act 1925 . . . . 25.2; 26.2
s 16 . . . . 19.14
19 . . . . 34.58
31 . . . . 1.9; 16.19; 17.4, 17.5, 17.7, 17.10, 17.11, 17.14, 17.21; 19.3, 19.4, 19.5; 22.21
(1)(ii) 17.5; 19.5

Trustee Act 1925 – *contd*
s 31(2) 19.3
32 . . . . 1.9; 16.18; 17.4, 17.7, 17.14; 18.10, 18.14; 19.7, 19.8; 22.18
69(2) 19.3, 19.7
Trustee Act 2000 . . . . 8.28; 11.8; 19.9, 19.16, 19.22, 19.30, 19.35, 19.36; 25.2; 26.2
s 1 . . . . 19.30, 19.45; 24.6; 27.12; 28.2; 29.3; 34.30
(1)(a), (b) 19.30
2 . . . . 11.10, 11.13; 19.30; 34.31
3 . . . . 11.10; 19.9, 19.10; 34.32
(1), (2) 19.10
(3) 11.12; 19.10
4 . . . . 19.9, 19.10, 19.11; 34.33
(1) 19.11
5 . . . . 19.9, 19.10, 19.12; 34.34
(3), (4) 19.12
6 . . . . 19.9, 19.11, 19.12; 34.35
(1) 19.10
8 . . . . 34.36
(1), (2) 11.11; 34.37
9 . . . . 11.10, 11.12
11 . . . . 19.9, 19.16; 34.38
(1) 19.17
12 . . . . 19.9, 19.16; 34.39
(1)–(3) 19.21
13 . . . . 19.9, 19.16; 34.40
(1), (2) 19.20
14 . . . . 19.9, 19.16; 34.41
(1), (2) 19.21
(3)(a)–(c) 19.21
15 . . . . 19.9, 19.16; 34.42
(1) 19.19
(2)(a), (b) 19.19
(4) 19.19
(5)(a)–(c) 19.19
16 . . . . 19.9, 19.16; 34.43
(1)(a), (b) 19.23
(2) 19.23
17 . . . . 19.9, 19.16; 34.44
(1)–(3) 19.23
18 . . . . 19.9, 19.16; 34.45
(1), (2) 19.23
19 . . . . 19.9, 19.16; 34.1, 34.46
(1) 19.24
(a), (b) 19.13
(2) 19.13
(a)–(c) 19.24
(5) 19.13
(a), (b) 19.24
(6), (7) 19.42
20 . . . . 19.9, 19.16; 34.47

Trustee Act 2000 – *contd*
s 20(1), (2) 19.24
(3)(a)–(c) 19.24
21 . . . . 19.9, 19.16, 19.26; 34.48
22 . . . . 19.9, 19.16, 19.45; 25.2; 26.2; 27.12; 28.2; 29.3; 34.49
(1)(a)–(c) 19.26
(2)(a)–(c) 19.27
23 . . . . 19..9, 19.16, 19.28; 34.50
24 . . . . 19.9, 19.16, 19.28; 34.51
25 . . . . 19.9, 19.16; 34.52
26 . . . . 19.9, 19.16; 34.53
(b) 19.22
28 . . . . . . 19.9, 19.45; 26.2; 27.12; 34.54
(1), (2) 8.29
(4) 8.30; 21.10
(b) 8.30
(5), (6) 8.29
29 . . . . 19.9; 34.55
(1) 8.29
(2), (3) 8.28
31 . . . . 34.2, 34.56
32 . . . . 34.3, 34.57
33 . . . . 34.4
(2)(a) 21.10
34 . . . . 34.58
(1) 34.1
35 . . . . 34.59
(3)(a) 8.30
39 . . . . 34.60
40(1) 34.2, 34.19, 34.22, 34.23
(3) 34.19, 34.22
Sch 1 . . . . 11.10, 11.11; 34.61
para 1–6 . . . . 19.30
7 . . . . 11.10; 19.30
Sch 2
para 25 . . . . 34.2
45 . . . . 11.10
(1)–(3) 34.19
46 . . . . 34.22
47 . . . . 34.23
Sch 4
Pt II 34.19, 34.22
Trusts of Land and Appointment of Trustees Act 1996 . . . . 11.8, 11.14; 19.31, 19.35
s 1 . . . . 34.14
(1)(a) 11.8
(2)(a) 11.8
2 . . . . 11.7; 34.15
3 . . . . 34.16
4 . . . . 16.2; 19.31; 34.17
(1) 11.8
5 . . . . 34.18
6 . . . . 19.32; 34.19
(1) 11.10; 19.32
(2) 19.32, 19.45

Trusts of Land and Appointment of Trustees Act 1996 – *contd*
s 6(3) 11.11
(9) 11.10; 19.36
7 .... 34.20
8 .... 19.32; 34.21
(1), (2) 11.12
9 .... 19.35; 34.22
(1) 11.13
(7) 11.13; 19.35
9A 34.23
(1) 11.13
(2)(b) 11.13
(3)(a)–(c) 11.13
10 .... 34.24
11 .... 19.37; 24.6; 25.2; 26.2; 27.12; 28.2; 29.3; 34.25
(1) 11.14; 19.45
(a), (b) 11.14
(2)(a) 11.14
12 .... 34.26
(1) 11.16, 11.17
(a), (b) 11.16
(2) 11.17
13 .... 19.34; 34.27
(3) 11.18
(1), (2) 11.18
(4)(a)–(c) 11.19
(5)(a), (b) 11.18
(6) 11.18
(a), (b) 11.18
(7)(a), (b) 11.19
(8) 11.19
18 .... 11.10; 34.28

Trusts of Land and Appointment of Trustees Act 1996 – *contd*
s 25(1) 33.17, 33.25; 34.3
(2) 33.1, 33.17
Sch 1 .... 11.7
para 1, 2 .... 34.29
Sch 3
para 3(1), (8) 34.3
6(1), (5) 33.17
25 .... 33.25
Sch 4 .... 33.1, 33.17
Variation of Trusts Act 1958 .... 31.4
Wills Act 1837 .... 21.11
s 1 .... 33.1
7 .... 33.2
9 .... 2.16, 2.17, 2.18; 21.1, 21.2, 21.5, 21.17; 33.3
15 .... 21.10; 33.4
18 .... 2.51; 33.5
18A 2.52; 4.7, 4.8; 33.6
18B 33.7
18C 2.52; 4.7, 4.8; 33.8
20 .... 4.5; 33.9
21 .... 21.3; 33.10
22 .... 33.11
24 .... 12.4; 33.12
29 .... 33.13
33 .... 16.25, 16.26, 16.30; 20.7, 20.12; 27.11; 29.3; 31.8; 33.14
Wills Act 1963
s 11 .... 6.2
Wills Act 1968
s 1 .... 21.10; 33.4, 33.18

Table of Statutory Instruments

[*All references are to paragraph number*]

Cancellation of Contracts made in a Consumer's Home or Place of Work etc Regulations 2008, SI 2008/1816 . . . . . 3.7
Civil Procedure Rules 1998, SI 1998/3132
r 57.1(2)(a) 2.14
PD 40A.15 . . . . . 10.9
Consumer Protection (Distance Selling) Regulations 2000, SI 2000/2334 . . . . . 3.9
Marriage (Same Sex Couples) Act 2013 (Consequential and Contrary Provisions and Scotland) Order 2014, SI 2014/560
art 2 . . . . . 33.24
Marriage (Same Sex Couples) Act 2013 (Consequential and Contrary Provisions and Scotland) Order 2014 – *contd*
Sch 1
para 19 . . . . . 33.24
Non-contentious Probate Rules 1987, SI 1987/2024
r 13 . . . . . 21.7
Rules of the Supreme Court 1965, SI 1965/1776
Order 65
r 14B 12.16
Stamp Duty (Exempt Instruments) Regulations 1987, SI 1987/516 . . 31.15
Schedule
Category M 31.19

Table of Cases

[*All references are to paragraph number*]

B

Banks v National Westminster Bank plc [2005] EWHC 3479 (Ch) 2.49
Banks v Goodfellow (1869-70) LR 5 QB 549 .... 2.19; 3.20
Barns v Barns [2003] HCA 9, (2003) 114 CLR 169, [2005] WTLR 1093 ....5.8
Barry v Butlin (1838) 2 Moo PCC 480, 12 ER 1089 ....2.26
Benham's Will Trusts, Re [1995] STC 210 ....22.30
Berry v IBS-STL (UK) Ltd (in liquidation) [2012] EWHC 666 (Ch), [2012] PTSR 1619, [2012] WTLR 1421...14.16
Birmingham v Renfrew [1937] HCA 52, 57 CLR 666.............................5.8
Blewitt, In the Goods of (1880) 5 PD 116 ....21.3
Bowen Buscarlet's Will Trusts, Re [1972] Ch 463, [1971] 3 WLR 742, [1971] 3 AlL ER 636 ....2.3
Burgess v Rawnsley [1975] Ch 429, [1975] 3 WLR 99, [1975] 3 All ER 142..........2.12

C

Cattermole Prisk [2006] 1 FLR 693, [2006] Fam Law 98 ....2.20
Chapman, Re; Hales v A-G [1922] 2 Ch 479..................................14.4
Cleaver (deceased), Re [1981] 1 WLR 939, [1981] 2 All ER 1018, (1981) 125 SJ 445 ...5.8
Colling, Re; Lawson v Von Winckler [1972] 1 WLR 1440, [1972] 3 All ER 729, (1972) 116 SJ 547.. 2.17; 21.2

D

D, Re [1982] Ch 237, [1982] 2 WLR 373, [1982] 2 All ER 37 ....30.12
D (Statutory Will), Re [2010] EWHC 2159 (Ch), [2012] Ch 57, [2011] 3 WLR 1218.. 30.11, 30.17
Dale (deceased), Re [1994] Ch 31, [1993] 3 WLR 652, [1993] 4 All ER 129....... 5.6, 5.8
Dorman (deceased), Re [1994] 1 WLR 282, [1994] 1 All ER 804, [1994] 2 FLR 52... 2.49; 12.15
Duddell (deceased), Re; Roundway v Roundway [1932] 1 Ch 585...................5.2

E

Esterhuizen v Allied Dunbar Assurance plc [1998] 2 FLR 668, [1998] Fam Law 527.. 21.14, 21.15, 21.16, 21.18

F

Frewen v Frewen (1874-75) LR 10 Ch App 610 ....2.48
Fuller v Strum [2001] EWCA Civ 1879, [2002] 1 WLR 1097, [2002] 2 All ER 87 .....2.25

G

G (TJ), Re [2010] EWHC 3005 (Fam), [2011] Med LR 89, [2011] WTLR 231 . . . 30.11, 30.16
Goodchild (deceased), Re; Goodchild v Goodchild [1997] 1 WLR 1216, [1997] 3 All ER 63, [1997] 2 FLR 644. . . . . 5.7
Gould v Kemp (1834) 2 My & K 304, 39 ER 959 . . . . 2.8
Gray v Richards Butler (supervision of execution) [2000] WTLR 143 . . . . 21.12, 21.14, 21.16, 21.18

H

HM (a child), Re; SM v HM [2012] Med LR 449, [2014] Med LR 40, [2012] WTLR 281 . . . . 18.3
Hall v Hall (1865-69) LR 1 P & D 481 . . . . 2.28
Hancock (deceased), Re [1998] 2 FLR 346, [1999] 1 FCR 500, [1998] Fam Law 520. . . 2.33
Heys (deceased), Re [1914] P 192 . . . . 2.12

I

Ilott v Mitson [2011] EWCA Civ 346, [2012] 2 FLR 170, [2011] 2 FCR 1 . . . . 2.36

J

J(C), Re [2012] WTLR 121 . . . . 30.16

K

Kenward v Adams [1975] CLY 3591 . . . . 2.20
Kinch v Bullard [1999] 1 WLR 423, [1998] 4 All ER 650, [1999] 1 FLR 66 . . . . 32.6
Knox v Till [2000] Lloyd's Rep PN 49, [2000] PNLR 67, [2002] WTLR 1147 . . . . 2.21

L

Langston, Re [1953] P 100, [1953] 1 WLR 581, [1953] 1 All ER 928 . . . . 4.7
Lewis' Will Trusts, Re [1985] 1 WLR 102, [1984] 3 All ER 930, (1984) 128 SJ 385. . . . . 13.30; 23.24

M

M (Statutory Will), Re [2009] EWHC 2525 (Fam), [2011] 1 WLR 344, [2010] 3 All ER 682 . . . . 30.11, 30.14, 30.16
McKee, Re [1931] 2 Ch 145 . . . . 2.3
Martin v Nicholson [2004] EWHC 2135 (Ch), [2005] WTLR 175 . . . . 31.18
Morris, Re; Lloyd's Bank Ltd v Peake [1971] P 62, [1970] 2 WLR 865, [1970] 1 All ER 1057 . . . . 2.24

N

NT v FS [2013] EWHC 684 (COP), [2013] WTLR 867 . . . . 30.11
Nathan v Leonard [2002] EWHC 1701 (Ch), [2003] 1 WLR 827, [2003] 4 All ER 198 . . . 2.43

P

P (Statutory Will), Re [2009] EWHC 163 (Ch), [2010] Ch 33, [2010] 2 WLR 253. . . . . 30.11, 30.12, 30.16
Palmer v Bank of New South Wales (1975) 7 ALR 671, 133 CLR 150, (1976) 50 AJLR 320 . . . . 5.8
Parker v Felgate (1883) 8 PD 171. . . . . 3.17

Phillips, Re [1938] 4 All ER 438 . . . . 12.16
Public Trustee v Till [2002] ZLR 508, [2002] WTLR 1169 . . . . 2.21

R

Ratcliffe (deceased), Re; Holmes v McMullan [1999] STC 262, [1999] BTC 8017, (1999) 96 (11) LSG 70 . . . . 22.30
Rogers (deceased), Re [2006] EWHC 753 (Ch), [2006] 1 WLR 1577, [2006] 2 All ER 792 . . . . 8.21, 8.33
Roundway v Roundway *see* Duddell (deceased), Re [1932] 1 Ch 585
Russell v IRC [1988] 1 WLR 834, [1988] 2 All ER 405, [1988] STC 195 . . . . 31.17

S

SM v HM *see* HM (a child), Re [2012] Med LR 449, [2014] Med LR 40, [2012] WTLR 281
Sansom v Peay (Inspector of Taxes) [1976] 1 WLR 1073, [1976] 3 All ER 375, [1976] STC 494 . . . . 16.21
Selby-Bigge (deceased), Re [1950] 1 All ER 1009, 66 TLR (Pt 1) 993, [1950] WN 231 . . . 21.6
Sen v Headley [1991] Ch 425, [1991] 2 WLR 1308, [1991] 2 All ER 636 . . . . 2.44
Sharp v Adam [2006] EWCA Civ 449, [2006] WTLR 1059, (2007-08) 10 ITELR 419 . . 2.19
Simpson (deceased), Re (1977) 121 SJ 224 . . . . 2.20
Sinclair (deceased), Re [1985] Ch 446, [1985] 2 WLR 795, [1985] 1 All ER 1066 . . . . . 2.52; 4.8
Southerden's Estate, Re; Adams v Southerden [1925] P 177 . . . . 4.10

U

Upton v Jeans (1895) 13 R 627 . . . . 20.4

W

Wilford's Estate, Re (1879) 11 Ch D 267 . . . . 2.12
Williams v Williams (1882) 20 Ch D 659 . . . . 7.1
Wilson v Bell (1843) 5 Ir Eq R 501 . . . . 2.12
Woolnough (deceased), Re; Perkins v Borden [2002] WTLR 595 . . . . 2.8

Z

Zehr, Re [1944] 2 DLR 670 . . . . 27.12; 28.2; 29.3

1 Introduction

1.1 The drafting of a Will is one of the most underrated services offered by legal professionals. It can be hard to persuade a client to pay anything approaching a reasonable fee and professionals themselves have regarded the drafting of a Will as something to be offered at a 'knock down' fee in the hope of attracting other more lucrative work. Yet of the services offered by legal professionals, the drafting a Will is one of the most important. A failure to make a Will before death can cause enormous problems and costs for those left behind, just as a poorly conceived or poorly drafted Will can lead to years of disagreement and dispute. A well drafted Will must take into account a whole series of considerations as to who should benefit and how, must take careful account of the tax implications and must be worded in such a way as all who read it subsequently will understand what to do.

1.2 The drafting of Wills is a complex business. The area is replete with ancient learning and obscure rules and the necessity for simple language is often overtaken by the testator's desire for complex and involved provision. At the same time the Will must take into account a complex and changing tax environment and its drafting can have real implications on the amount of tax that is paid. This is not something to be attempted without knowledge and experience and only then with careful reference to a well-established text.

1.3 In all its editions, this book has been intended to set out, in a clear and modern form, the considerations that apply to all aspects of Will drafting together with clear and helpful precedents. It is intended as a guide for the busy practitioner on the most commonly encountered issues and considerations that arise in Will drafting. It does not attempt to be a comprehensive treaty on all areas of Wills or Will drafting and neither does it seek to set out all the applicable taxation or available tax planning schemes.

Drafting

1.4 The purpose of a Will is to convey, in clear terms, what is to happen to the testator's estate after his death. In doing so the onus should be on precision, accuracy and effectiveness of communication. The discipline of using tried and tested set forms is an enormous benefit to clients and draftsmen alike and the use of plain language can help a clear thinker to express himself precisely and a muddled thinker to focus his mind.

1.5 In a good Will a complicated provision should be expressed simply, clearly and concisely in a manner which can be understood by clients and lawyers alike. However, the draftsman should remember that the client is mainly, if not exclusively, interested in the destination rather than the fine technical detail of the vehicle and the route used to get there. The draftsman, on the other hand, must take care to ensure that what he produces will achieve the client's aims: sloppy, vague, ambiguous and ill thought out attempts to impose plain language in place of meaningful and precise technical phrases do much more harm than good. The draftsman should, in all cases, exercise clear-headed, independent judgment in selecting and tailoring precedents for he who tries to force an ill-fitting precedent onto a client is also forcing a client into a precedent.

1.6 The advent of civil partnerships and of gender recognition has, unfortunately, added to the difficulty of adapting a suitable Will precedent. Very little needs to be said about civil partnerships, because the effect of the Civil Partnership Act 2004 is to make civil partners equivalent to heterosexual spouses[1]. However, a point which many draftsmen miss is that in the case of a widowhood interest (ie an interest which terminates on death or remarriage) express provision should also be made for termination on the formation of a civil partnership. Similarly, if it is to be effective, an interest limited in favour of a surviving civil partner ought to be made terminable on that civil partner 'dying, forming a new civil partnership or marrying'.

1 Civil partners are not necessarily homosexual, there being no concept or possibility of sexual consummation (exclusively by male–female vaginal penetration) in the formation of a civil partnership, nor of adultery (likewise) in the ending of it.

1.7 In deference to the Gender Recognition Act 2004 the Will draftsman should now be somewhat wary of unspecific class gifts to 'daughters' or 'sons'[1] in case of accidentally including or excluding a person who has changed gender when the testator did not intend that result. By way of example, a gift to 'my daughters born female' probably does the trick. Likewise a gift of 'my farm to my eldest son' should be clarified by naming the son lest his elder sister alter her gender and attempt to take the gift[2].

1 Or to nephews, nieces, grandsons, granddaughters etc.
2 An absurd example, perhaps, but hopefully the point is clear.

1.8 In respect of Wills made on or after 6 April 2010 drafting is simplified by the Perpetuities and Accumulations Act 2009 in two respects. First, this Act has abolished the statutory restrictions on accumulations that, over the last two centuries, have curtailed the power of trustees to accumulate income. This means that it is no longer necessary to restrict the power to accumulate to a period of 21 years, a formulation which tended to confuse clients. Accumulation is now permitted throughout the period of any trust and all that is needed is a power to accumulate in general terms. The second change brought about by the Perpetuities and Accumulations Act 2009 is that, for Wills made on or after 6 April 2010, the perpetuity period is now 125 years. This also serves to simplify Will drafting by removing the need to consider lives in being and the like. Whereas previously, a gift to children might have specified that it should vest at the age of 30 but the gift over to their children would have had to vest at the age of 21 years, it is no longer necessary to draft trusts with those discrepancies. Both of these matters are discussed further in **chapter 16**.

1.9 The Inheritance and Trustees Powers Act 2014 has extended significantly the statutory powers of maintenance and advancement contained in ss 31 and 32 of the Trustee Act 1925 and it may no longer be necessary to further extend those powers. This is further considered in **chapter 19**.

Precedents

1.10 This is a book of precedents and we fully expect that practitioners will turn to this book in order to see how to best express a testator's wishes or to see what different forms of words should be used. Precedents are, though, only examples. Consideration should always be given as to whether the particular wording is appropriate for the circumstances and whether suitable adaptations should be made to meet those circumstances. Similarly, the precedents appear at the end of the chapters because those chapters explain the law and background of those precedents and we urge the reader to consider the text as carefully as the precedents and to read the notes to the precedents as well.

1.11 Many of the precedents in this book give alternatives in square brackets and some optional additions are bordered by obliques[1]. When using these precedents the draftsman should take the greatest care in the choice (and printing) of alternatives and additions.

1 Particular cases in point are the alternatives '[husband]/[wife]/[civil partner]' and '[children]/[daughters]/[sons]' and the optional contingency provisions 'such as / and attain 25'.

2 General Considerations

2.1 Before proceeding to take instructions for the drafting of a Will there are a number of potential issues of which the draftsman must be aware. Usually it is unnecessary for the draftsman to delve too deeply into any of these but it is important that the draftsman is aware of them in order to ask suitable questions during the taking of instructions and to be aware of the need to take appropriate actions if any of these issues arise. This chapter intends to give a brief introduction to these issues and specialised texts should be consulted for more detailed discussions on any of the issues.

The intestacy rules

2.2 A full intestacy occurs where there is no disposition of a person's estate because he has not left a valid Will. A partial intestacy occurs when there is an incomplete disposition of a person's estate. This occurs where the testator has left a Will which either fails to dispose of all of his property or the whole of the beneficial interest in that property. The former sort of partial intestacy (eg where a testator disposes of all of his money and other personal property but fails to dispose of his house) is easily avoided by the Will draftsman making use of a comprehensive gift of residue.

2.3 The latter sort of partial intestacy is more subtle and causes more complications. It can occur, for example, when a testator makes provision for the disposition of a capital interest in property but fails to dispose of the intermediate income (or vice-versa). Similarly, if the property is left on the happening of a contingency but the provisions disposing of the property in the event of the contingency not being satisfied are inadequate this can again result in a partial intestacy[1]. Cases of apparent partial intestacy, particularly of the latter kind, can give rise to difficult questions of construction and distribution[2]. For these reasons, as well as the obvious reason that such partial intestacy is almost certainly not intended by the testator, the Will draftsman should make sure that the Will disposes of all the property of the testator without leaving the possibility of any partial intestacy of any kind.

1 As in *Re Bowen-Buscarlet's Will Trusts* [1972] Ch 463 where, as a result of a drafting mishap, the testator's Will gave a life interest in residue to his widow but did not provide for what was to happen thereafter.

2 The application of the intestacy rules to cases of partial intestacy is governed by Administration of Estates Act 1925 s 49 but, as *Re Bowen-Buscarlet's Will Trusts* [1972] Ch 463 and *Re McKee* [1931] 2 Ch 145 show, the outcome can be difficult to fathom.

2.4 The current statutory rules regarding the distribution of the residuary estate of an intestate are contained in the Administration of Estates Act 1925 ss 46 to 47A[1]. These rules have recently been changed by the Inheritance and Trustees' Powers Act 2014 which came into force on 1 October 2014. The current distribution under intestacy varies according to whether or not the intestate leaves a spouse or civil partner and whether they leave issue. If there is a spouse or civil partner but no issue the spouse or civil partner takes absolutely (even if brothers, sisters or parents survive). If the intestate leaves a spouse or civil partner and issue, the spouse or civil partner will take the personal chattels[2] absolutely (regardless of their value), a fixed sum (irrespective of the value of the estate), a life interest in one-half of the remainder of the residuary estate with the remainder (including the interest falling in on the spouse's death) being held on trusts prescribed by Administration of Estates Act 1925 s 47[3] for the issue. Currently the fixed sum is £250,000. Following the coming into force of the Inheritance and Trustees Powers Act 2014 it will increase with the Consumer Prices Index.

1 See **appendix 35.1–35.3**.
2 Defined at Administration of Estates Act 1925 s 55(1)(x): see **appendix 33.17**.
3 See **appendix 35.2**.

2.5 Prior to the enactment of the Inheritance and Trustees' Powers Act 2014 the spouse or civil partner's interest would have also been reduced if the intestate had left no issue but had left a parent, brother, sister, nephew or niece. However, the 2014 Act has removed all intestate rights of parents, brothers, sisters, nephews and nieces where the spouse or civil partner survives.

2.6 In general, people who die intestate leaving a partner and children have either given the question of the disposition of their estate no thought at all or mistakenly believe that their partner will inherit everything. This mistaken belief is particularly damaging in the case of unmarried cohabiting couples where a surprisingly large proportion believe that they acquire rights as 'common law husband and wife'. Mere cohabitees have, at this moment, no rights under the intestacy rules regardless of how long they have been cohabiting. Despite the harshness this may cause to cohabitees in long-term relationships this position is unlikely to change in the near future. The Law Commission examined this area and produced a draft bill which would have given certain unmarried partners who had lived together for five years (two years if they had a child together) the right to inherit under the intestacy rules[1]. However, the government has announced that these recommendations will not be implemented during this Parliament. Pure cohabitees, therefore, will remain unable to inherit under the intestacy rules for the foreseeable future.

1 Law Commission (LAW COM No. 331) – Intestacy and Family Provision Claims on Death.

2.7 The restrictive nature of the intestacy provisions and the fact that they do not give any rights to unmarried cohabiting couples is often not appreciated by the layman and the avoidance of their inflexible impact is often the best reason a Will draftsman can give for his employment.

Joint property

2.8 Property held jointly with another person or persons may be held under either a joint tenancy or a tenancy in common. This distinction is very important as only joint property held under a tenancy in common can pass under a Will. Property held under a tenancy in common forms part of the testator's estate and the testator's share of the joint property will pass under the Will or under intestacy. By contrast, property of any sort (whether land or personal property) which is held under a joint tenancy does not form part of the testator's estate (except for inheritance tax purposes). This is because on the death of a person entitled to property under a beneficial joint tenancy, the whole of the beneficial interest in the property automatically accrues to the surviving joint tenant(s) by right of survivorship and cannot therefore pass under that person's Will. The beneficial interest of the deceased person does not pass to another person but rather just ceases to exist at all[1]. This means that a legacy in a Will purporting to dispose of an interest in property held on a joint tenancy will fail. It is therefore vital that the draftsman establishes whether or not the testator holds any property on a joint tenancy and, if so, whether the testator wishes such property to pass by survivorship or whether he wishes the joint tenancy to be brought to an end in order that he can pass his share of the property under his Will[2].

1 Administration of Estates Act 1925 s 3(4).

2 A Will does not bring a joint tenancy to an end (*Gould v Kemp* (1834) 2 My & K 304) although, in an extreme case, it is possible that instructions given by joint owners in connection with Will-making might amount to a course of dealing or mutual agreement sufficient to end the joint tenancy (*Re Woolnough, Perkins v Borden* [2002] WTLR 595).

2.9 The distinction between joint property held under a joint tenancy and that held under a tenancy in common arises most frequently in relation to land but also applies to other property (such as bank accounts), which may also be held either jointly or as tenants in common.

2.10 The position regarding jointly owned land is that the legal interest (or legal title) must be held as joint tenants because a legal estate in land cannot be held on a tenancy in common. The beneficial interest in the land can, however, be held as tenants in common. Where this is the case the joint title holders are only trustees holding the legal interest in the land on trust for the beneficial owners in accordance with their tenancy in common. The beneficial interest in the land can be held as either joint tenants beneficially (where the survivor takes all), or as tenants in common (where each beneficial owner has a 'share' which can be disposed of by Will).

2.11 The distinction between joint property held on a joint tenancy and on a tenancy in common is not widely understood which means that many testators talk about having 'a share' of a property even though they own it as a beneficial joint tenant. If the draftsman simply takes the testator's word at face value and includes a gift of 'my share of the property at ...' this can open up the draftsman to potential negligence actions if it later turns out that the property in question was owned by the testator and another as beneficial joint tenants so that nothing passes under the gift in the Will. It is also important to note that, in the case of land, the absence of a restriction on the title is not determinative of the question whether the property is held as joint tenants or as tenants in common and the matter may need to be investigated further.

2.12 Where it is known that the client holds property as a joint tenant but does not wish it to pass under survivorship the solution is to 'sever' the beneficial joint tenancy. This does not alter the way in which legal title is held, but converts the beneficial interests into shares held on a tenancy in common meaning the client's share can pass under his Will. There are various ways of severing the joint tenancy including:

- notice to the other joint tenant(s);
- an act of any one of the joint tenants interested operating upon his own share;

- mutual agreement[1]; and
- a course of dealing between the joint tenants sufficient to intimate that their interests were mutually treated as constituting a tenancy in common[2].

In the case of land, a beneficial joint tenancy is most often severed by giving a notice in writing in accordance with Law of Property Act 1925 s 36(2)[3].

1 As in *Burgess v Rawnsley* [1975] Ch 429.
2 See, for example, *Wilson v Bell* (1843) 5 Ir Eq R 501. An agreement to make mutual Wills is effective for this purpose: *Re Wilford* (1879) 11 Ch D 267; *Re Heys* [1914] P 192.
3 An example and further discussion of service of a notice of severance can be found in **chapter 32**.

2.13 Clients often wish their interest in the joint property to pass under their Will but are unaware of whether they hold property as joint tenants or tenants in common. In this situation the recommended course is to serve a notice severing the joint tenancy (which may or may not exist) in order to make certain that the property does not pass by survivorship.

Contentious probate claims

2.14 A Probate Claim is a claim for the grant of probate of the Will, or letters of administration of the estate, of a deceased person; the revocation of such a grant; or a decree pronouncing for or against the validity of an alleged Will; not being a claim which is non-contentious (or common form) probate business[1]. A Will draftsman never wishes his Will to be at the centre of a contentious Probate Claim and should strive to avoid this happening. While it will never be possible to guarantee completely avoidance of such hostile litigation, if the draftsman is aware of the potential challenges to a Will it is easier to take steps to minimise the risk of such a claim being brought.

1 CPR 57.1(2)(a).

2.15 Probate Claims usually involve allegations of one or more of the following:
(1) That the testator did not properly execute his Will.
(2) That the testator lacked testamentary capacity to make a Will.
(3) That the testator did not know or approve the contents of his Will.
(4) That the testator was acting under undue influence when the Will was made.
(5) That the Will was made by fraud.

Improper execution

2.16 The ordinary formalities[1] for a properly executed Will are laid down in s 9 of the Wills Act 1837. Section 9 holds that no Will shall be valid unless:
(a) it is in writing, and signed by the testator, or by some other person in his presence and by his direction; and
(b) it appears that the testator intended by his signature to give effect to the will; and
(c) the signature is made or acknowledged by the testator in the presence of two or more witnesses present at the same time; and
(d) each witness either—
  (i) attests and signs the will; or
  (ii) acknowledges his signature;
  in the presence of the testator

1 Statutory Wills and the Wills of those on active service are exemptions from the ordinary formalities.

2.17 The requirements of s 9 are strict and a failure to follow them is likely to result in a successful challenge to the Will. Thus, if the witnesses sign the Will before the testator it will be invalid. Similarly, if the testator signs his name in the presence of one witness who signs and then acknowledges his signature in the presence of the two witnesses with the second witness signing, the Will is still invalid[1]. In this case the first witness would also have to sign again after the acknowledgement to be valid.

1 *Re Colling, Lawson v Von Winckler* [1972] 3 All ER 729.

2.18 The requirements of due execution and the draftsman's duty in respect of such execution are discussed further in **chapter 21**. It should be noted, provided the Will is executed under the supervision of the Will draftsman or some other person properly equipped and qualified to supervise execution and the qualified person gives evidence that s 9 was followed, this will usually suffice to extinguish any claim that the Will was not properly executed.

Lack of testamentary capacity

2.19 The test of testamentary capacity derives from the following well-known statement of Cockburn CJ in *Banks & Goodfellow*[1]:

> 'It is essential to the exercise of such a power [to make a Will] that a testator shall understand the nature of the act and its effects; shall understand the extent of the property of which he is disposing; shall be able to comprehend and appreciate the claims to which he ought to give effect; and with a view to the latter object, that no disorder of the mind shall poison his affections, pervert his sense of right, or prevent the exercise of his natural faculties – that no insane delusion shall influence his will in disposing of his property and bring about a disposal of it which, if the mind had been sound, would not have been made.'

That statement highlights the common law test of capacity and continues to be cited in modern Probate Claims. The test requires that four things must exist at the time of making a Will[2]:

(1) the testator must be capable of understanding that he is giving his property to one or more objects of his regard;
(2) he must be capable of understanding and recollecting the extent of his property;
(3) he must also be capable of understanding the nature and extent of the claims upon him both of those who he is including in his Will and those who he is excluding from his Will; and
(4) no insane delusion shall influence his Will in disposing of his property and bring about a disposal of it which, if the mind had been sound, would not have been made.

1 (1870) LR 5 QB 549 at 565.
2 *Sharp v Adam* [2006] EWCA Civ 449, [2006] WTLR 1059.

2.20 In cases in which the testator's capacity is in doubt the Will draftsman is put in a very difficult position. It is said that there is a 'golden rule' that where there is a doubt as to the testator's capacity, a medical practitioner should be present both to witness the Will and to examine the testator and make a record of his findings[1]. However, that is not, of itself, a touchstone of validity, but only a means of minimising disputes[2]. In addition, the involvement of such medical practitioner takes time and incurs expense which may be in conflict with the draftsman's duty to prepare a Will with all reasonable speed. The Law Society Guidance on preparing Wills provides that where it is not possible to obtain a medical opinion as to the testator's capacity then the solicitor should explain to the client that the absence of such a report might leave the Will open to later challenge and should ask the client to confirm that they nevertheless wish to continue. That advice and the testator's response should then be recorded on the file.

1 *Re Simpson* (1977) 121 Sol Jo 224; *Kenward v Adams* [1975] CLY 3591.
2 *Cattermole v Prisk* [2006] 1 FLR 693.

2.21 The question of the solicitor's duty in relation to mental capacity has been considered by the New Zealand Court of Appeal who held that ordinarily the question of capacity is outside the draftsman's professional expertise[1]. The court noted the fact that a solicitor who has suspicions about his testator client's mental capacity will meet confidentiality problems and conflicts of interest. In a subsequent decision at first instance, the court accepted that there could be a duty on a solicitor to consider and advise a testator about capacity but ordinarily a solicitor is bound to carry out the testator's instructions and the solicitor may not make inquiries of other persons about his capacity without his authority[2].

1 *Knox v Till* [2002] WTLR 1147.
2 *Public Trustee v Till* [2002] WTLR 1169.

2.22 The question of capacity is sometimes a matter which must be approached with some delicacy. A Will draftsman is always subject to the testator's instructions but if there is reason to doubt his mental capacity it is advisable to stick to the 'golden rule' and arrange for a medical practitioner to certify that he is capable. If the practitioner is satisfied that the testator is of sound mind he should be asked to act as an attesting witness.

2.23 **Chapter 3** deals with the taking of instructions and the following of the guidance there should help minimise future challenges to capacity and protect the draftsman from allegations of negligence in the preparation of the Will.

Knowledge and approval

2.24 Before a Will is admitted to probate the court must be satisfied that the testator knew and approved of the contents of the Will at the time he signed it[1]. The claim that a testator did not know and approve of the contents of the Will is usually pursued alongside a claim for want of capacity but they are two different claims and it is clear that a testator could have capacity but not know and approve of the contents of the Will and vice-versa.

1 *Re Morris, Lloyds Bank Ltd v Peake* [1970] 1 All ER 1057.

2.25 In an ordinary case, proof of testamentary capacity and proof of due execution of the Will are sufficient to establish knowledge and approval of the Will but where the circumstances of the Will are sufficient to found the court's suspicion, the person propounding the Will must prove affirmatively that the Will represents the wishes of the deceased[1]. Thus, for example, if the draftsman receives a benefit under the Will this is likely to exercise the court's suspicion and the court will require the person propounding the Will to prove knowledge and approval.

1 *Fuller v Strum* [2001] EWCA Civ 1879, [2002] All ER 87, [2002] 1 WLR 1097, [2002] FCR 608.

2.26 Unusual circumstances aside, following the guidance contained in **chapter 3** and taking instructions for the Will exclusively from the testator and in the absence of any person who might benefit under the Will and reading the Will over to the testator before execution, generally provides an adequate defence to any allegation that a testator did not know or approve the contents of the Will[1]. An appropriate attestation clause[2] is also of presumptive importance.

1 *Barry v Butlin* (1838) 2 Moo PCC 480.
2 See **chapter 21**.

2.27 Sometimes taking instructions by telephone from the principal beneficiary (often a child of the testator), or from the testator with the principal beneficiary present or posting a Will to the beneficiary for the testator to execute is unavoidable. However, the draftsman should be aware of the greater potential for a challenge on the basis of lack of knowledge and approval when such steps are taken and should take steps to minimise the risk or at least warn the testator of the risk of such a challenge. In a perfect world the Will draftsman would only ever take instructions from the testator alone, having first satisfied himself that the testator is who he claims to be.

Undue Influence

2.28 In the case of Wills, undue influence means coercion. As Sir J P Wilde put it[1]:

> 'Persuasion is not unlawful, but pressure of whatever character if so exerted as to overpower the volition without convincing the judgment of the testator, will constitute undue influence, though no force is either used or threatened.'

1 *Hall v Hall* (1868) LR 1 P&D 481 at 482.

2.29 Unlike inter vivos contracts there is no presumption of undue influence with regard to Wills and there must be positive proof of coercion overpowering the volition of the testator. Unfortunately, many of those unfamiliar with Wills are not aware of the distinction and challenges to Wills based on presumed undue influence are not unheard of. The best that a Will draftsman can do to avoid potential undue influence claims is to see the testator alone when taking instructions and executing the Will.

Fraud

2.30 Fraud is a serious matter which, in the case of Wills, usually involves falsifying the testator's signature. That is not something which should concern a Will draftsman provided he is satisfied that the person instructing him is who they claim to be.

Claims under the Inheritance (Provision for Family and Dependants) Act 1975

2.31 Under the Inheritance (Provision for Family and Dependants) Act 1975, a variety of people may make an application to the court for an award on the basis that the testator's Will or the law relating to intestacy fails to make reasonable financial provision for the applicant.

2.32 A claim lies only where the testator died domiciled in England and Wales[1] and should ordinarily be made within six months of the grant of representation being obtained[2] although permission may be given to make a claim out of time[3]. A large number of such claims are made every year. Some claims are brought in cases of intestacy but the more contentious claims are those brought by persons who believe that a Will has failed to make reasonable financial provision for them either because they are excluded from the Will completely or because they believe their interest under it is inadequate.

1 The Law Commission (Law Commission (LAW COM No. 331) – Intestacy and Family Provision Claims on Death) recommended removing the domicile pre-condition in certain circumstances but this recommendation was not been carried forward into the Inheritance and Trustees' Powers Act 2014.

2 Inheritance (Provision for Family and Dependants) Act 1975 s 4.

3 This book is not concerned with technical or procedural aspects of such claims. Reference should be made to specialist texts where appropriate.

2.33 The potential applicants under this Act are as follows:

(i) A spouse or civil partner of the deceased;
(ii) A former spouse or civil partner of the deceased;
(iii) A cohabitee who has been living as the husband or wife or civil partner of the deceased for the preceding 2 years;
(iv) A child of the deceased[1];
(v) A person who in the case of any marriage or civil partnership to which the deceased was a party was treated by the deceased as a child of the family in relation to the marriage or civil partnership;
(vi) Any person who was being maintained by the deceased immediately before his death.

1 This includes adult children. There are no special requirements which need to be satisfied before such an adult child can claim. In particular, there is no requirement that the adult child show some sort of moral obligation owed to him or her by the deceased or other special circumstances which entitle him or her to recover under the 1975 Act: *Re Hancock* [1999] 1 FCR 500.

2.34 For the purposes of the Will draftsman it is important only to be alert to the possibility that a claim might be made under the Act and to advise the testator accordingly. In order to avoid difficulty after death and as a matter of good practice the Will draftsman should inquire whether there is anyone in those categories and ask the testator to consider what provision (if any) is being made for those persons by his Will.

2.35 It is not the job of the Will draftsman to seek to persuade the testator to make provision for potential claimants even where it is apparent that a testator is set on a course likely to provoke a potential claimant to make a claim. Keeping an attendance note of the advice given and any comments of the testator is, however, advisable, in order to avoid or minimise future difficulty for the Will draftsman.

2.36 It does not follow that a person who is within one of the recognised classes of applicant will be able to make out a claim under the Act. When considering an application under the Act, the court may only make an order if it concludes that the testator's Will (or the law on intestacy) fails to make reasonable financial provision for the applicant. Sometimes it is reasonable to make no provision for a potential applicant. This is especially true if the potential applicant is independently wealthy and/or able to earn a living. Mature adult children with their own financial security and to whom the testator owes no special moral obligation will have considerable difficulty in maintaining a claim even if they are left nothing under their parent's Will[1]. There is, however, nothing that can be done to stop a determined applicant from pursuing a claim against the estate even if that claim is ultimately unsuccessful.

1 In *Ilott v Mitson* [2011] EWCA Civ 346, [2012] 2 FLR 170 the Court of Appeal re-emphasised that an adult child faces no greater 'hurdle' than any other applicant under the Act. Nevertheless, any claim is founded upon the provision (or lack of provision) not being reasonable and that is not easy to establish where no obligation or other reason to make provision exists.

2.37 If the court is satisfied that the testator's Will fails to make reasonable financial provision for the applicant it must then go on to consider what would be reasonable financial provision for the applicant in all of the circumstances. In the case of an application by a surviving spouse or civil partner, 'reasonable financial provision' means such provision it would have been reasonable for the testator to have made. In all other cases, 'reasonable financial provision' means such provision as it would have been reasonable for the applicant to receive for his maintenance (a term in respect of which there is no statutory definition).

2.38 Section 3 of the Act sets out a number of factors which the court must take into account at both stages of the process. These are:
(1) the size of the net estate;
(2) the financial needs and resources of the applicant, or which the applicant is likely to have in the foreseeable future;
(3) the financial needs and resources of the beneficiaries of the estate, or which such beneficiaries are likely to have in the foreseeable future;
(4) the financial needs and resources of any other applicant under the Act;
(5) the obligations and responsibilities owed by the testator to any applicant under the Act or to any beneficiary of the estate;
(6) any physical or mental disability of any applicant for an order or any beneficiary; and
(7) any other matter which the court may consider relevant, including the conduct of the applicant or the testator.

2.39 There are other factors which depend upon the identity of the applicant. Thus:

- Where an application is brought by a spouse, former spouse, civil partner or former civil partner the court must take into account the age of the applicant, the duration of the marriage or civil partnership and the contribution made by the applicant to the welfare of the family. In the case of an application by a spouse or civil partner where there has not been a decree of judicial separation, the court must have regard to the provision which the applicant might have expected to receive on divorce[1].
- In the case of an application made by a cohabitee, the court must consider the age of the applicant, the length of time that the applicant lived as the husband or wife or civil partner of the testator and any contribution made to the welfare of the testator's family[2].
- In the case of an application by a child or a person treated as the child, the court must consider whether the testator had assumed responsibility for the applicant's maintenance, the basis upon which he had done so, the length of time for which he had maintained the applicant and, in the latter case, whether or not he did so knowing the applicant was not his child and whether or not

anyone else had responsibility for the applicant's maintenance. The court must also consider the manner in which the applicant was being or was expected to be educated or trained[3].

- In the case of an application by a person who was being maintained by the testator, the court must have regard to the length of time for which the person had been maintained by the testator, and the basis upon which the testator had assumed responsibility for the applicant's maintenance[4].

1 Section 3(2).
2 Section 3(2A).
3 Section 3(3).
4 Section 3(4).

2.40 The factors set out above are to be determined at the date of the hearing of the application and so there is no way of completely preventing a claim when making a Will as the circumstances of the applicant and what is reasonable provision might change dramatically between the date of the Will and the date of the hearing of the application. Nevertheless, consideration of the possibility of such a claim and appropriate advice from the draftsman is likely to enable the testator to reduce the risk of a claim. Of course, the testator does not have to provide for such potential applicants and is free to exclude them but he should at least do so in the knowledge that there is a risk that a claim will be made under the 1975 Act.

2.41 Partly as a result of the ability of applicants to claim under the Act, it is no longer considered sensible or appropriate to provide a surviving spouse or civil partner with no more than an interest under a discretionary trust[1] or with a mere right of residence in the matrimonial home or with an income interest which determines on marriage or on the formation of a civil partnership.

1 A discretionary trust might be appropriate for a class of children but often leaves a spouse with no security, especially in the case of second marriages where the identity of the trustees may cause friction.

2.42 If the testator intends to exclude a child or some other person who would be expected to receive some provision in the Will, it is prudent for the testator to sign a letter explaining the reason or reasons why that person is excluded from the Will (or why they are to receive less than would otherwise be expected). A statement can then be included in the Will saying that no (or limited) provision is made for such a person for the reasons set out in the attached letter[1]. It is usually inappropriate to set out the reasons for excluding such person in the Will as they may be scandalous and refused probate. However, where the reasons are not scandalous they may be included in the Will. Such a declaration and accompanying letter will not prevent a claim being made but it is likely to prove that the testator did not merely exclude such person by mistake or because they were acting under an insane delusion and may help explain why the lack of provision is reasonable.

1 An example of such a declaration of exclusion is contained at **Form 20.3.**

2.43 Testators sometimes find the concept of their wishes being challenged and the uncertain nature of the challenge difficult. It is important to explain that the test of 'reasonable financial provision' is objective. The question is not whether the testator has been unreasonable but whether or not the provision made for the applicant is unreasonable, and this is something which may be altered by circumstances which occur after the Will is made and even by circumstances after his death. The statute therefore operates as a form of safety net for those persons closely related, or dependent, upon the testator. It is probably not possible to exclude the operation of the statute – even by agreement – but it is possible to include a clause forfeiting what provision is made in the Will in the event of a claim[1].

1 See *Nathan v Leonard* [2002] EWHC 1701 (Ch), [2003] 1 WLR 827.

Donatio mortis causa

2.44 The doctrine of *donatio mortis causa* is an anomaly as it concerns a gift which is neither totally testamentary nor totally inter vivos. Under the doctrine it is possible for a donor to make a conditional gift which will take effect on his death outside of and prior to the operation of any Will or the intestacy provisions. The essential requirements of a *donatio mortis causa* are that it is a gift made in contemplation of impending death, the gift is conditional on the donor's death and revocable until that event and that the subject matter of the gift or the essential indicia of the title of it (eg the title deeds)[1] is handed over to the donee before the donor's death.

1 *Sen v Headley* [1991] Ch 425, [1991] 2 All ER 636.

Foreign issues

2.45 Where a testator owns property overseas (including Scotland) or has a foreign residence, nationality or domicile then complexities can arise regarding the effectiveness of an English Will both as to assets in England and Wales and assets elsewhere. These issues are considered in more detail in **chapter 6**.

Changing circumstances

2.46 It should always be remembered by the draftsman and emphasised to the testator that a Will is not a 'once and for all' action[1]. Changing circumstances may make a previous suitable Will entirely unsuitable for the client and for this reason Wills should be kept under regular review by both draftsman and testator. The ways in which circumstances can require a change to a Will are numerous but the following are some of the most common:

- Ademption;
- Change of Law;
- Marriage / Civil Partnership;
- Divorce / Dissolving of Civil Partnership;
- Other Personal Circumstances.

1 A point emphasised in the Law Society Wills and Inheritance Protocol, page 76.

Ademption

2.47 Ademption occurs when a specific gift in the Will such as a house or a car ceases to be part of the testator's estate between the making of the Will and the testator's death. The result is the gift is adeemed and the proposed beneficiary receives nothing.

2.48 Ademption can happen in a number of different ways. The property can be intentionally transferred out of the estate, accidentally changed into another form or even converted to something different by a third party or Act of Parliament[1].

Regardless of the cause of the transfer or conversion if the property described in the Will no longer exists the gift will be adeemed and the proposed beneficiary will receive nothing under the gift.

1 *Frewen v Frewen* (1875) 10 Ch App 610.

2.49 Ademption can occur without testators realising it or without being aware that their actions are depriving their beneficiaries of an intended gift. Thus, a testator who has left a gift of 'my Jaguar car' may mistakenly assume that trading his Jaguar car for a Ferrari will just mean that the Ferrari goes to the beneficiary whereas in reality such a trade will result in the gift of the car being adeemed. Similarly, a testator who sells their house and puts the sale proceeds in a bank account believing that the beneficiary of a gift of the house will receive the sale proceeds instead may be depriving the principal beneficiary of their estate of any benefit. Gifts of funds in specified bank accounts are also particularly susceptible to ademption as banks can merge and accounts can be converted or merged to such an extent that it is not possible to identify what sums were intended for the beneficiaries[1]. Ademption can also happen by the actions of a third party, for example where shares in a company change their nature following a reorganisation of the company or where an attorney acting for the donor sells property that is the subject of a specific devise in the Will[2].

1 See *Re Dorman* [1994] 1 WLR 282.
2 See *Banks v Natwest Bank* [2005] EWHC 3479 (Ch).

2.50 A prudent draftsman should explain the risk of ademption of specific gifts and not only advise against gifts which are particularly susceptible to ademption but also advise of the need for the testator to regularly update their Will.

Marriage or Civil Partnership

2.51 A subsequent marriage or civil partnership automatically revokes a Will (unless the Will is made in the contemplation of marriage)[1]. This fact does not appear to be general knowledge among the public and there are many examples of testators dying intestate believing that the Will they had created prior to marriage or civil partnership would take effect. The consequences of marriage or civil partnership on the validity of a Will must be explained to the testator and if appropriate consideration should be made to making a declaration that the Will is made in contemplation of marriage or civil partnership[2].

1 Wills Act 1837 s 18. See **appendix 33.5**.
2 An example of such a declaration is contained at **Form 4.6**.

Divorce

2.52 A Will is not revoked if the testator's marriage or civil partnership is dissolved or annulled. However, unless a contrary intention appears in the Will, if a marriage or civil partnership is dissolved or annulled, gifts to the former spouse or civil partner and the appointment of the spouse or civil partner as executor will be rendered ineffective[1]. In these circumstances, the former spouse or civil partner is treated as if they had died on the date of the divorce or annulment rather than the gift failing or lapsing. The consequence of this is that gifts over remain operative notwithstanding the divorce or annulment. Thus, after a divorce a gift 'to my wife and if she predeceases me to X' will take effect as a valid testamentary gift to X[2].

1 Wills Act 1837 s 18A (marriage) and s 18C (civil partnership). See **appendix 33.6** and **33.8** respectively.

2 Originally s 18A provided that the gift to the former spouse lapsed and therefore, if the gift over was contingent on the wife predeceasing the testator, the gift would fail: *Re Sinclair* [1985] Ch 446.

Changing personal circumstances

2.53 Aside from marriage or civil partnership other major events in the testator's life are likely to require an alteration to the testator's Will. Births, deaths, adoptions, divorces, purchase of houses and moving countries may all require revisions to the testator's Will and the testator should be advised of this. Where the draftsman is working from a previous Will of the testator he should be particularly aware of any changes in the personal circumstances of the testator which necessitate alterations to the previous Will.

Change in law

2.54 Changes in law are most likely to require a review of a Will when it contains provisions designed to mitigate inheritance tax as inheritance tax legislation changes relatively regularly meaning that what was once a tax saving measure may no longer be effective. However, other changes in law may require alterations to existing Wills. A Will draftsman should keep well abreast of the current law and, if a change occurs which affects existing Wills, contact those clients to recommend that they update their Wills.

2.55 Many testators do not fully understand the importance of regularly reviewing their Will. The draftsman should explain the above concepts to the testator and advise them of the importance of regularly reviewing their Will. A failure to regularly review a Will may mean that a perfectly drafted Will is converted into a thoroughly unsuitable Will with negative publicity for the draftsman and drastic consequences for the beneficiaries.

Binding of wills

2.56 There are no restrictions on how a Will should be bound and there are a number of acceptable ways to bind a Will. Whatever method is adopted it should ensure that the Will is securely bound, that no pages are likely to come loose and that no additional pages can be added to the Will. While the probate registry has no formal policy as to their preference regarding how a Will should be bound, they do informally suggest that one of the best ways is a simple corner tag at the top of the Will holding the pages together. If a draftsman is uncertain as to the best way to bind a Will this is good advice to follow.

2.57 The biggest problem with the binding of Wills is if they are later un-bound in order to photocopy them (often in order to send them to the probate registry). If this happens it is very difficult for anybody to tell if any further testamentary document was attached to the Will but was then detached and this may lead to problems with obtaining a grant from the probate registry. For this reason, a Will should remain bound when photocopying and should not be un-bound unless it is intended to be revoked.

3 Taking Instructions

3.1 The importance of the proper taking of instructions for a Will cannot be overstated. Even the most talented draftsman will end up on the wrong end of multiple negligence claims as well as potentially being subject to professional disciplinary procedures if he or she fails to take proper care when taking instructions. If one or two matters in taking instructions are overlooked the resulting Will can be at cross-purposes to the intention of the testator and the testator's estate can be dragged into a bitter probate dispute. This chapter aims to set down advice which will help ensure that the testator's intention is accomplished and the draftsman is protected from the claims of disappointed beneficiaries.

Protocols and codes of practice

3.2 Any draftsman who is a member of a professional body must be aware of any protocols or codes of practice produced by his or her professional body and should have regard to such documentation when taking instructions and drafting a Will. The Law Society have issued an extensive 'Wills and Inheritance Protocol'[1] numbering some 83 pages and providing very detailed guidance as to the Law Society's 'preferred practice' in Will drafting, probate and estate administration. The adoption of the Protocol is mandatory for members of the Law Society's Wills and Inheritance Quality Scheme. Adoption of the Protocol is voluntary for other members of the Law Society but good practice would advise such other members to pay close attention to it regardless.

1 Publication date 3 July 2013.

3.3 The Society of Trust and Estate Practitioners ('STEP') have also prepared a code for members involved in Will preparation. The 'STEP Code for Will Preparation in England & Wales' provides a framework within which each STEP member who prepares Wills should operate. Adherence to the Code is mandatory for all STEP members who prepare Wills in England and Wales. The Institute of Professional Willwriters and the Institute of Scottish Professional Willwriters have also produced a Code of Practice for their members and again all members must comply with this Code.

3.4 It is recognised that while many draftsmen will be members of a professional body this is not a requirement and there remains no formal qualifications needed to draft a Will for another person. That being said, those who are not members of a professional body would nevertheless do well to follow the recommended practice in the professional codes and protocols in the interests of their clients and the avoidance of negligence claims.

Arrangements for taking instructions

3.5 Ideally prior to the meeting at which instructions are taken, the testator should be sent a list of documents or information which he or she should bring to the meeting. This should include documents proving his or her identity, copies of any previous Wills (if not held by the draftsman), copies of any Wills dealing with foreign property, names and addresses of family members and potential beneficiaries and details of all significant assets held by the testator. Bringing such documentation to the meeting will facilitate the taking of proper instructions and will also help alleviate the need for the draftsman to repeatedly refer back to the testator for further instructions, thus saving time and expense.

3.6 If at all possible, instructions should be taken from the testator at a face-to-face meeting in the absence of any potential beneficiaries. This will help avoid claims of lack of knowledge and approval, undue influence and fraud. It also allows the draftsman to make a better assessment of the testator's capacity and helps prevent claims on this basis as well.

3.7 If the testator is unable to attend a meeting in the draftsman's office for the purposes of giving instructions consideration must be made to visiting the testator at his or her home instead. In the case of a testator with a disability a home visit might come under reasonable adjustments which the draftsman may be required to make to comply with anti-discrimination law and policies.

3.8 If the contract for drafting a Will is made elsewhere other than the draftsman's office (eg the testator's home, workplace or hospital bed) then it must be remembered that the Cancellation of Contracts made in a Consumer's Home or Place of Work Regulations etc 2008[1] will apply. The Regulations will also apply if a contract already made is subsequently varied during a visit to the testator's home, work or hospital bed. The Regulations require the draftsman to give the testator written notice of the testator's right to cancel the contract within seven days. As it is rarely in the testator's best interests (particularly if they are ill) for the draftsman to wait seven days before preparing the Will the testator should be asked to give written instructions to allow the draftsman to start work within the seven days.

1 SI 2008/1816.

3.9 It is advisable to explain to the testator why a face-to-face meeting is preferable and why a Will drafted on the basis of instructions given in a different manner may be more susceptible to challenge. If it is not possible to have such a meeting or if the testator does not wish to have such a meeting the testator should be sent a checklist similar to the one contained at **3.25** and asked to complete it. Copies of the checklist and any other instructions as regards the Will or other contact from, or on behalf of, the testator (whether by phone, letter or email) should be maintained on the Will file. If there is no face-to-face meeting the draftsman should remember that if the contract for drafting a Will is made at distance the provisions of the Distance Selling Regulations[1] must also be complied with.

1 SI 2000/2334.

3.10 In the case where instructions were not made face-to-face and the draftsman is subsequently involved in the execution of the Will he should use this opportunity to confirm that the information provided in the checklist and other instructions were provided by the testator and that the testator remains happy with such instructions.

3.11 It may also not be possible for a meeting with the testator to take place in the absence of any potential beneficiaries. There are a variety of possible reasons for this – the testator may be infirm, need the assistance of a family member, have language problems or may simply not wish to have a meeting in the absence of the potential beneficiary. In these circumstances, the draftsman should explain why it is preferable to have the meeting (or at least part of it) in the absence of the potential beneficiary and how a Will made in their absence is less susceptible to challenge than one with them present. If the potential beneficiary is said to be needed to communicate with the testator (either because of language problems or because of a disability) consideration should be made for arranging an independent interpreter or assistant to attend instead of the potential beneficiary.

3.12 If the testator still wishes to have the potential beneficiary present or their presence is necessary this should be recorded on the attendance note. During the meeting the draftsman should be observant of the existence of any undue influence and carefully record any comments or prompting made by the potential beneficiary.

3.13 If couples wish to give joint instructions for their Wills at the same meeting the draftsman should confirm with each testator (ideally prior to the meeting) that they are happy to give instructions in the presence of each other given that sensitive matters may have to be discussed. It should also be explained to each testator that if a conflict of interest arises the draftsman may not be able to act for either or both of them and this would cover situations where one party wishes to change their Will without the knowledge of the other party. These explanations and each testator's response should be recorded in the attendance note and stored on the Will file.

Taking instructions

3.14 By necessity some Wills must be prepared on an urgent basis and such deathbed Wills are often the most important to the testator. In these circumstances, the draftsman may not be able to take all the steps he would otherwise take to guard against potential challenges to the Will. There may not be time to obtain a medical opinion, have an interview in the absence of potential beneficiaries, obtain past Wills, consider possible inheritance tax mitigation or ask all of the questions that the draftsman would ordinarily ask. Nevertheless the draftsman should still have regard to issues of capacity, undue influence and fraud and do his best to guard against such challenges as well as taking steps to avoid any major misunderstanding as to the disposition of the testator's estate. If it is in the testator's best interests, consideration should be made to drafting and executing a preliminary deathbed Will with a more considered and detailed Will prepared and executed at a future date if the testator survives their illness for such period.

3.15 Ideally the person taking the instructions should be the same person as the person drafting the Will. This helps prevent internal confusion or misunderstanding but may not always be practical. Where there are different people involved in the taking of instructions and the drafting of the Will, full and detailed attendance notes and a clear checking policy are essential.

3.16 When taking instructions it is crucial to prepare a detailed attendance note during or soon after the meeting. Such attendance notes will help prevent challenges to the Will by showing the testator had capacity to make a Will, was free from undue influence and that their intention was the same as that contained in the Will as executed. In addition, in the event of a mistake in drafting, a detailed attendance note will provide excellent evidence to support rectification and may prevent a long and costly probate dispute on this ground as well. If facilities are available consideration should also be made to making a video record of the meeting for added confirmation.

3.17 If there is a danger of the testator losing capacity between the drafting and the execution of the Will the Law Society have advised in its Protocol that the draftsman should get the testator to sign the attendance note to confirm it is an accurate record of his or her instructions. If the testator subsequently loses capacity the existence of the attendance note may allow the Will to be executed under the rule in *Parker v Felgate*[1]. If there is such a large risk of the testator losing capacity and it is practical to do so, consideration should also be made to the drafting and execution of the Will on the same occasion as the meeting if this is in the testator's best interests.

1 (1883) 8 P & D 171. The rule is that if a testator has given instructions to a solicitor at a time when he was able to appreciate what he was doing in all its relevant bearings, and if the solicitor prepares the Will in accordance with these instructions, the Will shall be valid even though at the time of execution the testator is capable only of understanding that he is executing the Will which he has instructed, but is no longer capable of understanding the instructions themselves or the clauses in the Will which give effect to them.

3.18 When taking instructions the draftsman should bear in mind the general considerations discussed in **chapter 2**. In particular, the question of testamentary capacity should be at the forefront of the draftsman's mind. In many cases the testator's capacity will not be in any doubt, however if there is any question as to capacity a medical opinion should be obtained. While the mere fact the testator is old, infirm or even has been diagnosed with dementia does not mean the testator lacks capacity, if any of these situations occur a medical opinion should be obtained (provided the testator consents and time allows).

3.19 The testator's permission to obtain such an opinion needs to be obtained and the testator may not give such consent. If this occurs, the draftsman should explain to the testator why a medical opinion is advisable and how in the absence of such opinion the Will may be more likely to be challenged. If the testator still refuses their consent this should be recorded on the attendance note.

3.20 In the absence of a medical opinion the draftsman's view on capacity should be recorded in the attendance note. This opinion should be based on the draftsman's view after having met and spoken to the testator and should have regard to relevant tests in *Banks v Goodfellow*[1] and the Mental Capacity Act 2005[2].

1 (1869–1870) LR 5 QB 549, 39 LJQB 237, 22 LT 813, [1861–73] All ER Rep 47.
2 The contents of these tests are discussed in **chapter 2**.

3.21 If the testator has made a previous Will (or Wills) the provisions of the earlier Will(s) should be compared to the testator's current instructions and any departures and the reasons for them discussed with the testator. In particular, if there is a sudden or dramatic change from a pattern of testamentary dispositions, this should be investigated thoroughly as unjustified dramatic changes are often indicative of lack of capacity or undue influence.

3.22 A suggested checklist of questions to ask a testator during the process of taking of instructions is contained at the end of this chapter. This checklist could either be sent to the testator for completion prior to the meeting or used as a basic checklist during a meeting. It is emphasised, however, that every testator is different and a checklist is merely a starting or guiding point and further tailored questioning will be needed depending on the circumstances of the testator. The aim of a draftsman must always be to find out the testator's testamentary wishes and how best these wishes might be accomplished. This is generally done by reference to 'open' questions such as 'who…', 'what…' and 'how much…' rather than closed questions which do not allow the testator to elaborate fully on what their wishes are.

Other matters

3.23 As part of the taking of instructions the draftsman is likely to have to give advice to the testator in terms of guiding them to making the disposition of their estate which best reflects their wishes. The contents of this advice will obviously change depending on the circumstances of the testator and their testamentary wishes. However, alongside advice (if appropriate) concerning what possible provisions would best reflect their testamentary wishes advice concerning some of the general considerations contained in **chapter 2** will also likely need to be given.

3.24 The testator should also be given advice as to the timescale of preparing a Will and when they can expect to receive a draft of the final Will as this will help to manage testator expectations. If instructions have been given over the phone, by way of a written document, via an intermediary or in any other way which did not involve a face-to-face meeting then when the Will is being sent out (especially if it is being sent via a potential beneficiary) consideration should be made to posting a second copy to the testator's home or other address to help guard against fraud. However, this additional step should not be seen as a substitute for other steps to guard against fraud and a face-to-face meeting is always advised.

Checklist

3.25

Contact details

Full Name(s): ....

Have you been known by any other name(s)? If so, please give details:

....

Address (including postcode):

....

....

Telephone Numbers (home): ....

(work): ....

(mobile): ....

Email: ....

Alternative Email: ....

Is there any reason for urgency in preparation of this Will (eg because of serious illness). If yes, please give details of required timeframe.

....

....

Personal details

Date of Birth: ....

Occupation/Profession: ....

Marital status (circle as appropriate): Single / Married / Civil-Partnership / Engaged / Cohabiting / Widowed / Widower / Divorced / Dissolved Civil-Partnership / Separated

Do you intend to marry / enter civil partnership or divorce / dissolve civil partnership in the near future?

....

If so, do you wish this Will to be made in anticipation of such change?

....

Is England and Wales your permanent home (domicile)?

....

If not,

Where is your permanent home (domicile)?

....

Do you intend to make England and Wales your permanent home?

....

Do you have English or Welsh nationality?

....

If married or in a civil partnership please give the following details about your spouse or civil partner:

Full name: ....

Date of Birth: ....

Address: ....

The country which is their permanent home (domicile):

....

Do you have any medical conditions (Dementia, Alzheimer's Disease etc) which affect your memory?

....

....

Do you have any disability or physical condition which will require special arrangements for meeting or communicating with this organisation?

....

....

Do you have any disability or physical condition which will require the assistance of any person when making and executing a Will?

....

....

Is anybody assisting or helping you in making this Will? If so, please provide the following details about them:

Their name: ....

Their relationship to you: ....

In what way they are helping you:

....

Their address:

....

....

....

Their phone number: ....

Their email: ....

Are you making this Will voluntarily and of your own free will?

....

Personal and family background

Are you a widow, widower or the survivor of civil partners?

....

If so:

When did your spouse or civil partner die?

....

What happened to his or her estate?

....

....

....

In particular, did your spouse or civil partner leave any property by Will or on intestacy to anyone other than yourself or a charity? Alternatively did they hold any property on a joint tenancy which passed to somebody other than you or a charity? Please give details:

....

....

If yes, what was the approximate value of the property left or passing to others?

....

Have you previously been divorced or had a Civil Partnership dissolved? ....

If so:

When did that marriage / Civil Partnership end?

....

Is there any ongoing obligation to pay maintenance? If so, please give details: ....

....

Do you have any children? If so, please provide details of their names, date of birth and addresses (if known): ....

....

....

....

Are all of your children the children of your relationship with your current spouse/ partner? If not, please give further details: ....

....

....

....

Do you have any children maintained by a former spouse / partner? If so, please give details:

....

....

....

Does your current spouse or partner have any children not detailed above? If so, please give details:

....

....

....

Does any former spouse or partner have any children which, you currently treat or at some time in the past have treated as your own? If so, please give details:

....

....

....

Are any of your children / your partner's children / your former partner's children dependent on you for financial support? If so, please state which:

....

....

....

....

Is there anybody else (adult or child) who is dependent on you (in whole or in part) for financial support. If so, please give details:

....

....

....

....

....

....

Financial situation

Do you have a pension(s)? If so please give details: ....

....

....

....

Do you have any life assurance policies (held individually or jointly with another)? Please give details (including whether or not they have been written in trust or assigned):

....

....

....

....

Do you have the benefit of any death in service scheme?

....

If so,

Have you made a nomination of who is to receive any payments under the scheme?

....

Is the nomination revocable?

....

Who is to receive payments and how much is to be received?

....

Do you have a business or businesses?

....

If so,

What is its name? ....

....

Is it incorporated or unincorporated?

....

What is its approximate value?

....

Is the business something which could continue after your death?

....

Are you in partnership with any other person?

....

If so,

What is the partnership name? ....

....

What is its approximate value?

....

Is the partnership something which could continue after your death?

....

Is there a partnership agreement?

....

Do you farm any land?

....

If so,

Do you do so alone or with another person or persons?

....

Is it something which could continue after your death?

....

Who owns the property in which you live? ....

Who else (if anybody) lives in the same property? ....
....

If you own your own home:

Do you own it with anyone else?

....

If it is owned with another, do you know if the house is owned by you as joint tenants or as tenants in common? ....

What is the property worth (approximately)? ....

Is there a mortgage? If so, how much is outstanding (approximately)? ....

Do you have mortgage protection insurance?

....

Are there any policies of life assurance linked to the mortgage?

....

Are there any other charges on the property? If yes, please give details:

....

Do you own any other land or real property in the UK? If so, please give the details requested above in relation to all other land or real property you own:

....

....

....

....

....

....

....

....

....

....

....

....

Approximately what is the value of your money in bank and building accounts?

....

....

Is any of this money held in a joint account? If so, please give details of who are the other account holders and the approximate value in the account:

....

....

Outside of the bank accounts detailed above do you have any other savings / bonds / investments etc? If so, please give details including their approximate value:

....

....

....

....

....

....

....

....

Do you have any valuable items (eg a car) which are in somebody else's possession? Please give details and approximate value:

....

....

....

....

....

Do you have any valuable items (eg a car) in your possession which belong to somebody else? Please give details and approximate value:

....

....

....

....

....

Other than land or real property or joint bank accounts detailed above do you own any other property jointly with another person? If so, please give details:

....

....

....

....

....

Do you have any particularly valuable digital or online assets (eg eBay accounts, PayPal accounts, Domain Names, Bitcoin, valuable digital photographs, gaming profiles etc). If so, please give details and approximate value:

....

....

....

....

....

....

....

....

Do you own any particularly valuable items not detailed above (eg expensive jewellery, car, antiques etc)? Please give details and approximate value:

....

....

....

....

....

....

....

Do you have any interest under any trust? If so, please give details:

....

....

Are you a trustee? If so, please give details:

....

....

....

Do you have a power of appointment over any trust assets? If so, please give details of the power and the assets over which it is exercisable:

....

Do you expect to inherit any property?

....

If so:

From whom do you expect to inherit? ....

....

....

....

Have you been given any promises or assurances that you will inherit the property? If so, please give details of such promises or assurances:

....

....

....

....

Roughly how much do you expect to inherit? ....

....

....

Have you made any gifts over £3,000[1] to any person or payments to any trust in the last seven years? If so, please give details of to whom the gift or payment were made and when the gifts or payments were made:

....

....

....

....

....

Foreign property

Do you own any land, houses, real property or interest in land (including timeshares) outside England and Wales? If so, please provide details including location and approximate value: ....

....

....

....

Have you taken the advice of a local lawyer in the jurisdiction in which the property is situated?

....

....

....

....

....

Have you made a foreign Will dealing with such property?

....

....

....

....

....

....

Do you wish your UK Will to deal with such property?

....

....

....

....

....

....

Summary of financial situation

In total, what is the approximate value of your assets which you wish to be distributed under your UK Will?

....

....

....

Liabilities

Please detail all your liabilities (debts, loans etc) including to whom they are owed, when they are due and if they have security (ie if they have a right over some asset of yours if you do not pay).

....

....

....

....

....

....

....

....

....

....

....

Litigation

Are you involve in any ongoing litigation or do you anticipate being involved in such litigation in the future? If so, please give details including the value of the claim and the likely level of costs which will be incurred:

....

....

....

....

....

....

....

Appointment of executors

(The executors will have the responsibility of getting in / realising your assets and distributing your estate in accordance with your Will)

(Only one executor needs to be appointed but you should not appoint more than four executors and trustees. The order in which they are appointed is irrelevant to their powers and duties).

If married, in a civil partnership or other relationship as a couple do you want your spouse/partner to be one of your executors? ....

....

Other executor (if desired):

Name: ....

Relationship to you: ....

Address: ....

....

....

....

Is this executor to be appointed with your spouse/partner or only if you are the survivor? ....

Other executor (if desired):

Name: ....

Relationship to you: ....

Address: ....

....

....

Is this executor to be appointed with your spouse/partner or only if you are the survivor? ....

Other executor (if desired):

Name: ....

Relationship to you: ....

Address: ....

....

....

Is this executor to be appointed with your spouse/partner or only if you are the survivor? ....

Other executor (if desired):

Name: ....

Relationship to you: ....

Address: ....

....

....

....

Is this executor to be appointed with your spouse/partner or only if you are the survivor? ....

Appointment of trustees

Do you wish for your executors to also be your trustees?

....

....

....

If not:

Please give details of the reason why:

....

....

Please give details of your desired trustees including name and address: ....

....

....

....

....

....

....

....

Appointment of guardians

(A guardian will have responsibility for a child / children under 18 if there is no surviving parent with parental responsibility)

Are you are responsible for children under the age of 18?

....

(If the answer is no the following questions in this section can be skipped)

If yes, please give the child's or children's name(s) and age(s):

....

....

....

....

Have you previously appointed a guardian(s) for this child or children?

....

If so, please provide the following details for each guardian:

....

Name: ....

Relationship to you: ....

Address: ....

....

....

....

Do you wish to replace this guardian?...

If not, do wish to use this Will to appoint a guardian(s) for this child or children?

....

Please provide the following details for each new guardian:

Name: ....

Relationship to you: ....

Address: ....

....

....

....

Child or children for which they are to be guardian: ....

....

Name: ....

Relationship to you: ....

Address: ....

....

....

....

Child or children for which they are to be guardian: ....

....

Funeral wishes

Would you like to express any particular desires concerning your funeral and what will happen to your body after your death (burial, cremation etc)?

....

....

....

....

Have you made a pre-paid funeral plan? If so, please give details: ....

....

....

....

....

....

Specific gifts and legacies

Are there any specific gifts or sums of money that you would like to leave?

....

....

Gift 1

Name of Beneficiary (person or organisation receiving gift):

....

Relationship or connection to you: ....

Is this beneficiary a person under 18 years old? ....

Address: ....

....

....

....

Description of Gift/Sum of Money:

....

....

Is this to be free of inheritance tax? (The tax will be met out of residue)

....

Gift 2

Name of Beneficiary (person or organisation receiving gift):

....

Relationship or connection to you: ....

Is this beneficiary a person under 18 years old? ....

Address: ....

....

....

....

Description of Gift/Sum of Money:

....

....

....

Is this to be free of inheritance tax? (The tax will be met out of residue)

....

Gift 3

Name of Beneficiary (person or organisation receiving gift):

....

Relationship or connection to you: ....

Is this beneficiary a person under 18 years old? ....

Address: ....

....

....

....

....

Description of Gift/Sum of Money:

....

....

Is this to be free of inheritance tax? (The tax will be met out of residue)

....

Gift 4

Name of Beneficiary (person or organisation receiving gift):

....

Relationship or connection to you: ....

Is this beneficiary a person under 18 years old? ....

Address: ....

....

....

....

....

Description of Gift/Sum of Money:

....

....

....

Is this to be free of inheritance tax? (The tax will be met out of residue)

....

(Please attach details of further gifts if appropriate)

Gift of the rest of your estate (your residuary estate)

If you are single what would you like to happen to your residuary estate? Please give details of respective percentages or shares if appropriate:

....

....

....

....

....

If you are married / in a civil partnership / in a relationship what would you like to happen to your residuary estate if you die before your spouse / partner?

....

....

....

....

....

If you are married / in a civil partnership / in a relationship what would you like to happen to your residuary estate if you survive your spouse / partner?

....

....

....

....

....

Powers of attorney

Would you like to grant Powers of Attorney so that members of your family or others whom you choose could deal with your personal and / or financial affairs in your later years (including if you lose capacity)?

....

If so:

What person(s) (if any) would you like to deal with your personal affairs?

....

....

....

....

If you have chosen two or more people would you like them to have the power to act independently or would you like them to have to agree on any decision?

....

....

What person(s) (if any) would you like to deal with your financial affairs?

....

....

....

....

If you have chosen two or more people would you like them to have the power to act independently or would you like them to have to agree on any decision?

....

Previous Wills and Codicils

Have you made a Will or Codicil before?

....

....

If so,

Please give the approximate dates of such Will(s) and Codicil(s) and who prepared the documents:

....

....

....

Do you have copies of such Wills and Codicils or can copies be obtained?

....

(If yes, such copies should be given to the person drafting your Will)

What is the main motivation for making this new Will? (passing of time / change of wishes / marriage / divorce / death of beneficiary etc)

....

....

....

What are the main things you wish to change between your previous Will and the new Will?

....

....

....

....

....

....

Other issues or potential problems

Have you promised or indicated that you intend to leave certain property to a specified person / group of people? If so, please give details of this promise or indication:

....

....

....

....

....

Is there somebody who you do not wish to include as a beneficiary who might expect to be included as a beneficiary? If so, please give details:

....

....

....

....

....

Are there any problems which may arise about your Will(s) or in the family generally? Please give details:

....

....

....

....

....

Are there any other points or factors relevant to your estate or your Will which have not been detailed above? Please give details: ....

....

....

....

....

1 This is current annual exemption figure and should be changed if the annual exemption figure changes.

4 Opening and Revocation

4.1 The practice followed in this book is to begin a Will with the name and address of the testator, a statement that all previous Wills are revoked and a statement that the document constitutes the testator's last Will. In this book, the date of the Will appears at the end in the testimonium and attestation clause because it is thought that if it is located there the insertion of the date is less likely to be forgotten[1]. There is, however, nothing improper about inserting the date at the beginning or anywhere else in the Will, although it would be unusual to place the date somewhere other than at the beginning or end of the Will. **Form 4.2** is an example of an opening containing the date of the Will while the other forms presuppose that the date will be inserted at the end of the Will. If the date is inserted in the opening, care should be taken to ensure no alternative date is inserted anywhere else in the Will.

1 Testimonium and attestation clauses containing the date are contained in **chapter 21**.

Identity of the testator

4.2 The full name and address of the testator should be given for clarity. If the testator has used an alias or a different name to his birth name or has changed his name it may be necessary to state this alternative name as well. Where a testator is generally known by his or her birth name and uses this name in formal documents, it is usually unnecessary to state any alternative names in the Will. However, where the alternative name has been used by the testator in official documents such as a marriage certificate or documents of title it is advisable to include reference to the alternative name(s) in the opening. It is not, however, necessary to describe how the name came to be changed, for example, by reciting that it was changed by deed poll or the particular date on which it was changed.

4.3 There are five fairly common situations in which an alternative name may need to be stated:

(1) Where the testator has changed his name by assuming another name, with or without formalities. In these circumstances, it is usually advisable to make reference to his former name.
(2) Where the testator has used two names fairly indiscriminately. In this case, both names should be stated in the Will, because it is likely that some documents of title are in one name and some in the other.
(3) Where the testator has habitually used his forenames in a different order from that in which they were given, for example, George Albert instead of Albert

George. In these circumstances, it is advisable to recite both names.

(4) Where the testator has never used the full names he was given at birth but has, throughout his life, been known by a different name. If the testator has always used his birth names in official documents and only used his alternative name informally it will not be necessary to include his alternative name but, for the sake of clarity, it would be advisable to do so.

(5) Where the testator has anglicised a foreign name. If the testator holds no assets in his original foreign name there may be no need to refer to such name. However, if some official documents retain the original foreign name then it should be recited as well.

Form 4.3 is an example of an opening which recites the testator's alternative name.

4.4 Some testators will share the same name as other members of their family. This often results from a family tradition of naming the eldest son after their father. Whenever the testator shares the same name as his father, son, grandfather, grandson, brother, uncle or nephew (or the equivalent in the case of a testatrix) care should be given to correctly identify the testator in the Will. In some circumstances, this may be done by giving the address of the testator. However, given the possibility of a son living with his father or vice-versa or the prospect of the testator leaving the home he is currently living in it is better practice to state the date of birth of the testator to help distinguish the testator from other members of the family who share the same name. **Form 4.4** is an example of such an opening.

Revocation by act of the testator

4.5 A Will is revoked by destruction, by the burning, tearing, or otherwise destroying of the Will by the testator or by some other person in his presence and by his direction with the testator having the intention of revoking it[1]. A Will is also revoked by a written declaration of an intention to revoke the Will executed in the same manner as a Will. Executing a new Will does not automatically revoke a previous Will as a Will is only revoked by a subsequent Will to the extent that the later Will is inconsistent with the earlier one. Otherwise it may just be considered to be a codicil of the previous Will. For this reason, and also because the testator may have forgotten having made an earlier Will, it is generally desirable to include an express revocation clause in a new Will.

1 Wills Act 1837 s 20, **appendix 33.9**.

4.6 When the testator has property in foreign jurisdictions and has made a foreign Will disposing of such property it must be clarified whether or not the testator wishes to revoke that foreign Will. Assuming the testator does not want to revoke the foreign Will the revocation clause should be carefully limited to property in this jurisdiction as a broad revocation clause may accidentally revoke the foreign Will. **Form 4.5** is an example of a revocation clause limited to property in the United Kingdom. Foreign issues are discussed further in **chapter 6**.

Revocation by marriage or civil partnership

4.7 A Will is revoked by marriage[1] or by the formation of a civil partnership[2] unless it appears from the Will itself that it was made in expectation of that marriage or civil partnership and is not to be revoked by it. In order for a Will not to be automatically revoked it must be clear from the Will itself (not merely the surrounding circumstances) that it is not intended to be revoked by marriage or civil partnership. The Will can be of unlimited duration but it is not possible to make a Will in the expectation of marrying or forming a civil partnership with a yet unidentified person. The testator must make the Will expecting to marry a specific person or to form a civil partnership with a specific person for the Will not to be revoked by the occurrence of that event.

The forms used in this book use the phrase 'expecting to marry' or 'expecting to form a civil partnership' but no specific words are needed so long as the Will indicates the expected marriage or civil partnership[3].

1 Wills Act 1837 s 18A, inserted by the Administration of Justice Act 1982 s 18(2) with effect from 1 January 1983 but subsequently substituted by the Law Reform (Succession) Act 1995 s 3 with effect from 1 January 1996. See **appendix 33.6**.

2 Wills Act 1837 s 18C, added by the Civil Partnership Act 2004 s 71, Sch 4 para 2. See **appendix 33.8**.

3 In *Re Langston* [1953] 1 All ER 928, a Will leaving everything 'unto my fiancée Maida Edith Beck' was held to be made in contemplation of marriage because of its reference to fiancée and hence not revoked by the testator's marriage to Ms Beck.

By decree of divorce or nullity or dissolution of civil partnership

4.8 A Will is not revoked if the testator's marriage or civil partnership is dissolved or annulled. However, unless a contrary intention appears in the Will, if a marriage or civil partnership is dissolved or annulled, gifts to the former spouse or civil partner and the appointment of the spouse or civil partner as executor will be rendered ineffective[1]. In these circumstances, the former spouse or civil partner is treated as if they had died on the date of the divorce or annulment rather than the gift failing or lapsing. The consequence of this is that gifts over remain operative notwithstanding the divorce or annulment. Thus, after a divorce a gift 'to my wife and if she predeceases me to X' will take effect as a valid testamentary gift to X[2].

1 Wills Act 1837 s 18A (marriage) and s 18C (civil partnership). See **appendix 33.6** and **33.8** respectively.

2 Originally s 18A provided that the gift to the former spouse lapsed and therefore, as the gift over was contingent on the wife predeceasing the testator, the gift failed: *Re Sinclair* [1985] Ch 446.

4.9 An example of a Will made in contemplation of divorce or annulment of a marriage or civil partnership is contained at **Form 4.8**.

Conditional revocation

4.10 Revocation may be conditional and if the condition is not satisfied, the Will prior to such revocation remains in force[1]. In general, conditional revocation is inadvisable as it leaves the disposition of the testator's estate in a position of uncertainty. However, it may be of some practical use if the testator wishes to make a Will in contemplation of marriage but does not want that Will to take effect until and unless the marriage takes place. An example of such a Will is contained in **Form 4.7**.

1 *Re Southerden's Estate, Adams v Southerden* [1925] P 177.

PRECEDENTS

4.11

FORM 4.1

Standard Opening and Revocation of Earlier Wills

I, [*full name*] of [*address*] revoke all earlier Wills and declare this to be my last Will.

FORM 4.2

Opening and revocation with date of Will at beginning[1]

I, [*full name*] of [*address*] revoke all earlier Wills and declare this Will dated [*insert date*] to be my last Will.

1 The practice of this book is to include the date of the Will in the testimonium and attestation clause for the reasons contained at **4.1**. However, there is nothing improper about including the date of the Will in the opening as per this form. If the date is included in the opening there is no need to include it in the testimonium and attestation clause.

FORM 4.3

Opening where the testator has used two or more alternative names[1]

I, [*more common name*] [*formerly*]/[*also*] known as [*alternative name*] of [*address*] revoke all earlier Wills and declare this to be my last Will.

1 See note at **4.2–4.3**.

FORM 4.4

Opening distinguishing testator from relatives with the same name[1]

I, [*full name*] (born on [*date*]) of [*address*] revoke all earlier Wills and declare this to be my last Will.

1 See note at **4.4**.

FORM 4.5

Opening and revocation limited to UK property

I, [*full name*] of [*address*] revoke all earlier Wills so far as they relate to my property in the United Kingdom.

FORM 4.6

Opening where Will is to remain in force after marriage or civil partnership[1]

I, [*full name*] of [*address*] revoke all earlier Wills and declare this to be my last Will. This Will is made expecting to [*marry*] [*form a civil partnership*] with [*name*] and is not to be revoked by this [*marriage*]/[*civil partnership*] taking place.

1 See note at **4.7**.

FORM 4.7

Will conditional on marriage or civil partnership taking place[1]

I, [*full name*] of [*address*] make this Will expecting to [*marry*]/[*form a civil partnership with*] [*name*]. My Will dated [*date*][2] shall remain in force until my intended [*marriage*]/[*civil partnership*] revokes it after which this document constitutes my last Will.

1 Note that no general words of revocation should be included in this clause.
2 Insert date of testator's existing Will.

FORM 4.8

Opening where Will is made in contemplation of divorce/ annulment[1]

I, [*full name*] of [*address*] revoke all earlier Wills and declare that I make this Will expecting my [*marriage to*]/[*civil partnership with*] [*name*] to be [*dissolved*]/ [*annulled*].

1 See notes at **4.8**.

5 Joint, Mutual and Reciprocal ('Mirror') Wills

5.1 Joint, mutual and reciprocal (also called 'mirror') Wills are Wills which govern the distribution of the estate of more than one person. However, despite this common thread they have very different consequences.

Joint Wills

5.2 A joint Will[1] is a single document which embodies the Wills of two (or more) persons. Essentially A and B make a single Will which disposes of all A's assets and all of B's assets. On the death of each testator probate is obtained of the joint Will in respect of that particular deceased. A joint Will must be expressed to be a joint Will and contain the joint dispositions of the testators. It is revocable at any time – by either of the testators during their joint lives or by the survivor after the death of one of them. Joint Wills are very unusual in this jurisdiction[2]. Joint Wills are not recommended and the draftsman should actively discourage testators from making a joint Will. They are inappropriate, and whatever is the objective, it can be better achieved by individual Wills. Even if the purpose of a joint Will is to exercise a joint power of appointment, this can be achieved better by individual Wills in which each testator exercises the power in the same terms.

1 See **Form 5.1.**
2 But not totally unheard of: *Roundway v Roundway* [1932] 1 Ch 585.

Reciprocal / mirror Wills

5.3 Reciprocal or mirror Wills[1] are where two people (generally a couple) make Wills in essentially identical terms. Each Will made is independent and separate to the other Will and (in contrast to a mutual Will) is freely revocable. The only connection between the two (or more) Wills is that they are in substantially the same terms and are generally made by couples acting together[2]. Reciprocal Wills are very common for couples where each person wishes to leave their estate to the other or, if the other person has pre-deceased them, to the children. Reciprocal Wills are generally the most suitable Wills for a couple to prepare as they do not limit the survivor's power to revoke or alter the Will if circumstances so require.

1 See **Form 5.2**.
2 Any two (or more) people can make reciprocal Wills regardless of whether they are a couple, cohabitees, family members, friends or strangers.

Mutual Wills

5.4 Mutual Wills[1] are separate Wills executed under an agreement that they will not be revoked or altered once one of the parties to the agreement has died[2]. Once one of the parties has died the other party is bound by the agreement not to revoke their Will. While they can still technically revoke their Will (either expressly or by a subsequent marriage or civil partnership) they will be in breach of the mutual Will agreement. This means that when they die the executors of their new Will will be granted probate but will hold the estate on trust to give effect to the terms of the original (mutual) Will.

1 See **Form 5.3**.
2 The agreement may, however, permit the alteration of some terms if the other provisions are retained. The agreement may also permit the revocation of the agreement during the lifetime of the parties if they both agree.

5.5 Contractual principles are important as the enforceability of mutual Wills is dependent on the strength of the agreement made between the parties and not the terms of distribution of the estate. As the remedy (a declaration of trust) available to the beneficiaries of the original Will is an equitable one its availability will depend on equitable principles and the beneficiaries' claim will be vulnerable to equitable defences.

5.6 The most common use of mutual Wills is where a couple makes mutual Wills leaving the bulk of their respective estates to each other for life and then to their children. There is, however, no need for the second testator to obtain a benefit under the Will of the first to die in order for the agreement to be binding[1]. There is also nothing limiting mutual Wills to any class of testators and cohabitees and siblings also occasionally make mutual Wills.

1 *Re Dale* [1993] 4 All ER 129.

5.7 A mere desire that the Wills should not be revoked is not sufficient to create mutual Wills, there must be a clear agreement or contract not to revoke[1]. An agreement for mutual Wills between the parties may be oral or in writing in a separate document but in view of the importance of the agreement the best practice is to record the precise terms of the agreement in the Will.

1 *Re Goodchild* [1997] 3 All ER 63.

5.8 Mutual Wills, like joint Wills, should generally be discouraged by the draftsman. While there may be some circumstances in which they are appropriate they are affected by factors beyond the testators' control, are generally overly restrictive, are often much less effective than the testators believe and, generally speaking, are much more likely to lead to litigation than reciprocal Wills. Some of the possible problems which are generally not foreseen by clients and which can undermine the desirability or effectiveness of a mutual Will include:

(i) A future change in circumstances after the death of the first-to-die which requires the survivor to use the assets in a way different to that which was agreed.

(ii) The costs to the original beneficiaries of enforcing the agreement if the survivor revokes the Will.
(iii) The inherent possibility of arguments as to the enforceability of the agreement and the extent of the assets bound by the mutual Will agreement.
(iv) The possibility of a claim under the Inheritance (Provision for Family and Dependants) Act 1975 which might deprive the intended beneficiaries of some, if not all, of the intended inheritance[1].
(v) The fact there is nothing preventing the survivor from depriving the intended beneficiaries of the intended inheritance by disposing of the assets during his lifetime (eg by spending it or making lifetime gifts)[2].
(vi) The possibility that the existence of the mutual Will goes unnoticed. If the survivor hides or destroys the mutual Will and makes a new Will in contravention of the mutual Will the new Will may be unchallenged if nobody is aware of the existence of the mutual Will.

1 It is unclear whether property governed by a mutual Will would be available to satisfy a claim under the 1975 Act. The Australian High Court held that it would be so available in *Barns v Barns* [2006] WTLR 1093 but this has not been tested in this jurisdiction yet.

2 An issue addressed in Australia (see, for example, *Birmingham v Renfrew* (1937) 57 CLR 666 and *Palmer v Bank of New South Wales* (1975) 7 ALR 671) but, as yet, unresolved in this jurisdiction; see: *Re Dale (deceased)* [1994] Ch 31 and *Re Cleaver* [1981] 1 WLR 939.

5.9 The testators' attention should be drawn to these potential problems and it should be explained to them that these are some of the reasons why mutual Wills are generally not appropriate and that, taking account of the problems and difficulties of mutual Wills, in many situations it is better to merely trust the other party to honour a moral obligation. Draftsmen should, however, be wary of recording this moral obligation in the Will as it can encourage a disgruntled intended beneficiary to make a claim under the Inheritance (Provision for Family and Dependants) Act 1975 as moral obligations are one of the factors to be considered under s 3 of that Act.

5.10 It is recognised that, despite these warnings, clients may insist on mutual Wills and therefore precedents for this have been provided. If mutual Wills are made the Law Society's advice[1] that it is advisable to consider giving a copy of the mutual Will agreement to a third party (to prevent the survivor concealing its existence) should also be heeded by the draftsman.

1 Law Society, Wills and Inheritance Protocol, publication date 3 July 2013, paragraph 10.5.3.

PRECEDENTS

5.11

FORM 5.1

Clause creating Joint Will[1]

This is the joint Will[2] of us [(*names*), both of (address)] [(*name*) of (*address*) and (*name*) of (*address*)] made by us jointly. We have agreed that this joint Will is not intended to be mutually irrevocable and we are both free to alter the disposition of our estates in any way and at any time.

1 Joint Wills should be actively discouraged and this precedent is included for information purposes only. See notes at **5.2**.
2 A joint Will must be expressed to be a joint Will and contain the joint dispositions of the testators.

FORM 5.2

Clause reciting the creation of reciprocal but not mutual Wills[1]

This Will is not one of two mutual Wills. [*Name*] is making a Will in similar terms to this Will but we have agreed that our Wills are not mutual Wills and each of us shall be free to revoke his or her Will at any time whether before or after the death of the other and be under no obligation or trust to dispose of any of his or her property in accordance with the terms of these Wills.

1 It is suggested that this clause appears immediately after the revocation clause.

FORM 5.3

Clause creating a mutual Will[1]

This Will is made by agreement with [my wife/civil partner] [*name*] that we will make mutual Wills each of which is a mirror image of the other and that except by [written[2]] agreement between us [made by deed[3]] neither Will shall be revoked or altered except to:

i) change any administrative provisions of the Will[4];

ii) nominate an alternative beneficiary if the residuary beneficiary dies before the survivor of us;

iii) [revoke or reduce any legacy][5].

1 It is suggested that this clause appears immediately after the revocation clause.
2 There is nothing to stop the agreement being varied orally but, in view of the potential for litigation arising from mutual Wills, it may be more appropriate to restrict amendments to ones agreed in writing.
3 Particularly where the Wills are not to be revoked during the lifetime of the testators, a deed should be preferred to an agreement under hand.
4 It is sensible and practical to allow alteration of administrative provisions to reflect changing circumstances and, in particular, to allow the changing of executors if one of the executors dies or becomes incapacitated or unwilling to act.
5 The addition of the words in square brackets provides more flexibility to the mutual Will agreement. In particular these words would allow a legacy to be revoked or reduced which may be desirable if the main concern is to preserve the residue for the residuary beneficiary.

FORM 5.4

Agreement underpinning a mutual Will[1]

This Agreement dated [*(date)*] is made between:

(1) [*Name*]; and

(2) [*Name*].

1.1 We are making reciprocal Wills which will constitute mutual Wills [but we have recognised that circumstances may change and that it is desirable that the survivor of us should be able to change his or her Will within certain limits][2].

1.2 It is our intention that our residuary beneficiary [*name*][3] shall take the bulk of the estate passing under the Will of the survivor.

2. We have therefore agreed that:

2.1 During our joint lives, neither of us will revoke or change the terms of his or her Will except by [written[4]] agreement with the other [made by deed[5]].

2.2 The survivor will not revoke his or her Will nor vary it except:

2.2.1 to change any administrative provisions of the Will, for example, the appointment of executors and trustees;

2.2.2 to nominate an alternative beneficiary if the residuary beneficiary dies before the survivor of us;

[2.2.3to revoke or reduce any legacy][6].

1 This is a precedent for an agreement which is contained in a separate document to the Will. For the reasons expressed at **5.7** it is generally better to record such agreement in the Will as per **Form 5.3**.

2 The addition of the words in square brackets provides more flexibility to the mutual Will agreement.

3 This is a simple example. More often there are multiple beneficiaries from two family groups and the mutual Wills are designed to protect the interests of the relatives of the first to die while giving the survivor more or less complete control of his estate during his lifetime.

4 There is nothing to stop the agreement being varied orally but, in view of the potential for litigation arising from mutual Wills, it may be more appropriate to restrict amendments to ones agreed in writing.

5 Particularly where the Wills are not to be revoked during the lifetime of the testators, a deed should be preferred to an agreement under hand.

6 The addition of the words in square brackets provides more flexibility to the mutual Will agreement. In particular these words would allow a legacy to be revoked or reduced which may be desirable if the main concern is to preserve the residue for the residuary beneficiary.

6 Foreign Issues and Declarations as to Jurisdiction

6.1 When foreign issues are involved there are two separate questions. The first concerns the formal validity of the Will (ie is it recognised as a valid document?). The second question concerns the essential validity of the Will (ie what law is applicable to its provisions and whether the provisions of the Will are valid according to that law?). An understanding of these questions is vital for the draftsman whenever a Will involves foreign issues, in particular where there is property situated outside of England and Wales. These issues will not only affect the advice which should be given to the testator but also the actual drafting including, if appropriate, limiting the jurisdictional effect of the Will.

Formal validity

Wills made outside England and Wales

6.2 Section 11 of the Wills Act 1963 provides that a Will shall be treated as properly executed 'if its execution conformed to the internal law in force in the territory where it was executed, or in the territory where, at the time of its execution or of the testator's death, he was domiciled or had his habitual residence, or in a state of which, at either of those times, he was a national'. This means that, for example, a Will executed validly in Japan will be recognised as validly executed in England even if it would not have been validly executed according to the requirements of England and Wales.

'International wills'

6.3 The concept of an 'International Will' which would be acceptable in every country has been in existence for some time. The Convention Providing a Uniform Law on the Form of an International Will was signed on 26 October 1973. This provided that a Will drawn up and executed in accordance with its provisions would be valid in any other State which is a signature to the Convention. In theory therefore, a French Will executed in accordance with its provisions would be recognised in England and Wales and an English Will executed in accordance with its provisions would be recognised in France.

6.4 The requirements of an International Will under the Convention are set down in the Annex to the Convention and include that in addition to two witnesses, an authorised person (in England and Wales this is a solicitor or notary public[1]) must also witness and attest to the Will and that if there is more than one page to the Will each page must be numbered and signed. These requirements and the other requirements are detailed more fully in the Annex to the Convention[2].

1 Section 28 of the Administration of Justice Act 1982.
2 Available at http://www.unidroit.org/instruments/succession.

6.5 The Convention was given legislative effect in England and Wales in ss 27 and 28 of the Administration of Justice Act 1982 but these sections have not yet been brought into force and there is no indication that they are likely to be brought into force in the near future. Many of the other signatures to the Convention have also not brought its effect into force in domestic law. However, it has entered into force in the following countries: Belgium, Bosnia and Herzegovina, Canada[1], Croatia, Cyprus, Ecuador, France, Italy, Libya, Niger, Portugal and Slovenia. In theory, these countries will recognise a Will drawn up and executed in accordance with the Convention. However, a draftsman wishing to draft a Will to be recognised in these countries would still be advised to consult a lawyer in the relevant jurisdiction to confirm the practical application of the Convention in that jurisdiction.

1 It is in force in Manitoba, Newfoundland, Ontario, Alberta, Saskatchewan, Prince Edward Island, New Brunswick, Novia Scotia and British Columbia but notably not in force in Quebec.

Essential validity

6.6 To understand this area it is vitally important that the concepts of domicile, immovable property and movable property are clear to the draftsman and to the testator. These concepts are key to the operation of English and Welsh private international law of succession and will affect what dispositions can be made in a Will governed by the law of England and Wales.

Domicile

6.7 In England and Wales a person's domicile is, for practical purposes, synonymous with his permanent home. It is where they intend to spend the rest of their life. Everybody has a domicile but nobody may have more than one. Everybody is born with a domicile of origin as a matter of law but this can change through dependency (if the person is under 16 or lacks capacity and the domicile of the person they are dependent on changes) or through choice (eg moving to another country and intending to remain there forever). A child born to unmarried parents takes the mother's domicile while a child born to married parents takes the domicile of its father (unless the parents are living apart and the child is living with the mother in which case he takes her domicile).

6.8 If a person acquires a domicile of choice by moving to a new country with the intention of remaining there forever but subsequently changes their mind they will resurrect their domicile of origin until or unless they acquire a new domicile of choice. Most people have an obvious domicile but, for some, it can be difficult to determine.

6.9 It should be remembered that foreign jurisdictions may have a radically different concept of domicile and many are more reliant on concepts of residence or nationality which are quite different and (from the English and Welsh perspective) less permanent.

6.10 In the UK there is also a concept of fiscal domicile for inheritance tax purposes by which a person who does not have a domicile in England and Wales under the general law may nonetheless be deemed domiciled in the UK for inheritance tax purposes[1]. Essentially the deemed domicile provisions provide that, subject to certain exceptions a person will be deemed domiciled in the UK if he was domiciled in the UK within the previous three years or was resident in the UK in not less than 17 of the previous 20 years. The importance of this is that UK inheritance tax is charged on the worldwide estate of a person with domicile in the UK. Where questions of inheritance tax mitigation are concerned the deemed domicile of a testator is therefore as important as his actual domicile.

1 Inheritance Tax Act 1984 s 267.

Immovables and movables

6.11 For practical purposes the term 'immovable' can be equated with land and interests in land (eg a mortgagee's interest in land) and the term 'movable' can be equated with everything else. Generally speaking it is easy to tell if something is immovable or movable but in cases of uncertainty (eg a partner's interest in partnership land) reference should be made to specialist texts for further analysis. It is also noted that as foreign jurisdictions have their own concepts of what constitutes immovable and movable property some things may be found to be immovable under English and Welsh law but movable under the law of a foreign jurisdiction.

English private international law of succession

6.12 The English private international law of succession is derived from a variety of sources but the essential rules can be found in *Dicey, Morris & Collins, The Conflict of Laws*. Although *Dicey* is not an authority per se, it is generally treated as such and the rules relating to succession contained within it are not seriously questioned. The following are the essential rules which will apply in the absence of legislation specifying otherwise:

- The essential validity of a Will of movables or a gift of movables in a Will is governed by the law of the testator's domicile at the time of his death[1].
- The essential validity of a Will of immovables or a gift of immovables in a Will is governed by the law of the country where the immovables are situated.
- A Will is to be interpreted in accordance with the law intended by the testator. In the absence of indications to the contrary, this is presumed to be the law of his domicile at the time when the Will is made[2].

1 Note here it is the domicile at the time of his death and not the time of the making of the Will which is important.

2 Note here it is the domicile at the time of making the Will and not his domicile on his death which is important.

6.13 These rules mean that if a Will is drafted in England and Wales for a testator domiciled in England or Wales then all his gifts of movables will be governed by

English and Welsh law. However, gifts of immovable property situated in a foreign country will be governed by the law of that foreign country and English rules may be irrelevant. This is particularly important when the property is in a country which has concepts of forced succession as this may dramatically restrict the testator's testamentary freedom in relation to some or all of his assets. For example, if an English domiciled testator has a house in country X which requires that all property on a person's death should go to his children then a provision in his English Will leaving the house to his parents will be ineffective and it will be given to his children.

6.14 Knowledge of the existence of forced succession of some assets under foreign law may influence the testator's disposition of assets located in England and Wales and so it may be worthwhile to consult a foreign lawyer even if the Will being drafted is only intended to deal with local assets.

6.15 These rules demonstrate why it can be very important for the draftsman to establish the testator's domicile and what foreign property he owns prior to giving advice and drafting the Will. Whenever a draftsman is advising or drafting a Will for a testator with a foreign domicile or who owns immovable property abroad the draftsman is strongly advised not to draft a Will with international scope without taking advice from a lawyer in the correct jurisdiction. This is because the drafting of a foreign Will is a specialist topic which requires specialist advice. There is nothing in this book which ought to lead a Will draftsman to set about drafting a foreign Will.

6.16 When a testator has foreign property which is governed by a foreign Will or by foreign intestacy or forced heirship rules it will usually be advisable to restrict the jurisdictional scope of the English Will. **Forms 6.1–6.3** are included as precedents for when it is desired to restrict the jurisdiction of the Will because of the existence of foreign assets which are to be governed by some other document or rule.

6.17 Great care should also be taken with revocation clauses in Wills. Without appropriate questioning it is possible to fail to establish the existence of a foreign Will and to include a revocation clause revoking such foreign Will by mistake. The questionnaire at the end of **chapter 3** is designed to help minimise the risk of this and similar mistakes occurring.

EU Regulation No 650/2012

6.18 EU Regulation No 650/2012 provides an important addition to the draftsman's knowledge whenever a testator holds property in another EU country. As detailed above the general rule is that for a testator domiciled in England and Wales his movable property will be governed by domestic law but his immovables will be governed by the law of state in which they are situated.

6.19 Regulation 650/2012 changes the position with regard to most EU states. The Regulation applies to the succession of all persons dying after 17 August 2015[1]. It provides that for deaths occurring after this date a single national law of succession will apply to the whole of the testator's estate (both movables and immovables). A key concept in the Regulation is that of 'habitual residence' because the default law which will apply to a testator's whole estate 'shall be the law of the State in which the deceased had his habitual residence at the time of death'[2]. Thus, if a testator dies habitually resident in Spain in September 2015 but with property in France it will be Spanish law will apply to both his movable and immovable property.

1 Article 83 of Regulation 650/2012.
2 Article 21. Article 21 goes on to state that if it is clear that from all the circumstances of the case that the deceased was manifestly more closely connected with another State than the State of his habitual residence then the law of that other State shall apply to his succession.

6.20 The Regulation also provides for a testator to make a choice of law to apply to his estate which can replace the default application of the law of the State of habitual residence. Under Article 22 a testator may choose the law of any State whose nationality he possesses at the time of making the choice or at the time of his death.

6.21 The UK opted out of the Regulation but it applies to all other States in the EU except Ireland (who also opted out[1]) and Denmark (who did not participate in its adoption[2]). While the UK has opted out of the Regulation it remains of importance to UK based draftsmen because it will affect the succession of estates of testators who have property in other EU States. This is because under Article 20 the law specified or chosen to apply shall apply whether or not it is the law of a Member State and therefore the Regulation applies whether or not the State whose law is to apply has opted in or out of the Regulation[3]. This means that if a testator dies post August 2015 and is habitually resident in the UK but has a property in France (eg a holiday home) then it will be UK law which applies to all of his estate including the property in France. The same would be true if he died resident in France but had UK nationality and made a declaration that UK law should apply to the disposition of his estate. This is an important change as previously the immovable property in France would be governed by French law which has fixed rights of inheritance.

1 Recital 82.
2 Recital 83.
3 Unless the specified or chosen law to be applied is 'manifestly incompatible with the public policy of the forum' (Article 35). This is unlikely to be the case with the application of UK law in other EU Member States and is more likely aimed towards the law of countries outside the EU.

6.22 If a testator has property in another EU State the draftsman should be aware of the Regulation and consider it when advising the testator. In particular, if the testator is (or may be) habitually resident in another EU State but holds UK nationality (or will acquire it in the future) and wishes for his estate to be governed by UK law then the draftsman should consider inserting a declaration that the testator wishes for his estate to be governed by UK law. An example of such a declaration is contained at **Form 6.4**. Again the prudent draftsman may still wish to consult a lawyer in the other State to confirm if there are any other issues arising from the foreign nature of the assets.

Location of declarations as to jurisdiction

6.23 Some draftsmen prefer that all declarations are grouped together at the end of the Will. There is nothing wrong with such an approach. However, it is generally considered advantageous to have the jurisdiction of the Will clarified at the start of the Will and, for this reason, it is more common for declarations concerning the jurisdictional extent of a Will to be placed at the beginning of a Will. This book adopts a similar approach.

PRECEDENTS

6.24

FORM 6.1

Jurisdiction excluded for foreign immovables[1]

This Will does not relate to my immovable property in [*name of country*]/[outside England and Wales] which is the subject of [a separate Will] [separate Wills]

1 This precedent is for use where the testator domiciled in England and Wales has immovable property elsewhere. It is anticipated that the testator will have a foreign Will dealing with such foreign immovables.

FORM 6.2

Jurisdiction limited to Property in England and Wales[1]

This Will relates only to my property in England and Wales and does not affect any other property.

1 This precedent is for use where the testator has property throughout the world and wishes his Will to only dispose of his English and Welsh property. It is anticipated that the testator will have other foreign Wills dealing with his other property.

FORM 6.3

Jurisdiction limited to Immovable Property in England and Wales[1]

This Will relates only to my immovable property in England and Wales and does not affect any other property.

1 This precedent is for use in the situation in which a foreign domiciled testator requires a Will disposing of his English and Welsh immovable property only. It is anticipated that the balance of the testator's estate will be dealt with under a foreign Will or foreign intestacy provisions.

FORM 6.4

Declaration of choice of law under EU Regulation 650/2012[1]

I hereby declare that the dispositions of property contained in this Will shall be governed by and take affect according to the law of England and Wales

1 See notes at **6.22**. Such a declaration will only be effective for deaths on or after 17 August 2015 and only if the testator holds UK nationality at the date of the Will or the date of his death. There is no strict need to make such a declaration if the testator is habitually resident in and most clearly connected with the UK.

7 Funeral Wishes

Declarations concerning funeral arrangements and disposal of the testator's body

7.1 Despite what many believe, it is the executors and not the testator who have the right to dispose of the testator's corpse[1]. Regardless of this, many testators want to express wishes concerning their funeral and the disposal of their body in their Will in the hope or expectation that their executors will abide by these wishes. The inclusion of such wishes may also help to reduce the risk of painful and expensive disagreement among the testator's family and loved ones after his or her death. The draftsman should therefore enquire as to whether the testator wishes to include such directions.

1 *Williams v Williams* (1882) 20 Ch D 659.

7.2 If the testator does wish to include such directions the testator should be reminded that such directions are not legally binding and that there is no guarantee that they will be followed. This is especially so if the testator's wishes are impractical and the testator should be asked to consider whether his wishes are ones which it will be practical for the executors to perform.

7.3 The testator should also be reminded that as the funeral will take place very shortly after his death he should consider expressing the same wishes informally (either orally or in a letter) to those likely to make the funeral arrangements in order to prevent the funeral and burial/cremation taking place prior to the Will being found and read. This is especially the case if the Will is hidden or kept in a location other than the testator's house. The more detailed or important the instructions, the more vital it is that the existence and content of such instructions is known by those likely to undertake preparations for the funeral. Otherwise there is a real danger of causing significant emotional distress to loved ones who prepared and organised one type of funeral and burial only to discover later (when the Will is read) that the testator wished to have a different type of funeral and burial. If the testator has entered into a prepaid funeral arrangement it is similarly vital for this to be known prior to the funeral taking place[1].

1 See **Form 7.4**.

7.4 In many situations the best approach is for the testator to leave a copy of funeral wishes with those who are likely to help make preparations for the funeral and then in the Will simply state:

'I have given [written] instructions concerning my funeral arrangements to [*name(s)*].'

A copy of these instructions can be kept with the Will if the testator so wishes. If this is the case those in the provision above should be informed that there is another copy being held with the Will in case their copy is lost or misplaced.

Expenses

7.5 Executors may incur all reasonable expenses in connection with the funeral and burial or cremation of the testator as a testamentary expense without any direction in the Will. Exceptional or unusual expenses should be authorised by the Will, although that is not a complete safeguard because the Will might not be proved – in which case those who incurred the expenses may be liable.

Cremation

7.6 It is the executors, not the testator, who have the right to dispose of the testator's corpse and it is no longer unlawful to cremate the corpse of a testator who has left directions to the contrary (though for obvious reasons this may be inadvisable). If the testator wishes to have his or her ashes scattered in a particular location, research should be undertaken to confirm whether this is permitted as some organisations or locations prohibit the scattering of ashes on their land and even national parks and other similar organisations may ask that the scattering of ashes be limited.

Donation of the body and organs

7.7 The donation of bodies is covered by Human Tissue Act 2004. This Act provides that anatomical examination etc will be lawful if given with the appropriate consent. The consent may be given by the deceased (or by certain other nominated people) and such consent may be given in a Will[1]. If the testator wishes to have his or her body donated they should be reminded that their body may be refused or returned after use and therefore the testator may also wish to cover this eventuality as well. A testator who wishes to donate their body is well advised to undertake enquires of the donee institution and make direct arrangements with them. This will help prevent refusal of the body and other awkward situations for the executors.

1 Human Tissue Act 2004 s 3(5).

7.8 The donation of organs for transplantation is also governed by the Human Tissue Act 2004 and, again, consent is required. While such consent can be included in a Will it is generally impractical to do so as in view of the speed with which actions need to be taken for transplantation it will likely be too late to implement the testator's wishes by the time the Will is read. A testator who wishes to donate organs for transplantation is better advised to carry a donor card and inform loved ones and medical staff of his or her intentions.

PRECEDENTS

7.9

FORM 7.1

Objection to cremation[1]

I do not wish to be cremated.

1 See note at **7.6**.

FORM 7.2

Direction for cremation[1]

I wish to be cremated [and to have my ashes deposited/scattered at [ ]].

1 See note at **7.6**.

FORM 7.3

Direction for funeral service

I wish my funeral service to be held at [ ].

FORM 7.4

Funeral arrangements: prepaid funeral[1]

I direct that my funeral shall be undertaken by [ ] of [*address*] with whom I have deposited money for my funeral expenses [*under plan number #*].

1 See note at **7.3**.

FORM 7.5

Direction for burial

I wish to be buried.

FORM 7.6

Direction for burial with reference to specific plot

I wish to be buried [*in the family grave at …*]/[*in the plot where my wife is buried*][1].

1 It is important to consider whether the direction is capable of fulfilment in order to avoid or, at least, reduce the risk of painful and expensive disagreement among the family.

FORM 7.7

Donation of the body[1]

I wish my body to be donated to [*donee institution*] [and I have made arrangements for this with the appropriate authorities][2]. I wish my body or any part of it which is not disposed of by or on behalf of [*name institution*] to be [*buried*]/[*cremated*][3]. Any expense incurred in giving effect to these wishes shall be an executorship expense.

1 See note at **7.7**.
2 If a testator wishes that his or her body should be used for medical purposes after his or her death it is advisable to make direct arrangements with the donee institution prior to his or her death.
3 A donation will not necessarily dispose of the body as it may be refused or returned after use and therefore the body's disposal should still be considered.

8 Appointment of Executors and Trustees

Definitions

8.1 The term 'executor' is used in this chapter and throughout the book to refer to the person responsible for the administration of the testator's estate regardless of that person's gender. While the term 'executrix' may be used where a woman is appointed alone or the term 'executrices' if a number of women are appointed together, it is considered that it is simpler and causes less confusion if the person appointed is merely referred to as an executor which is widely used as a gender-neutral term.

Advice to testator

8.2 The draftsman should advise the testator about the roles and responsibilities of executors in order to allow the testator to choose the correct person or persons. This is an express requirement for those acting under the Law Society Wills and Inheritance Protocol[1], the STEP Code for Will Preparation in England and Wales[2] or the Institute of Professional Willwriters Code of Practice[3] and is good practice for all other draftsmen. This advice should include advice concerning the desirability of appointing people who the testator trusts and who can work together and an explanation of the rules concerning the costs and expenses of executors.

1 Publication date 3 July 2013, paragraph 11.4.
2 Paragraph 1(xiii).
3 Paragraph 5.4.

8.3 The testator should also be advised that whoever he appoints has the power to hire solicitors or other professionals in the course of the administration of the estate and that such fees, provided they are reasonable and properly incurred in the administration of the estate, will be an expense of the estate. Without this advice some testators will not wish to appoint lay people who, though appropriate, the testator fears might not be able to manage some of the technical parts of the administration of the estate. Similarly the testator should be made aware of the fact that even if he appoints a lay person, fees for solicitors and other professionals may still be incurred.

8.4 The maximum number of executors who will be granted probate is four[1] and therefore though it is technically possible to appoint more than four this is inadvisable. Equally it is always inadvisable for the testator to appoint a single executor without a substitutional provision as this may leave the estate without an appointed testator if the original executor pre-deceases the testator or becomes unable or unwilling to act. A minor or a person who otherwise lacks capacity will not be granted probate. However, if there are other executors they will be granted probate and power will be reserved to the person lacking capacity until they gain or regain capacity. The court also has the power in special circumstances to pass over the executor(s) appointed in the Will and to grant letters of administration to another person if they think it necessary or expedient to do so[2] but such power is only exercised in exceptional circumstances.

1 Senior Courts Act 1981 s 114(1).
2 Senior Courts Act 1981 s 116.

Executors and trustees

8.5 While generally speaking the same people are appointed as executors and trustees, the roles are different and there is no obligation to appoint the same people to both roles. The role of an executor is, broadly speaking, to collect in the testator's estate, to clear it of debts and liabilities and to distribute the estate in accordance with the Will[1]. A trustee's role depends on the terms of the trust and therefore can be very different to an executor's role.

1 In holding the balance of the estate prior to distribution the executor or executors are often said to be holding it on trust for the beneficiaries and so, in this role, are sometimes considered to be acting as trustees and not executors.

8.6 If there is no possibility of a continuing trust arising under the Will the testator need only appoint executors and does not need to appoint trustees[1]. If a trust does unexpectedly arise the executors would ordinarily become trustees by implication. If there is a possibility of a continuing trust arising it is generally considered good practice to expressly appoint trustees (usually the executors but it can be different people)[2]. Even if a trust is unlikely to arise it is often wise to appoint the executors as trustees in case of an unexpected trust arising and this is the practice adopted in the majority of the forms included in this book. If there are any specialised trusts deliberately created by the Will these trusts should also have trustees expressly appointed which may or may not be the same people as the testator wishes to administer their estate.

1 See **Forms 8.1–8.4**.
2 See **Form 8.5**.

8.7 It is usually convenient to appoint the same people as executors and trustees and this is the common practice unless there is a compelling reason not to do so. Examples of such cases include estates where there might be foreign property, estates of authors where separate literary executors may be desirable and estates in which separate trustees might be needed to run a continuing business. Sometimes a testator will want professional executors to realise his estate but decides that it is better if members of the family are responsible for the administration of any trust created. It may also be that the terms of a trust created under a Will are such that the testator feels that somebody other than the named executors would be better suited or qualified to act as a trustee. Similarly, if more than one trust is created the testator may wish to name different trustees for each trust.

8.8 When there are interests in succession under a trust, the appointment of a beneficiary as both executor and trustee has potential to produce a conflict of interest. If the Will gives power to the trustees to use capital for the benefit of a life tenant it is generally unwise to appoint either the life tenant or the remaindermen as trustees because of a possible conflict of interests and paralysis of the administration. The possibility of a conflict should always be a relevant factor in choosing executors and trustees.

8.9 Where it is intended to appoint the same people as executors and trustees it is advisable to limit those appointed as trustees to 'those of my executors who obtain probate of this Will'. This helps to avoid complications if one of the executors declines to take probate and ensures that those administering the estate are actually the same as those administering any trust arising under the Will.

Common appointments

8.10 The following are the most commonly appointed executors:

1) One or more members of the testator's family;
2) A beneficiary, usually the principal beneficiary;
3) A disinterested family friend[1];
4) A business acquaintance of the testator;
5) One of the testator's professional advisers (solicitor, accountant etc);
6) A trust corporation (such as the trust administration arm of a bank or an incorporated solicitors' firm).

1 This is particularly common when the interests of minors need to be balanced against those of adult beneficiaries.

Appointment of a beneficiary

8.11 If the estate is small and the assets can be administered easily, the principal beneficiary is often the most appropriate choice. They can administer the estate with minimal cost and ensure that the small estate is not unnecessarily reduced through expenses. They also tend to have good knowledge of the circumstances and wishes of the testator and can administer the estate with a personal touch which would be lacking if a solicitors' firm or a trust corporation was appointed. However, even when the estate is small and uncomplicated there are still situations where the principal beneficiary would be inappropriate: for example if they were legally incompetent, very elderly or if there was family tension or even, simply, if the principal beneficiary indicated that they did not wish to be executor.

8.12 Sometimes the appointment of a professional adviser can be combined with that of a responsible family member. This can have the advantage of the use of the skills of the professional advisor combined with the personal touch of the family member. Again, in some situations this may be inappropriate.

8.13 If a spouse or civil partner is appointed it should be remembered that if the marriage or civil partnership is dissolved or declared void both the gifts to the former spouse/civil partner and their appointment as executor will be void[1].

1 See note at **3.10**.

Appointment of a friend or business acquaintance

8.14 The appointment of a disinterested family friend is particularly common when the interests of minors need to be balanced against those of adult beneficiaries under a trust. The appointment of a business acquaintance is most useful if the testator has a substantial interest in an ongoing business which may be difficult or complicated to realise.

8.15 In considering a friend or a business acquaintance the testator should remember that the administration may be burdensome to an executor who has no personal interest in the estate and has his own affairs to attend to. In these circumstances consideration should be made to making a gift to the proposed executor to compensate him/her for acting as executor. Unless otherwise stated it will be presumed this gift is conditional on him/her acting as executor but this should be clarified to avoid uncertainty and possible future conflict[1].

1 See **Form 10.16**.

Appointment of solicitors

8.16 The testator may wish to appoint his solicitors as his executors – a practice encouraged by most firms as it ensures a continuing connection with the client and his estate. Future executorships are regarded almost as part of the goodwill of the practice and so firms are anxious that appointments should relate to the practice rather than to an individual partner. Many draftsmen will have to be careful how they approach this issue as some regulatory bodies have rules concerning how this issue can be raised and agreed[1].

1 For example, the Law Society Inheritance and Wills Protocol, paragraph 11.4.

8.17 The appointment of a solicitors' firm will operate as an appointment of the partners in the firm at the date of the Will (not the date of death) unless the clause contains express provision to the contrary. In many situations it may be more convenient to appoint the partners at the date of death of the testator and this option is included in the forms.

8.18 Problems can arise if a solicitors' firm changes its name, amalgamates with another firm, incorporates or becomes a limited liability partnership. These problems can generally be resolved by drafting sufficiently wide definitions of 'the Firm' or 'my solicitors' and the appointment clause should therefore be drafted wide enough to cover all of these situations. Unfortunately, there is no satisfactory drafting solution to the situation where an existing firm is dissolved or ends and either no new firm is created or two (or more) firms are created but none are the direct successors to the old firm. In these circumstances, it is best for the testator to execute a new Will or a codicil updating or replacing the executors.

8.19 Where it is desired to appoint certain solicitors but the solicitors have formed a corporate body the corporate body itself should not be appointed executor because it is not a trust corporation and therefore cannot act as an executor. Instead the owners, directors or members (whichever may be the most appropriate in the circumstances) of the corporate body should be appointed. However, it is often the case that solicitors who have incorporated will also form a trust corporation as a separate entity and, if this is the case, that trust corporation can be appointed instead of the owners, directors or members[1].

1 See **Form 8.15**.

8.20 As a LLP is also a form of incorporated practice the LLP itself should not be appointed as an executor. Instead, its members should be appointed[1]. LLP's also often form trust corporations as separate entities and, if this is the case, that trust corporation can be appointed instead[2].

1 See **Form 8.12**.
2 See **Form 8.15**.

8.21 If the clause merely appoints the partners in a traditional partnership and the firm subsequently converts to an incorporated practice or a LLP this may not be sufficient to appoint the members of the incorporated practice or LLP[1]. For this reason, the draftsman should draft the definition of the firm in such a way so as to cover and subsequent incorporation or conversion to a LLP as is done in **Forms 8.10–8.14**.

1 In *Re Rogers (deceased)* [2006] 2 All ER 792 Lightman J held that on those particular facts the appointment of the partners in a firm was effective to appoint the profit sharing (but not the salaried) members of a limited liability partnership. He also added that testators ought to make express provision for who should be appointed if the firm incorporates or becomes an LLP.

8.22 It is generally not recommended for the testator to appoint named partners in a firm as it causes complications if the named partners leave, retire or die. It is also not in the best interests of the firm as they run the risk of losing the business if the named partners join another firm. Where named partners are appointed the firm may invite the testator to change his executors after the named partner leaves, retires or dies and some firms will maintain a register of executorships in order to know when to make such an invitation.

Appointment of accountants

8.23 **Form 8.14** includes provision for the appointment of accountants as executors alongside solicitors. This can be sensible where the administration is likely to be complex, involving, for example, the winding up of a business or resolution of difficult tax issues. However, it should be borne in mind that taxation issues relating to the administration of trusts and estates are specialist topics in respect of which even the testator's accountants may require separate advice. It should also be noted that the appointment of a solicitor and an accountant from different firms is likely to lead to greatly increased administration charges if both are to do their job properly. In the event of disagreement or dispute between the executors or the beneficiaries the additional expense consequent on appointing both solicitors and accountants can quickly become disproportionate.

Appointment of a trust corporation

8.24 The appointment of a trust corporation is sometimes the most sensible option where, for example, the family are in dispute and professional advisers, business colleagues or family friends will simply be drawn into the dispute if they are appointed. Unfortunately, some (but not all) trust corporations will renounce probate if made aware of a family dispute as they do not wish to be involved in any dispute. A trust corporation can also be appropriate if the testator has a very large or complicated estate and does not believe his or her family and professional advisors to have enough time, experience or resources to administer his estate in the best possible way.

8.25 In other situations, the appointment of a trust corporation is inappropriate and may cause more harm than good. Some of the problems which can arise if a trust corporation is appointed include the high cost, the corporation's impersonal nature[1], its often cumbersome administrative machinery and, sometimes, the physical distance between its administrative centre and where the beneficiaries live.

1 Which can be seen as an advantage in the context of a bitter family dispute but otherwise might result in the estate being administered without as much regard to the personal or emotional background of the situation as might be expected if a family member was administering the estate.

Appointment of the public trustee

8.26 It is possible to appoint the Public Trustee as executor and/or trustee but the appointment will only have effect if the Public Trustee consents to act. For this reason it is advisable to seek confirmation of a willingness to act from the Public Trustee prior to executing the Will[1]. Generally speaking the Public Trustee is only used as an executor and trustee of last resort.

1 The contact details for the Public Trustee are available on the justice.gov.uk website.

Power to charge fees

8.27 If solicitors or other professionals or a trust corporation are being appointed or may be appointed in the future, express provision enabling the executors and trustees to charge fees should be provided in the Will as in **Forms 8.10–8.16.**

8.28 Without such express provision a professional executor or trustee may still be able to charge fees but the power is limited. Thus, under the Trustee Act 2000, a trustee or personal representative acting in a professional capacity can charge 'reasonable remuneration'[1] for any services he provides but only if he:

(a) Is not a sole trustee, and
(b) Each other trustee has agreed in writing that he may be remunerated[2].

1 'Reasonable remuneration' is defined as 'such remuneration as is reasonable in the circumstances for the provision of those services to or on behalf of that trust by that trustee', Trustee Act 2000 s 29(3).
2 Trustee Act 2000 s 29(2), see **appendix 34.55**.

8.29 Similarly, without an express provision a trust corporation can still charge 'reasonable remuneration' (without the limitation imposed on professional trustees as to receiving written consent from the co-trustees) for services it provides[1]. While for both the professional trustee and the trust corporation the default charging provisions do cover services capable of being provided by a lay trustee[2] it is still desirable to insert an express charging provision. Without such a provision a professional trustee will still have to obtain the written consent of his co-trustees before charging and if they are a sole trustee they will not be able to charge at all. Furthermore, in the case of both the professional trustee and the trust corporation what is considered 'reasonable remuneration' may not be the level at which the professional trustee or trust corporation would usually charge which may result in them refusing to act as executor. An express charging provision also reduces the risk of future litigation concerning what is or is not reasonable remuneration and draws everybody's attention to the fact there will be charges incurred.

1 Trustee Act 2000 s 29(1), see **appendix 34.55**.
2 Trustee Act 2000 s 28(1), (2), (5)–(6), see **appendix 34.54**.

8.30 In the case of an express remuneration clause, a professional trustee's remuneration is to be regarded as remuneration, not as a gift[1], for the purposes of Wills Act 1837 s 15[2] meaning there is no risk of the remuneration being invalid if the professional trustee witnesses the Will. Charges made are automatically regarded as an administrative expense for the purposes of Administration of Estates Act 1925 s 34(3)[3] and there is no need for the Will to state this.

1 Trustee Act 2000 s 28(4), see **appendix 34.54**.
2 Which provides that gifts to an attesting witness are void. See **appendix 33.4**.
3 Trustee Act 2000 ss 28(4)(b), 35(3)(a), see **appendix 34.54**. Administration of Estates Act 1925 s 34 concerns the order of application of assets and is not reproduced in the appendix.

8.31 The charging clause can be included as a declaration at the end of the Will and **Form 8.16** is an example of such a declaration. This may be appropriate if the executors initially appointed are lay persons but there is the possibility of a professional being appointed in the future. In general, however, it is better practice to incorporate the charging clause in the clause appointing executors and trustees[1]. This emphasises its importance to the appointees and ensures that the testator is aware of its significance.

1 As in **Forms 8.10–8.15**.

Final points

8.32 Three final points should be mentioned. First, the testator may wish to leave a legacy to his executor. There is a presumption that any legacy to the executor is conditional on him or her accepting the office of executor. The position as to whether the gift to the appointed executor is or is not conditional on them acting as an executor should be made clear[1]. Second, the testator sometimes expresses a wish that the executors should use the services of a particular firm of solicitors. It is convenient to include such a wish in the appointment clause rather than elsewhere in the Will[2]. The remarks at **8.16–8.22.** also apply to such a wish. Third, there is sometimes concern about the liability of executors/trustees if the estate suffers loss and provisions can be included to offer them additional protection. This is dealt with in **chapter 19**.

1 See **Form 10.16**.
2 See **Form 8.8**.

PRECEDENTS

8.33

FORM 8.1

Appointment of a sole executor with alternative executor[1]

I appoint as my executor [*name*] of [*address*] but if [he/she] is unable[2] or unwilling to act or if [he/she] dies before proving my Will I appoint [*name*] of [*address*].

1 It is undesirable to appoint a sole executor without a substitutional provision and so no precedent for this has been included. But if this was desired the deletion of the words 'but if… [*address*]' would achieve this object.

2 'Unable' includes the executor's predeceasing the testator but also extends to the executor's inability to act for other reasons, such as mental incapacity.

FORM 8.2

Appointment of the testator's partner as executor with children as alternatives[1]

I appoint as my executor my [wife/husband/civil partner] [*name*] of [*address*] but if [he/she] is unable[2] or unwilling to act or if [he/she] dies before proving my Will I appoint as my executors those of my children who survive me.

1 It is envisaged that the next clause will be:

> 'If my [wife/husband/civil partner] survives me by thirty days I give the whole of my estate to [him/her] but if this gift fails the following provisions of my Will shall apply.'

The separation of the appointment of the widow as executor from her contingent gift is desirable because otherwise her appointment as executor will also be contingent.

2 'Unable' includes the executor's predeceasing the testator but also extends to the executor's inability to act for other reasons, such as mental incapacity.

FORM 8.3

Appointment of beneficiaries as executors[1]

I appoint as my executors my [residuary] beneficiaries [who have attained 18 at my death][2].

1 This kind of appointment can be useful when the testator wishes the beneficiaries to act as executors but the circumstances import a degree of uncertainty, for example, 'to those of my brothers and sisters who survive me', or where there is a substitutional gift of the residue which may well take effect. Consideration should be given to the need to amend this clause if a codicil is executed which changes the [residuary] beneficiaries.

2 This is desirable if one or more of the residuary beneficiaries may be minors.

FORM 8.4

Appointment of two executors where there is no possibility of a trust arising

I appoint as my executors [*name*] of [*address*] and [*name*] of [*address*] [but if either or both of them are unable[1] or unwilling to act or if either or both of them die before proving my Will I also appoint as my executor [*name*] of [*address*]][2].

1 'Unable' includes the executor's predeceasing the testator but also extends to the executor's inability to act for other reasons, such as mental incapacity.

2 It may be desirable for the testator to consider the appointment of an alternative executor in the event of one predeceasing him.

FORM 8.5

Appointment of executors and trustees where a trust may arise[1]

1 I appoint as my executors [*name*] of [*address*] and [*name*] of [*address*].

2 I appoint as my trustees those of my executors who obtain probate of this Will[2].

3 In this Will the expression 'my Trustees' means (as the context requires) those of my executors who obtained probate and the trustees for the time being of any trust arising under this Will.

1 See note at **8.5**.

2 See note at **8.6**.

FORM 8.6

Appointment of executors with different people appointed as trustees[1]

1 I appoint as my executors [*name*] of [*address*] and [*name*] of [*address*].

2 I appoint as my trustees [*name*] of [*address*] and [*name*] of [*address*].

3 In this Will the expression 'my Trustees' means the trustees for the time being of this Will and of any trust arising under it [other than the (*Trust A*) trustees who are referred to as ("Trust A Trustees") which shall mean the trustees for the time being of Trust A.][2]

1 It is unusual for the executors not to be appointed as the original trustees but it sometimes is appropriate. See note at **8.7**. In some cases, the executors will be able to transfer the trust property to the trustees at an early stage of the administration. In other cases, for example, where the trust property is the residuary estate, it will only be transferred when the administration of the estate is complete.

2 This should be included if the Trust A trustees are to be given different powers and administrative provisions to the trustees of the other trustees.

FORM 8.7

Appointment where different trustees appointed for a particular trust[1]

1 I appoint as my executors [*name*] of [*address*] and [*name*] of [*address*].

2 I appoint as my trustees to [(*name of Trust A*)] [*name*] of [*address*] and [*name*] of [*address*][2].

3 I appoint as my trustees [to all other trusts arising under this Will] those of my executors who obtain probate of this Will[3].

4 Unless the context requires otherwise the expression 'my Trustees' means the trustees for the time being of any trust arising under this Will.

1 See note at **8.7**.
2 The clause appointing a different trustee to a different trust can also sometimes be found in the provisions creating that particular trust.
3 See note at **8.7**.

FORM 8.8

Appointment of executors with wish expressed regarding solicitors to be employed[1]

1 I appoint as my executors [*name*] of [*address*] and [*name*] of [*address*] [but if either or both of them are unable[2] or unwilling to act or if either or both of them die before proving my Will I also appoint as my executor [*name*] of [*address*].

2 I appoint as my trustees those of my executors who obtain probate of this Will[3].

3 In this Will the expression 'my Trustees' means (as the context requires) those of my executors who obtain probate and the trustees for the time being of any trust arising under this Will.

4 I wish my Trustees to employ as their solicitors [*name*] of [*address*] or any other firm corporation or limited liability partnership[4] which at my death has succeeded to and carries on its practice.

1 See note at **8.32**.
2 'Unable' includes the executor's predeceasing the testator but also extends to the executor's inability to act for other reasons, such as mental incapacity.
3 See note at **8.5**.
4 See the notes at **8.16–8.22**.

FORM 8.9

Appointment of the Public Trustee as executor and trustee[1]

1 I appoint the Public Trustee as my executor and trustee.

[2 I wish my executor and trustee to employ as their solicitors [*name*] of [*address*] or any other firm corporation or limited liability partnership[2] which at my death has succeeded to and carries on its practice.]

1 An appointment of the Public Trustee does not have effect unless the Public Trustee consents to act so it is advisable for a testator to seek confirmation of a willingness to act in advance. The Public Trustee has statutory power to charge for acting as executor/trustee and so no professional charging clause is necessary.
2 See the notes at **8.16–8.22**.

FORM 8.10

Appointment of solicitors' firm where there is no possibility of a trust arising

1 I appoint as my executors the partners [at my death][1] in the firm of [*name*] of [*address*] ('the Firm').

2 The expression 'the Firm' means not only [*name*] but any other firm which at my death has succeeded to and carries on its practice including

a firm which has been incorporated or has formed a limited liability partnership.

3 The expression 'partners' means the persons commonly described as partners in the Firm including salaried partners[2] and, in the case of an incorporated practice or limited liability partnership, the directors, members and beneficial owners of any share of the Firm.

4 I wish not more than [two] of the partners in the Firm to apply for probate of this Will.

5 Any of my executors who is a solicitor may charge fees for work done by him or his firm (whether or not the work is of a professional nature) on the same basis as if he were not one of my executors but employed to carry out the work on their behalf[3].

1 See note at **8.17**. In the absence of these words the partners at the date of the Will will be appointed.
2 Following the decision in *Re Rogers (deceased)* [2006] 2 All ER 792 (see **8.21** above) if salaried partners are to be included the Will must expressly include them.
3 See notes at **8.27–8.31** as to why an express charging clause is desirable.

FORM 8.11

Appointment of members of solicitors' firm as executors and trustees

1 I appoint as my executors the partners [at my death][1] in the firm [*name*] of [*address*] ('the Firm') and I appoint as my trustees those of my executors who obtain probate of this Will[2].

2 The expression 'the Firm' means not only [*name*] but any other firm which at my death has succeeded to and carries on its practice including a firm which has been incorporated or has formed a limited liability partnership.

3 The expression 'partners' means the persons commonly described as partners in the Firm including salaried partners[3] and, in the case of an incorporated practice or limited liability partnership, the directors, members and beneficial owners of any share of the Firm.

4 In this Will the expression 'my Trustees' means (as the context requires) those of my executors who obtain probate and the trustees for the time being of any trust arising under this Will.

5 I wish not more than [two] of the partners in the Firm to apply for probate of this Will.

6 Any of my Trustees who is a solicitor may charge fees for work done by him or his firm (whether or not the work is of a professional nature) on the same basis as if he were not one of my Trustees but employed to carry out the work on their behalf[4].

1 See note at **8.17**. In the absence of these words the partners at the date of the Will will be appointed.
2 See note at **8.6**.
3 Following the decision in *Re Rogers (deceased)* [2006] 2 All ER 792 (see **8.21** above) it is apparent that if salaried partners are to be included the Will must expressly include them.
4 See note at **8.27–8.31** as to why an express charging clause is desirable.

FORM 8.12

Appointment of members of solicitors' LLP as executors and trustees

1 I appoint as my executors the members [at my death][1] of the firm [*name*] of [*address*] ('the Firm') and I appoint as my trustees those of my executors who obtain probate of this Will[2].

2 The expression 'the Firm' means not only [*name*] but any other firm which at my death has succeeded to and carries on its practice including a firm which has been incorporated or has formed a limited liability partnership.

4 In this Will the expression 'my Trustees' means (as the context requires) those of my executors who obtain probate and the trustees for the time being of any trust arising under this Will.

5 I wish not more than [two] members of the Firm to apply for probate of this Will.

6 Any of my Trustees who is a solicitor may charge fees for work done by him or his firm (whether or not the work is of a professional nature) on the same basis as if he were not one of my Trustees but employed to carry out the work on their behalf[3].

1 See note at **8.17**. In the absence of these words the partners at the date of the Will will be appointed.
2 See note at **8.6**.
3 See note at **8.27** as to why an express charging clause is desirable.

FORM 8.13

Appointment of solicitors together with lay trustee as executors and trustees

1 I appoint as my executors the partners [at my death][1] in the firm ('the Firm') and [*lay trustee name*] of [*address*].

2 I appoint as my trustees those of my executors who obtain probate of this Will[2].

3 The expression 'the Firm' means not only [*name*] but any other firm which at my death has succeeded to and carries on its practice including a firm which has been incorporated or has formed a limited liability partnership.

4 The expression 'partners' means the persons commonly described as partners in the Firm including salaried partners[3] and, in the case of an incorporated practice or limited liability partnership, the directors, members and beneficial owners of any share of the Firm.

5 In this Will the expression 'my Trustees' means (as the context requires) those of my executors who obtain probate and the trustees for the time being of any trust arising under this Will.

6 I wish [*lay trustee name*] and not more than [one] of the partners in the Firm to apply for probate of this Will.

7 Any of my Trustees who is a solicitor may charge fees for work done by him or his firm (whether or not the work is of a professional nature)

on the same basis as if he were not one of my Trustees but employed to carry out the work on their behalf[4].

1 See note at **8.17**. In the absence of these words the partners at the date of the Will will be appointed.
2 See note at **8.6**.
3 Following the decision in *Re Rogers (deceased)* [2006] 2 All ER 792 (see **8.21** above) if salaried partners are to be included the Will must expressly include them.
4 See note at **8.27** as to why an express charging clause is desirable.

FORM 8.14

Appointment of members of a solicitors' firm and an accountants' firm as executors and trustees[1]

1 I appoint as my executors the partners [at my death][2] in the firm [*name*] of [*address*] ('the Solicitors' Firm') and the partners [at my death][3] in the firm [*name*] of [*address*] ('the Accountants' Firm').

2 I appoint as my trustees those of my executors who obtain probate of this Will[4].

3 In this Will the following expressions have the meanings assigned to them:

3.1 'my Trustees' means (as the context requires) those of my executors who obtain probate and the trustees for the time being of any trust arising under this Will;

3.2 'the Solicitors' Firm' means not only [*name*] but also any other firm which at my death has succeeded to and carries on its practice including a firm which has been incorporated or has formed a limited liability partnership;

3.3 'the Accountants' Firm' means not only [*name*] but also any other firm which at my death has succeeded to and carries on its practice including a firm which has been incorporated or has formed a limited liability partnership;

3.4 the expression 'partners' means the persons commonly described as partners in the Firm including salaried partners[5] and, in the case of an incorporated practice or limited liability partnership, the directors, members and beneficial owners of any share of the Firm.

4 I wish not more than [one] of the partners in the Solicitors' Firm and not more than [one] of the partners in the Accountants' Firm to apply for probate of this Will.

5 Any of my Trustees who is a solicitor or an accountant may charge fees for work done by him or his firm (whether or not the work is of a professional nature) on the same basis as if he were not one of my trustees but employed to carry out the work on their behalf[6].

1 See the note at **8.23**.
2 See note at **8.17**. In the absence of these words the partners at the date of the Will will be appointed.
3 See note at **8.17**. In the absence of these words the partners at the date of the Will will be appointed.
4 See note at **8.6**.
5 Following the decision in *Re Rogers (deceased)* [2006] 2 All ER 792 (see **8.21** above) if salaried partners are to be included the Will must expressly include them.
6 See note at **8.27** as to why an express charging clause is desirable.

FORM 8.15

Appointment of a trust corporation as executors and trustees[1]

1 I appoint [*trust corporation's name*] as my executor and trustee.

2 The conditions on which [*trust corporation's name*] acts as executor last published before the date of this Will shall apply and the said trust corporation shall be remunerated in accordance with the scale of fees current at my death as varied from time to time during the administration of any trust arising under this Will[2].

1 See note at **8.24**. If a trust corporation is appointed, it is advisable to contact the trust corporation before the Will is executed to confirm they are willing to act. The trust corporation may also have a standard appointment clause which they wish to be used which, depending on its contents, may be more appropriate.

2 See note at **8.27** as to why an express charging clause is desirable.

FORM 8.16

Professional charges clause[1]

Any of my Trustees in a profession, including a sole trustee, may charge for work done by him or his firm (whether or not the work is of a professional nature) on the same basis as if he were not one of my trustees but employed to carry out the work on their behalf and a trust corporation may be paid fees according to the scale fees which it charges from time to time[2].

1 The express charging provision would usually be included in the provisions appointing the executor but occasionally it may be more appropriate to include as a separate clause. See **8.31**.

2 See note at **8.27** as to why an express charging clause is desirable.

9 Appointment of Guardians

9.1 In all circumstances where a testator has minor children the testator should be advised to consider appointing a guardian of the children to act after the testator's death. If a guardian is so appointed, then if there is no surviving parent with parental responsibility on the death of the testator, the appointed guardian will be given parental responsibility for the minor children[1]. This is a significant responsibility with parental responsibility defined as 'all rights, duties, powers, responsibilities and authority which by law a parent of a child has in relation to the child and his property'[2] and accordingly it must be considered carefully.

1 If there is a surviving person with parental responsibility the appointment will take effect on their death.

2 Children Act 1989 s 3(1).

9.2 Those governed by the Law Society Wills and Inheritance Protocol are required to give the testator specified advice regarding the appointment of guardians[1] but all other draftsmen should give similar appropriate advice concerning the appointment of guardians if the testator has minor children. This advice should include the effect of the appointment, the role of a guardian, what happens if no appointment is made, that an appointment can be made by Will or by a separate document and (if applicable) the rights of the child's other parent. The role of a guardian is a very important role and it has significant responsibilities and so the testator should be advised to consider very carefully who they wish to appoint as a guardian.

1 Law Society Wills and Inheritance Protocol, Publication date 3 July 2013, paragraph 11.5.

9.3 It is important to remember that not all parents will have parental responsibility and so not all parents may be able to appoint guardians. If a father and mother are married when the child is born both will have parental responsibility[1]. However, if the father and mother were unmarried only the mother will have automatic parental responsibility. The father can acquire parental responsibility (i) if he marries the mother[2]; (ii) if he becomes registered as the child's father; (iii) if he and the mother make a 'parental responsibility agreement'; or (iv) if the court (on his application) orders that he shall have parental responsibility for the child[3]. Step-parents[4] and second female parents[5] likewise do not automatically have parental responsibility but can acquire it in a similar way to an unmarried father. If the testator desires that his or her children be cared for by an unmarried father, a second female parent or by a step-parent then steps should be taken for the other parent to acquire parental responsibility or, if there is insufficient time to do so, the other person should be appointed as a guardian.

1 Children Act 1989 s 2(1).
2 A combination of the Children Act 1989 s 2(1) read with the Family Law Reform Act 1987 s 1(2)–(4).
3 Children Act 1989 s 4(1).
4 Children Act 1989 s 4A.
5 Children Act 1989 s 4ZA.

Appointment

9.4 The appointment of guardians and the rights they have are governed by the Children Act 1989. Under the Act a parent[1] with parental responsibility may appoint a guardian by Will or by a document which they date and sign and which provides that the appointment only takes effect on their death. While in many circumstances it will be most appropriate to make the appointment in a Will there will be some occasions where it would be better made in a separate document. This might include situations where time is of the essence and there is a risk that the testator might die before the Will can be executed or where the testator is likely to revoke their Will in the future but will not wish to revoke the appointment of a guardian[2].

1 This does not include a step-parent as they (unlike unmarried fathers or second female parents) cannot become registered as the child's parent.
2 The appointment of a guardian in a Will or codicil is revoked if the Will or codicil is revoked: Children Act 1989 s 6(4).

9.5 It is possible to appoint more than one guardian. It is also possible for both parents to appoint separate guardians but for obvious reasons couples should be advised to consult one another and appoint the same person or persons if possible.

9.6 The appointment of a guardian can either be conditional on the testator being the sole surviving parent[1] or it can be unconditional[2]. If the appointment is unconditional then if on the testator's death there is a surviving parent with parental responsibility the appointment will only take effect on the death of the surviving parent. It will take effect even if the surviving parent appoints a different guardian, in which case both appointees will be guardians. In the case of married couples it is generally better practice for the appointment to be conditional as it allows the survivor to choose the most appropriate person or persons to be appointed without being constrained by the person chosen when the first-to-die passed away. For practical reasons it is also common that the same persons are appointed guardians of all the testator's minor children but circumstances may make this unsuitable. In particular, if there have been children from different relationships it may be appropriate to make different appointments for different children and provision for this is made in **Forms 9.4** and **9.5**.

1 See **Form 9.2**.
2 See **Form 9.1**.

9.7 An appointed guardian may appoint another guardian to act in the case of his or her death[1]. This is a statutory power and therefore there is no requirement to refer to this power in the Will. However, it may be sensible to include reference to this power in the Will if the appointed guardian is likely to be unaware of this power.

1 Children Act 1989 s 5(4).

9.8 The High Court also has an inherent jurisdiction to appoint a guardian but it is much more desirable for the testator to make his or her own appointment rather than relying on the inherent jurisdiction of the High Court.

Revocation

9.9 A signed and dated document revoking the appointment of a guardian will revoke the appointment even if it the appointment is contained in an unrevoked Will or codicil[1]. If the appointment was made in a separate document the appointment is also revoked by destruction of that document[2] while if the appointment was made by Will the revocation of the Will also revokes the appointment[3].

1 Children Act 1989 s 6(2).
2 Children Act 1989 s 6(2), (3).
3 Children Act 1989 s 6(4).

9.10 A later appointment revokes an earlier appointment (including one contained in an unrevoked Will or codicil) unless it is clear that the later appointment was to appoint an additional guardian rather than replace the original guardian. Draftsmen should therefore take considerable care to make this point clear if they are asked to appoint an additional guardian in a later document.

9.11 An appointment of the testator's spouse as a guardian is also automatically revoked by the subsequent dissolution or annulment of the marriage unless a contrary intention appears in the appointment[1]. If the testator seeks to appoint their spouse as guardian the draftsman should clarify this point with the testator and prepare the Will accordingly[2].

1 Children Act 1989 s 6(3A).
2 See **Form 9.3**.

Other points

9.12 The testator should be advised to obtain the consent of the proposed guardian prior to making a provision appointing them as a guardian. A failure to do so may lead to the guardian disclaiming the guardianship which would be undesirable for all concerned. A guardian can disclaim his appointment by a signed document but this must be made within a reasonable time of the guardian first knowing that the appointment has taken effect[1].

1 Children Act 1989 s 6(5).

9.13 The interrelationship between guardians and trustees means that careful consideration should be made as to whether or not the chosen guardians should also be appointed as trustees of any trust created under the Will. On one hand, the guardians are best placed to know the needs of the children and they have the task of providing for those needs and therefore it may make sense for them to also be trustees. On the other hand, if they are appointed as trustees they can be placed in a conflict of interest if the children are beneficiaries under the trust. As guardians they should act in the children's best interests but as trustees they should be neutral when they judge the conflicting claims of the different beneficiaries. This problem is particularly obvious when the residue is held on discretionary trusts and the children are discretionary beneficiaries. In a case such as this, the most sensible position is sometimes to appoint two professional (or otherwise independent) trustees to act alongside one of the guardians.

PRECEDENTS

9.14

FORM 9.1

Appointment of testamentary guardians[1]

I appoint [*name*] of [*address*] and [*name*] of [*address*] as guardians of any of my children under eighteen.

1 This form is for use where the appointment of guardians is not conditional on being the sole surviving parent.

FORM 9.2

Appointment of testamentary guardians conditional on being surviving parent

1 If I am the sole surviving parent with parental responsibility for my children then I appoint [*name*] of [*address*] and [*name*] of [*address*] as guardians of any of my children under eighteen.

2 My appointed guardians have the power to appoint guardians to act after their death[1].

1 It is not necessary to include this power as it is a statutory power. However, it can be helpful to expressly draw the appointees' attention to this power.

FORM 9.3

Appointment of spouse not intended to be revoked by dissolution of marriage[1]

1 I appoint [(*name of spouse*)] of [*address*] and [*name*] of [*address*] as guardians of any of my children under eighteen.

2 The appointment of [(*name of spouse*)] shall not be revoked by any annulment or dissolution of my marriage to them.

1 This form is for use when the spouse does not already have parental responsibility and needs to be expressly appointed but such appointment is not to be revoked if the marriage is annulled or dissolved.

FORM 9.4

Appointment of different guardians for different children

1 [If I am the sole surviving parent with parental responsibility for my children then] I appoint [*name*] of [*address*] and [*name*] of [*address*] as guardians of any of [(*names of children)*] who are under eighteen and I appoint [*name*] of [*address*] and [*name*] of [*address*] as guardians of any of [(*names of children)*] who are under eighteen.

2 My appointed guardians have the power to appoint guardians to act after their death[1].

1 It is not necessary to include this power as it is a statutory power. However, it can be helpful to expressly draw the appointees' attention to this power.

FORM 9.5

Appointment of different guardians for children from different marriages[1]

1 [If I am the sole surviving parent with parental responsibility for my children then] I appoint [*name*] of [*address*] and [*name*] of [*address*] as guardians of any of my children by [X] who are under eighteen and I appoint [*name*] of [*address*] and [*name*] of [*address*] as guardians of any of any of my children by [Y] who are under eighteen.

2 My appointed guardians have the power to appoint guardians to act after their death[2].

1 This form is the similar to **Form 9.4** save that it identifies the children by parents rather than name. It can be appropriate if the existing children's parents are known and there is a prospect of future children being born to existing parents.

2 It is not necessary to include this power as it is a statutory power. However, it can be helpful to expressly draw the appointees' attention to this power.

10 Legacies

The use and type of legacies

10.1 Legacies are used for a variety of reasons. Gifts of small sums of money (pecuniary legacies) are often used as a means of remembering friends or relatives who are not intended to participate in a gift of residue, whilst specific gifts of particular assets (such as homes or chattels) (specific legacies) are a means of passing on particular assets to particular people.

10.2 Legacies are grouped into general, demonstrative and specific. A general legacy is one where the subject matter is not distinguished or payable from other property included in the estate. It follows that most gifts of money – pecuniary legacies – are general legacies. Demonstrative legacies consist of a pecuniary legacy payable out of a particular fund. Such a legacy does not fail by the total or partial failure of the fund out of which it was directed to be paid but then becomes payable out of the general personal estate and it does not abate with the general legacies until after the particular fund is exhausted.

10.3 A specific legacy is a legacy of some thing or of some interest forming part of the testator's estate. The use of a specific legacy for gifts of money should be avoided (eg a gift of a specific bank account). Future events often defeat the original intention of the testator and can be a fertile source of family disharmony as well as creating problems relating to their true meaning. Specific legacies are best reserved for bequests of real property, chattels and securities.

10.4 In this chapter we consider the use of pecuniary, general or demonstrative legacies. Specific gifts of chattels, property and of business interests are dealt with in **chapters 11, 12** and **13** respectively.

Gifts free of inheritance tax

10.5 Inheritance tax on unsettled UK property is a testamentary expense to be paid out of the estate and not by any particular beneficiary. The Will may vary the incidence of inheritance tax by express direction or make express provision clarifying the position. In the ordinary case the normal direction to pay inheritance tax out of the residue merely makes this clear although in the case of chattels which may be out of the UK an express direction is considered essential.

10.6 If some gifts are expressed to be tax-free and others are not, the problem of 'double grossing-up' may arise. If legacies are subject to double grossing-up a small inheritance tax advantage can result at the expense of time-consuming computations, likely to outweigh any tax saving in cases of low value. This is discussed further in **chapter 23**.

10.7 Unless the testator desires otherwise, it is advisable to include words expressly freeing pecuniary legacies from inheritance tax, or to include a general declaration freeing legacies from inheritance tax as in **Form 10.1**.

The priority and timing of legacies

10.8 In a solvent estate, and in the absence of express direction from the testator, a legacy will be payable in the normal course of the administration of the estate. In most cases that means at the point where the residue has been ascertained and when the executor can be certain that the subject matter of the legacy is not needed for the payment of debts and expenses. In any case an executor is not bound to distribute the estate before the expiry of a year from the deceased's death[1] but that is not to say that distribution cannot be postponed for much longer in cases of uncertainty or complexity or that an executor is prevented from making earlier payment where there is no reason for doubt.

1 Administration of Estates Act 1925 s 44.

10.9 Subject to express direction in the Will (see **Form 10.7**), interest is payable on pecuniary legacies at the simple rate of 0.3% from the expiry of the executor's year[1] (the rate varies and should be checked).

1 See paragraph 15 to Practice Direction 40A of the Civil Procedure Rules.

10.10 Where the estate is solvent but insufficient to pay all of the gifts and legacies, then the residuary gifts abate first. If after that there is insufficient to pay the legacies then (subject to any provision of the Will and to charges on the property itself) pecuniary legacies abate first (proportionately) and thereafter those assets that are subject to specific legacies[1].

1 Administration of Estates Act 1925 s 34(3) and Sch 1 Part II.

The satisfaction of debts and the presumption against 'double portions'

10.11 Without more, a legacy to a person to whom the testator owes money at the time of death will be presumed to be in payment of the indebtedness. So where a legatee of £1,000 is owed £500 by the testator the estate will pay the legatee the £1,000 but not the additional £500. The presumption can be altered by the terms of the Will (see **Form 10.18**). Similarly, where a legatee owes a debt to the estate they must bring such debt into account and will be paid only the net sum (eg a legatee of £500 who owes £250 will receive only £250). For releases of debts see **12.14** and **Forms 12.23–12.25**.

10.12 A payment by a person in the position of a parent to their child is presumed to be a 'portion' and will cause a legacy to that child to adeem wholly or partially.

So, where a father leaves £5,000 to each of his three sons but then pays one of them £2,500 in his lifetime that will cause a partial ademption of the legacy so that the son will receive only £2,500 from the Will. This presumption can also be altered by the terms of the Will (see **Form 10.11**).

Nil rate band legacies

10.13 Although less common after the introduction of transferable nil rate bands, it is possible to create a legacy of a sum equivalent to the nil rate band applicable to the estate. This is commonly used as a means of making a gift that will not cause tax to be borne by the estate in circumstances where the residuary beneficiary is exempt (usually a spouse). Such legacies are considered in more detail in **chapter 23**.

Legacies to the draftsman

10.14 A legacy in favour of a solicitor or draftsman who drafted the Will, will be valid, provided that person does not also witness the Will. However, such legacies are frowned upon by professional bodies, who are concerned that such gifts may be procured in breach of the draftsperson's professional obligations. The Law Society Protocol requires every practice to have a written policy setting out how a draftsman will deal with the professional conduct issues arising from gifts and legacies to those drafting Wills or persons connected with them. The policy must include a requirement for the client to obtain independent advice regarding such gifts and for the draftsperson to obtain written confirmation of that advice subject only to a limited exceptions in cases where the client is a member of the beneficiary's family and the gift is not disproportionate to their and other family member's expectations.

PRECEDENTS

10.15

FORM 10.1

Declaration that legacies are free of inheritance tax and other duties[1]

The legacies [*given by this Will*] [*at clauses [ ] to [ ]*] shall be paid free of inheritance tax and other taxes or duties payable as a result of my death.

1 See the note at **10.5–10.7**.

FORM 10.2

Pecuniary legacy

I give £[ ] to [*name*] [*free of inheritance tax*[1]].

or

I give the following legacies [*free of inheritance tax*[1]]:

(a) £[ ] to [*AB*] of [*address*]

(b) £[ ] to [*CD*] of [*address*]

etc.

1 It is sensible expressly to provide that legacies are free of inheritance tax if, as is usually the case, that is what the testator intends. See the note at **10.5–10.7**.

FORM 10.3

Specific pecuniary legacy[1]

I give to [*name*] [*any money in my safe*] [*free of inheritance tax*[2]].

1 Such gifts are unusual and testators should be advised to avoid them. See the notes at **10.3**.
2 It is sensible expressly to provide that legacies are free of inheritance tax if, as is usually the case, that is what the testator intends. See the note at **10.5–10.7**.

FORM 10.4

Demonstrative pecuniary legacy[1]

I give £ to [*name*] to be paid primarily out of money standing to my credit at my death with [*Building Society*] but if such credit is insufficient at my death then this gift is payable out of my residuary estate. [*This gift is made free of inheritance tax*[2].]

1 Such gifts have certain advantages but are usually best avoided. See notes at **10.3**.
2 It is sensible expressly to provide that legacies are free of inheritance tax if, as is usually the case, that is what the testator intends. See the note at **10.5–10.7**.

FORM 10.5

Legacy subject to inheritance tax[1]

I give £[ ] to [*name*] subject to his bearing any inheritance tax attributable to it.

1 See the note at **10.5–10.7**. If any gifts are expressed to be subject to inheritance tax, the Will ought not to contain a direction (for example, as in **Form 10.1**) for inheritance tax to be paid out of residue as the two provisions relating to inheritance tax will conflict. If a general direction is omitted the inheritance tax on gifts not bearing their own tax will be payable out of residue under statutory provisions.

FORM 10.6

Priority legacy[1]

I give £[ ] to [*name*] to be paid immediately after my death and to rank in priority to all other gifts made by this Will. [*This gift is made free of inheritance tax*[2].]

1 This provision has three consequences. If the estate is solvent, it requires the executors to pay the legacy as soon as sufficient funds are available without waiting until the estate is ready for general distribution. If the estate is insolvent, the legacy will be payable in full (if possible) out of the moneys available for the payment of pecuniary legacies and will not abate proportionally with other legacies. Finally, interest on the legacy will run from the date of death and not from the first anniversary of the testator's death.

2 It is sensible expressly to provide that legacies are free of inheritance tax if, as is usually the case, that is what the testator intends. See the note at **10.5–10.7**.

FORM 10.7

Direction as to Interest

I direct that all legacies payable by this Will shall bear interest at the simple rate of [*3%*] on but not before [*one year*] from my death.

FORM 10.8

Legacies to two beneficiaries with provision for accruer

I give [£1,500] to each of [*AB*] and [*CD*] but if either of them dies before me I give [£3,000] to the survivor. [*This gift is made free of inheritance tax*[1].]

1 It is sensible expressly to provide that legacies are free of inheritance tax if, as is usually the case, that is what the testator intends. See the note at **10.5–10.7**.

FORM 10.9

Legacy to be divided between two or more beneficiaries

I give [*free of inheritance tax*[1]] £[ ] to be divided equally among those of the following who survive me:

[*AB*] of [*address*];

[*CD*] of [*address*];

[*EF*] of [*address*];

etc.

1 It is sensible expressly to provide that legacies are free of inheritance tax if, as is usually the case, that is what the testator intends. See the note at **10.5–10.7**.

FORM 10.10

Legacy to a minor – provision for payment to minor if over 16 and otherwise to parent or guardian[1]

I give [*free of inheritance tax*[2]] £[ ] to [*name*] and if at my death he is under sixteen years old it may be paid to his parent or guardian for his benefit or if he has attained the age of sixteen years it may be paid to the beneficiary himself and either payment shall be a discharge to my Trustees.

1 Although the gift vests on the testator's death, a minor cannot give a valid receipt for it unless married. Without specific authority the trustees would be able to pay the legacy to a person with parental responsibility for the beneficiary while under 18 but in many cases it is desirable to provide that a beneficiary between the ages of 16 and 18 should himself give a good receipt for the legacy.

2 It is sensible expressly to provide that legacies are free of inheritance tax if, as is usually the case, that is what the testator intends. See the note at **10.5–10.7**.

FORM 10.11

Direction regarding 'double portions'

In paying any legacies in this Will I direct that no account shall be taken of previous payments or gifts made by me in my lifetime.

FORM 10.12

Legacy to grandchildren

I give [*free of inheritance tax*[1]] £[ ] to be divided equally among [*my grandchildren living at my death*]/[*those of my grandchildren who survive me and attain the age of eighteen years*][2].

1 It is sensible expressly to provide that legacies are free of inheritance tax if, as is usually the case, that is what the testator intends. See the note at **10.5–10.7**.

2 In the case of either alternative it is recommended that the executors are given power to pay sums to minor grandchildren or to their parents or guardians, as in **Form 19.1**. If the second alternative is to be used the executors could find themselves holding a fund for the grandchildren for very many years. Where professional executors or trustees are appointed by the Will their charges for the management of the fund may have the effect of depleting it so the provision may only be appropriate where there is a substantial fund for investment. The argument in favour of gifts to children and grandchildren being vested (see **16.13–16.24**) suggests that it would be better to exclude an age contingency provision.

FORM 10.13

Legacy to grandchildren – alternative method

(a) I give £ to be divided equally among those children of my son [*AB*] [*who are living at my death*]/[*who survive me and attain the age of eighteen years*][1].

(b) I give £ to be divided equally among those children of my daughter [*CD*] [*who are living at my death*]/[*who survive me and attain the age of eighteen years*][2].

[*This gift is made free of inheritance tax*[3].]

1 See footnote 2 to **Form 10.12**.
2 See footnote 1 above.
3 It is sensible expressly to provide that legacies are free of inheritance tax if, as is usually the case, that is what the testator intends. See the note at **10.5–10.7**.

FORM 10.14

Legacy of specific amount to each grandchild

I give [*free of inheritance tax*[1]] £[ ] to each of my grandchildren [*living at my death*]/[*who survives me and attains the age of eighteen years*][2].

1 It is sensible expressly to provide that legacies are free of inheritance tax if, as is usually the case, that is what the testator intends. See the note at **10.5–10.7**.
2 See footnote 2 to **Form 10.12**.

FORM 10.15

Legacy to grandchildren with substitution of great grandchildren

I give [*free of inheritance tax*[1]] £[ ] to be divided equally among those of my grandchildren who survive me [*and attain the age of eighteen years*][2] but if any of them dies before attaining a vested interest leaving children then those children shall [*on attaining the age of eighteen years*][2] take the share which their parent would have inherited if he or she had survived me.

1 It is sensible expressly to provide that legacies are free of inheritance tax if, as is usually the case, that is what the testator intends. See the note at **10.5–10.7**.
2 See footnote 2 to **Form 8.12.** The more so in the case of the great grandchildren.

FORM 10.16

Legacy to executor

I give [free of inheritance tax[1]] £[ ] to [*name*] and this legacy [*is*]/[*is not*][2] conditional on his acting as my executor [*and trustee*].

1 It is sensible expressly to provide that legacies are free of inheritance tax if, as is usually the case, that is what the testator intends. See the note at **10.5–10.7**.
2 It is desirable to make clear whether or not the legacy is conditional on the executor/ trustee accepting the appointment as there is a presumption that a legacy to an executor is conditional on acceptance of the office.

FORM 10.17

Legacy to employee if still employed

I give [*free of inheritance tax*[1]] £[ ] to [*name*] if he is in my employment at my death and not under notice whether given by him or me to leave and this legacy is in addition to any sum due to him for wages which I might owe at the date of my death[2].

1 It is sensible expressly to provide that legacies are free of inheritance tax if, as is usually the case, that is what the testator intends. See the note at **10.5–10.7**.
2 It is desirable to make clear that the legacy is in addition to any sums owing to the employee if, for example, wages are payable in arrears.

FORM 10.18

Direction regarding Legacies to Creditors

Insofar as any of the legacies in this Will are given to persons to whom I owe money, I declare that the legacies are given in addition to the payment of the debts owing to them and are not to be in satisfaction of such debts

FORM 10.19

Inflation-proof legacy

I give [*free of inheritance tax*[1]] to [*name*] the sum which has the same value at my death as [£1,000] has at the date of this Will to be calculated by my trustees having regard to the Retail Prices Index in the month in which this my Will is executed and in the month of my death having regard to any re-basing of the Index which might have occurred in the meantime[2].

1 It is sensible expressly to provide that legacies are free of inheritance tax if, as is usually the case, that is what the testator intends. See the note at **10.5–10.7**.

2 The trustees will have to assess the current value of the specified sum by reference to the RPI. It is not sensible to provide a vague direction as to the means of calculation. The clause could go further and set out the mechanics of the calculation but that ought to be obvious. There is no substitute for reconsidering a Will regularly in the light of changed circumstances.

FORM 10.20

Gift of a number of inflation-proof legacies

I give [*free of inheritance tax*[1]] to each of the legatees named below the sum which has the same value at my death as the amount specified against his name had at the date of this Will, such sum to be calculated by my trustees having regard to the Retail Prices Index in the month in which this my Will is executed and in the month of my death having regard to any re-basing of the Index which might have occurred in the meantime.

[*AB*]: [£1,000]

[*CD*]: [£2,500]

[*EF*]: [£5,000].

1 It is sensible expressly to provide that legacies are free of inheritance tax if, as is usually the case, that is what the testator intends. See the note at **10.5–10.7**.

11 Specific Gifts of Real Property and Rights of Occupation

Simple gifts of land

11.1 A gift of a person's house or home is very often a gift of their most valuable asset. This must be considered carefully when establishing the effect of the Will, since a new Will inserting a gift of a person's residence may effect a dramatic change of disposition. Similarly, where such gift might fail (eg because the home has been sold) one or more persons may feel significantly aggrieved.

11.2 It is important for the draftsperson to consider the testator's power to make the gift. Most obviously it should be checked that the testator owns the home and owns the interest they think they have. Where the property is owned jointly it is essential to sever any joint tenancy since without this the gift in the Will will be ineffective. Further discussion of severance and an example of a notice of severance is contained at **32.6**.

11.3 As with all gifts of specific property an accurate description is important. In the case of a house it will usually suffice to use the postal address. Sometimes, however, more will be needed. There is no need to extend the description to refer to rights and restrictions that affect the property as it will be taken on the same terms as those on which the testator holds it. Similarly, if the property is subject to tenancies the beneficiary will take subject to them.

Mortgages

11.4 A debt which is charged on the testator's property such as a mortgage is payable out of the property charged, unless the Will expresses a contrary intention[1]. The normal form of direction to pay debts out of residue is not sufficient: there must be an express reference to the mortgage debt[2]. The reference to 'any charge' covers not only a legal but also an equitable charge.

1 Administration of Estates Act 1925 s 35, see **appendix 33.16**.
2 See **Form 11.1**.

11.5 It is important to inquire about mortgages when taking instructions. There may be mortgage protection or other policies, the proceeds of which are intended to go towards the discharge of the debt but which may fall into residue unless express provision is made. This may not accord with the wishes of the testator. Care should also be taken with policies of insurance held on trusts which are payable at the discretion of trustees having regard to a letter of wishes or similar direction of the testator which may be out of date by the time the Will is made. Many testators do not realise that the disposition of policies held on trust is not something which can be controlled by Will but which must be dealt with by giving a direction to trustees during the testator's lifetime.

Ademption[1]

11.6 A risk common to all specific gifts, but of most importance in the case of gifts of land, is the risk of ademption, most obviously from the home having been sold prior to the testator's death. A possible solution is illustrated in **Form 11.8**; the use of the well-known phrase 'principal private residence' is to provide for the testator changing his residence between the date of his Will and the date of his death.

1 Ademption is discussed further in **Chapter 2** at **2.47–2.50**.

Minors

11.7 A gift of real property to a beneficiary who may be a minor at the death of the testator will normally be effected through an express trust created by the Will. A simple gift to a minor will not be effective to pass the legal estate to the minor but instead operates as a declaration that the property is held in trust for the minor[1].

1 Trusts of Land and Appointment of Trustees Act 1996 s 2 and Sch 1, see **appendix 34.15** and **34.29**.

Gifts of land on trust

11.8 Any trust of property (whether express, implied, resulting or constructive[1]) which consists of or includes land is a trust of land[2]. In every trust of sale of land there is implied, despite any provision to the contrary, a power for the trustees to postpone sale of the land[3].

1 Trusts of Land and Appointment of Trustees Act 1996 s 1(2)(a), see **appendix 34.14**.
2 Trusts of Land and Appointment of Trustees Act 1996 s 1(1)(a), see **appendix 34.14**.
3 Trusts of Land and Appointment of Trustees Act 1996 s 4(1), see **appendix 34.17**.

Gifts of Beneficial share

11.9 Testators may not own the whole beneficial title but share their ownership with one or more other beneficial owners. Where their share is held as tenants in common it will form part of their estate on death and so can form the subject matter of a specific gift[1].

1 See **Form 11.6**.

Powers of Management of Land[1]

11.10 Trustees' powers of management of land are derived from the Trusts of Land and Appointment of Trustees Act 1996 and the Trustee Act 2000, which heavily amended the former Act in this regard[2]. Trustees of land have in relation to the land subject to the trust all the powers of an absolute owner[3]. The power also applies to personal representatives[4]. The powers of management of land may be extended or restricted by the Will[5]. The duty of care applies to trustees of land when exercising their powers of management of land[6] but that, too, can be excluded if desired[7].

1 See also notes in **Chapter 19** at **19.31–19.38**.
2 Trustee Act 2000 Sch 2 Part II para 45.
3 Trusts of Land and Appointment of Trustees Act 1996 s 6(1), see **appendix 34.19**.
4 Trusts of Land and Appointment of Trustees Act 1996 s 18, see **appendix 34.28**.
5 Trustee Act 2000 s 9, see **appendix 34.37**.
6 Trusts of Land and Appointment of Trustees Act 1996 s 6(9), Trustee Act 2000 s 2, Sch 1, see **appendix 34.19**, **34.31** and **34.60**.
7 Trustee Act 2000 Sch 1 para 7, see **appendix 34.60**.

11.11 Trustees may acquire freehold or leasehold land[1] in the UK as an investment, for occupation by a beneficiary, or for any other reason[2]. The term 'freehold or leasehold land' has a specific definition[3] and because of that trustees cannot acquire any undivided share in land in England and Wales under the statutory power, since an undivided share exists only in equity and cannot subsist as a legal estate. Where it is thought that trustees might need to invest in an undivided share of land an express power to that effect should be included[4].

1 'Land' is defined in the Interpretation Act 1978: it includes buildings and other structures; land covered with water; and any estate, interest, easement, servitude or right in or over land.
2 Trusts of Land and Appointment of Trustees Act 1996 s 6(3) and Trustee Act 2000 s 8(1), (2), see **appendix 34.19** and **34.36**.
3 The terms 'freehold or leasehold land' is specifically defined to mean, in relation to England, Wales and Northern Ireland, a legal estate (including in relation to Northern Ireland land held under a fee farm grant), and in relation to Scotland, the estate or interest of the proprietor if the dominium utile, or in the case of land not held on feudal tenure, the estate or interest of the owner, or a tenancy: Trustee Act 2000 s 8(2), see **appendix 34.36**.
4 This is most often necessary where trustees are to hold a share of a property occupied by a beneficiary who is a co-owner. See **Forms 11.8** and **11.9** which include such a power.

11.12 Trustees acquiring land as an investment are under duties to have regard to the standard investment criteria and to obtain and consider proper advice[1], and also the statutory duty of care[2], if it has not been limited or excluded by the Will or trust instrument, but if they are acquiring land for a non-investment purpose, for example, for occupation by a beneficiary, trustees will only be subject to the statutory duty of care. The powers may be restricted or excluded[3] or made subject to consents[4]. As part of general power of investment, trustees may invest in loans secured on land[5].

1 See **appendix 26.33**.
2 See **appendix 26.60**.
3 Trusts of Land and Appointment of Trustees Act 1996 s 8(1) and Trustee Act 2000 s 9, see **appendix 34.21** and **34.37**. The power in the Trustee Act 2000 s 8(1) is more limited than the power in Trustee Act 2000 s 3 in that it only permits trustees to lend on the security of land situated in the UK, but wider in that it permits trustees to lend on the security of land for purposes other than investment.
4 Trusts of Land and Appointment of Trustees Act 1996 s 8(2), see **appendix 34.21**.
5 Trustee Act 2000 s 3(3), see **appendix 34.32**. This power is also subject to the trustees having regard to the standard investment criteria, the requirement to obtain proper advice (unless the exclusion applies), and the statutory duty of care.

Delegation to beneficiaries

11.13 Trustees of land acting together jointly as trustees are given power to delegate by power of attorney to any beneficiary or beneficiaries of full age and beneficially entitled to an interest in possession in land any of their functions which relate to the land, for any period or indefinitely[1]. Beneficiaries to whom functions have been delegated are, in relation to the exercise of those functions, in the same position as trustees with the same duties and liabilities[2]. The duty of care[3] applies to trustees in deciding whether to delegate any of their functions to beneficiaries[4] but, if the delegation is not irrevocable[5], the trustees remain under a continuing duty to keep the delegation under review[6] and, if the circumstances make it appropriate to do so, must consider whether there is a need to exercise any power of intervention that they have[7] and if they consider that there is a need to exercise such a power they must do so[8].

1 Trusts of Land and Appointment of Trustees Act 1996 s 9(1), see **appendix 34.22**.
2 Trusts of Land and Appointment of Trustees Act 1996 s 9(7), see **appendix 34.22**.
3 Trustee Act 2000 s 2, Sch 1, **appendix 34.31** and **34.60**.
4 Trusts of Land and Appointment of Trustees Act 1996 s 9A(1), see **appendix 34.23**.
5 Trusts of Land and Appointment of Trustees Act 1996 s 9A(2)(b), see **appendix 34.23**.
6 Trusts of Land and Appointment of Trustees Act 1996 s 9A(3)(a), see **appendix 34.23**.
7 Trusts of Land and Appointment of Trustees Act 1996 s 9A(3)(b), see **appendix 34.23**.
8 Trusts of Land and Appointment of Trustees Act 1996 s 9A(3)(c), see **appendix 34.23**.

Consultation with beneficiaries

11.14 In the exercise of any function relating to land subject to the trust[1], trustees of land are under a duty 'so far as practicable' to consult the beneficiaries of full age and beneficially entitled to an interest in possession in the land[2], and so far as consistent with the general interest of the trust to give effect to the wishes of those beneficiaries, or (in the event of a dispute) the majority by value[3]. This applies unless expressly excluded[4].

1 Trusts of Land and Appointment of Trustees Act 1996 s 11(1), see **appendix 34.25**.
2 Trusts of Land and Appointment of Trustees Act 1996 s 11(1)(a), see **appendix 34.25**.
3 Trusts of Land and Appointment of Trustees Act 1996 s 11(1)(b), see **appendix 34.25**.
4 Trusts of Land and Appointment of Trustees Act 1996 s 11(2)(a), see **appendix 34.25**.

11.15 The duty to consult with beneficiaries adds appreciably to the burdens and difficulties of the trustees and in general the authors recommend its routine exclusion[1]. The duty to consult is particularly something to exclude in relation to a gift by Will where it is intended that any land shall be sold and the proceeds divided. Sometimes there are special reasons for not doing so such as a co-ownership trust of a house in which the co-owners are going to live, in a trust to provide a residence for a beneficiary, or any other land where it is intended that a beneficiary will occupy it. In such cases it will usually be desirable to provide the occupying beneficiary with the assurance of knowing that trustees must consult him.

1 See **Form 19.14** for a form of general exclusion.

The right of occupation

11.16 The Trusts of Land and Appointment of Trustees Act 1996 makes provision for a right of occupation for a beneficiary 'who is beneficially entitled to an interest in possession' in land subject to a trust of land at any time[1] if at that time either the purposes of the trust include making the land available for his occupation (or for the occupation of a class of which he is a member or of beneficiaries in general)[2]; or the land is held by the trustees so as to be so available. This is subject to the right not being available if the land is either unavailable or unsuitable for occupation by him[3].

1 Trusts of Land and Appointment of Trustees Act 1996 s 12(1), see **appendix 34.26**.
2 Trusts of Land and Appointment of Trustees Act 1996 s 12(1)(a), see **appendix 34.26**.
3 Trusts of Land and Appointment of Trustees Act 1996 s 12(1)(b), see **appendix 34.26**.

11.17 The statutory right of occupation is not confined in its application to residential property held on trust, but can be relevant to any kind of land in England and Wales held on trust which is capable of being occupied by a beneficiary, such as a farm or business premises. However, the statutory right is only available in respect of a beneficiary who is beneficially entitled to an interest in possession in the land[1]. No right is conferred on a beneficiary if the land is either unavailable or unsuitable for his occupation[2].

1 Trusts of Land and Appointment of Trustees Act 1996 s 12(1), see **appendix 34.26**. Interest in possession is not defined for these purposes but probably connotes a lesser interest than that contemplated by the use of the same words in Inheritance Tax Act 1984 Part III Chapter II.
2 Trusts of Land and Appointment of Trustees Act 1996 s 12(2), see **appendix 34.26**.

11.18 Trustees may impose reasonable conditions on a beneficiary in relation to his occupation of land[1] including payment of outgoings[2] and assuming any other obligation in relation to the land or any activity conducted there[3]. Where two or more beneficiaries are entitled to occupy land, trustees may exclude or restrict the entitlement to occupy of one or more but not all of them, but may not do so unreasonably or to an unreasonable extent[4]. If a beneficiary is excluded trustees can require compensatory provision to be made for anyone excluded by a beneficiary in occupation[5]. The trustees might also impose conditions on the occupying beneficiary including a condition that a beneficiary who occupies the land may be required to pay a 'rent' to an excluded beneficiary or beneficiaries[6], or a condition that he forgoes benefit from another part of the trust fund so that a compensating additional benefit from that other part is received by the excluded beneficiary or beneficiaries[7].

1 Trusts of Land and Appointment of Trustees Act 1996 s 13(3), see **appendix 34.27**.
2 Trusts of Land and Appointment of Trustees Act 1996 s 13(5)(a), see **appendix 34.27**.
3 Trusts of Land and Appointment of Trustees Act 1996 s 13(5)(b), see **appendix 34.27**.
4 Trusts of Land and Appointment of Trustees Act 1996 s 13(1), (2), see **appendix 34.27**.
5 Trusts of Land and Appointment of Trustees Act 1996 s 13(6), see **appendix 34.27**.
6 Trusts of Land and Appointment of Trustees Act 1996 s 13(6)(a), see **appendix 34.27**.
7 Trusts of Land and Appointment of Trustees Act 1996 s 13(6)(b), see **appendix 34.27**.

11.19 The powers of exclusion or restriction must be exercised having regard to the intentions of the person who created the trust[1], the purposes for which the land is held[2] and the circumstances and wishes of the beneficiaries who are entitled to occupy the land[3]. A testator may include an express declaration of his intentions in a Will and can provide that a property is to be retained in specie for the purpose of providing a particular beneficiary with a home. In doing so the testator will strongly influence what is subsequently done with the land because the powers of exclusion or restriction cannot be exercised so as to prevent a person who is in occupation of land from continuing to occupy the land[4] in a manner likely to result in his ceasing to occupy the land[5] unless he consents or the court has given approval[6]. Should the matter come to court the testator's intentions and the purposes for which the land is held will be taken into account[7].

1 Trusts of Land and Appointment of Trustees Act 1996 s 13(4)(a), see **appendix 34.27**.
2 Trusts of Land and Appointment of Trustees Act 1996 s 13(4)(b), see **appendix 34.27**.
3 Trusts of Land and Appointment of Trustees Act 1996 s 13(4)(c), see **appendix 34.27**.
4 Trusts of Land and Appointment of Trustees Act 1996 s 13(7), see **appendix 34.27**.
5 Trusts of Land and Appointment of Trustees Act 1996 s 13(7)(a), see **appendix 34.27**.
6 Trusts of Land and Appointment of Trustees Act 1996 s 13(7)(b), see **appendix 34.27**.
7 Trusts of Land and Appointment of Trustees Act 1996 s 13(8), see **appendix 34.27**.

Providing for a right of residence by Will

11.20 There are two approaches to giving a beneficiary the right to live in a property. The first is to create a life interest in the property, eg to hold on trust for life[1]. The second is to grant a mere right of occupation which may or may not be subject to terms of occupation[2]. Granting a life interest does more than just grant a right of occupation. It entitles the life tenant to the net rents until sale and the income produced by the proceeds of sale of the property if sold. Sometimes the granting of a life interest to the beneficiary is the best way of achieving the testator's wishes. If, for example, the beneficiary's health were to require him to move out of the house to sheltered accommodation or a nursing home, the testator might wish him to have the interest from the sale proceeds to supplement his income. In such cases it is also useful to include a power to advance capital[3] to the life tenant in case the income is not sufficient to pay the fees of a nursing home or similar.

1 **Form 11.7**.
2 **Form 11.9**.
3 **Form 11.8**.

11.21 Where the testator only wants to grant a right of occupation and not a life interest the occupying beneficiary will not be entitled to the net rents until sale or the income produced by the proceeds of sale of the house if sold and so, if it is intended that the proceeds of sale are to be invested in a replacement property, the Will should make express provision for that event[1]. If the intention is that the beneficiary will become entitled to the rents or the interest generated by investment of the proceeds of sale then the testator really intends that he should have a life interest. A problem which often arises is that account is not taken of the liability for outgoings and insurance. If the trustees are to bear these liabilities a separate fund will have to be provided. Even if the liabilities are to be imposed on the beneficiary, if there is no fund held back for the trustees they will not be able to enforce the beneficiary's obligations should that prove necessary.

1 See **Forms 11.9–11.11**.

11.22 Often the testator's intention is to provide furnished accommodation. Serious consideration should be given to making an outright gift of the furnishings to the proposed occupant. If this is not done, it is impracticable to place an obligation on the occupant to 'maintain and replace as occasion requires' because, over a period of time, the intended benefit becomes a burden. As ordinary household furniture is not durable, a life interest is also inappropriate. The precedents are not intended to apply to furnishings which constitute valuable assets in themselves.

Inheritance tax

11.23 Inheritance tax is payable out of residue in the absence of a direction to the contrary. **Form 11.5** is an example of a gift which bears its own inheritance tax. In cases in which the testator directs that any inheritance tax is to be borne by the beneficiary but any mortgage is to be paid out of residue, care should be taken to ensure that the testamentary provision makes it clear whether the beneficiary's inheritance tax liability relates to the value of the house subject to the mortgage or to its value after repayment of the mortgage.

11.24 A gift of a house subject on trust for life[1] will create an immediate post death interest in possession and so the property will be treated for inheritance tax as within the estate of the beneficiary (creating a further charge on that person's death). A gift of a right of occupation[2] will usually be regarded as a similar qualifying interest in possession but if complete certainty is required (eg in order to secure the spouse exemption where the widow/er is to be the beneficiary) it is suggested that a trust for life is the better course. A series of trusts for life or rights of occupation, or trusts which confer rights of occupation on more than one beneficiary are best avoided and if used, the inheritance tax consequences should be carefully considered.

1 **Form 11.8**.
2 **Forms 11.9, 11.10, 11.11**.

PRECEDENTS

11.25

FORM 11.1

Simple gift of house free of mortgage

I give to [*name*] my house known as [*postal address*] [and I direct that any charge[1] on my house shall be discharged out of my residuary estate].

1 This will include a statutory charge, an equitable charge or any other financial charge on the property as well as a mortgage.

FORM 11.2

Simple gift of house to two or more persons as tenants in common[1]

I give my house known as [*postal address*] to [AB] and [CD] in equal shares but if one of them dies before me his share shall [form part of my residuary estate]/[be taken by [EF]].

or

I give my house known as [*postal address*] to [AB] and [CD] as tenants in common in equal shares[1] or to the survivor of them.

or

I give my house known as [*postal address*] as tenants in common in equal shares[1] to those of the persons named below who survive me

[AB];

[CD];

[EF].

or

I give my house known as [*postal address*] to the persons named below in the shares indicated:

[AB] one half;

[CD] one quarter;

[EF] one quarter.

If any beneficiary named dies before me then the benefit he would have taken if he had survived me shall be [added proportionally to the other shares]/[shared equally among the surviving beneficiaries][2].

1 A gift to two or more persons without words of severance will constitute a gift to them as joint tenants. If they survive the testator, they can, of course, elect to take the gift as tenants in common. If, however, one of them pre-deceases the testator (or survives the testator and dies before an assent in favour of the beneficiaries as tenants in common has been executed) the whole of the

property will pass to the survivor(s). If the gift is to beneficiaries in specified shares they will take as tenants in common and, if one beneficiary pre-deceases the testator, his share will fall into residue. It is better to provide for possible contingencies rather than to allow the position to be regulated by the application of the general law if one beneficiary dies before the testator as it is then clear that the consequence was intended and has not resulted from chance.

2 This can be adapted and used with this or the earlier provisions of this form. In some cases, a suitable adaption may be:

> 'shall be taken by his widow [or if his widow does not survive me by those of his children who survive me].'

FORM 11.3

Simple gift of house to two or more persons as joint tenants[1]

I give my house known as [*postal address*] to [AB] and [CD] as beneficial joint tenants [or to the survivor of them].

1 The effect is that if both AB and CD survive the testator but one of them dies before severing the joint tenancy, the survivor will take the whole interest by survivorship. The inclusion of the words in brackets is not essential but is desirable. See footnote 1 to **Form 11.2**.

FORM 11.4

Gift of immovable property – provision for description

I give to [*name*] my [freehold] [leasehold][1] land fronting to [xxx] which is [registered at HM Land Registry under title number [ ] *or* [which I hold by a conveyance [*or* assignment, lease etc] dated [ ] and made between etc].

1 Leaseholds are personal property, not real property.

FORM 11.5

Gift of house – subject to inheritance tax[1]

I give to [*name*] my house known as [*postal address*] but subject to his bearing any inheritance tax attributable to its value.

1 See the note at **11.22**.

FORM 11.6

Gift of interest in a house held as tenant in common

I give to [*name*] my beneficial share and interest in the house known as [*postal address*].

FORM 11.7

Gift of testator's residence

I give to [*name*] the house that constitutes at my death my principal private residence[1] [and if doubt exists as to which is my principal private residence the decision of my Trustees shall be final and binding].

1 The term 'principal private residence' has been used because it has a well-established meaning as a result of capital gains tax legislation. There is unlikely to be any doubt as to which constitutes the

testator's principal private residence. For capital gains tax purposes he will probably have made an election. If the testator has a house abroad and one or more houses in the UK, it would be as well to describe the property as 'my principal private residence in the United Kingdom'. Where there is no possibility of the testator having a second home, it would be sufficient to refer to 'the house that constitutes my residence at my death'. Although the Will speaks from death it is thought desirable to make it clear that the provision relates to the testator's principal residence at the time of his death and not at the date of the Will.

Form 11.8

Gift of Property on Life Interest

My Trustees shall hold [*description of property*] [the property that constitutes my principal private residence at my death] [the property][1] on trust as follows:

1 To pay the income to [AB] for life.

2 Thereafter to hold the capital [upon the trusts of my residuary estate set out below[2].

3 [During the lifetime of [AB] my Trustees shall have power in their absolute discretion to pay or apply all or any part of the capital of this trust to or for the benefit of [AB] notwithstanding the interest of those persons at clause [2] above][3].

4 During [AB]'s lifetime and for so long as this trust includes the Property my Trustees:

(a) Shall not sell the Property without the consent of [AB];

(b) Shall allow [AB] to occupy the Property providing [he/she] complies with any obligations imposed by (c);

(c) Shall be free to impose such conditions as to the payment of insurance, outgoings and expenses of and relating to the property as they think fit;

(d) If at any time [AB] shall request in writing the Trustees shall sell the Property and shall apply the whole or any part of this trust in the purchase of another property whether freehold or leasehold and shall hold the same upon the trusts contained in this clause as if references to the property in this clause were a reference to the replacement property;

(e) In purchasing a replacement in accordance with the previous power my Trustees may join with any person in purchasing an undivided share of land.

1 See the footnote to **Form 11.7** above.
2 It is assumed that the life tenant is not also a beneficiary under the residuary estate. If, however, they are this provision can be amended.
3 This sub-clause introduces useful flexibility for trustees but is not essential.

FORM 11.9

Gift of house to trustees to permit occupation as a residence[1]

I give my house known as [*postal address*] ('the House')[2] to my Trustees on trust [for sale] on the following terms:

1 My Trustees shall permit [AB] ('the Occupant') to live in the House free of charge[3] so long as he wishes.

2 While the Occupant is living in the House my Trustees shall not sell it without his consent.

3 When the Occupant has ceased to live in the House my Trustees shall hold it [as part of my residuary estate]/[*appropriate gift over*][4].

4 [At the Occupant's request my Trustees may sell the House and buy another to be held on trust [for sale] on the same terms as the House][5].

5 In purchasing a replacement in accordance with the previous power my Trustees may join with any person in purchasing an undivided share of land[6].

1 This precedent should not be used for the purpose of inheritance tax mitigation. It serves a practical purpose where inheritance tax savings are not the prime consideration.
2 If the testator wishes to include their home wherever it is it would be preferable to use the definition in **Form 11.8** (of their principal private residence).
3 If terms are to be imposed on the Occupant's right to live in the House, use **Form 11.10**. If not, the testator should consider setting aside a fund out of the residuary estate from which the trustees can pay for repairs and the like.
4 See footnote 2 to **Form 11.8**.
5 The wording of this clause gives the trustees the express power they need to acquire an alternative house. They cannot spend more than the proceeds of the sale of the present house. For a provision enabling them to spend more, see clause 7 of **Form 11.10**.
6 This provision is intended to give the trustees power to own a proportion (ie a beneficial interest) of a property.

FORM 11.10

Gift of house to trustees to permit occupation as a residence – alternative[1]

I give my house known as [*postal address*] ('the House')[2] to my Trustees on trust for sale on the following terms:

1 My Trustees shall permit [AB] ('the Occupant') to live in the House without payment to them so long as he wishes and so long as he keeps the House in repair, insures it and pays all outgoings relating to it[3].

2 While the Occupant is entitled to live in the House my Trustees shall not sell it without his consent.

3 When the Occupant has ceased to be entitled to live in the House my Trustees shall hold it [as part of my residuary estate]/[*appropriate gift over*][4].

4 At the Occupant's request my Trustees may sell the House and buy another to be held on trust for sale on the same terms as the House.

5 In purchasing a replacement in accordance with the previous power my Trustees may join with any person in purchasing an undivided share of land[5].

6 Any surplus arising from the sale and purchase shall [form part of my residuary estate]/[*as in Clause 3*].

7 My Trustees may use money from my residuary estate to make up the difference between the cost of purchase and the cost of sale[6].

1 This precedent should not be used for the purpose of inheritance tax mitigation.

2 If the testator wishes to include their home wherever it is it would be preferable to use the definition in **Form 11.8** (of their principal private residence).

3 It is still sensible, even where a beneficiary is obliged to pay the expenses, for the testator to provide a fund out of which the trustees can pay for the work if the beneficiary fails to do so or take action to compel the beneficiary to comply with his obligations.

4 See footnote 2 to **Form 11.8**.

5 This provision is intended to give the trustees power to own a proportion (ie a beneficial interest) of a property.

6 It is only practicable to empower the trustees to use funds from the residuary estate if there is a continuing trust relating to it. It is undesirable that the occupant should be able to require the trustees to acquire an alternative house and particularly to provide additional funds for it. For that reason the trustees are given a discretionary power only.

FORM 11.11

Gift of a furnished house to trustees to permit occupation as a residence[1]

I give my house known as [*postal address*] ('the House') with the furniture, curtains, carpets and other articles of household use or ornament in it ('the Furnishings') to my Trustees on trust [for sale] on the following terms:

1 My Trustees shall permit [AB] ('the Occupant') to live in the House and have the use of the Furnishings free of charge[2] for so long as he wishes.

2 While the Occupant is living in the House my Trustees shall not sell the House nor the Furnishings without the Occupant's consent.

3 When the Occupant ceases to live in the House my Trustees shall hold the House and the Furnishings [as part of my residuary estate]/[*appropriate gift over*][3].

4 [*as in the previous forms*][4].

1 This precedent should not be used for the purpose of inheritance tax mitigation.

2 If obligations to repair and insure the House are to be imposed on the Occupant, clause 1 should be amended to read:

> '1 My Trustees shall permit AB ('the Occupant') to live in the House without payment to them so long as he wishes and so long as he keeps the House in repair, insures it and pays all outgoings relating to it and to have the use of the Furnishings free of charge for so long as he wishes.'

with consequential amendments to 2 and 3 following the wording of clauses 2 and 3 of the preceding form. It is suggested, however, that any maintenance obligation should not extend to the Furnishings.

3 See footnote 2 to **Form 11.8**.

4 The concluding provisions of the preceding forms can be adapted if necessary.

12 Specific Gifts of Chattels and Other Personal Property

Need for a gift of chattels

12.1 Where a testator is giving the whole of his estate to his spouse there is no need to include a separate gift of chattels. Where, however, the Will is more complex a separate gift of chattels is desirable to avoid chattels having to be divided between residuary beneficiaries.

12.2 A trust that includes chattels (for example, to hold them for a person's life) should be actively discouraged. Not only is it inconvenient but it raises problems of maintenance, fair wear and tear, insurance, safe-keeping and taking inventories. A trust of chattels most often arises where a testator creates a life interest of the whole of the estate. Where that happens it is preferable for chattels to be excluded from the life interest and to be the subject of an absolute gift. This is particularly so where the life tenant is the testator's widow. Perhaps the one exception is where a right to occupy a house as a residence is given and the testator wishes the contents to remain in the house. Even so, the testator should think hard about whether an absolute gift of the contents is more appropriate. A precedent for this is **Form 11.11**.

Inheritance tax and gifts of chattels

12.3 Inheritance tax on chattels situated in the UK will be borne by residue as a testamentary expense but chattels situated elsewhere will bear their own inheritance tax. As noted in a previous chapter[1], in the ordinary case, the normal direction to pay inheritance tax out of the residue merely makes this clear but where chattels may be out of the UK an express direction is essential. If valuable chattels are to be given subject to inheritance tax an express direction will be required.

1 See **10.5–10.7**.

Gifts of personal chattels

12.4 Gifts of chattels are almost always specific. It should always be made clear in the Will whether the gift is to relate to a particular item owned when the Will is made or to any item which, at death, corresponds to the description given in the Will. In default of a clear direction the Wills Act 1837 s 24[1] provides that a Will 'speaks from death' unless a contrary intention is expressed. The expression, for example, 'my car' may refer to the car the testator owns at the date of his Will or, by virtue of s 24, the car he owns at death. If there may be ambiguity the matter should be put beyond doubt by the terms of the Will (contrast **Forms 12.1** and **12.2**). Forethought should also be given to the possibility of the testator's owning more than one of the specified chattel (eg two cars) at his death.

1 Wills Act 1837 s 24, see **appendix 33.12**.

12.5 Problems also arise when the subject matter of the gift is one of a number of similar items, for example, a piece of jewellery. Practitioners are well aware of the difficulties which can arise on distribution in giving effect to inadequate descriptions such as 'my dress ring'. It is therefore important to take pains to obtain detailed descriptions of such items, bearing in mind that, even where only one such item exists at the date of the Will, there is the possibility of others being acquired subsequently.

12.6 Where a testator wishes to make a general gift of personal chattels, it is convenient to refer to 'personal chattels as defined by Administration of Estates Act 1925 s 55(1)(x)'[1]. The definition was changed by the Inheritance and Trustees Powers Act 2014 to mean:

> 'tangible movable property, other than any such property which—
> - Consists of money or securities for money, or
> - Was used at the death of the intestate solely or mainly for business purposes, or
> - Was held at the death of the intestate solely as an investment'.

The definition therefore excludes money, securities for money, chattels used solely for business purposes and investments.

1 Administration of Estates Act 1925 s 55, reproduced at **appendix 33.17**.

12.7 Special care should be taken in the case of chattels which have a business use. Once again a good example is a car which the testator may refer to as 'my car' when in fact it belongs to a company. The use of a car for both business and private purposes may prevent its being a 'personal chattel' as defined. If the statutory definition (above) is used it will depend upon whether the car was 'solely or mainly' used for business purposes. If it is not, it will be an open question for the interpretation of the Will. Care should be taken that the gift will achieve the testator's desires.

Collections

12.8 Whether or not a collection of items will fall within the new statutory definition will depend upon whether they are held for investment purposes. That will primarily depend upon whether the testator collected them for pleasure or in order to make money. Given the uncertainty it is preferable for them to be expressly included or excluded. Often the testator has a specific idea of what he wants to do with a particular collection but has no idea what to do with ordinary chattels.

Rights of selection of chattels

12.9 The testator who has little or no idea what to do with ordinary chattels often has some vague desire that friends or relatives should be given a right to select mementoes or keepsakes from his possessions. Generally a testator who cannot decide what to do with his own chattels is only saving up trouble for others and so the inclusion of rights of selection should be discouraged where possible. Practitioners will be aware that disputes concerning chattels often arise in the context of litigation concerning the administration of estates and are often the cause of the dispute. However, testators can be quite determined to give a right of selection and so **Forms 12.14–12.18** have been included in this section.

12.10 The possibilities covered by these forms include a gift to trustees subject to various alternative rights of selection[1]; a mere right of selection and distribution with the items not selected falling into residue[2]; a gift of such item as is selected with provision for the resolution of disputes where beneficiaries cannot agree[3]; an absolute gift coupled with a non-binding direction to make a distribution in accordance with a memorandum of wishes[4]; and a gift to children in equal shares subject to division and distribution in specie by trustees[5].

1 See **Form 12.14**.
2 See **Form 12.15**.
3 See **Form 12.16**.
4 See **Form 12.17**.
5 See **Form 12.18**.

12.11 These forms are not exhaustive of the variety of possible schemes of distribution which testators desire. The important thing in each case is to be clear. As with all testamentary dispositions it is important to establish what is given and to whom but there should also be a long-stop date by which rights of selection or powers of distribution must be exercised. The timing may also have inheritance tax consequences: a gift over by a specific legatee in accordance with the testator's wishes within two years of the testator's death will be treated for inheritance tax purposes as having been made by the testator's Will[1] as will a discretionary distribution by trustees within the same period[2].

1 Inheritance Tax Act 1984 s 143 (**appendix 36.6**) and see **Form 12.17**.
2 Inheritance Tax Act 1984 s 144 (**appendix 36.7**) and see **Form 12.14**.

Chattels subject to a charge

12.12 In the case of chattels subject to a charge there are two typical situations: credit sale and hire purchase. With a credit sale, ownership of the chattel is vested in the testator and will pass to the beneficiary under the Will. The amount outstanding under the agreement is a debt which may be payable out of residue unless express provision is made for the beneficiary to discharge it[1]. The ownership of goods held under a hire purchase agreement is not vested in the testator although, where the Consumer Credit Act 1974 applies, the hirer's rights pass on death to the personal representatives who can transfer the rights to the beneficiary. In other cases there is the difficulty that some agreements prohibit a transfer of rights and others even provide for termination of the agreement on the death of the hirer. A gift of 'my personal chattels' will not include any chattels that are subject to a hire purchase agreement or any other agreement under which the testator does not own the goods.

1 See **Forms 12.19** and **12.20**.

12.13 The simple solution is to refer specifically to any goods which the testator holds under a hire purchase or similar agreement and to provide for the outstanding balance to be paid out of the residue. This is best done in the clause constituting the gift[1]. Whatever the strict legal position, it is likely that the finance company will accept payment in full and transfer ownership. The other possibility is to express the gift in such a way that the beneficiary must, if he wishes to take it, accept it subject to the liability of the hire purchase agreement, whatever that may be[2].

1 See **Form 12.19**.
2 See **Form 12.20**.

Releases and gifts of debts

12.14 Debts are choses in action[1] and so can be given by Will. **Form 12.22** is an example. Where a legatee owes a debt to the estate they must bring such debt into account and will be paid only the net sum (eg a legatee of £500 who owes £250 will receive only £250).Testators often want to release debtors from debts due to them but it is unwise to include a general forgiveness of debts in a Will as this might include debts incurred subsequently and those which the testator does not regard as such: strictly this would include the balance of a current bank account. It is better to identify the debtor and the debt and include a release by way of specific gift. For examples of releases see **Forms 12.23–12.25**.

1 Ie the testator does not have immediate enjoyment of the debt, merely a right to recover it by action.

Gifts of shares

12.15 A simple gift of shares should be distinguished from a gift of a business or an interest in a business in which the testator is a participant[1]. The simple gift of a holding in a public company as in **Forms 12.26** and **12.27** does not normally require any special inheritance tax consideration and is no different from any other specific gift.

1 For gifts of business interests see **chapter 13**.

12.16 Shares in private limited companies will often have restrictions upon their transfer or sale or else be subject to rights of pre-emption in favour of other shareholders. Clients should be warned of this possibility when attempting to include such shares by way of bequest and encouraged to investigate the company's articles of association.

Gifts of bank accounts

12.17 It is generally inadvisable to make a gift by reference to a particular bank account, for example of 'all my money in my NatWest current account'. First, testators often change accounts without considering the effect of this upon their Wills[1]. Second, the nature of bank accounts means that the balance within the account can be affected by all sorts of things so that the size and nature of the gift will vary according to what monies were in the account at the time of death. To be effective the account balance must belong to the deceased after their death and so must not, for example, be held jointly with some other person. Notwithstanding these warnings because it is a gift many testators wish to give, a precedent for such a gift is at **Form 12.28**.

1 See *Re Dorman* [1994] 1 All ER 804.

PRECEDENTS

12.18

FORM 12.1

Bequest of car owned at date of Will

I give to [*name*] my car, registered number [ ][1].

1 If the car is not owned at death the gift will, of course, fail.

FORM 12.2

Bequest of car owned at date of death

I give to [*name*] the car I own at the date of my death[1].

1 The draftsman must guard against the possibility of the testator owning more than one car. If the car may be subject to a hire purchase or finance agreement, see **Forms 12.19** and **12.20**.

FORM 12.3

Bequest of Baxter Prints[1]

I give to [*name*] my framed Baxter Prints the 'Ascent of Mont Blanc', catalogue numbers 336, 336A, 336B and 336C.

1 This form is used as an example of a precedent in which it is possible to define the subject matter of the gift with great precision.

FORM 12.4

Bequest of collection by reference to inventory[1]

I give to [*name*] the collection of [antique silver] which is specified in detail in [my insurance policy [No.] with [ ]].

1 Definition by reference to an inventory can sometimes be useful, particularly where it relates to a valuable collection. For insurance purposes, the testator is likely to ensure that additional items acquired are added to the inventory. There are obvious pitfalls and the testator should be warned that the items appearing in the inventory at his death will constitute the gift.

FORM 12.5

Bequest of specific items by reference to inventory – alternative method[1]

The schedule to this Will applies to gifts of chattels.

Schedule

1 I have left with this Will a list of chattels (being a valuation prepared for insurance purposes). Each item bears a number and the number shown in brackets after a chattel specified in paragraph 2 of this schedule corresponds

with the number in the list used for insurance purposes. That list is not a testamentary document but has been placed with this Will to assist my Trustees in identifying the gifts specified in paragraph 2.

2 I give to the person named in the first column below the chattel or chattels specified against his name in the second column

Donee	Chattel
[*name*]	(a) My Tissot gold watch and bracelet (42)
	(b) My gold cufflinks (30)
[*name*]	My Avis gold watch and bracelet (43)
[*name*]	My silver inkstand (23)

etc.

1 Where a testator makes specific gifts of a number of chattels it is convenient to use a schedule for this purpose. In this form the inventory contained in an insurance document has been used. Such inventories usually contain a detailed description of each article and sometimes a photograph.

FORM 12.6

Bequest of chattels as defined by Administration of Estates Act 1925[1]

I give to [*name*] my personal chattels as defined by Administration of Estates Act 1925 s 55(1)(x) [except those which are the subject of specific gifts in this Will or in any Codicil to it].

1 See the note at **12.4–12.7**.

FORM 12.7

Bequest of personal chattels as defined by Administration of Estates Act 1925 with additions[1]

I give to [*name*] my personal chattels as defined by Administration of Estates Act 1925 s 55(1)(x) and also:

1 [all my medical text books];

2 [all my surgical instruments].

1 This example is used to emphasise that, while items such as books would fall within the general definition of s 55, items for business purposes would be excluded. See the note at **12.4–12.7**.

FORM 12.8

Bequest of personal chattels as defined by Administration of Estates Act 1925 with exceptions[1]

I give to [*name*] my personal chattels as defined by Administration of Estates Act 1925 s 55(1)(x) except the following:

1 [any pictures and prints];

2 [any car].

[The items excluded from this gift shall form part of my residuary estate[2].]

1 See the note at **12.4–12.7**.
2 Alternatively the specific items referred to could be given to another donee.

FORM 12.9

Bequest of personal chattels as defined by Administration of Estates Act 1925 with additions and exceptions[1]

I give to [*name*] my personal chattels as defined by Administration of Estates Act 1925 s 55(1)(x) but this gift:

1 includes any [car which is used partly for business purposes[2]];

2 excludes any [pictures and prints].

1 See the note at **12.4–12.7**.
2 This can cause complications if the donee does not also receive the business so care should be taken to ensure that the two gifts are not inconsistent.

FORM 12.10

Bequest of furniture and household effects

I give to [*name*] all my furniture curtains carpets and articles of household use or ornament.

FORM 12.11

Bequest of jewellery and personal effects

I give to [*name*] all my clothing jewellery and articles of personal use or adornment.

FORM 12.12

Bequest of contents of house[1]

I give to [*name*] those of my personal chattels [*in any house in which I live at my death*] which constitute:

1 furniture or articles of household use or ornament;

2 jewellery or articles of personal use or adornment;

3 books, photographs and [physical]/[published or written][2] articles relating to [any sport hobby or other pastime][3].

1 This form and the next have been included with some misgivings. The draftsman should strive to find an alternative to 'the contents of my house'. It is a form that can give rise to problems, for example, where chattels normally contained in the testator's house have been put into storage, have been lost and are recovered after the testator's death or some of which have been used to furnish the testator's room in a nursing home while the rest have been left in his home. In this precedent the reference to the chattels being contained in a testator's residence could well be omitted.

2 Although in the context of the preceding paragraphs the word 'articles' must mean 'physical articles', when placed beside 'books' and 'photographs' a reference to 'articles' might be construed as a reference to 'writings' only. Such ambiguity should be avoided.

3 A greater degree of precision may be required in defining the subject of the gift than the testator has considered.

FORM 12.13

Bequest of contents of house – alternative form[1]

I give to [*name*] the contents of the house in which I reside that are chattels.

1 See footnote to the preceding precedent. It would almost certainly be better to use one of the **Forms 12.5–12.9**.

FORM 12.14

Bequest of personal chattels selected by beneficiaries[1]

I give those of my personal chattels which are articles of personal use or adornment or articles of household use or ornament to my Trustees on the following trusts:

1 To transfer to [*name*] such items as in the opinion of my Trustees [s/he] reasonably requires for [his/her] personal use[2].

or

1 To transfer to [*name*] the items [s/he] selects provided that their value does not in the opinion of my Trustees exceed [£] *or* [one quarter of the total value of the items from which the selection is made][3].

or

1 To permit my personal friends to select as mementoes one item each[4] from the personal chattels to which this trust relates and in giving effect to this provision my Trustees in their absolute and unfettered discretion:

1.1 shall decide who are the persons entitled to select mementoes;

1.2 may permit more than one item to be selected if together they constitute a set or match one another; and

1.3 shall transfer the ownership of any item selected or allotted to the person concerned.

2 Any personal chattels not transferred under 1 above within one year[5] shall form part of my residuary estate.

1 See the note at **12.9–12.11**. Many testators wish one or more beneficiaries to be permitted to select items from their personal chattels. Often the testator is not clear in his own mind what he really intends to happen. Sometimes he intends, for example, that friends and acquaintances should each select a keepsake or that a relative should select items of furniture for use in his own home but not to sell. Practitioners are well aware of the difficulty of drafting a satisfactory provision and the problems which can arise from interpreting such a provision. The authors have tried to overcome the problems encountered in practice but every case is different. It should be noted that this form expressly vests the ownership of the personal chattels in the trustees so as to give them a degree of control over the selection and then provides for them to transfer the ownership of the selected items to the beneficiary. This is preferable to a provision such as:

'I give to AB such of my personal chattels as he selects.'

2 A testator often wants the intended beneficiary to enjoy the chattel and has a strong objection to the beneficiary selecting an item merely to convert it into cash.

3 This provision is intended to prevent the avaricious beneficiary selecting virtually all the personal chattels.

4 A provision designed to restrict the selection to personal keepsakes.

5 It is important to introduce a time limit for the completion of an exercise of this sort. One year is generally convenient but a period of up to two years would take advantage of Inheritance Tax Act 1984 s 144: see **appendix 36.7**.

FORM 12.15

Gift of jewellery to daughter with right of selection and distribution, default gift into residue[1]

I give to my daughter [*name*] absolutely such of my jewellery as she may select within six months after my death and any such articles not selected by her within the said time shall be distributed by her within a further six months amongst such of my female relatives and such of the wives, widows and female cohabitees for the time being of such of my male relatives as she shall in her absolute and unfettered discretion select and any such articles not distributed by her within one year of my death shall fall into and form part of my residuary estate[2].

1 See the note at **12.9–12.11**.

2 This is only a gift of the jewellery which the daughter wishes to select or distribute. She might select everything but if there is anything which is neither selected nor distributed it will fall into residue.

FORM 12.16

Gift of pictures to children to select with provision for disagreement[1]

I give to each of my children one of my [*Bill Maltman Watercolours of Lake District Hills*] and I direct that my children should agree which painting each of them is to have but in the event that they cannot agree within six months of my death the decision of my trustees[2] as to which child should take which painting shall be final and binding.

1 See the note at **12.9–12.11**.

2 If one or more of the children are trustees then provision should be made for an independent trustee or some other independent person to make this decision. For example, in place of 'my trustees' substitute 'my trustees other than any trustee who is one of my children'.

FORM 12.17

Absolute gift of personal chattels to children with non-binding request as to distribution in accordance with memorandum[1]

I give to my children[2] my personal chattels as defined by Administration of Estates Act 1925 s 55(1)(x) not otherwise disposed of[3] by this my Will in equal shares absolutely and without imposing any trust or binding obligation upon my children I request that my personal chattels be distributed in accordance with any existing or future memorandum[4] of my wishes left by me.

1 See the note at **12.9–12.11**. This form should *not* be adapted for use by a testator who cannot make up his mind about the identity of legatees and the sums payable to them. It creates a gift to the children coupled with a non-binding indication as to the applicable wishes.

2 This is an absolute gift to the children who are therefore entitled to the chattels if they do not distribute them in accordance with a memorandum of wishes whether one can be found or not. It is unlikely to be appropriate to make a gift in these terms in favour of the trustees. However, the clause could be adapted as a gift to trustees to hold as part of the residuary estate in the following manner:

'I give to my trustees my personal chattels as defined by Administration of Estates Act 1925 s 55(1)(x) not otherwise disposed of by this my Will to hold as part of my residuary estate but without imposing any trust or binding obligation upon them I request that my personal chattels be distributed in accordance with any existing or future memorandum of my wishes left by me.'

If the chattels are distributed in accordance with the testator's wishes within two years of the death this gift will take advantage of Inheritance Tax Act 1984 s 143: see **appendix 36.6**.

3 This gift could be used in conjunction with one of the earlier gifts because it only affects property not otherwise disposed of.

4 The memorandum will not be incorporated into the Will where the Will refers to either an existing or a future document: *University College of North Wales v Taylor* [1908] P 140. It is not desirable that the memorandum should be incorporated in this situation.

FORM 12.18

Bequest of personal chattels as defined by Administration of Estates Act 1925 – gift to trustees for distribution equally among children[1]

I give to my Trustees my personal chattels as defined by Administration of Estates Act 1925 s 55(1)(x) to be distributed among those of my children who survive me as my Trustees shall think fit and without imposing any binding obligation I direct that my Trustees shall endeavour to share them (as nearly as possible) equally having regard to their nature and value.

1 See the note at **12.9–12.11**. A gift in these terms does not include a gift over into residue. If the trustees cannot distribute the chattels in specie they will have to sell and divide the proceeds of sale.

FORM 12.19

Bequest of chattels in possession of testator but not owned by him[1]

I give to [*name*] [*any car*] in my possession at my death and I direct that if it is in my possession under the terms of a hire purchase agreement an agreement for lease purchase or similar agreement my Trustees shall take such steps as are practical to vest ownership of [*the car*] in [*name*] at the expense of my residuary estate.

1 See the note at **12.12–12.13**. For financial reasons, motor cars in particular are often in the testator's possession under an agreement with a finance company. Testators are inclined to regard the cars as their own property although the ownership is not vested in them. The testator is often unaware of the legal niceties of the agreement he has entered into and this precedent has been drafted to try to cover any such agreement. If the testator insists on the car itself being transferred to the beneficiary, he should be warned that, because of the terms of the agreement, it may be impossible to give effect to his wishes.

FORM 12.20

Bequest of chattels subject to financial agreement[1]

I give to [*name*] [*any car*] owned by me or in my possession at my death but only on condition that he pays to my Trustees

1 Such sum as they are required to pay in order to discharge:

1.1 any credit sale agreement; or

1.2 any loan obtained to finance the purchase of [*the car*]; or

1.3 any other similar financial obligation.

2 Such sum as they are required to pay under the terms of any hire purchase agreement an agreement for lease purchase or similar agreement in order to enable the ownership of [*the car*] to be transferred to him.

1 See the note at **12.12–12.13**. This form requires the beneficiary to discharge any financial obligation of the testator relating to his acquisition of the car including liabilities which would otherwise be paid out of his residuary estate.

FORM 12.21

Cost of delivery to or vesting in beneficiary[1]

The cost of delivering any gift to a beneficiary or vesting it in him shall be an executorship expense [as shall be the cost of the upkeep of the gift until delivery or vesting].

1 In the ordinary course, it is for the beneficiaries to make their own arrangements to collect gifts. The extent of this rule is uncertain. Generally it is not treated as requiring, for example, a devisee to bear the cost of an assent in his favour. The words in square brackets oust the usual rule applicable to specific gifts but they may not be appropriate in all cases, for example, to a specific devise or a gift of livestock. In the case of residuary gifts the cost of upkeep is always a testamentary expense.

The cost of tracing a beneficiary is often said to be borne by the beneficiary: *Re Phillips* [1938] 4 All ER 438. However, although in the early 20th century, RSC Ord 65 r 14B did indeed provide that the costs of court inquiries to ascertain the person entitled to a legacy or share be paid out of the legacy unless the court otherwise directed, that provision was repealed and not replaced in 1959 and decisions such as *Re Phillips* may no longer be reliable.

FORM 12.22

Gift of a debt

I give to [*name*] the debt of £[ ] and all interest and arrears owing[1] at the date of my death from [*debtor*].

1 See the note at **12.14**. It is important to specify that all interest is included to avoid difficult questions as to the passing of arrears.

FORM 12.23

Release of simple debt[1]

I release [*name*] from the debt of £[ ] and all interest owing.

1 See the note at **12.14**. The release of a debt constitutes a legacy in favour of the debtor so that if the debtor dies before the testator, the release will lapse and the debt will remain owing out of the debtor's estate. For a clause also releasing the estate see **Form 12.25**. The release of the debt will enable the debtor to require the release of any security but **Form 12.24** may be preferred where the debt is secured.

FORM 12.24

Release of security[1]

I release [*name*] from the debt of £[ ] and all interest owing on the security of [*property charged*]. [The cost of discharging the security shall be an executorship expense].

1 See the note at **12.14** and the footnote to **Form 12.23**.

FORM 12.25

Release of debt and the debtor's estate[1]

I release [*name*] from the debt of £[ ] and all interest owing and if he dies before me his personal representatives shall have the benefit of this provision.

1 See the note at **12.14**.

FORM 12.26

Gift of shares[1]

I give to [*name*] [*number*] [*one pound ordinary shares in ABC plc*].

1 See the note at **12.15**.

FORM 12.27

Gift of shares – alternative form[1]

I give to [*name*] my holding of shares in [*ABC plc*].

1 See the note at **12.15**.

FORM 12.28

Gift of sums of money in a Bank Account[1]

I give to [*name*] all the monies at the time of my death in the bank account I hold with [ ] bank with account number [ ]

1 Such gifts are, generally speaking, inadvisable, see **12.17**.

13 Business Interests

13.1 Gifts of business interests involve different considerations to other gifts from the testator's estate and the draftsman must take extra care when advising a testator as to potential options and when drafting clauses to dispose of any business interest. A failure to deal appropriately with business interests can result in the failure to maximise tax relief, the loss of a substantial asset or, possibly worst of all, in a costly and complicated dispute as to what the business consists of and who owns what part of it. However, with appropriate drafting and advice the majority of problems relating to business interests can be avoided.

Tax reliefs

Business Relief

13.2 The most obvious reason why the disposal of business interests should be considered separately to the disposal of other assets is because of the existence of business relief. Business relief is extremely valuable because it is usually granted at 100%. This means that if an asset attracting full business relief is given to a beneficiary under the Will there will be no inheritance tax to pay on the business asset regardless of its value, who it goes to or whether the nil-rate band is used up or not.

13.3 It is particularly important for the draftsman to understand both business relief and agricultural relief if there is any consideration of making a nil-rate band discretionary trust as the reliefs can easily operate to pass far more than intended under the discretionary trust leading to negligence claims and other litigation. A nil-rate band discretionary trust of 'the maximum sum which I can give without any inheritance tax being payable on my death' will not only pass the remaining nil-rate band but also any property subject to business or agricultural relief leaving the residuary beneficiaries with much less than expected. For example, if a testator had an unused nil-rate band, general assets of £300,000 and a business worth £2 million and gave a specific legacy using the above nil-rate band formula the specific legacy would pass his entire estate and the residuary beneficiaries would be left with nothing.

13.4 The requirements for the availability of business relief are set out in Part V, Chapter 1 of the Inheritance Tax Act 1984, to which the reader is referred for full details. Business relief is either granted at 50% or 100%. It is granted at 100% for the following types of business interests[1]:

(i) Property consisting of a business or interest in a business (this includes businesses of sole traders and shares in a partnership but does not include any business not carried out for gain)[2];

(ii) Unquoted securities in a company which give control of the company to the transferor;

(iii) Unquoted shares in a company.

1 Inheritance Tax Act 1984 s 105.
2 Inheritance Tax Act 1984 s 103(3).

13.5 Business relief is granted at the reduced rate of 50% for the following types of business interests[1]:

(i) Quoted shares or securities in a company which give control of the company to the transferor;

(ii) Land, buildings or machinery which were used wholly or mainly for the purposes of a business carried on by a company of which the transferor then had control or by a partnership of which he was a partner;

(iii) Land, buildings or machinery which was used wholly or mainly for the purposes of a business carried on by the transferor and was settled property in which he was beneficially entitled to an interest in possession.

1 Inheritance Tax Act 1984 s 105.

13.6 It is important to note that an asset used in a business will not attract business relief unless it is either passed as part of a business or is a business in itself. Thus, if a car used in a business is transferred during the testator's lifetime it will not attract business relief unless the whole business is also passed. This is less important for a gift under a Will because the entire business will be included in the deemed transfer on death but is still important to understand as it will affect how the relief is applied between the specific gift and the rest of the estate.

13.7 Business relief is only available if the property had been owned by the testator for the two years prior to his or her death[1]. However, if the testator inherited the property from their spouse then the testator can also count their spouse's period of ownership[2]. Furthermore, if the property was given to them as a lifetime gift or by Will and attracted business relief when it was given to them, the requirements as to time shall not apply[3]. Property bought to replace previous business property will also, provided other conditions are met, be deemed to have been held for the period in which the replaced property was held[4].

1 Inheritance Tax Act 1984 s 106.
2 Inheritance Tax Act 1984 s 108.
3 Inheritance Tax Act 1984 s 109.
4 Inheritance Tax Act 1984 s 107.

13.8 If a particular asset is not used wholly or mainly for the purposes of a business for the two years prior to the testator's death it will not attract business relief. However, if part of the asset is used exclusively for the business (eg a room in a building) then it will be considered as a separate asset and business relief may be granted for that part of the asset.

13.9 The existence of business relief is an important consideration for the testator. If 100% relief exists, consideration should be given to the testator giving such property to a non-exempt beneficiary (ie somebody other than a spouse, civil partner or charity) because otherwise the inheritance tax relief can be seen to be 'wasted' or not fully taken advantage of. This rationale is diminished if the exempt beneficiary will hold the property in such a way as to maintain business relief.

13.10 If the testator has property which could potentially attract business relief but does not at the moment, consideration should be given as to whether the testator wishes to do anything to assist with obtaining business relief in the future. For example, if the time limit has not yet been complied with (eg the testator has only held the business property for one year) it may be advisable for the testator to leave the business to his spouse who is an exempt beneficiary. She could then add her period of ownership to it and it would attract business relief within one year and then it could be given to a son or daughter free of inheritance tax. If the testator left the business property to his son directly it would be liable for inheritance tax as it would not have been owned by the testator for the required two years.

13.11 Another potential option would be to leave the assets potentially attracting business relief (eg shares in an unquoted company) to the non-exempt beneficiary (the son) conditionally on the testator having owned the assets for the required period of time and, if not, leaving it to an exempt beneficiary (the spouse)[1]. Of course, the spouse would thereby become absolutely entitled to any shares which were not owned for the required time and there would be no obligation on her to pass the shares to the son on her death and this may make such a condition unsuitable in some circumstances.

1 See **Form 13.3** for such a bequest.

Agricultural Relief

13.12 If the testator's business involves farming there is likely to be a considerable crossover between business relief and agricultural relief. Like business relief, agricultural relief is usually given at 100%[1] meaning that if the property has 100% agricultural relief there will be no tax to pay regardless of its value or who it is given to. The full requirements for the granting of agricultural relief are contained in Part V, Chapter 2 of the Inheritance Tax Act 1984. However, in summary they are that:

(i) The property must be located in the UK, the Channel Islands, the Isle of Man or the European Economic Area;

(ii) The land is agricultural property. This includes agricultural land or pasture and any buildings (including farmhouses and cottages) which are occupied are used for agricultural purposes and are proportionate in size to the farming activity. It also includes woodland and stud farms.

1 Inheritance Tax Act 1984 s 116.

13.13 The relief is only granted on the agricultural value and not market value of the property meaning that any developmental or hope value attached to agricultural land cannot be considered[1]. Similarly, a farmhouse or cottage which has a high market value because of its location will only be given the agricultural value of the farmhouse or cottage. Farmhouses and cottages which are not occupied by somebody involved in using the land for agriculture will not qualify for relief.

1 If this land was held as part of a business the increased value could potentially attract business relief.

13.14 Similar considerations should be made by the testator and draftsman if there is property which attracts (or could potentially attract) agricultural relief as if there is property which attracts (or could potentially attract) business relief. In particular, it should be considered whether or not it is advisable to leave the agricultural land to a non-exempt beneficiary to make full use of the agricultural relief.

13.15 If the testator has an interest in a farming business it is likely that much of the property of the business will be entitled to both agricultural relief and business relief. If property attracts both agricultural relief and business relief, only agricultural relief will apply[1]. However, even if the testator's business is related to farming (and hence the majority of the assets are covered by agricultural relief) it is important to understand the extent of business relief as some assets related to agriculture may not qualify for agricultural relief but may qualify for business relief. For example farm equipment, machinery, harvested crops and livestock will not qualify for agricultural relief[2] but such assets are likely to be granted business relief if they are used as part of a farming business. Similarly, if the farming land is located wholly or partly outside the UK, the Channel Islands, the Isle of Man or the European Economic Area, agricultural relief will not apply to those assets but business relief may apply as it is not subject to the same jurisdictional limits as agricultural relief.

1 Inheritance Tax Act 1984 s 114.
2 Growing crops transferred with the land will, however, be entitled to agricultural relief.

Gift of a business interest

13.16 If the testator has an interest in a business he may simply wish for the business interest to be sold and the proceeds distributed as part of his residuary estate. This is usually the simplest aim to achieve and requires the least amount of work by the draftsman. Aside from considering whether the trustees should be given the power to run the business prior to selling it[1] whether the net profits and proceeds of sale should be given to a specific person[2] and ways in which the value of the business can be maximised, there is not much for the draftsman to consider.

1 See note at **13.33**.
2 See **Form 13.5**.

13.17 The position is more difficult where the intention is for a beneficiary (or a number of beneficiaries) to take over, or be given the opportunity to take over, the business. In these circumstances consideration should be given to taking steps to ensure the succession of the business during the testator's lifetime as it may be difficult or even impossible to organise effective and trouble free succession by Will. The method of succession and the most effective way to transfer a business interest will depend on what sort of a business interest it is – sole trader, incorporated, or partnership.

13.18 While it is sometimes possible to include provisions which will allow a gift of a business to take place even if there has been some restructuring of the business whether by incorporation, takeover or merger[1] a testator should be advised to reconsider any gift of a business whenever there has been a restructuring of his business to ensure that his wishes can still be accomplished.

1 See **Form 13.6**, **Form 13.7** and **Form 13.9**.

Sole Trader

13.19 Whenever a testator wishes to give a gift of a business interest the draftsman should be clear as to what assets are to be transferred with the business interest and what assets are to be distributed under the rest of the testator's estate. This is particularly important in the case of a sole trader because sole traders often intermingle business and personal assets and it can be unclear what assets are considered to be part of the business interest transferred and what assets are considered to be non-business assets.

13.20 The word 'business' has no legally defined meaning. This means that a simple gift of 'my business' could, narrowly construed, be taken to only pass the right to use the trade name of the testator and to operate as the successor to the testator's business. Alternatively, the phrase, construed widely, could cover all the stock, machinery and other equipment such as computers or laptops which have been used, even occasionally, in the business as well as the freehold or leasehold of the premises in which the business is operated. For this reason it is inadvisable to draft a clause which merely refers to 'my business' or 'my interest in X business' because it is likely to result in confusion and conflict and possibly litigation to resolve exactly what was transferred under the clause. Instead, it is strongly advised that any gift of an interest in a business, particularly a sole trader, should specify precisely what assets are to be transferred under the gift[1].

1 See **Form 13.4**.

13.21 It is also recommended to expressly state that the gift is subject to taking over the liabilities of the business. Not only does this provide clarity but it also stops a beneficiary from seeking to take all the assets of the business but leaving all the business debts and other trade liabilities to be borne by the estate.

Company

13.22 The biggest restriction on the transfer of a business interest in a company is the terms of the company's governing documents, namely the Memorandum and the Articles of Association. In particular these documents may provide for the company or other shareholders to have rights of first refusal on any of the testator's shares at either fixed prices or market value. These or other company provisions and rules may prevent the testator from making an effective gift of his shares of the company. Consequently, such documents should be checked prior to any attempt to dispose of any business interest in a company via Will.

13.23 On the other hand the company's governing documents may not only provide for the transfer of shares but may also give the testator other rights such as the right to appoint somebody on his death to be a director of the company or to some other role. Again, this further illustrates the importance of examining the constitutional documentation whenever the testator wishes to dispose of an interest in a company.

Partnership

13.24 The potential succession to a partnership or the gift of a partnership share will be governed by the provisions of the partnership agreement and these provisions must be consulted before any consideration is given to passing an interest in a partnership. The partnership may be governed by a formal Partnership Agreement drawn up and subscribed to by the partners but if there has not been one made by the partners the partnership will be governed by the default provisions in the Partnership Act 1890.

13.25 A testator who has an interest in a partnership cannot transfer his interest in a partnership unless there is an express provision in the partnership agreement permitting him to do so. The default provisions do not provide for the transfer of a partnership interest. Rather the default provisions provide that the partnership will be dissolved by the death of a partner[1]. It is also somewhat unusual for a Partnership Agreement made by the partners to provide for the transfer of a partnership interest (especially an unrestricted right to transfer the partnership interest). If there is a right for the testator to transfer his partnership interest in the Partnership Agreement the Agreement will likely also provide for the method of transferring the interest and such procedure should be followed if appropriate.

1 Partnership Act 1890 s 33.

13.26 In the absence of a provision allowing the testator to transfer his share in a partnership the testator is usually restricted to providing for what should happen to his share of the partnership property on any dissolution of the partnership and any debts owed to him by the partnership which, in the absence of any other provision, would fall into residue.

Limited Liability Partnerships ('LLPs')

13.27 The ability of a testator to leave his interest in a LLP to any person will be governed by the terms of the LLP Agreement and this must be consulted prior to drafting any provisions governing this interest. The LLP Agreement will likely provide for the surviving partners to buy out the testator's interest at a predetermined price or by reference to a specified mechanism for determining its value. If the LLP Agreement does provide for any payment it may be possible to bequeath this payment under the Will[1].

1 See **Form 13.9**.

Chattels Used By a Business

13.28 Special considerations should be given when dealing with chattels which are used in a business. If it is intended that they should pass to whoever is to receive the business interest the draftsman must be careful to draft the provision passing the business interest sufficiently broad enough to pass the associated chattels[1].

1 See note at **13.20**.

13.29 If the intention is to pass the chattels to another person it must first be confirmed that the testator owns the chattel in question and is able to transfer it by Will. A good example is a car which the testator may refer to as 'my car' when in fact it belongs to a company and therefore is not his to give. If it is clear that the testator does own the asset, the provision making the bequest should be drafted carefully to make sure that it accomplishes the intention. For example, a gift of chattels by reference to the statutory definition of 'personal chattels'[1] will not be sufficient to pass any chattels which are used solely or mainly for business purposes and therefore the clause giving the chattels may need to be amended slightly[2]. Care should also be taken to co-ordinate any bequest of chattels or a particular chattel with a bequest of the business because if the bequest of the business is drawn too widely it may inadvertently include items which the testator wishes to be the subject of different bequests.

1 Administration of Estates Act 1925 s 55(1)(x), see **appendix 33.17**.
2 See **Form 13.2**.

Farming Business

13.30 A farming business will usually be run as a sole trader, through a company or by a partnership and therefore the comments above will apply to it according to how it is held. However, it is worth taking particular care whenever the business of the testator involves farming. Sometimes it is very clear on what basis the farming business is being run and what the business consists of, but traditionally farming businesses have been run through informal family based agreements where it is unclear what the ownership shares are, whether it is run as a partnership or not, what are business assets and what are personal assets. The draftsman should therefore take particular care to establish the background before he advises the testator in relation to the bequest of any interest in a farming business. Otherwise the consequences can be very far-reaching[1].

1 Such as in *Re Lewis's Will Trusts* [1984] 3 All ER 930 where the testator left a bequest of 'my freehold farms' when he actually owned three quarters of the shares in a company which owned the farm with the result that the gift failed.

13.31 The existence of agricultural relief and its cross-over with business relief should also encourage the draftsman to establish exactly what assets the testator has an interest in and his intentions as regards those assets before drafting any provisions relating to the farming business. If used correctly the combination of agricultural relief and business relief can result in substantial inheritance tax savings but, equally, poorly thought out provisions can result in unnecessary inheritance tax charges. A classic example is a testator farmer who makes a lifetime gift of the farmland to his son and then leaves the farmhouse in which he currently lives to his son by Will. The separation of the farmland from the farmhouse will mean the farmhouse loses its agricultural relief so on his death a substantial charge to inheritance tax will be made. On the other hand, had the testator made a gift of the farmland and farmhouse by Will, no inheritance tax would likely have been payable on the farmhouse.

13.32 A particular difficulty with farming businesses is that often the farming business is the testator's main or only asset and while the testator wishes to keep the farm together and give it to one particular child (typically the one who has stayed on the farm and helped the testator the most) he also wishes to provide for his widow and other children. Such a situation is never easy but the most effective solution is often to give the farming child the option to purchase the farm (often with provisions allowing for gradual repayment) with the money received by the estate from the purchase (if the farming child choose to exercise the option) being used to provide for the other beneficiaries. If the option is not exercised then the farm would fall to be sold and distributed in accordance with the default provisions of the Will. The precise workings of any such option can vary dramatically as regards the extent of the farming business purchased, the price, the timeframe for exercising the option, the notices to be served and the payment schedule. A basic sample option agreement for a farming business is contained at **Form 13.11**. However, the draftsman is reminded that option agreements are an individual topic in themselves and must be carefully tailored to the particular circumstances of the testator and his family.

Trustees' powers

13.33 Whenever there is a bequest of a business interest, consideration should be given as to whether to give the trustees the power to carry on the business, and if so, for how long. In the absence of express provision, personal representatives only have the power to continue the testator's business so far as is necessary to enable it to be sold as a going concern. For many different reasons it may be desired to give the trustees more extensive powers to enable them to run the business. These reasons could include everything from the desire to protect a family member who is employed in the business; to running the business for long enough for another family member or acquaintance to take over; to a desire to give a beneficiary a regular income through the payment of the net profits of the business[1]; to a belief that the value of the business will be greatly increased in a few years' time.

1 See **Form 13.5**.

13.34 If it is desired to grant the trustees more extensive powers to run the business, additional provisions should also be considered. In particular, it should be considered whether to provide for the trustees to be indemnified for any loss or whether they should be entitled to receive and retain any remuneration for their role in running the business. An example of the powers which can be granted to trustees in these circumstances is included in **Form 19.9**.

Business executors

13.35 It is possible to appoint business executors who are different from the other executors in the Will and who will only have responsibility for the administration of business assets. Whether or not this is appropriate will depend on the nature of the business and its assets and the identity of the general executors. While in some circumstances it will be advisable to appoint separate business executors it also often adds an extra layer of complication and increases the potential for disputes to have separate executors and therefore should not be done unless necessary.

13.36 If separate business executors are appointed they should be expressly given the power to administer the testator's business assets and the extent of these business assets should be carefully defined to ensure there is no confusion or dispute as regards what assets fall to be administered by which set of executors. **Form 13.12** is an example of a provision appointing separate business executors.

PRECEDENTS

13.37

FORM 13.1

Specific Gift of Agricultural or Business Property – by reference to the available relief

I GIVE free of tax to those of my children who survive me and attain 25 in equal shares all of my assets:

(i) That are or would be reduced for the purposes of inheritance tax [by 100%][1] by reason of their meeting the definition of Relevant Business Property in section 105(1) of the Inheritance Tax Act 1984.

(ii) Whose agricultural value would or could be reduced [by 100%][2] by reason of their meeting the definition of Agricultural Property in section 115(2) of the Inheritance Tax Act 1984[3].

1 The words in square brackets would exclude assets that attract only 50% relief, including assets used within the business but not owned by it. To omit it, however, may mean that this gift will attract some taxation. Since it is expressed to be free of tax, if the residue is exempt, it would have to be grossed up for the purposes of calculating inheritance tax.

2 There are relatively few instances of agricultural property not qualifying for 100% relief. The more limited relief (at 50%) applies in circumstances where the land is let on neither an Agricultural Holding or a Farm Business Tenancy and the owner is not entitled to vacant possession within 12 months. However, the words in square brackets may be desired for the reasons expressed above.

3 It would still be possible for some part of the value of this gift to attract tax because of its non-agricultural value. Therefore, it is possible that some part of this gift could bear tax, with the resulting possibility of grossing up if the residue is exempt. The alternative is to make the gift subject to tax.

FORM 13.2

Gift of chattels including a chattel used in business to somebody other than the successor to the business[1]

I give to [*name*] my personal chattels as defined by Administration of Estates Act 1925 s 55(1)(x) but this gift also includes:

1. Any [car] which is also used for business purposes.
2. Any computer, laptop, tablet, mobile phone or similar device which is used partly for personal use and partly for business use [save any device permanently located in the business premises][2].

1 Care should be taken that this does not conflict with any gift of the business itself. See note at **13.20**.

2 Such a clause should be carefully considered to ensure that the successor to the business has all necessary use of computers used in the business.

FORM 13.3

Gift of shares in unquoted company to non-exempt beneficiary conditional on testator owning the shares for the preceding two years[1]

1 I give to [*name of non-exempt beneficiary*] all my shares in [*(A company)*] provided such shares satisfy the minimum period of ownership under section 106 of the Inheritance Act 1984.

2 If any of the shares mentioned in the preceding sub-clause do not satisfy the minimum period of ownership or the aforementioned gift does not take effect for any reason I give such shares to [*name of exempt beneficiary*].

1 See note at **13.11**.

FORM 13.4

Gift of business of which testator is sole proprietor[1]

1 I give to [*name*] my business ([known as (*name*)] *or* [of (*description of business*)]) carried on by me at my death.

2 This gift:

2.1 includes the goodwill, equipment, machinery, plant, stock-in-trade, vehicles, computers or other similar devices and all the other assets used in the business or owned by the business together with the [leasehold] property known as [ ] and together with all balances standing to the credit of such business at any bank or similar financial organisation and all debts owed to the business together with the benefit of all contracts relating to such business.

2.2 is subject to:

(a) taking over all liabilities in connection with the business[2] and indemnifying my estate against all liability in relation to the above gift whether such liabilities arose before or after my death;

(b) bearing any inheritance tax attributable to this gift[3];

(c) [observing the provisions of the lease of the property];

1 See note at **13.19–13.21**.
2 It is advisable to make the gift of the business subject to the liabilities of the business. See note at **13.21**.
3 There should not be any inheritance tax payable on this gift as it should be granted 100% business relief. However, it is prudent to include such a provision in case any inheritance tax is payable (eg if some assets were not held for sufficient time prior to the testator's death).

FORM 13.5

Gift of sole trader business to trustees with requirement that the net profits and proceeds of sale be held on trust[1]

1 I give to my Trustees my business ([known as (*name*)] *or* [of (*description of business*)]) carried on by me at my death.

2 This gift:

2.1 includes the goodwill, equipment, machinery, plant, stock-in-trade, vehicles, computers or other similar devices and all the other assets used in the business or owned by the business together with the [leasehold] property known as [ ] and together with all balances standing to the credit of such business at any bank or similar financial organisation and all debts owed to the business together with the benefit of all contracts relating to such business.

2.2 is subject to:

(a) taking over all liabilities in connection with the business[2] and indemnifying my estate against all liability in relation to the above gift whether such liabilities arose before or after my death;

(b) bearing any inheritance tax attributable to this gift[3];

(c) [observing the provisions of the lease of the property];

3 My trustees shall hold the said business and the net profits of such business and the net proceeds of sale of the said business or any part of it upon trust to pay such annual net profits or income from the net proceeds of sale for [*(name)*] for life and then to [*(name)*][4].

1 If such a gift is used it is vital to give the trustees adequate powers to run the business. See note at **13.33–13.34**.

2 It is advisable to make the gift of the business subject to the liabilities of the business. See note at **13.21**.

3 There should not be any inheritance tax payable on this gift as it should be granted 100% business relief. However, it is prudent to include such a provision in case any inheritance tax is payable (eg if some assets were not held for sufficient time prior to the testator's death).

4 Further administrative and other provisions beyond the provisions included in this form will need to be included to ensure that the trust created can be run smoothly. Such provisions are dealt with elsewhere in this book. See, for example, **chapters 16** and **17**.

FORM 13.6

Gift of shares in company[1]

1 I give to [*name*]:

1.1 my holding of shares in [*A Limited*];

1.2 all dividends and interest accrued at my death.

2 If any of the shares comprised in this gift are as a result of a takeover amalgamation or reconstruction represented by a different holding sub-clause 1 above shall take effect as a gift of that holding.

1 The company's constitutional documents should be checked to ensure that it is possible to leave a bequest of this nature. See note at **13.22–13.23**.

FORM 13.7

Gift of shares and loan account in company[1]

1 I give to [*name*]:

1.1 my holding of shares in [*A Limited*];

1.2 all dividends and interest accrued at my death;

1.3 all undrawn remuneration and fees due to me from the company;

1.4 any loans I may have made to the company which are outstanding at my death.

2 If any of the shares comprised in this gift are as a result of a takeover amalgamation or reconstruction represented by a different holding sub-clause 1 above shall take effect as a gift of that holding.

1 The company's constitutional documents should be checked to ensure that it is possible to leave a bequest of this nature. See note at **13.22–13.23**.

FORM 13.8

Gift of interest in partnership[1]

1 In the exercise of the power in the partnership agreement dated [ ] I give to [*name*] [my share and interest in that partnership, its capital, assets and profits] [or] [the price payable for my share and interest in that partnership, its capital, assets and profits][2].

2 This gift is subject to [*name of beneficiary*]:

(a) indemnifying my residuary estate to the satisfaction of my Trustees from all liabilities of the partnership;

(b) [accounting for any sum owing to me from the partnership profits at my death or constituting profits to the date of my death][3];

(c) accepting as binding on him so far as is applicable all the terms of the partnership agreement;

(d) bearing any inheritance tax attributable to this gift[4].

1 It will not be possible to make this gift unless there is a provision in the partnership agreement providing for such a gift. See note at **13.24–13.26**.
2 Some partnership agreements will provide that instead of bequeathing the interest in the partnership the continuing partners will buy out the testator's share and that this sum can then be bequeathed to whoever the testator chooses.
3 Alternatively the trustee may wish to make a gift of such sum to the beneficiary.
4 There should not be any inheritance tax payable on this gift as it should be granted 100% business relief. However, it is prudent to include such a provision in case any inheritance tax is payable (eg if some assets were not held for sufficient time prior to the testator's death).

FORM 13.9

Gift of interest in LLP or any sums payable by LLP[1]

1 I give to [*name*] all my interest in [*name*] LLP ('the LLP'), its capital, assets and profits and all sums received and payable from the LLP. This gift shall include:

1.1 Any payment received or payable from the LLP or its directors, members, partners or owners after my death whether ex-gratia or to represent my interest in the LLP or for any other reason.

1.2 All loans, dividends, interest, remuneration, fees or similar payments owed to me by the LLP.

1.3 Any shares in the LLP.

2 The expression 'the LLP' means not only [*name*] LLP but also:

2.2 Any other LLP which has taken over, merged or amalgamated with the LLP.

2.3 Any incorporated company or other body which has succeeded to the business of the LLP.

1 The terms of payment (if any) for the testator's interest in the LLP will be governed by the terms of the LLP Agreement and it is highly advisable to consult such document prior to drafting any clause bequeathing an interest in the testator's share. See the note at **13.27**.

FORM 13.10

Specific Gift of Agricultural Property – simple form

I GIVE all my share and interest in the farm and business known as [ABC Farm] to those of my children who survive me and attain 25 in equal shares

FORM 13.11

Gift of option to purchase farming business and freehold farm[1]

1 I give to [*name*] ('the Grantee') the option to buy from my Trustees the business of farmer carried on by me at my death.

2 The purchase if effected shall:

2.1 include the goodwill, equipment, machinery, plant, stock-in-trade, vehicles, computers or other similar devices and all the other assets used in the business or owned by the business together with the [leasehold] property known as [ ] and together with all balances standing to the credit of such business at any bank or similar financial organisation and all debts owed to the business together with the benefit of all contracts relating to such business.

2.2 is subject to:

(a) taking over all liabilities in connection with the business[2] and indemnifying my estate against all liability in relation to the above gift whether such liabilities arose before or after my death;

(b) bearing any inheritance tax attributable to this gift[3];

(c) [observing the provisions of the lease of the property];

3 My Trustees shall give written notice to the Grantee of this right within [# weeks][4] of my death.

4 The Grantee shall exercise this option by giving written notice to my Trustees within [# months][5] of my death.

5 The price to be paid by the Grantee shall be:

5.1 [#% of][6] the market value at my death of the business and property as defined in Inheritance Tax Act 1984 ss 160 and 168;

5.2 paid as to [#%] upon exercising the option and as to the balance when and on such terms as my Trustees think fit.

6 The cost of any conveyance or transfer required to give effect to this gift shall be [an executorship expense] [borne by the Grantee].

7 The Trustees shall have the power to carry on the aforementioned business for so long as they think fit and with the same powers as if they were beneficially entitled[7] and in the exercise of this power my Trustees shall have the right to:

(i) form a company to carry on the business;

(ii) employ in the business any assets of my residuary estate[8];

(iii) be employed in the business and to retain for themselves any reasonable remuneration paid[9];

(iv) be directors of any such company and to retain for themselves any reasonable remuneration paid[9];

(v) be indemnified out of my residuary estate for any loss incurred[10].

1 See the note at **13.32**. This form will be useful where, for example, the testator wishes his son to carry on his business but the business constitutes the main asset of his estate and he also wishes to provide for his widow and other beneficiaries. Circumstances in general and, in particular, the amount of money required to provide for other beneficiaries, will dictate the terms of the option.

2 It is advisable to make the gift of the business subject to the liabilities of the business. See note at **13.21**.

3 There should be no inheritance tax payable on this gift as most assets should be granted agricultural relief and those which are not (eg farm machinery, livestock etc) should be granted 100% business relief. However, it is prudent to include such a provision in case any inheritance tax is payable (eg if some assets were not held for sufficient time prior to the testator's death).

4 The period within which notice of the option ought to be given and accepted should be tailored to the business in question. There may be issues such as the care and feeding of livestock or sowing and harvesting of crops that require immediate attention and so may demand very rapid action by the executors and/or the option holder. On the other hand the accounts might be in such a state that there is no realistic prospect of ascertaining the price payable until many months after the death.

5 The trustees will likely not wish to carry on the business for longer than is necessary. It is therefore usually desirable that the grantee should be required to exercise the option at the earliest possible time. In some circumstances, the grantee's state of knowledge may be such as to enable him to exercise the option before the precise cost is known but it would be impractical to impose a time limit which takes no account of the date on which the cost of exercising the option will be ascertained.

6 The testator will often desire to give the option holder a discount when purchasing the farming business either out of benevolence or a desire to provide an incentive to purchase the farm and continue with the business.

7 Whatever the terms of the option, the trustees will require powers to carry on the business and an indemnity during the period between the death of the testator and the exercise of the option. Such provisions can be contained either within the option itself or in the clause dealing with the trustees' powers but it is generally more suitable to include them in the option itself.

8 This clause enables assets of the estate generally to be used in the business. Without this express authority, executors and trustees would be restricted to assets used by the testator himself in the business.

9 This clause is needed because of the general rule that a trustee may not profit from his office.

10 When trustees carry on a business under a power in a Will they are personally liable for any debts incurred. To prevent their right of indemnity being limited to assets used in the business an express right to resort to the whole of the residuary estate can be given but caution should be exercised in including this far-reaching power.

FORM 13.12

Appointment of Separate Business Executors[1]

1 I appoint [*name*] of [*address*] and [*name*] of [*address*] as my executors and trustees for all purposes except those relating to the assets given by clause [*insert clause containing gift of business*].

2 I appoint [*name*] of [*address*] and [*name*] of [*address*] as my executors and trustees in relation to the assets given by clause [*insert clause containing gift of business*].

3 Unless the context otherwise requires, in this Will the expression 'my Trustees' means the executors and trustees appointed under sub-clause 1 of this clause and the expression 'my Business Trustees' means the executors and trustees appointed under sub-clause 2 of this clause[2].

1 See note at **13.35–13.36**.
2 Such a definition could also be included in a separate definitions section in the Will but it is thought to be more appropriate here.

14 Charities and Charitable Giving

Introduction

14.1 The charity sector has expanded greatly in recent years and it is now more common than ever for testators to leave gifts, often of very large sums, to charity in their Will. Currently the annual value of bequests to charity in the UK is estimated at somewhere between £1.5 and £2 billion. A draftsman must therefore be able to deal with requests of clients to draft effective Wills containing charitable bequests and must be aware of the potential pitfalls in drafting such Wills. This is especially so given that some charities, mainly because of the importance of legacy income to their total income, have gained a reputation as rather aggressive litigators with the consequence that a poorly drafted charitable provision could well result in litigation.

14.2 Aside from purely benevolent reasons, charitable giving is also particularly attractive to testators because of its favourable inheritance tax position. All charitable gifts attract no inheritance tax[1] and if gifts amounting to a certain percentage of the testator's net estate are made, a reduced inheritance tax charge may be made against part or all of the testator's estate[2]. This means that the testator concerned with maximising his inheritance tax savings should actively consider making charitable bequests.

1 Inheritance Tax Act 1984 s 23.
2 See note at **14.6–14.11** below.

Whether a gift is charitable

14.3 The question of whether a gift is charitable or not has resulted in substantial legal jurisprudence but in most situations will not be of concern to the draftsman. Most testators simply wish to leave a sum of money or a percentage of their estate to a charity or charities registered with the Charities Commission and if a charity has been registered with the Charities Commission then it is conclusively presumed to be a charity and any gift to it will be charitable[1].

1 Charities Act 2011 s 37.

14.4 It is only where the gift is to somebody other than a registered charity that the draftsman will need to concern himself with whether the gift is charitable or not. The Charities Act 2011 provides a definition of 'charity'[1] and 'charitable purpose'[2]. In order for a purpose to be charitable it must fall within one of the purposes listed in s 3(1) of the Act[3] and must also be for the public benefit[4]. It is also noted that if the executors or trustees are given an option about whether to apply the gift for charitable or non-charitable purposes (eg a gift for 'charitable or other purposes which my trustees in their sole discretion may select') then it is not a charitable gift even if the trustees do apply the gift for charitable purposes[5]. A full analysis of precisely what gifts are charitable and what are not falls beyond the scope of this book and reference should be made to specialised textbooks if the draftsman cannot easily identify whether an intended gift is or is not a gift for a charitable purpose.

1 Charities Act 2011 s 1.
2 Charities Act 2011 s 2.
3 These purposes are the prevention or relief of poverty; the advancement of education; the advancement of religion; the advancement of health or the saving of lives; the advancement of citizenship or community development; the advancement of the arts, culture, heritage or science; the advancement of amateur sport; the advancement of human rights, conflict resolution or reconciliation or the promotion of religious or racial harmony or equality and diversity; the advancement of environmental protection or improvement; the relief of those in need because of youth, age, ill-health, disability, financial hardship or other disadvantage; the advancement of animal welfare; the promotion of the efficiency of the armed forces of the Crown or of the efficiency of the police, fire and rescue services or ambulance services; or any other purpose which are analogous or within the spirit of any of the recognised charitable purposes.
4 The mere fact that a purpose falls within s 3(1) is not sufficient to make it charitable. It must also be for the public benefit.
5 *Re Chapman, Hales v A-G* [1922] 2 Ch 479.

14.5 The draftsman should also be aware of the provisions of the Equality Act 2010 when advising testators in relation to charitable giving. In most practical situations the question of discrimination will not arise but some testators may wish to restrict gifts in ways which engage the Equality Act. A restriction on a charitable gift by reference to colour will take effect as if the reference to colour was ignored[1] while a restriction on a charitable gift by reference to any other protected characteristic[2] may be permitted if it is a proportionate means of achieving a legitimate aim or to prevent or compensate a disadvantage linked to the protected characteristic[3].

1 Equality Act 2010 s 193(4).
2 These are age; disability; gender reassignment; marriage and civil partnership; pregnancy and maternity; race; religion or belief; sex; sexual orientation (Equality Act 2010 s 4).
3 Equality Act 2010 s 193.

Reduced rate of inheritance tax

14.6 In addition to charitable gifts being free from inheritance tax, if a testator leaves a certain percentage of his property to charity (or a registered Community Amateur Sports Club), then his estate may be able to claim a reduced rate of inheritance tax (36%) on the rest of his estate or on a particular component of his estate. The relevant provisions are contained in Schedule 1A of the Inheritance Tax Act 1984. In order to work out whether the reduced rate can apply and over what part of the estate (if any) it applies, a testator's estate is broken down into three components:

- Survivorship – assets which pass by survivorship;
- Trust Assets – assets held in trust which form part of the testator's estate;
- General – all assets that the testator owns outright or as a tenant in common.

14.7 A fourth component (gifts with reservation) can also qualify to pay tax at the reduced rate but only if it is merged with one of the other components.

14.8 If the testator makes from any component a charitable gift of 10% or more of the net estate of that component (as calculated in accordance with the provisions of Schedule 1A) then the chargeable part of that component will only bear inheritance tax at 36%. For example, if a testator has general net assets of £750,000, a nil-rate band of £325,000 and leaves a charitable legacy of £42,500 he will have a chargeable estate of £382,500 but because the charitable gift of £42,500 is 10% of the net estate he will only pay inheritance tax at 36% (£137,700) instead of 40% (£153,000).

14.9 There are also provisions to allow for the merger of components to gain the maximum benefit. This means that if a gift in one component is sufficiently large it can ensure an inheritance tax saving across two or more components.

14.10 It is essential for the draftsman to be aware of the reduced rate of inheritance tax provisions as, if used correctly, they can result in a win-win situation for all concerned. More money can be given to charity, less inheritance tax can be paid and, ultimately, the beneficiaries can receive more money[1]. The draftsman should therefore bear this in mind when advising the testator as to the level of charitable gifts which he or she might wish to make. Helpfully, the HMRC website contains a very useful reduced rate calculator which can be used to calculate the minimum level of gift which must be left to charity in order to qualify for the reduced rate of inheritance tax[2].

1 For example, if the net estate (calculated in accordance with the relevant provisions) is £575,000, a gift to charity of £50,000 (less than 10% of the net estate) would result in inheritance tax of £210,000 being payable and the beneficiaries receiving £315,000 whereas a larger gift to charity of £57,500 (10% of the net estate) would result in inheritance tax of £186,300 being payable and the beneficiaries receiving £331,200 (an extra £16,200). This example is 'Example 2' of the 'Worked Examples' on the HMRC website – http://www.hmrc.gov.uk/inheritancetax/pass-money-property/charity-examples.htm).

2 http://www.hmrc.gov.uk/tools/iht-reduced-rate/index.htm.

14.11 As the value of the testator's estate may fluctuate over time a gift of a fixed sum may require regular amendment in order to ensure that it meets the 10% test. To avoid this, consideration should be given to a formula clause which will ensure that a gift of 10% (subject to maximum or minimum levels if desired) is always left to charity and the reduced rate of inheritance tax is always obtained[1]. If, however, no such clause is used and the gift to charity is insufficient to obtain the reduced rate of inheritance tax (or no gift to charity at all is made) the Will can be varied by the beneficiaries to increase the gift to charity to the required amount.

1 See **Forms 14.1** and **14.2**.

Gifts to charity

14.12 Gifts to charity can take many forms – pecuniary legacies, gifts of personal property, gifts of land, gifts of a share of residue or a gift on a charitable trust. While clauses providing for a gift to a charity are often similar to a gift to an individual they do need certain additions and amendments in order to make the charitable gift both effective and trouble-free.

14.13 One of the practical problems relates to receipt of the gift and finding somebody who can give a proper receipt to the executors or trustees for the gift. This is particularly a problem if the charity is not incorporated as then a gift will take effect as a gift to each member. Express provisions concerning receipts are particularly important in such scenarios but are advisable in all situations in order to provide certainty and clarity to assist those administering the estate. In addition, in the case of many charities, particularly smaller charities where those running the charity may not always keep the registered officers up to date, it is often prudent to give the trustees the additional protection of providing that they may accept in full discharge, the receipt of anybody who appears to be a proper officer of the charity as well as anybody who actually is a registered officer of the charity.

14.14 The other major issue which draftsmen need to be aware of when drafting charitable bequests is in relation to a charity's potential to merge, amalgamate, change name or cease to exist. If the provisions of the Will are not drafted with sufficient foresight and/or are not updated properly subsequent changes to the charity beneficiary can lead to the gift going to an unintended beneficiary or failing completely. Not only does this affect the gift itself but it also has potential to affect the underlying tax on the rest of the estate as it may prevent the estate from claiming a reduced rate of inheritance tax[1].

1 See note at **14.6–14.11**.

14.15 Mistakes in the name of a charity should no longer occur given that the vast majority of charities are registered with the Charity Commission and can be checked on their website[1] with considerable ease. Nevertheless it is still advisable to include both the charity's name and number to ensure that there is absolutely no confusion as to which charity was intended. There also remain some charities which are not registered with the Charity Commission and particular care should be taken to ensure that the names of these charities are recorded correctly.

1 http://www.charitycommission.gov.uk/

14.16 More difficult are the cases where charities merge or cease to exist. Some efforts have been made to alleviate the problems with s 311 of the Charities Act 2011 which provides that where two charities merge (and the merger is registered in the register of charity mergers) a gift to one of the charities will take effect as a gift to the new charity. This, however, provides no assistance if the gift is to a named charity and the merger happens before death because then there is no valid gift to any existing charity and the gift will fail[1]. For this reason it is advisable to include a provision to prevent the lapse of such gifts and to give the power to the trustees to pay the gift to the most suitable charity in the event that the gift fails.

1 *Berry v IBS-STL(UK) Ltd* [2012] EWHC 666 (Ch).

14.17 Whenever it is intended to make a bequest to a charity it should be considered whether to contact the charity in question as many of the larger charities will have standard clauses which they like donees to use when creating a Will. Contacting the charity is particularly important if the testator wishes to give the charity an unusual gift or there is a chance that the charity would not accept the gift (perhaps because of the underlying principles of the charity or because the charity does not have the resources or knowledge to cope with such a gift).

14.18 Contacting the charity is also very important if the testator wishes his legacy to be put to a particular use. Most charities are anxious to give effect to a benefactor's wishes but sometimes there are practical or legal difficulties and sometimes policy decisions of the charity will prevent the charity from using the gift in the desired way. If the charity cannot be contacted or cannot formally agree to the request then it is usually more sensible to make an unconditional gift to the charity with a non-binding expression of desire as to its use[1] rather than to make a conditional gifts which would run the risk of total failure if the condition is not able to be fully complied with.

1 See **Form 14.5**.

14.19 Difficulties also arise where the testator wants to give a gift to a local branch of a national charity. In such cases some charities will have standard wording which they like to be used in order to enable such a gift to be given effect to but in the absence of this it is usually advisable to make provision for an effective gift to the national charity coupled with a non-binding expression of desire concerning its local application[1].

1 See **Form 14.6**.

14.20 Special considerations should also be made when it is intended to make a charitable gift of part of residue. This is because the division of residue between exempt and non-exempt beneficiaries can make calculation of the respective shares very difficult having regard to the inheritance tax being borne by each gift. It is therefore strongly advised to include a provision allowing for the respective shares to be calculated without taking into account inheritance tax and then take the respective inheritance tax from the non-exempt residuary beneficiaries[1].

1 See **Form 14.7**.

14.21 If the testator wishes to make a gift to charity but does not know or cannot decide which charities to benefit, consideration should be given to creating a charitable trust which would give the trustees the power to choose the charities to benefit. **Form 14.8** is an example of a standard charitable trust.

PRECEDENTS

14.22

FORM 14.1[1]

Formula gift to charity to ensure that the reduced rate of inheritance tax is available in relation to general component of estate[2]

1.1 I give [*name of charity*] [registered under Charity No.][3] (the charity) such a sum as together with any other gifts to charity made under my Will or any codicil shall constitute a donated amount equal to 10% of the baseline amount in relation to the general component of my estate.

1.2 [If for whatever reason the charity has ceased to exist or is otherwise unidentifiable and the gift is liable to fail for this reason this gift shall take effect as a gift to [*name of charity*] [registered under Charity No.] but otherwise take effect according to the provisions of this clause][4].

1.3 My Trustees in making payment of the legacy given by this clause

1.3.1 shall be entitled to accept in full discharge the receipt of the secretary, treasurer or other officer of the charity concerned [or any person appearing to be such an officer][5];

1.3.2 may appropriate assets not otherwise specifically bequeathed to satisfy (or partly satisfy) this legacy without the consent of any beneficiary under my Will or any codicil.

1.4 I hereby confer on my Trustees the power in their absolute discretion to make or withdraw an election under paragraph 7 of Schedule 1A Inheritance Tax Act 1984[6] in relation to any other eligible part of my estate whether or not the general component is the qualifying component and to make or withdraw an election under paragraph 8 of that Schedule[7].

1.5 Terms in this clause have the same meaning as in Schedule 1A Inheritance Tax Act 1984 and the reference to a gift to charity means a gift attributable to property to which section 23 Inheritance Tax Act 1984 applies[8].

1.6 [The legacy given by this clause shall in no event[9]:

1.6.1 be less than £[ ] whether or not the lower rate of tax shall be applicable; or

1.6.2 be more than £[ ] (the upper limit) even if the consequence of this restriction in the value of this legacy the lower rate of tax shall not apply].

1.7 If for whatever reason including the provisions of this clause or the abolishment of inheritance tax or the repeal of Schedule 1A of Inheritance Tax Act 1984 the lower rate of tax shall not be applicable this legacy shall [be equal to the amount of the upper limit] [be the sum of £[ ]] [lapse][10].

1 This form is adapted from the model form provided by STEP.
2 This form is drafted to ensure that the reduced rate of inheritance tax is available over the general

component of the testator's estate only. To ensure the reduced rate of inheritance tax is available over more than just the general component of the estate, **Form 14.2** should be used.

3 It is advisable to state both the charity's name and registered number if available. See notes at **14.15**.

4 This provision is an addition to the model form provided by STEP and is designed to provide a second charity to help ensure the gift is still effective in case the original charity ceases to exist. This may be particularly suitable if the original charity is a small charity and the second charity is a large charity which is unlikely to unexpectedly cease to exist

5 The words in square brackets provide additional protection for the trustees and, particularly in the case of smaller and less formal charities, may be well advised. See the notes at **14.13**.

6 This paragraph allows for an election to join one or more of the components to the general component for the purposes of maximising tax benefit.

7 This paragraph allows for the opting out of the reduced rate of inheritance tax. Sometimes it will be simpler and more cost efficient to opt out of the reduced rate and the executors should be given the power to so do. For example, if the testator left his house to charity it would not ordinarily need to be valued as there would be exempt from inheritance tax. However, if his executors were to claim the reduced rate of inheritance tax they would need to have the house professionally valued and the cost of doing this might outweigh the benefits.

8 This section includes registered Community Amateur Sports Clubs as charities.

9 This clause is inserted if it is desired to place an upper and/or lower limit on the gift to charity.

10 This sub-clause provides for what is to happen in the event that the reduced rate of tax is not available for whatever reason. The testator may wish to make a gift regardless of this or they may wish for the gift to lapse.

FORM 14.2[1]

Formula gift to charity to ensure that the reduced rate of inheritance tax is available in relation to more than one component of estate[2]

1.1 I give [*name of charity*] [registered under Charity No.][3] such a sum as together with any other gifts to charity made under my Will or any codicil and also any property passing to charity forming part of such of the survivorship component and settled property component as are comprised in my estate, shall constitute a donated amount equal to 10% of the baseline amount in relation to the aggregate of the general component and [survivorship component] [and] [settled property component] [and] [reservation of benefit property][4] of my estate.

1.2 [If for whatever reason the charity has ceased to exist or is otherwise unidentifiable and the gift is liable to fail for this reason this gift shall take effect as a gift to [*name of charity*] [registered under Charity No.] but otherwise take effect according to the provisions of this clause][5].

1.3 My Trustees in making payment of the legacy given by this clause

1.3.1 shall be entitled to accept in full discharge the receipt of the secretary, treasurer or other officer of the charity concerned [or any person appearing to be such an officer][6];

1.3.2 may appropriate assets not otherwise specifically bequeathed to satisfy (or partly satisfy) this legacy without the consent of any beneficiary under my Will or any codicil.

1.4 I hereby confer on my Trustees the power in their absolute discretion to make or withdraw an election under paragraph 7 of Schedule 1A Inheritance Tax Act 1984[7] in relation to any other eligible part of my estate whether or not the general component is the qualifying component and to make or withdraw an election under paragraph 8 of that Schedule[8].

1.5 Terms in this clause have the same meaning as in Schedule 1A Inheritance Tax Act 1984 and the reference to a gift to charity means a gift attributable to property to which section 23 Inheritance Tax Act 1984 applies.

1.6 [The legacy given by this clause shall in no event[9]:

1.6.1 be less than £[ ] whether or not the lower rate of tax shall be applicable; or

1.6.2 be more than £[ ] (the upper limit) even if the consequence of this restriction in the value of this legacy the lower rate of tax shall not apply.]

1.7 If for whatever reason including the provisions of this clause or the abolishment of inheritance tax or the repeal of Schedule 1A of Inheritance Tax Act 1984 the lower rate of tax shall not be applicable this legacy shall [be equal to the amount of the upper limit] [be the sum of £[ ]] [lapse][10].

1 This form is adapted from the model form provided by STEP.
2 This form is designed to ensure that the reduced rate of inheritance tax is available over more than just the general component of the estate. If it is only intended to obtain the reduced rate of inheritance tax over the general component **Form 14.1** should be used. It is noted that this alternative clause only defines the amount of legacy to be left under the Will. In order for the relief to be available over more than just the general component an election will have to be made under paragraph 7 of Schedule 1A to merge the different components.
3 It is advisable to state both the charity's name and registered number if available. See notes at **14.15**.
4 The words in square brackets should be included or deleted depending on which components are intended to be merged with the general component. If all components are intended to be used then all the words in square brackets in this sub-clause should be used.
5 This provision is an addition to the model form provided by STEP and is designed to provide a second charity to help ensure the gift is still effective in case the original charity ceases to exist. This may be particularly suitable if the original charity is a small charity and the second charity is a large charity which is unlikely to unexpectedly cease to exist.
6 The words in square brackets provide additional protection for the trustees and, particularly in the case of smaller and less formal charities, may be well advised. See the notes at **14.13**.
7 This paragraph allows for an election to join one or more of the components to the general component for the purposes of maximising tax benefit.
8 This paragraph allows for the opting out of the reduced rate of inheritance tax. Sometimes it will be simpler and more cost efficient to opt out of the reduced rate and the executors should be given the power to so do. For example, if the testator left his house to charity it would not ordinarily need to be valued as there would be exempt from inheritance tax. However, if his executors were to claim the reduced rate of inheritance tax they would need to have the house professionally valued and the cost of doing this might outweigh the benefits.
9 This clause is inserted if it is desired to place an upper and/or lower limit on the gift to charity.
10 This sub-clause provides for what is to happen in the event that the reduced rate of tax is not available for whatever reason. The testator may wish to make a gift regardless of this or they may wish for the gift to lapse.

FORM 14.3

Pecuniary legacy to charity

(a) I give £[ ] to [*name of charity*] [registered under Charity No.][1] ('the charity').

(b) The receipt of a person who [is] [appears to be][2] a proper officer of the charity shall be a full discharge to my Trustees.

1 It is advisable to state both the charity's name and registered number if available. See notes at **14.15**.

2 The use of the words 'appears to be' provides additional protection to the trustees and, particularly in the case of smaller and less formal charities, may be well advised. See notes at **14.13**.

FORM 14.4

Pecuniary legacy to charity with provision for the charity ceasing to exist[1]

(a) I give £[ ] to [*name of charity*] [registered under Charity No.][2] ('the charity').

(b) The receipt of a person who [is] [appears to be][3] a proper officer of the charity shall be a full discharge to my Trustees.

(c) If for whatever reason the charity has ceased to exist or is otherwise unidentifiable and this gift is liable to fail for this reason this gift shall not fail but take effect as a gift to my Trustees who shall divide the gift in such shares as they see fit and pay it to the charity or charities which they in their sole discretion consider most nearly fulfils the objects I intended to benefit.

1 This clause is designed to enable the gift to continue to be effective as a charitable gift even if the charity ceases to exist. In this case the gift will take effect as a gift to the trustees who are to pay it to the charity or charities which they feel closest represents the objects of the original charity.

2 It is advisable to state both the charity's name and registered number if available. See notes at **14.15**.

3 The use of the words 'appears to be' provides additional protection to the trustees and, particularly in the case of smaller and less formal charities, may be well advised. See notes at **14.13**.

FORM 14.5

Gift to charity with non-binding purpose request[1]

(a) I give £[ ] to [*name of charity*] [registered under Charity No.][2] ('the charity').

(b) It is my wish without creating a binding obligation on the charity that this gift is used for [*(its projects in Ethiopia) (its education work with girls) (its research into bowel cancer) etc.*].

(c) The receipt of a person who [is] [appears to be][3] a proper officer of the charity shall be a full discharge to my Trustees.

[(d) If for whatever reason the charity has ceased to exist or is otherwise unidentifiable and this gift is liable to fail for this reason this gift shall not fail but take effect as a gift to my Trustees who shall divide the gift in such shares as they see fit and pay it to the charity or charities which they in their sole discretion consider most nearly fulfils the objects I intended to benefit.][4]

1 Whenever the testator wishes a gift to be put to a particular use it is recommended to contact the charity to see if such use is possible. See notes at **14.18.**

2 It is advisable to state both the charity's name and registered number if available. See notes at **14.15**.

3 The use of the words 'appears to be' provides additional protection to the trustees and, particularly in the case of smaller and less formal charities, may be well advised. See notes at **14.13**.

4 This sub-clause is designed to enable the gift to continue to be effective as a charitable gift even if the charity ceases to exist. In this case the gift will take effect as a gift to the trustees who are to pay it to the charity or charities which they feel closest represents the objects of the original charity.

FORM 14.6

Gift to national charity with non-binding request that it be used for a local branch of the charity[1]

(a) I give £[ ] to [*name of charity*] [registered under Charity No.][2] ('the charity').

(b) It is my wish without creating a binding obligation on the charity that this gift is used for the benefit of the branch located at [*insert address*] or if that branch is no longer in existence then for the benefit of the nearest branch of the charity to the above address.

(c) The receipt of a person who [is] [appears to be][3] a proper officer of the charity shall be a full discharge to my Trustees.

[(d) If for whatever reason the charity has ceased to exist or is otherwise unidentifiable and this gift is liable to fail for this reason this gift shall not fail but take effect as a gift to my Trustees who shall divide the gift in such shares as they see fit and pay it to the charity or charities which they in their sole discretion consider most nearly fulfils the objects I intended to benefit.][4]

1 Whenever the testator wishes a gift to be put to a particular use it is recommended to contact the charity to see if such use is possible. See notes at **14.18**.

2 It is advisable to state both the charity's name and registered number if available. See notes at **14.15**.

3 The use of the words 'appears to be' provides additional protection to the trustees and, particularly in the case of smaller and less formal charities, may be well advised. See notes at **14.13**.

4 This sub-clause is designed to enable the gift to continue to be effective as a charitable gift even if the charity ceases to exist. In this case the gift will take effect as a gift to the trustees who are to pay it to the charity or charities which they feel closest represents the objects of the original charity.

FORM 14.7

Gift of share of residue

1.1 My Trustees shall divide my residuary estate into [*(two)*] equal shares which they shall hold on trust as to:

(a) One share for [*(name)*] of [*address*] absolutely

(b) One share for [*name of charity*] [registered under Charity No.][1] ('the charity') and the receipt of a person who [is] [appears to be][2] a proper officer of the charity shall be a full discharge to my Trustees.

1.2 In calculating the shares of my residuary estate my Trustees shall not take into account any inheritance tax payable and attributable to my residuary estate and then after the division the shares subject to inheritance tax shall have such tax attributed to them[3].

1.3 If for whatever reason the charity has ceased to exist or is otherwise unidentifiable and this gift is liable to fail for this reason this gift shall not fail but take effect as a gift to my Trustees who shall divide the gift in such shares as they see fit and pay it to the charity or charities which they in their sole discretion consider most nearly fulfils the objects I intended to benefit.][4]

1 It is advisable to state both the charity's name and registered number if available. See notes at **14.15**.

2 The use of the words 'appears to be' provides additional protection to the trustees and, particularly in the case of smaller and less formal charities, may be well advised. See notes at **14.13**.

3 This clause is to prevent complicated calculations of the shares taking into inheritance tax and simply divides up the estate without taking into account inheritance tax. See notes at **14.15**.

4 This sub-clause is designed to enable the gift to continue to be effective as a charitable gift even if the charity ceases to exist. In this case the gift will take effect as a gift to the trustees who are to pay it to the charity or charities which they feel closest represents the objects of the original charity.

FORM 14.8

Gift on charitable trust[1]

(a) I give to my Trustees £[ ][2] to be held as to income and capital to pay to such charity or charities as my Trustees shall in their absolute discretion think fit.

(b) [It is my wish without creating a binding obligation on my Trustees that this gift is used for the benefit of charities who work [*(with children) (in Africa) (fighting cancer) (assisting the homeless) etc*][3].

(c) The receipt of a person who [is] [appears to be][4] a proper officer of the charity shall be a full discharge to my Trustees.

(d) In this clause 'charity' shall have the same meaning as in the Charities Act 2011.

1 This form merely provides the basics of the trust. Further provisions may be desirable if the trustees are to have more extensive powers than their statutory powers.

2 This form is based on a situation where the trust fund is comprised from a pecuniary legacy but it could be easily adapted to a case where a share of residue comprises the trust fund.

3 Additional wishes concerning the application of the trust fund could be included if desired or the trustees can be given the a very broad discretion by removing this sub-clause altogether.

4 The use of the words 'appears to be' provides additional protection to the trustees and, particularly in the case of smaller and less formal charities, may be well advised. See notes at **14.13**.

15 Digital Assets

Digital assets

15.1 The phrase 'digital assets' covers a myriad of different and distinct assets, but is broadly understood to mean assets stored in a digital or online form. It covers information stored on computers, tablets, mobile phones and other devices. It can also cover email accounts, social media profiles and online storage resources (Dropbox, the Cloud etc) as well as financial assets such as the balances in PayPal, eBay or online bank accounts.

15.2 It is essential for the modern draftsman to consider digital assets when preparing a Will and will only become even more so as time progresses and more of the digital generation start thinking about making a Will. A failure to consider digital assets and the effect of Will provisions on such assets will not only cause great trouble for the testator's family and loved ones but may also leave the draftsman vulnerable to a negligence claim.

15.3 While the financial value of social media profiles are likely to be relatively limited[1] the financial value of other digital assets will not be. The most valuable domain names are sold for millions of pounds while balances in PayPal accounts, gambling accounts, eBay accounts, and other similar accounts may also be very financially valuable. Similarly if the testator is a photographer, writer, graphic designer or equivalent their online content may constitute a very significant proportion of their net estate.

1 Though some, particularly those of the famous or infamous, may have a not insignificant commercial value.

15.4 If no thought is given to digital assets there is a real danger of significant financial loss occurring due to the executors being either unaware of or unable to realise assets in online accounts, in digital content or stored in an electronic form. There is also potential for significant emotional distress to family and friends of the testator due to them being unable to close social media profiles[1] or unable to access accounts which could give an insight into the testator's last thoughts or actions in a suspicious death[2].

1 Which results in the additional risk of the deceased's identity being stolen and used for criminal purposes.
2 As was the case following the death of British model Sahar Daftary whose estate (unsuccessfully) sought access to her Facebook account to show she had not committed suicide.

Current rules

15.5 There is a dearth of rules and formal guidance as to the treatment of digital assets. This is largely because the area has developed (and continues to develop) so quickly that legal rules have not had sufficient time to develop to match it. Added to this is the international nature of digital assets which makes them uniquely difficult to legislate and provide for. This has meant digital assets are either shoehorned into existing legal principles designed for a different class of assets or, alternatively, fall outside all formal legal rules. Both situations can cause significant problems for the draftsman when attempting to provide his client with the best possible service.

15.6 When drafting provisions concerning digital assets it is vital to take note of any terms and conditions or terms of service relating to a digital asset as they may affect how it can be used after death. For example, the majority of email accounts are only licensed to the user, meaning that after they die the email address and all its contents revert back to the provider. Similarly, despite what many members of the public believe, when a person buys music on iTunes they only purchase a licence to listen to the music and not the music itself meaning the songs in a person's library cannot be passed on to the next generation, regardless of any provision in the Will. Furthermore, many social media sites and other digital accounts contain rules prohibiting a person from logging into another person's account which can affect the way certain digital assets can be passed on and prevent a beneficiary from inheriting an account even if they have the testator's username and password. The terms of service may also set down the consequences of the death of an account holder and the procedure to be followed by any personal representatives.

Practical problems concerning digital assets

15.7 There are a number of practical problems concerning digital assets. The first problem concerns identification. Unlike a house or a large chattel the executors and descendants of the testator are not certain to just discover the existence of a digital asset. There is no physical item to spot and unless the testator has brought the existence of the asset to somebody's attention there is a real risk it will remain unnoticed and unrealised.

15.8 The second problem concerns realisation. Even if the executors are aware of the existence of the assets, the absence of usernames, passwords, pin codes and logins can exclude the executors from being able to fulfil the testator's wishes. The exclusion does not need to be permanent, as even a temporary exclusion or a delay can effectively destroy the assets. For example, most email accounts are deleted forever if they are not used for a few months while betting accounts and online bank accounts often provide that if they are not used for a certain period then the accounts can be closed and the proceeds in the account disposed of. Domain names with .uk endings will terminate unless the personal representative has transferred them to another person within one year after the death of the holder or at the end of their appointment (whichever is first)[1]. Therefore, even if the personal representative is eventually able to gain access to the account it may be fruitless if too much time has passed.

1 Nominet, Term 18, accurate as of September 2014.

15.9 The third problem concerns jurisdiction. The majority of digital assets are international in nature and therefore jurisdiction can be a very difficult area. The rights and powers of the executors may depend on what sort of digital asset it is and where the company behind the asset is legally based[1]. If a particularly valuable digital asset was based in USA it might therefore be inappropriate to restrict the UK Will to only UK based assets. This is something the draftsman must consider carefully when drafting any jurisdictional provisions in the Will.

1 For example, PayPal is registered as a Luxembourg bank while Yahoo's headquarters are in the USA.

15.10 Unless a testator has diligently read all the terms and conditions of any domain name registry, online bank account and social media account the testator is unlikely to know where the underlying company is based. If the asset is particularly valuable the prudent draftsman will research the governing law and provide appropriate advice concerning how best to leave the asset under this law (if he is able to so advise). However, given the number of digital assets it is unlikely to be practical to do so for every asset and so the draftsman may have to make a choice as to whether or not to restrict the jurisdictional scope of the Will with the knowledge that this may hinder the ability to deal with certain digital assets.

15.11 Other practical problems which can exist can be the lack of sufficient technical knowledge on behalf of the executor/recipient to be able to realise or access the assets, how to accommodate a testator's wish to hide certain digital assets from their beneficiaries while at the same time passing on other digital assets and the general difficulties inherent in acting in an area of such rapid change.

Digital asset list

15.12 In order to avoid the two principle problems of identification and realisation of digital assets the testator should be advised to make a list of all his digital assets and make a note of the method of accessing them. This can be done by completing a document such as the sample 'Digital Asset List' contained at **Form 15.7** or alternatively there are a number of online companies which will provide such a service. Both options have different advantages and disadvantages and it may be a matter for the testator's possible preference. The use of an online company will keep the information safe from physical theft or destruction but not electronic theft or the closure of the company. On the other hand a physical document is easier to keep with the Will and often seen as easier to create but does suffer from the danger of physical theft and destruction. Whichever method is used the testator should be advised that the record should be regularly updated and kept in a manner whereby it will be easily available to his executors after his death. Any document containing usernames, passwords or logins should not be incorporated into the Will as a Will is a public document.

Gifts of digital assets

15.13 Digital assets can be of very different natures; from the content on a computer, to a domain name, to the balance in an online account. This makes a broad brush approach hard to provide for especially as many of them are more properly classified as a chose in action than a concrete asset. Unless specific provision is given the digital assets will be shoehorned under existing provisions. Online bank accounts will pass under provisions relating to bank accounts, content on computers are likely to pass with the computer and the majority of other digital assets will most likely fall under residue.

15.14 As a very general rule, the handling of digital assets in the Will is equivalent to the handling of chattels in a Will and the advice concerning chattels contained in **chapter 12** should be followed subject to the necessary amendments to reflect the digital nature of the assets. This means that express provision should be made for any particularly valuable assets but the balance can most likely be given as a collective gift.

15.15 There will be some particular digital assets which are particularly valuable from a financial point of view but the majority are likely to be of more sentimental value than financial value. There is also likely to be a large number of different digital assets and this will often make it impractical to give a separate gift of each asset to a different beneficiary. For practical purposes the most suitable solution is often for the testator to give specific gifts of any particularly valuable or sentimental digital assets and then to leave the rest of the assets to a named individual (accompanied by a memorandum of wishes if the testator so desires)[1] or to fall into residue. If it is intended to give a general gift of 'Digital Assets' a definition of digital assets should be contained in the Will. A sample definition is contained in **Form 15.5** and **Form 15.6**.

1 See **Form 15.8**.

Caveat

15.16 The digital world evolves rapidly and the type, form and content of digital assets can change dramatically over the space of a short period of time. For this reason great care must be taken when providing for assets of a digital nature and gifts of digital assets in a Will should be reviewed regularly. However, despite the difficulties inherent in providing for legacies of a digital nature it is far more detrimental to the client to fail to consider or provide for such assets at all.

PRECEDENTS

15.17

FORM 15.1

Gift of Balance in an Online Account[1]

I give to [*name*] the balance existing in my [*PayPal/eBay/online betting account(s)*] at the date of my death.

1 Gifts of balances in online bank accounts are subject to the same risks as the gifts of balances in ordinary bank accounts (see note at **12.17**) and for this reason are generally inadvisable.

FORM 15.2

Gift of Domain Name

I give to [*name*] all rights and interest I hold in the domain name [*name*][1] and I direct my executor to take all steps required to transfer the domain name to [name].

1 If the domain name is connected with a business, care should be taken to coordinate any bequest of the business with the gift of the domain name.

FORM 15.3

Gift of Contents of Computers

I give to [*name*] the contents of all laptop and desktop computers I own or use[1] [on condition that [*name*] be permitted to copy any documents or files used in connection with my business][2].

1 The legal ownership of contents kept on computers owned by a third party (eg an employer) but used by the testator is uncertain and the third party may refuse access to such content. For this reason it is advisable for all testators to keep a back-up of any personal information stored on a third party's computer.

2 Many computers will be used both for personal and business purposes. The testator is likely to wish for the personal material to be given to his family but the business documents and files to be available to assist with the organisation and running of the business.

FORM 15.4

Gift of Digital Assets by Reference to List[1]

I give to the person named in the first column below the digital asset or assets specified against his or her name in the second column.

Donee	Digital Asset(s)
[*name*]	[*description*]
[*name*]	[*description*]
[*name*]	[*description*]

[*name*] [*description*]

[*name*] [*description*]

1 This form may be suitable for use where there are a large number of specific gifts of digital assets which the testator seeks to make.

FORM 15.5

Gift of all Digital Assets to Specified Beneficiary

I give to [*name*] all digital assets as defined below[1] and held by me at the date of my death and not otherwise disposed of by this Will or any codicil thereto.

'Digital Assets' includes files and information stored on my digital devices including but not limited to my desktop and laptop computers, hard-drives, phones, tablets and any similar device. It also includes all files and information stored online via online storage sites and Cloud based storage as well as all my interest in email accounts, social network accounts, domain names, web-hosting accounts, digital music, digital video, digital photographs and my interest in PayPal, eBay and other equivalent online-only financial accounts. Furthermore it includes all similar digital or online assets which currently exist or may exist at the date of my death.

1 Such definition could equally be contained in a collection of definitions or declarations contained at the start or end of the Will.

FORM 15.6

Gift of all Digital Assets to a Specified Beneficiary with non-binding request to deal with in accordance with Memorandum of Wishes

I give to [*name*] all digital assets as defined below[1] and held by me at the date of my death and not otherwise disposed of by this Will or any codicil thereto and request without imposing any trust or binding obligation that such digital assets be dealt with in accordance with any existing or future memorandum of wishes[2] left by me.

'Digital Assets' includes files and information stored on my digital devices including but not limited to my desktop and laptop computers, hard-drives, phones, tablets and any similar device. It also includes all files and information stored online via online storage sites and Cloud based storage as well as all my interest in email accounts, social network accounts, domain names, web-hosting accounts, digital music, digital video, digital photographs and my interest in PayPal, eBay and other equivalent online-only financial accounts. Furthermore it includes all similar digital or online assets which currently exist or may exist at the date of my death.

1 Such definition could equally be contained in a collection of definitions or declarations contained at the start or end of the Will.
2 A sample Memorandum of Wishes is contained at **Form 15.8**.

FORM 15.7

List of Digital Assets[1]

Digital Asset	Username	Password (P) / Password Hint (PH)	Approximate Value
Contents of Computers and Devices			
eg Content of Dell laptop	*Jimmy*	*jd14 (P)*	*Emotional only*
[Computer]			
[Laptop]			
[External Hard Drive]			
[Tablet]			
[Mobile Phone 1]			
[Mobile Phone 2]			
Email Accounts			
eg Hotmail	*jimdoe@hotmail.com*	*Date of Birth (PH)*	*N/A*
[Hotmail]			
[Gmail]			
[Work]			
Social Networks			
eg Facebook	*jimdoe@hotmail.com*	*jimmy14 (P)*	*N/A*
[Facebook]			
[Twitter]			
[Instagram]			
[LinkedIn]			

Domain Names			
eg DoesDoors.com	*jimdoe*	*My first dog (PH)*	*£3,000*
Bank Accounts			
eg Natwest A/C 321654	*Customer No: 10101 Online Pin: (My Date of Birth)*	*Password1* (P)*	*£20,000*
[Paypal]			
Storage Sites / Accounts			
eg Flickr	*jimdoe14*	*photoking (P)*	*N/A*
[Dropbox]			
[Cloud Storage 1]			
[Cloud Storage 2]			
[Music Storage]			
[Video Storage]			
Other			
eg Paddy Power A/C	*johnbetsdoe*	*jdbetting (P)*	*£3,000*
[Blog]			
[Betting Account]			
[eBay]			
[Amazon]			
[Bitcoin]			
[Airmiles]			

[Gaming Accounts]			

Signed: ______________________________

Dated: ______________________________

1 This is merely a sample list and will need to be adapted to cover the testator's particular assets.

FORM 15.8

Memorandum of Wishes for Digital Assets[1]

This is the Digital Asset Memorandum of *[insert name]*. Unless stated otherwise in my Will or any codicil thereto I ask (without imposing any legal obligation) that the instructions contained in this Memorandum are followed when dealing with the digital assets listed below. I also ask (without imposing any legal obligation) that this Memorandum is considered when dealing with any digital assets not specifically mentioned in my Will or in the table below.

Digital Asset	**Username**	**Password (P) / Password Hint (PH)**	**Wishes**	**Notes**
Contents of Computers and Devices				
eg Content of Dell laptop	*Jimmy*	*jd14* (P)	*Delete all save 'Work' folders which should go to Bill Burns*	*Nothing valuable*
[Computer]				
[Laptop]				
[External Hard Drive]				
[Tablet]				
[Mobile Phone 1]				

[Mobile Phone 2]				
Email Accounts				
eg Hotmail	*jimdoe@ hotmail.com*	*Date of Birth* (PH)	*To Jane Doe (or if deceased, John Doe) who should save any emails they wish and then delete account*	–
[Hotmail]				
[Gmail]				
[Work]				
Social Networks				
eg Facebook	*jimdoe@ hotmail.com*	*jimmy14* (P)	*Close account*	*Allow family to download any photos/ videos they wish before closing*
[Facebook]				
[Twitter]				
[Instagram]				
[LinkedIn]				
Domain Names				
eg DoesDoors. com	*jimdoe*	*My first dog* (PH)	*To Jane Doe, Jill Doe, John Doe*	–
Bank Accounts				
eg Natwest A/C 321654	*Customer No: 10101 Online Pin: (My Date of Birth)*	*Password1** (P)	*Left as in Will*	*Online Pin: (My Date of Birth)*

[Paypal]				
Storage Sites / Accounts				
eg Flickr	*jimdoe14*	*photoking* (P)	*Leave open*	*I wish everybody to enjoy my photos*
[Dropbox]				
[Cloud Storage 1]				
[Cloud Storage 2]				
[Music Storage]				
[Video Storage]				
Other				
eg Paddy Power A/C	*johnbetsdoe*	*jdbetting* (P)	*Proceeds to Jane Doe then close*	–
[Blog]				
[Betting Account]				
[eBay]				
[Amazon]				
[Bitcoin]				
[Airmiles]				
[Gaming Accounts]				

Signed: ________________________________

Dated: ________________________________

1 This is merely a sample memorandum and will need to be adapted to cover the testator's particular assets.

16 Residuary Gifts

16.1 A residuary gift is the 'sweep all' provision in a Will, intended to provide for the disposition of the whole of the testator's estate insofar as not already gifted by the earlier parts of the Will. Many testators will envisage a Will that deals with each of their assets in a specific way and with no residuary clause because they believe that they will have provided for everything. However, any Will, even one containing many specific gifts, should contain a residuary gift to avoid an unforeseen partial intestacy.

16.2 The traditional way of dealing with residuary gifts is to vest the residue in the trustees on trust for sale with power to postpone the sale. Where there is an outright gift of the residue and no continuing trust will come into being, it may be better not to vest the residue in trustees but to rely on the powers of executors to give effect to the terms of the Will. There will, of course, have to be provision for administration of the estate so far as is necessary. Where the residuary estate will or may be subject to a trust, it is suggested that it is vested in the trustees on an express trust for sale with power to postpone the sale. In the case of land, a power to postpone the sale is implied by Trusts of Land and Appointment of Trustees Act 1996 s 4 but it may be desirable to include an express power to postpone for the personalty which, invariably, will form part of the residuary estate.

16.3 **Form 16.1** sets out standard administration trusts including a trust for sale with power to postpone sale. It is intended to be introductory to the clauses contained in **Form 16.2** and subsequent forms. The form also contains various directions concerning the payment of debts and expenses. In many cases the statutory powers of executors and trustees to pay debts and expenses will suffice. Express provision has been made for the sake of certainty and in order to vary statutory provisions where appropriate. The reader is referred to the notes to the form itself. It is, in many cases, not necessary to include an express trust for sale but many practitioners continue to do so and lay executors often appreciate an express statement of their powers.

Survivorship clause

16.4 It is important to make an informed decision whether a residuary gift[1] should be contingent on the beneficiary's surviving the testator by a stated period. The object of the requirement is to prevent a beneficiary who only survives the testator by a short period from benefiting. In origin, this was also intended to prevent a second levy of estate duty in quick succession, but Inheritance Tax Act 1984 s 141, which gives inheritance tax relief in the event of a beneficiary's dying within five years of the testator, may result in the inclusion of a survivorship clause not being necessary for this purpose. Nevertheless, the inclusion or exclusion of the clause can have inheritance tax consequences and it ought not to be included without thought being given to those consequences.

1 Sometimes this is something which ought to be done in the case of a non-residuary gift.

16.5 The introduction of a transferrable nil-rate band between spouses and civil partners has had the immediate consequence that in the case of Wills for married couples and civil partners survivorship clauses are much less important than was previously the case and in many cases their inclusion will be detrimental. This is illustrated by the following example:

> H and W are married with children. Neither has been married before[1]. Their combined estates are taxable. Prior to the introduction of the transferrable nil-rate band H and W might have been advised to make Wills including a nil-rate band discretionary trust with debt and/or charge scheme provisions included. This would be done in order to avoid wasting the nil-rate band.
>
> Suppose each leaves the whole of his or her estate to the other subject to the other surviving for 30 days. In the alternative each leaves his or her estate to the children. If W survives H but dies within 30 days the gift to W is ineffective and H uses his nil-rate band in full. W then uses her nil-rate band in full on her death and, provided the estates have been equalised, the two dispositions are as tax-efficient as possible.

That situation is now no more advantageous than the case in which there is no survivorship clause because the transferability of H's nil-rate band to W means that H will not waste any of his nil-rate band if his Will leaves everything to W on her surviving him. Indeed, the absence of a survivorship clause may be advantageous if, for example, W dies in a different fiscal year after the nil-rate band has increased. This is because if H does not use any of his nil-rate band W's personal representatives are able to claim double the nil-rate band at the time of her death which will be greater than her nil-rate band plus H's at the time of his death.

1 If either is entitled to an enhanced nil-rate band because of a previous marriage or civil partnership the inclusion of a survivorship clause will remain useful because only one nil-rate band may be transferred.

16.6 Inheritance tax is not the only reason for including survivorship clauses. Administrative convenience might also justify the inclusion of a survivorship clause. Most importantly, the testator can have good reasons for including a survivorship clause as a means of controlling the ultimate destination of his estate. In the case of second marriages the use of a survivorship clause is helpful both as a means of controlling the destination of property and as a means of avoiding the waste of an already enhanced nil-rate band. Survivorship clauses are also particularly useful where the testator wishes to confer a benefit on the named person only, as in the case of a pecuniary legacy given as an acknowledgment of friendship or personal services. A survivorship clause under which the gift is deemed to lapse may then be required. One example, which is becoming more common, is the case of an unmarried couple with no children. Each may wish to benefit the other but include a survivorship clause so that his or her estate does not inadvertently end up in the hands of the other's relatives in the event of deaths in quick succession. Similar principles may apply to civil partners.

16.7 Inheritance Tax Act 1984 s 92[1] permits the use of a survivorship clause without adverse inheritance tax consequences if the period for survival does not exceed six months. One month or 30 days is the usual period used. Apart from the factors described above, such provisions are designed to cover the situation which arises where two people are involved in a common calamity and one survives the other by a few days.

1 Where property is held for a person on condition that he survives for a period of not more than six months and he does not do so, the Inheritance Tax Act 1984 applies as if the alternate provision had effect from the beginning of the period.

16.8 It is rare for there to be any advantage in extending the period beyond one month, although inheritance tax mitigation may sometimes require a longer period. The longer the period prescribed, the greater the inconvenience and uncertainty because the estate cannot be administered until after the expiry of the period.

16.9 If it is thought desirable to extend the period of survival, it is unwise to apply the survivorship clause to the appointment of an executor as it will not be possible to obtain a grant of probate within the prescribed period.

16.10 If two persons die in circumstances where it is uncertain which of them died first, the following statutory rules apply.

(1) Where the persons concerned are husband and wife or civil partners:
   (a) if the older dies testate, he is presumed to have predeceased the younger[1];
   (b) if the older dies intestate then in the administration of *his* estate, the younger is presumed to have predeceased him[2].

(2) Where the persons concerned are not husband and wife or civil partners, the older is presumed to have predeceased the younger whether he dies testate or intestate[3].

1 Law of Property Act 1925 s 184, see **appendix 33.15**.
2 Administration of Estates Act 1925 s 46(3), as amended, see **appendix 35.1**.
3 Law of Property Act 1925 s 184 unaffected by the amendment to Administration of Estates Act 1925 s 46, see **appendix 35.1**.

16.11 The application of the general rule that the elder is presumed to have predeceased the younger is not restricted to spouses or civil partners but it is to those relationships that they most commonly apply. The special rule as to intestate succession applies only to spouses and civil partners.

16.12 In the case of husband and wife or civil partners, if the husband is older than the wife and has left a Will leaving the whole of his estate to the wife or to X if the wife predeceases him and the statutory rules come into operation, the husband will be deemed to have predeceased the wife, his estate will pass to her and her estate will then be applied in accordance with her Will or intestacy. A survivorship clause will avoid this outcome. If the husband had died intestate, his estate would not pass to the wife but would be administered according to the rules of intestacy on the assumption that the wife had predeceased him. The wife's estate would, of course, be administered according to her Will or intestacy without the husband's estate being added to it. For these purposes, it matters not, therefore, whether the younger of the two dies testate or intestate.

Age contingent gifts

16.13 It is usual to make a residuary gift to the testator's children a class gift[1]. The question then arises whether the gift should be made contingent on the beneficiaries attaining a stated age and if so what age. Many testators take the view that they do not want a young beneficiary to have that right to capital which a vested interest confers. It is common, therefore, to provide that a gift does not vest until a beneficiary attains a specified age. The testator's wishes and the circumstances of individual cases will dictate whether gifts to minors would vest on the death of the testator or be made subject to an age contingency.

1 See **Forms 16.5–16.8**

16.14 Careful consideration should be given to the inheritance tax consequences of introducing age contingencies which are discussed in more detail at **22.17–22.21**. It is thought that in many situations the testator's concern about inheritance tax will be overridden by their concern not to vest interests in immature beneficiaries. As a result, in this chapter, age contingencies are employed which may be inefficient for inheritance tax purposes. Some of the matters besides inheritance tax of which the draftsman should take note are considered below.

16.15 In the case of Wills made on or after 6 April 2010, the Perpetuities and Accumulations Act 2009 (which came into force on that day) has the effect of introducing a single perpetuity period of 125 years[1]. No other perpetuity period may be specified and the 125-year period will apply whether or not the Will specifies a perpetuity period. A testator may limit the duration of a trust by specifying that all the income and capital must be distributed within, for example, 21 years of his death[2] but this does not have the effect of foreshortening the perpetuity period. For the purposes of age contingencies, the effect of imposing a unitary perpetuity period of 125 years is that there is a much reduced likelihood of a disposition infringing the Rule against Perpetuities. Thus, in previous editions, the delayed vesting of gifts to the testator's children (lives in being at the testator's death) would not contravene the rule that all interests must vest within the perpetuity period, but gifts to more remote issue carried the risk (subject to the 'wait and see' provision) of offending the Rule if a vesting age greater than 21 was specified. This meant that Wills made before 6 April 2010 could provide for children to take vested interests at the age of 25 or 30 years but that substitutional gifts to grandchildren required an age contingency of 21 years or less.

1 Perpetuities and Accumulations Act 2009 s 5(1): see **appendix 34.7**.
2 As in **Form 27.4**.

16.16 The Perpetuities and Accumulations Act 2009 has continued the 'wait and see' provisions[1] introduced by the 1964 Act so that, unlike the position at common law, a disposition is not void simply because it might not vest until too remote a time. Until it is established that an interest will not vest until after the end of the perpetuity period, the interest is treated as if it were not subject to the Rule against Perpetuities. Furthermore, if it is established that an interest will not vest in time, that does not affect the validity of things previously done in relation to that interest. This, together with a single perpetuity period of 125 years, greatly simplifies the application of the Rule and simplifies will-drafting. It also means that testators need not limit themselves to a 21-year age contingency in substitutional gifts since it is very likely that their grandchildren will attain the age of 30 or 35 years within the 125-year perpetuity period.

1 Perpetuities and Accumulations Act 2009 s 7: see **appendix 34.9**.

16.17 Wills made before 6 April 2010 are still governed by the previous rules even though the testator dies after that date.

16.18 Where the vesting of capital is postponed until an age greater than 18, Trustee Act 1925 s 31 will result in the beneficiary's interest in income vesting at 18. The Will may, of course, provide for income to be used for a contingent beneficiary prior to his attaining 18 or at a prescribed age over 18. There is, however a constraint on the contingent age being greater than 18 in that, if the inheritance tax advantages, such as they are, of a s 71D trust – the successor to the now redundant accumulation and maintenance trust[1] – are to be enjoyed, the right to receive income should not be postponed beyond 25.

1 It is no longer possible to create an accumulation and maintenance trust within Inheritance Tax Act 1984 s 71 and pre-existing trusts have now ceased to come within the section.

16.19 Prior to 6 April 2010 there was a second constraint which was that there would be an infringement of the Rule against Accumulations if the right to receive income did not vest within 21 years of the testator's death. This took effect subject to the saving provisions of the Perpetuities and Accumulations Act 1964 s 4. The Perpetuities and Accumulations Act 2009 has abolished the restrictions on accumulations[1] for Wills made on or after that date. This means that a power to accumulate need not be limited to 21 years. As a result Will drafting is much simplified and it is now possible to include a clause giving power: 'during the whole of the period in which a beneficiary has a contingent interest to accumulate such income as is not so applied and to invest that income as an addition to the capital of the share to which that beneficiary is entitled'. One consequence is that it is now possible for a Will to provide that the Trustee Act 1925 s 31 shall apply with a non-statutory age contingency.

1 Perpetuities and Accumulations Act 2009 s 13 which declares that the Law of Property Act 1925 ss 164 to 166 and the Perpetuities and Accumulations Act 1964 s 13 cease to have effect.

16.20 The decision whether to create a vested interest or an interest contingent upon age may also be governed by other inheritance tax considerations. The vestiges of the inheritance tax interest in possession regime, 'immediate post death interests', are discussed in **chapter 22**.

16.21 Capital gains tax is also relevant because it is only where an interest in capital is vested in a beneficiary that a disposal by the trustees will be treated as a disposal by the beneficiary under the Taxation of Chargeable Gains Act 1992 s 92, ranking for the full yearly exemption from that tax. In *Sansom v Peay*[1], however, it was held that relief from capital gains tax on the sale of a house was available although the occupant did not have a vested interest in the house. The taxpayers were the trustees of a discretionary trust with power to purchase a house and permit one or more of the discretionary beneficiaries to reside in it. They did this and permitted all the discretionary beneficiaries (being a husband, wife and children) to reside there without payment. It was subsequently sold at a profit and the court held that the profit was not subject to capital gains tax because the house was 'the only or main residence of the persons entitled to occupy it under the terms of the settlement'[2]. It is notable that in the circumstances of this case, the beneficiaries (or at any rate the husband and his wife) would almost certainly have had an 'interest in possession' for inheritance tax purposes even though they only had a contingent interest in the house itself.

1 [1976] 3 All ER 375, [1976] 1 WLR 1073. Where the contingent interest carries the right to the intermediate income, the contingent beneficiary is, of course, in the same position (for income tax purposes) as if he had a vested interest.

2 Taxation of Chargeable Gains Act 1992 s 225.

16.22 If tax considerations are the driving force and the gifts are not otherwise significant for inheritance tax purposes (either because the estate is small or because it is very large) it is the liability to income tax which often results in a vested interest being preferred to a contingent interest. Where the interest is vested, the income is, ultimately, treated as that of the beneficiary himself and does not attract income tax at the rate applicable to trusts[1].

1 The rate applicable to trusts is currently 45%. The dividend rate applicable to trusts is now 37.5%. There is now a special trust tax rate in respect of the first £1,000 of income and particular beneficial treatments apply to trusts for vulnerable beneficiaries.

16.23 Where the income is distributed to a contingent beneficiary the beneficiary may, with some inconvenience, offset or reclaim some of the tax but the ability to do so depends upon the beneficiary's circumstances. Where the income is accumulated, it cannot be recovered because when paid over it is treated as capital in the hands of the beneficiary. In most cases this is a financial disadvantage to the beneficiary although, where he is liable to higher rate tax, it may sometimes be better for him to receive the accumulated income as capital.

16.24 A further consideration which may be relevant is that there is greater scope for the variation of a trust where the interests of the beneficiaries are vested rather than contingent or subject to the exercise of a discretion. In making the choice between vested and age contingent gifts the advantages must be weighed against the disadvantages in each case. Some of the main considerations have been mentioned. Others include the risk of a beneficiary inheriting when immature, the personalities of those concerned (both testator and beneficiaries) and the kind of assets that make up the trust fund.

Lapse and class gifts

16.25 A gift (of whatever nature) to a child or remoter descendant of the testator will not necessarily lapse if the beneficiary dies before the testator because the Wills Act 1837 s 33[1], provides for the beneficiary's issue to take. The statutory provisions may be excluded either by an express substitutional provision[2] or by a general declaration[3].

1 See **appendix 33.14**.
2 For example, **Forms 16.6**, **16.8** and particularly **16.9**.
3 For example, **Form 20.8**.

16.26 It is usually better, however, to make express substitutional provision in the Will rather than to rely on the statutory provision in order to avoid difficulty and uncertainty, for example, as to whether the Will expresses a contrary intention so as to exclude the operation of the section. The testator rarely thinks about the possibility without prompting and should always be asked what he intends if a beneficiary dies before him. This is particularly important where the gift is in favour of a child or grandchild. A failure to seek express instructions may result in s 33 applying in a manner which may be contrary to the wishes of the testator.

16.27 Class gifts are subject to the class closing rules. If the class consists of the children of the testator, it must, of necessity, close with his death. In the case of class gifts in favour of the issue of the testator or another, gifts following a prior life interest and contingent gifts, it is essential to make it clear when the class closes and to have regard to the rule against perpetuities.

Discretionary trusts

16.28 A desire for flexibility may result in a discretionary trust being used to give effect to the testator's wishes. The disadvantage of a discretionary trust (sometimes a major disadvantage) is that the testator places outside his own control the detailed disposition of the property. It has, however, many advantages.

16.29 Discretionary trusts are often used for inheritance tax mitigation[1] but there are other uses for the discretionary trust unrelated to inheritance tax. A discretionary trust can be used where the testator wishes to make provision for his family in the event of his untimely death while the children are still financially dependent on him. An example would be a man in his early forties, married with three teenage children all of whom are at school. He wishes to cover the possibility of his wife and himself being killed in an accident. In that event, he wants his estate to be used for the benefit of the children along the same lines as he and his wife might have used their resources if they had been alive. The requirements of the children are not likely to be identical. At the time of his death one may have completed his education and be in reasonable employment and the other two may still be at school or college. **Form 16.19** is designed for this use of a discretionary trust. **Form 16.20** demonstrates another use for a discretionary trust.

1 See note at **23.21–23.23**

PRECEDENTS

16.30

FORM 16.1

Creation of trust for sale with debts, inheritance tax etc to be paid out of proceeds

My Trustees shall hold [the rest of[1]] my estate[2] on trust for sale [with power to postpone sale[3]] to pay executorship expenses[4] and debts including mortgages secured on real or leasehold property[5] and any inheritance tax in respect of property passing under this Will or which becomes payable because of my death[6] on any lifetime transfer by me[7] or payable because of my death on property in which I hold a beneficial interest as joint tenant[8]. My Trustees shall hold the residue ('my residuary estate') on the trusts of the following clauses.

[*Continue with appropriate provisions as illustrated in the following forms.*]

1 If the residuary gift is made after legacies then the gift should usually be expressed as a gift of 'the rest of' the testator's estate. If it is a gift of the whole of the estate then the words 'the rest of' can be excluded.

2 If there is a possibility of the testator having a power of appointment exercisable by Will the draftsman might include here the words 'including property over which I have a general power of disposition by my Will'.

3 It will not always be necessary or desirable to include an express trust for sale. In many cases this is now a matter of choice rather than compulsion. The inclusion of an express power to postpone sale is unnecessary but may assist lay executors to comprehend their task.

4 In previous editions the term 'executorship expenses' was preferred to 'testamentary expenses' on the basis that it describes the nature of the expenses more accurately. Indeed, it was the phrase used before 'testamentary expenses' became common. Nonetheless, many draftsmen now prefer 'testamentary expenses'.

5 This provision ought not to be included as a 'catch all'. If it is intended to relate to a specific gift, it is better to include the provision in the clause relating to the gift. If the mortgaged property is part of the residue, the direction serves no useful purpose.

6 The residue will bear inheritance tax in the absence of a direction to the contrary and, therefore, the inclusion of this clause is not strictly necessary. If the testator wishes some gifts to be made subject to inheritance tax and others free of inheritance tax, the draftsman must bear in mind that problems of 'double grossing-up' can arise and advise the testator accordingly.

7 This provision is intended to cover any inheritance tax chargeable on lifetime gifts as a result of the testator dying within seven years of the gift. Its inclusion may be inappropriate. Without it, the donee will be liable for any additional inheritance tax payable.

It is unwise to include this provision if no potentially exempt transfer has been made by the testator. If potentially exempt transfers have been made, the gifts to which the clause relates should be specified. The danger of including all gifts is that unexpected consequences may ensue. For example, the testator may make future lifetime gifts, intending that the donee should be liable for any inheritance tax which arises, but forgetting the general direction in his Will.

8 As above, this provision should not be included unless it is intended to relate to a particular property. If so, the gift to which the provision relates should ordinarily be specified. In the absence of express provision, the surviving joint tenant will be liable for the inheritance tax of the testator's half share.

FORM 16.2

Gift to spouse or civil partner to be followed by substitutional gift[1]

My Trustees shall pay my residuary estate to my [wife]/[husband]/[civil partner][2] but if this gift fails the following provisions of my Will shall apply[3].

1 In many Wills this primary gift to the surviving spouse or civil partner is not a residuary gift at all but is made without it being necessary to ascertain residue because the spouse or civil partner is

the sole executor and universal legatee. That is a different situation from the one contemplated by this clause, which presupposes that other gifts – such as small legacies – have been made before ascertaining residue.

2 If a survivorship clause is desired include the words: 'if [she]/[he] survives me by thirty days'. See the note at **16.4–16.12**.

3 Continue with alternative provisions such as those in **Form 16.7** or **16.8**.

FORM 16.3

Gift to spouse or civil partner for life

My Trustees shall pay the income from my residuary estate to my [wife]/[husband]/[civil partner] during [her]/[his] lifetime and after [her]/[his] death [*continue as required with appropriate gift over, for example, as in **Form 16.7 or 16.8***][1].

1 The draftsman always has to consider whether the gift over is to be contingent on the remaindermen surviving both the testator and the life tenant or only the testator. Generally it is considered that the remaindermen need only survive the testator. Otherwise it may not be possible to ascertain the remaindermen for many years and it may be difficult to vary the trust if it proves necessary to do so while the life tenancy is in existence so that complicated provisions may need to be included in the Will to accommodate the uncertainty of future events.

FORM 16.4

Gift to spouse/civil partner limited for life or until remarriage or formation of civil partnership[1]

My Trustees shall pay the income from my residuary estate to my [wife]/[husband]/[civil partner] until [her]/[his] death or remarriage or formation of a [new] civil partnership[2] [or [her]/[his] cohabiting with a [man]/[woman][3]] and after [her]/[his] interest ceases [*continue with appropriate gift over, for example, as in **Form 16.7 or 16.8***].

1 Because a life interest in favour of a surviving spouse is an immediate post-death interest in possession to which the spouse exemption applies which does not use up any of the testator's nil-rate band, this is now a very tax-efficient means of making provision for a spouse whilst still retaining control over the destination of property.

Many Will draftsmen advise against providing for the life interest to cease on remarriage or on the formation of a civil partnership because of the difficulties which may ensue. Interests terminable on remarriage or the formation of a civil partnership can give rise to litigation and, in particular, claims under the Inheritance (Provision for Family and Dependants) Act 1975. Nonetheless, such interests are often desired, especially by testators in second marriages.

2 A limited interest can end by death, remarriage or the formation of a civil partnership. In order effectively to cater for the demands of a testator it is necessary to provide for all three possibilities.

3 If the testator also wishes the life interest to be terminated by cohabitation, the words in square brackets should be included. The testator should be advised of the practical problems which arise from a cohabitation provision. Whether cohabitation exists is a question of fact and can be difficult to establish with certainty. To provide for the opinion of the trustees to prevail might place a heavy burden on the trustees and could result in the life tenant suffering an injustice. Most draftsmen advise against the inclusion of a cohabitation clause for these reasons and because it can be a fertile source of family disputes.

FORM 16.5

Vested gift to children with substitutional gift to grandchildren

My Trustees shall divide my residuary estate equally among those of my children who survive me [and attain 21[1]] but if any of them dies before me [*or* before attaining 21[2]] his children shall take equally [upon attaining 21[3]] the share which their parent would otherwise have inherited.

1 Since the commencement of the Perpetuities and Accumulations Act 2009 on 6 April 2010 this age contingency in the substitutional gift need not be fixed at 21 years but could be greater. See note at **16.19**.

2 Use the alternative if the gift to the deceased child is age contingent. For a discussion of the inheritance tax consequences of these provisions. See note at **22.17–22.21**.

3 See footnote 1 above.

FORM 16.6

Vested gift to children with substitutional gift to any surviving spouse of deceased child but otherwise to grandchildren

My Trustees shall divide my residuary estate equally among those of my children who survive me but if any of them dies before me then [his/her] spouse shall take the share which [he/she] would otherwise have inherited or if he is not survived by his spouse his children shall take equally [upon attaining 21][1] the share which he would otherwise have inherited.

1 Since the commencement of the Perpetuities and Accumulations Act 2009 on 6 April 2010 this age contingency in the substitutional gift need not be fixed at 21 years but could be greater. See note at **16.19**. For a discussion of the inheritance tax consequences of these provisions following Finance Act 2006, see note at **22.17–22.21**.

FORM 16.7

Gift to children at 25[1] with substitutional gift to grandchildren

My Trustees shall divide my residuary estate equally among those of my children who survive me [and attain 25] but if any of them dies before me [*or* before attaining a vested interest[2]] his children shall take equally [upon attaining 21][3] the share which their parent would otherwise have inherited.

1 For a discussion of the inheritance tax consequences of these provisions following the Finance Act 2006, see note at **22.17–22.21**.

2 Use the alternative if the gift to the deceased child is age contingent.

3 Since the commencement of the Perpetuities and Accumulations Act 2009 on 6 April 2010 this age contingency in the substitutional gift need not be fixed at 21 years but could be greater. See note at **16.19**.

FORM 16.8

Gift to children at 21[1] with substitutional gift to issue

My Trustees shall divide my residuary estate equally among those of my children who survive me [and attain 21] but if any of them dies before me [*or* before attaining a vested interest[2]] his issue[3] shall [upon attaining 21[4]] take equally [per stirpes[5]] the share which my deceased child would otherwise have inherited but none of my issue[6] shall be entitled to benefit while his parent is eligible.

1 For a discussion of the inheritance tax consequences of these provisions following the Finance Act 2006, see note at **22.17–22.21**.

2 Use the alternative if the gift to the deceased child is age contingent.

3 'Issue' means children, grandchildren and so on. 'Children' is limited to the first generation.

4 Since the commencement of the Perpetuities and Accumulations Act 2009 on 6 April 2010 this age contingency in the substitutional gift need not be fixed at 21 years but could be greater. See note at **16.19**.

5 Most draftsmen provide for a division per stirpes rather than per capita.
6 'Issue' means children, grandchildren and so on. 'Children' is limited to the first generation.

FORM 16.9

Gift to those of issue whom spouse or civil partner with life interest appoints with default gift to children

My Trustees shall pay the income from my residuary estate to my [wife]/[husband]/[civil partner] during [her]/[his] lifetime and after [her]/[his] death divide the capital among those of my issue living at the death of my [wife]/[husband]/[civil partner] as [she]/[he] by deed or by will appoints or if [she]/[he] makes no appointment [divide it equally among those of my children who survive my [wife]/[husband]/[civil partner]].

FORM 16.10

Gift to brothers, sisters, brothers-in-law and sisters-in-law with substitutional gift to nephews and nieces[1]

(1) My Trustees shall divide one half of my residuary estate equally among those of my brothers and sisters who survive me but if any of them dies before me his or her children shall take equally the share which their parent would otherwise have inherited.

(2) My Trustees shall divide the other half of my residuary estate equally among those of the brothers and sisters of my [wife]/[husband]/[civil partner] who survive me but if any of them dies before me his children shall take the share which their parent would otherwise have inherited.

(3) If the trust in subclause 1 fails then subclause 2 shall apply to the whole of my residuary estate and if the trust set out in subclause 2 fails then subclause 1 shall apply to the whole of my residuary estate.

1 This clause is intended to operate on the death of the survivor of a husband and wife or civil partners without issue. In these circumstances, it is common for them to want what is left from their joint estates on the death of the survivor of them to pass equally to their respective families. Each of their Wills would make a gift to the residuary estate to the other and the above would be the operative clause on the death of the survivor of them.

FORM 16.11

Gift to specified charities in equal shares[1]

(1) My Trustees shall divide my residuary estate equally among the following charities:

[*List of names and addresses and, if available, registered numbers*][2].

(2) If for whatever reason any of the above charities has ceased to exist or is otherwise unidentifiable my Trustees shall pay its share to the charity or charities which they in their sole discretion consider most nearly fulfils the objects I intended to benefit.

(3) The receipt of a person who [is] [appears to be][3] a proper officer of the charity shall be a discharge to my Trustees.

1 See also **chapter 14**.
2 See note at **14.15**.
3 The use of the words 'appears to be' provides additional protection to the trustees and, particularly in the case of smaller and less formal charities, may be well advised. See the note at **14.13**.

FORM 16.12

Gift to charities in such shares as the trustees see fit[1]

(1) My Trustees shall pay my residuary estate to all or any of the following charities in such shares as my Trustees think fit:

[*List of names, addresses and registered numbers of charities*][2].

(2) If for whatever reason any of the above charities has ceased to exist or is otherwise unidentifiable my Trustees shall pay its share to the charity or charities which they in their sole discretion consider most nearly fulfils the objects I intended to benefit.

(3) The receipt of a person who [is] [appears to be][3] a proper officer of the charity shall be a discharge to my Trustees.

1 See also **chapter 14**.
2 See note at **14.15**.
3 The use of the words 'appears to be' provides additional protection to the trustees and, particularly in the case of smaller and less formal charities, may be well advised. See the note at **14.13**.

FORM 16.13

Gift for specified charitable objects

(1) My Trustees shall pay my residuary estate[1] in such manner as my Trustees think fit to charities having as their objects:

[*Specify the objects, for example, the welfare of handicapped children, medical research, the welfare of the aged, the welfare of animals*.]

(2) The receipt of a person who [is] [appears to be][2] a proper officer of the charity shall be a discharge to my Trustees.

(3) [If the preceding trusts of this Will fail to apply my residuary estate for general charitable purposes as my Trustees think fit.]

1 This clause can easily be adapted where the general charitable gift is to apply if a particular trust (not being the residue) fails.
2 The use of the words 'appears to be' provides additional protection to the trustees and, particularly in the case of smaller and less formal charities, may be well advised. See the note at **14.13**.

FORM 16.14[1]

Division of residue among a number of persons in fractional shares[2]

My Trustees shall divide my residuary estate among the following in the shares specified:

(a) To AB: one half;

(b) To CD: one quarter;

(c) To EF and GH or the survivor of them: one quarter[3].

1 A partial intestacy will occur if any of AB, CD or EF and GH predecease the testator. The following **Forms 16.15** and **16.16** include gifts over in order to counter this possibility and might be adapted in order to minimise the risk of a partial intestacy unless that is what the testator wants. Alternatively, a general disposition of residue to charity might be included as in clause (4) to **Form 16.18**.

2 Note that if the gifts are to persons who include persons with a mixture of exempt and non-exempt inheritance tax statuses the notes to **Form 16.17** should be heeded.

3 The gift in subclause (c) is a gift to EF and GH as joint tenants which may be useful where they are husband and wife or civil partners. If a gift to residuary legatees as tenants in common is intended it might be expressed, 'to EF and GH in equal shares: one quarter' but in such a case the most sensible course isjust to give each one eighth.

FORM 16.15

Division of residue among a number of persons in percentage shares with gift over to children and provision for accruer of lapsed shares[1]

(1) My Trustees shall divide my residuary estate among the following in the shares specified:

(a) To AB: 50%;

(b) To CD: 25%;

(c) To EF: 25%[2].

(2) If any of the persons named in subclause (1) dies before me leaving a child or children living at my death then such child or children shall take in equal shares the share of my residuary estate which their parent would otherwise have inherited.

(3) If any share or shares of my residuary estate given by subclauses (1) and (2) hereof shall lapse or fail then such share or shares shall accrue to the other share or shares which have not lapsed or failed in the proportions which they bear to one another so that no share of my residuary estate shall be undisposed of by this subclause.

1 Note that if the gifts are to persons who include persons with a mixture of exempt and non-exempt inheritance tax statuses the notes to **Form 16.17** should be heeded.

2 It is important to ensure that these add up to 100%. This is an obvious point to make but given the number of historic occasions in which they do not add up to 100% a draftsman is advised to double check this.

FORM 16.16

Division of residue among a number of persons in percentage shares with no gift over to children but instead provision for accruer of lapsed shares[1]

(1) My Trustees shall divide my residuary estate among the following in the shares specified:

(a) To AB: 50%;

(b) To CD: 25%;

(c) To EF: 25%[2].

(2) If the named beneficiary above dies before me their share shall lapse and Wills Act 1837 s 33[3] shall not apply to the provisions of this clause[4].

(3) If any share or shares of my residuary estate given by subclauses (1) and (2) hereof shall lapse or fail then such share or shares shall accrue to the other share or shares which have not lapsed or failed in the proportions which they bear to one another so that no share of my residuary estate shall be undisposed of by this subclause.

1 Note that if the gifts are to persons who include persons with a mixture of exempt and non-exempt inheritance tax statuses the notes to the next form should be heeded.

2 Again, it is important to ensure that these add up to 100%.

3 See **appendix 33.14**.

4 This provision excludes the effect of Wills Act s 33 so that if a descent beneficiary predeceased the testator their share shall not go their children but shall accrue to the other beneficiaries of the clause. See note at **20.7**.

FORM 16.17

Division of residue among a substantial number of exempt and non-exempt beneficiaries[1]

(1) My Trustees shall divide my residuary estate in twenty equal parts (each of which is referred to as a 'share') and to pay:

(a) four shares to my brother [*name*] or if he dies before me to his widow or if he has no widow to those of his children who survive me in equal shares;

(b) four shares to my sister [*name*];

(c) two shares to my nephew [*name*] or if he dies before me to those of his children who survive me in equal shares;

(d) two shares to my niece [*name*] or if she dies before me to her husband [*name*];

(e) three shares to [*name of charity*] [registered under Charity No.][2];

(f) three shares to [*name of charity*] [registered under Charity No.][3];

(g) two shares to the [*name of charity*] [registered under Charity No.][4].

(2) If any of the gifts set out above fails it shall be added proportionally to the gifts which do not.

(3) The receipt of a person who [is] [appears to be][5] a proper officer of the charity shall be a discharge to my Trustees.

[(4) In calculating the shares of my residuary estate my Trustees shall not take into account any inheritance tax payable and attributable to my residuary estate and then after the division the shares subject to inheritance tax shall have such tax attributed to them[6].]

[(5) If the preceding trusts of this Will fail to apply my residuary estate for general charitable purposes as my Trustees think fit[7].]

1 Where the testator wants to mix exempt and non-exempt shares of residue great care must be exercised. This is because the division of residue between exempt and non-exempt beneficiaries can make calculation of the respective shares very difficult having regard to the inheritance tax being borne by each gift. It is therefore strongly advised to include a provision allowing for the

respective shares to be calculated without taking into account inheritance tax and then take the respective inheritance tax from the non-exempt residuary beneficiaries

2 It is advisable to state both the charity's name and registered number if available. See note at **14.15**.

3 See foonote 2 above.

4 See footnote 2 above.

5 The use of the words 'appears to be' provides additional protection to the trustees and, particularly in the case of smaller and less formal charities, may be well advised. See note at **14.13**.

6 See footnote 1 above.

7 This clause can easily be adapted where the general charitable gift is to apply if a particular trust (not being the residue) fails.

FORM 16.18

General discretionary trust of residue[1]

(1) In this clause:

(a) 'the Trust Fund' means my residuary estate.

(b) 'my Beneficiaries' are the following:

[*specify the discretionary beneficiaries*].

(2) My Trustees shall hold the Trust Fund upon the following trusts:

(a) For not more than 125 years from my death to apply the capital of the Trust Fund for the benefit of such of my Beneficiaries as my Trustees think fit.

(b) To apply the income of the Trust Fund for the benefit of such of my Beneficiaries as my Trustees think fit or to accumulate the whole or any part of it.

(c) Within 125 years of my death to end these trusts by distributing the Trust Fund among such of my Beneficiaries as my Trustees think fit.

(d) To exercise their discretionary powers over capital or income when and how they think fit without having to make payments to or for the benefit of all my Beneficiaries or to ensure equality among those who have benefited.

(3) My Trustees shall have the following powers[2]:

(a) To retain or sell any of the assets constituting the Trust Fund;

(b) To invest as if they were beneficially entitled and this power includes the right to invest:

(i) in unsecured interest free loans to any Beneficiary;

(ii) in non-income producing assets including policies of life assurance (with power to pay premiums out of income or capital);

(iii) in property for the occupation of any Beneficiary[3];

(c) To use the income or capital of the Trust Fund for or towards the cost of maintaining or improving any property forming part of the Trust Fund;

(d) To make loans which may be interest free;

(e) To borrow money on such terms as they think fit (including the giving of security) and to use it for any purpose for which the capital of the Trust Fund may be used;

(f) In exercising the statutory power of appointing new trustees to appoint a professional person and give him the right to charge for work done by himself or his firm.

(4) [If the above trusts fail to divide my residuary estate equally among the following charities:]

1 This residuary gift is designed for a testator who wishes to benefit a comparatively large group of beneficiaries, probably because he has no close relatives. This is certainly a case in which one would expect him to supply his trustees with a written statement setting out in detail the guidelines he wishes his trustees to follow in exercising their discretion.

2 The circumstances of the case will govern the powers given to the trustees. The powers listed below are merely examples of possible powers which could be given to trustees and the draftsman must fully consider what are appropriate powers to give to the trustee in the circumstances of the trust. See **chapter 19** for a discussion of some of the possible powers to grant to the trustees.

3 The draftsman should remember that the exercise by the trustees of this sub-clause might, in the right circumstances, result in the beneficiary so occupying obtaining a post-death interest in possession with the associated inheritance tax consequences. See **chapter 22**.

FORM 16.19

Discretionary trust of residue for testator's children[1]

(1) My Trustees shall hold my residuary estate ('the Trust Fund') on the following discretionary trust:

(a) To apply the capital of the Trust Fund for the benefit of such of my children as my Trustees think fit;

(b) To apply the income of the Trust Fund for the benefit of such of my children as my Trustees think fit or to accumulate all or any part of it;

(c) When all my children have attained [25] or died under that age to end the trust by distributing the Trust Fund among such of my children as my Trustees think fit;

(d) If any of my children dies before me or while this trust is in existence his children shall be included among those in whose favour my Trustees may exercise their discretion;

(e) My Trustees may exercise their discretionary powers over capital and income when and how they think fit and need not make payments to or for the benefit of all those in whose favour they can exercise their discretion nor ensure equality among those who are benefited.

(2) My Trustees shall have the following powers:

[*Include requisite powers. See, for example, **Form 16.18**, subclause (3)*].

1 This is primarily designed to provide for dependent children both of whose parents have died. See the note at **16.28–16.29**. It is, however, suitable for other circumstances. As the interests of prospective beneficiaries must vest during the lifetime of the testator's children, the Rule against Perpetuities has no adverse application.

17 Minors

17.1 Providing for minors is a common reason for making a Will and the issues that arise are therefore frequently encountered. In **chapter 9** we have considered the appointment of guardians to exercise parental responsibility over children. In this chapter we go on to consider the issues that arise in making smaller gifts or legacies to children and in larger gifts or portions of residue. The landscape is shaped by the different tax treatments that apply and so we have set out the principal options open to testators at the end of this chapter and provided precedents for each.

Receipt clauses

17.2 Minors are prevented from owning or holding property in their own name. This presents practical problems for executors where Wills contain small gifts (eg of personal items) or legacies of small sums of money. The executor does not wish to become a trustee of these items pending the individual's majority but otherwise has no clear means of obtaining a good receipt for the legacy[1]. For that reason it is common for Wills to provide either that the receipt of the minor is sufficient discharge for the executor or else to provide that a receipt from the minor's parent or guardian is sufficient. See **Forms 17.1** and **17.2**.

1 Children Act 1989 s 3(2) confers the authority upon a person with parental responsibility and this, together with a guardian's previous powers to hold property on the child's behalf, is probably sufficient authority. There is, however, no clear authority and an executor cannot always know who holds parental responsibility.

Trustee powers

17.3 For larger gifts the main consideration will be to ensure that the minor does not become wholly entitled to the principal sum too early, whilst at the same time ensuring that income or capital can be paid to them in order to meet their needs. These considerations can sometimes clash with the similar necessity to ensure that such provision is tax efficient and so it is important to understand the competing considerations imposed by the different legislation[1].

1 See para **17.6** below. Any gift that vests capital later than the age of 25 will not attract the inheritance tax advantages below and may be taxed as a relevant property trust.

17.4 Prior to income and capital vesting, trustees require powers to accumulate income, to apply income to or for the benefit of the minor and power to advance capital ahead of the individual's entitlement. Such powers are provided by statute in Trustee Act 1925 ss 31 and 32[1]. The former necessity of widening these powers by express provision in the Will has now been removed by the widening of these powers in the Inheritance and Trustees' Powers Act 2014[2]. It is still possible, though, to include express powers for accumulation of income or the advancement of capital, although in either case care will be needed to ensure that any desired tax advantages are not forfeited[3].

1 See **appendix** at **34.2** and **34.3**.
2 Sections 8 and 9 widened the statutory powers in a manner common to many precedents.
3 All the tax treatment referred to below require such income as is applied, or such capital as is advanced, to be paid or applied to the minor or for their benefit so a power that is wider than this will mean such reliefs are not available.

17.5 Following the Inheritance and Trustees Powers Act 2014 trustees have power:

- During any infants' minority to accumulate any income in which they have any interest in, whether vested or contingent, and to pay such income to their parent or guardian, if any, or otherwise apply for or towards his maintenance, education or benefit, the whole or such part as they think fit[1]. Upon reaching the age of 18 the minor, if he retains an interest in the income, will become entitled to the income[2].
- To pay or apply capital to or for the advancement or benefit of any person with a vested or contingent interest in that capital.[3] The former restriction of the power to one half of the capital has been removed.

1 Trustee Act 1925 s 31 as amended, see **appendix** at **34.2**.
2 Section 31(1))(ii), see **appendix** at **34.2**.
3 Trustee Act 1925 s 32 as amended, see **appendix** at **34.3**.

Inheritance tax

17.6 The inheritance tax treatment of gifts to minors within Wills depends upon (i) whether the minor became entitled to their interest under the Will of a parent; (ii) the age when they will become entitled to the income and the capital of the trust together with (iii) the powers to pay income or to advance capital to them.

17.7 The most favourable treatment is conferred upon trusts qualifying under the Inheritance Tax Act 1984 s 71A. That requires that the minor become entitled to both the income and to the capital of the trusts at the age of 18 and that:

- The trust be contained within the Will of a 'deceased parent'. It is not possible to create these trusts in the Will of, for example, a grandparent or uncle.
- For as long as the minor is under the age of 18 they are entitled to the whole of the income or any income that is applied for their benefit.
- For as long as the minor is under the age of 18 any capital that is applied will be applied for their benefit.

These requirements will be met by the application of the statutory powers within the Trustee Act 1925 ss 31 and 32. Alternatively, it is possible to create express or wider powers provided that such powers still meet the requirements set out above.

17.8 If these requirements are met then the relevant property charges that would otherwise apply to the trust, for example on applying capital for the minor's benefit prior to their becoming 18, are avoided, and no charge will arise upon the minor reaching the age of 18 (and so becoming absolutely entitled to the capital).

17.9 The age of 18 is often considered as too young, particularly where the gift involves substantial amounts of capital. Section 71D of the Inheritance Act 1984 confers some (more limited) advantages upon trusts that do not ensure that income and capital vests before the age of 18 but which do ensure that it will vest before the person attains the age of 25 and which otherwise meets the requirements set out above[1]. If the trusts do meet these requirements then relevant property charges will be avoided for the period prior to the beneficiaries' reaching the age of 18 and there will be no charge upon the beneficiary reaching the age of 18 or becoming wholly entitled to the capital and income before that age. However, for the period between their being 18 and 25 the relevant property charges will apply. Due to the manner in which these are calculated, however, they are likely to be small, at no greater than 4.2% of the fund (at current rates).

1 Substituting 25 for the age of 18.

17.10 The inheritance tax treatment of trusts that do not meet these qualifications will depend upon the nature of the interest of the beneficiary in them. One option is to give the minor a life interest that will qualify as an immediate post death interest. Indeed, where a gift is made to a person over the age of 18 conditional on reaching an age such as 30 their entitlement (unless expressly excluded) is to the income of that fund and so their entitlement will be an immediate post death interest. For persons under the age of 18 it is necessary to exclude the provisions of Trustee Act 1925 s 31 that would otherwise provide for income to be accumulated.

17.11 Another option is to provide that the minor is to be absolutely entitled to the income and capital. Since minors cannot hold the capital until reaching the age of 18 the income will be accumulated until they reach the age of 18 and capital can be – but does not have to be – advanced for their benefit. The effect is therefore similar to a trust qualifying under s 71A and HMRC have confirmed that they will not regard the existence of the powers to accumulate income in Trustee Act 1925 s 31 as preventing the minor from being absolutely entitled[1]. This option is particularly useful where the gift is by someone other than a parent since in such circumstances s 71A will not apply even if all the other conditions of that section are met.

1 In the answers to a series of questions put to them by STEP and CIOT in 2006, published in "Trust Taxation" by Chamberlain and Whitehouse.

17.12 It should not be forgotten that a relevant property trust is not always disadvantageous. If the estate is below the nil rate band then the regime will have no relevance. Even above the nil rate band the taxes are not a substantial proportion of the whole fund although the administrative costs can be burdensome. In some cases the ability to avoid the straightjackets of ss 71A or 71D may often be considered to be worth the cost, and can mean that considerable flexibility can be imported into the trust.

Income and capital gains tax

17.13 The Finance Act 2005 introduced a class of trusts known as trusts for 'vulnerable persons'. Where trusts qualify, it is open to the trustees to elect for them to be taxed so that the income and the capital is subject to tax rates as if it were the income and capital of the beneficiary. This avoids the rates that apply to trustees, which will often be higher than those applied to minor beneficiaries.

17.14 For a minor to qualify as a vulnerable person they must be under the age of 18 and at least one of their parents must have died. A qualifying trust for a relevant minor must then be contained within the Will of a deceased parent of that minor and must meet the following requirements:

- For so long as the minor is under the age of 18 they are entitled to the whole of the income or any income that is applied is applied for their benefit.
- For so long as the minor is under the age of 18 any capital that is applied will be applied for their benefit.

These requirements will be met by the application of the statutory powers within the Trustee Act 1925 ss 31 and 31. Alternatively, it is possible to create express or wider powers provided that such powers still meet the requirements set out above.

17.15 The similarity to the requirements of the Inheritance Act 1984, s 71A is deliberate, and was introduced by amendment in the Finance Act 2013. It means that most trusts that meet the requirements for the favourable Inheritance Tax treatment will also be capable of qualifying for this advantageous income and capital gains tax treatment.

17.16 Of course, other trusts will have similar results. A trust in which the minor is entitled to the income as it arises will be taxed as their income. Similarly, a bare trust will be taxed for both income and capital gains trust purposes as the income and capital of the minor.

Summary of options

17.17 In drafting the Will of a *parent* the draftsman is able to consider the whole range of options provided by the tax legislation in deciding what provision will best suit the relevant child. In deciding what provision to make the balance will usually need to be struck between obtaining the relevant tax advantage, whilst ensuring that capital does not vest too early. Often, therefore, the main question will be the likely extent of the provision.

17.18 The options open to a parent are:

- A trust vesting the income and capital upon the minor becoming 18, thereby avoiding inheritance tax charges (s 71A) and being capable of being taxed at the beneficiaries' rates for income and capital gains tax[1].
- A trust vesting the income and capital before the minor reaches the age of 25, thereby obtaining the advantages of s 71D (charges only between the age of 18 to 25) but not the income and capital gains tax advantages[2].
- A trust conferring an interest in possession, for inheritance tax purposes thereby being taxed as if it is their property and for income tax the income will be theirs[3].
- A bare trust, taxed for all purposes as the beneficiaries' property[4].
- Some other provision (eg vesting capital at age 30), which will (if entitlements to income are excluded) be taxed as a relevant property trust.

1 **Form 17.3**.
2 **Form 17.4**.

3 **Form 17.5**.
4 **Form 17.6**.

17.19 Where the testator is not a parent of the child then neither of the first two options will apply. Grandparents or other persons will therefore need to consider conferring an interest in possession or creating a simple bare trust or else taking the disadvantages of a relevant property trust.

PRECEDENTS

17.20

FORM 17.1

Small Legacy to Minor With receipt clause

I GIVE the sum of £500 to my grandchild [*name*] and declare that his receipt shall be sufficient discharge for my executors.

FORM 17.2

Receipt clause for minors – guardians and parental responsibility

In this Will wherever a person under the age of 18 is entitled I declare that it shall be a sufficient discharge for my trustees to transfer or pay the same to that person's parent or guardian or any other person with the responsibility for their care or welfare.

FORM 17.3

Age 18 Trust[1]

The residue of my estate shall be divided between such of my children who survive me and reach the age of 18 years in equal shares absolutely.

1 This precedent will qualify under s 71A as well as for the favourable treatment of trusts for 'vulnerable persons' provided that it is contained within the Will of a parent.

FORM 17.4

Age 18–25 Trust with express powers of accumulation and advancement[1]

1 The residue of my estate shall be divided between such of my children who survive me and reach the age of 25 years in equal shares absolutely:

1.1 My trustees shall accumulate the income of any person under the age of 25 and shall, have power at their discretion, apply it to or for or towards his maintenance, education, or benefit.

1.2 My trustees shall have power at their absolute discretion to advance all or any part of the capital of any person contingently entitled thereto to or for their benefit.

1.3 Upon reaching 25 the child shall become absolutely entitled to the income and capital of the trust, including any accumulated income.

1.4 My trustees may not pay or apply any of the income or any of the capital of any persons contingently entitled thereto other than for their benefit.

1 This precedent will qualify under s 71D.

FORM 17.5

Immediate post death interest for a person under 18 (excluding Trustee Act s 31)[1]

1 I GIVE to such of my children who survive me an equal share of my residue to be held upon the following trusts:

1.1 The income thereof shall be paid to them until they reach the age of [30] years ('the qualifying age').

1.2 Upon reaching the qualifying age they shall become entitled absolutely to the income and capital of the trust.

1.3 Pending attaining the qualifying age my trustees shall have power to pay or apply all or any part of the income or capital of the trust to or for their maintenance advancement or benefit as they thing fit.

1.4 In the event of any child failing to attain the qualifying age their interest shall be held upon the trusts of the other shares hereof.

1.5 Section 31 Trustee Act 1925 shall not apply to these trusts.

1 This trust may be used to provide for minors or older children either where the Will is not that of a parent or where the desire is to vest the capital at some age later than 18. The intention is to confer an immediate post death interest in the child and so the Trustee Act 1925 s 31 is disapplied.

FORM 17.6

Bare Trust for a Minor[1]

The residue of my estate shall be held by my trustees for each of [my grandchildren] in equal shares absolutely.

1 This trust entitles the child – even if a minor – to the income and capital. However, because they are under 18 the trustees will have power to accumulate income and to advance capital to or for their benefit. For inheritance tax and for income and capital gains tax these trusts are taxed as belonging to the minor. They should be considered in cases where the residue is not substantial and/or in cases where the Will is not that of a parent. The example given here is of the division of residue in the Will of a grandparent.

18 Disabled and Vulnerable Beneficiaries

18.1 In providing for beneficiaries who are disabled or otherwise vulnerable it is necessary to take into account a number of competing considerations. Flexibility is usually the watchword but that is made more difficult by the restrictions required in order to obtain favourable tax treatment. Where means tested benefits are, or could become, a relevant issue then further considerations arise. Striking a balance is the key, and a solution that works well in one case may well not work in another situation.

Flexibility

18.2 Disabilities come in many different forms. Some beneficiaries may have limited difficulties and be able to both earn an income and to manage money. For such people the considerations are probably no different than for any other adult. However, other people may have difficulty in earning money or may be unable to manage their own money. It is for such people that trusts described as 'discretionary trusts' are usually created.

18.3 The purpose of a trust will usually be twofold. First, it will provide a vehicle for the management of the inheritance by trustees. Where a person is unable to manage their property and affairs the consequence of making substantial absolute provision for them in a Will, will be to require the appointment of a Deputy by the Court of Protection to manage their affairs. Whilst there are many advantages to this form of management it tends to be expensive if a professional is involved and bureaucratic if not. A security deposit is required and the response of the Court of Protection and Public Guardian's Office is not always as swift or helpful as might be wished for. In such circumstances, a trust is frequently a preferred option and very often a Deputyship can be avoided altogether if a trust holds all or the substantial part of their assets[1].

1 For an illuminating discussion of the contrast between a Deputyship and a trust see the decision in *SM v HM* [2012] COPLR 187.

18.4 The second purpose will be to ensure that the individual is entitled to means tested benefits. As discussed below, such benefits can be substantial and their availability will mean that the trust can provide a 'top up' or for 'extras'. If, however, the trust causes benefits to be lost then a substantial amount of it will have to be used to make up what could have been received by benefits in any event.

18.5 The key to meeting these objectives is flexibility. Flexibility will mean that the trust can be managed in such a way as to meet the beneficiaries' needs whilst still retaining their autonomy and permitting them to manage their funds so far as possible. Flexibility should mean that the trust can be disregarded for the purposes of benefits or altered in the event of its not doing so. Flexibility also means that unforeseen changes in the future, whether in the beneficiaries' needs or in changes to the legislation can be met by changes to the terms of the trust.

Inheritance tax

18.6 Tax is not the only, or even the principal, consideration. Nevertheless, all trusts have a tax context and qualifying trusts for disabled persons are given certain advantages by the Inheritance Tax Act 1984 ss 89 to 89B.

18.7 Where a trust qualifies under the Inheritance Tax Act 1984 s 89 such trusts are treated as if the disabled beneficiary had a qualifying interest in possession. It follows that the capital of the trust will form part of their estate and no relevant property charges will arise.

18.8 In order to qualify for treatment under the Inheritance Tax Act 1984 s 89 it is necessary for the trust to secure certain benefits for a person defined as a 'disabled person'. A disabled person is now[1] defined by reference to Schedule 1A of the Finance Act 2005 as being:

(a) a person who by reason of mental disorder within the meaning of the Mental Health Act 1983 is incapable of administering his or her property or managing his or her affairs;
(b) a person in receipt of attendance allowance;
(c) a person in receipt of a disability living allowance by virtue of entitlement to the care component at the highest or middle rate;
(d) a person in receipt of personal independence payment by virtue of entitlement to the daily living component;
(e) a person in receipt of an increased disablement pension;
(f) a person in receipt of constant attendance allowance; or
(g) a person in receipt of armed forces independence payment.

1 Following the Finance Act 2013.

18.9 The definition is by reference to the time of the creation of settlement so, whilst it is possible for the person to lose their entitlement within the above, it is vital that they qualify when the property goes into the trust. Here, again, flexibility is the watchword since trustees who, for whatever reason, find their beneficiary does not qualify for favourable tax treatment may well wish to remove the restrictions that would otherwise be required to have such treatment.

18.10 Where a person meets the definition of a disabled person then, in order to qualify under s 89, the trust must ensure that (i) no interest in possession in the trust exists and (ii) if any of the settled property or income arising from it is applied during the disabled person's life for the benefit of a beneficiary, it is applied for the benefit of the disabled person. These requirements will not be treated as not having been met only by reason of the powers conferred by the Trustee Act 1925 s 32.

18.11 Where a person will not (or may not) meet the requirements of s 89, other options are available to the draftsperson. Firstly, it may be possible to consider a qualifying post death life interest, in order to obtain the same favourable treatment as under s 89. Indeed, in some cases such a trust may prove to be more attractive since there is no requirement or necessity to apply capital only for the benefit of that beneficiary[1]. Second, it may be possible to create a fully discretionary trust. Such a trust will be taxed as a relevant property trust but will not be as restrictive as that required in order to benefit from the provisions of s 89.

1 The income of the trust will be treated as being that person's for the purposes of means tested benefits. They may, though, meet the requirements for a qualifying trust for vulnerable persons since a trust that requires all the income to be paid to a disabled person is within that definition.

Income and capital gains tax

18.12 For income and capital gains tax it is possible for the trustees of a trust that meets the requirements for a qualifying trust for the benefit of a 'vulnerable person' to elect for the trust to be taxed, essentially, at the same rates of tax as if the income or capital gains were those of the vulnerable person.

18.13 Vulnerable persons include a 'disabled person' and the legislation uses the same definition for a disabled person as that for the Inheritance Tax Act s 89[1]. However, the definition must be met at the relevant time and so it is possible for a trust that has acquired the advantages of s 89 to retain those advantages whilst not having them for income and capital gains because the beneficiary no longer meets the definition of a disabled person.

1 Paragraph **18.8**.

18.14 A trust will be a qualifying trust if it provides that during the lifetime of the trusts or until the termination of the trusts (if that occurs before the disabled beneficiary's death) it secures that:

- If any of the property is applied for the benefit of a beneficiary, it is applied for the benefit of the disabled person; and
- Either the disabled person is entitled to all the income (if there is any) arising from the property or, if such income is applied for the benefit of a beneficiary, it is applied for the benefit of the disabled person.

A trust will meet these requirements notwithstanding the trustees having the powers conferred by Trustee Act 1925 s 32.

18.15 It is worth observing that whilst intended to reflect the requirements of the Inheritance Tax Act s 89 they are not precisely identical and it is possible for a trust to not meet the requirements of s 89 whilst meeting those above. For example, a trust that requires the income to be paid to the beneficiary will fall outside of s 89 because the beneficiary will thereby have an interest in possession but will meet the requirements above.

Means tested benefits

18.16 The state provides a range of benefits for persons with and without disabilities, some but not all of which, are subject to means testing. Means tested benefits include income support, universal credit, child tax credit, housing benefit and the pension credit guarantee. In addition local authorities frequently provide care or assistance, either at home or in residential facilities, and will assess the means of a person in order to decide whether and to what extent they must contribute to the costs of such care.

18.17 The capital and income limits vary somewhat according to the particular benefit being considered. Similarly, the applicable legislation and guidance for deciding whether and what counts as a person's income or capital will vary from benefit to benefit. Nevertheless, the general principles are relatively fixed and have remained so for some time.

18.18 First, a person's *income* will be assessed. Income over a particular level will disqualify from entitlement, income under a level will reduce the entitlement to benefits. In deciding what income a person has the relevant agency will take into account income that they are entitled to. They will not (and cannot) take into account monies to which a person is not entitled. Nevertheless, trustees that consistently apply an amount of income to a beneficiary may well find that person as being treated as being entitled to that income.

18.19 Second, a person's *capital* will be assessed. Again, capital over a certain level will disqualify for benefits or in some cases will reduce the available benefits based upon an assumed income from that capital. The relevant agency will disregard capital to which a beneficiary has no entitlement, so that capital held in trusts where the trustees have the discretion whether or not to pay it to the beneficiary should be – and usually is – disregarded.

18.20 In drafting trusts for the purposes of means tested benefits the most important requirement, therefore, is to ensure that the beneficiary has no entitlement to either income or to capital. Such considerations are consistent with the general need for flexibility and are not necessarily at odds to the requirements of the tax legislation set out above since, whilst that legislation places prohibitions on what else trustees can do with income or capital, it does not require that beneficiaries have an entitlement to that income or capital.

Drafting considerations and options

18.21 Freed from the restraints of the tax legislation a draftsman will consider a number of features designed to improve the circumstances of a disabled person. For example, it is common to provide for payments to be made direct to carers or for the benefit of charities involved with the care of the individual or to ensure that dependants of the individual can receive benefits directly from the trust. For these reasons the advantages of a widely drafted discretionary trust may well outweigh the advantages that would come from conforming to the requirements of the tax legislation.

18.22 On the other hand, where it is felt that the trustees will or might wish the trust to meet the requirements of the tax legislation it is important to provide sufficient flexibility so that the trustees can adapt, both to changes in the legislation and to changes in the beneficiaries' circumstances (which might, for example, disqualify the trusts from the tax benefits). Indeed, there is a good case to draft a simple and wide discretionary trust which the trustees can then appoint as required within the two year period.

18.23 Assuming, though, that the testator is clear about the desired tax advantages and the basic form of the trust then the draftsman can – in very broad terms – choose between the following options:

- A wide discretionary trust providing for flexible provision but not conferring the advantages for either inheritance tax or for income and capital gains tax[1].
- A discretionary trust qualifying under Inheritance Tax Act s 89 and as a qualifying trust for vulnerable persons[2].
- An interest in possession trust, capable of being an immediate post death interest and also a qualifying trust for vulnerable persons[3].

1 **Form 18.1**.
2 **Form 18.2**.
3 **Form 18.3**.

PRECEDENTS

18.24

FORM 18.1

Wide form discretionary trust[1]

1 My residue shall be divided into three equal shares as follows:

1.1 As to one third for [my son Jason] or if he does not survive me to such of his children as are alive at my death and reach the age of 18 years.

1.2 As to one third for [my daughter Alison], or if she does not survive me to such of her children as are alive at my death and reach the age of 18 years.

1.3 As to one third for the benefit of [my son Charles] as set out at clause [2] hereof.

AND I declare that if any person shall fail to acquire an interest under the above trusts then such share shall accrue to the other shares.

2 In this clause:

(a) 'The Principal Beneficiary' shall mean [Charles].

(b) 'The Family Beneficiaries' shall mean my children and grandchildren.

(c) 'The Trust Period' means the period ending 125 years after my death,

2.1 The share at 1.3 above shall be held by my Trustees on such trusts or interests as they shall, not being fewer than two in number, appoint provided that (i) no appointment shall be made so as to prejudice any prior appointment or any previous payment of capital and income and (ii) no such appointment can be made after the end of the Trust Period and (iii) any such appointment shall cause the income and capital to vest within the Trust Period.

2.2 Subject to clause 2.2 during the lifetime of the Principal Beneficiary my Trustees shall hold the capital and the income of the trust:

(a) To pay or apply the income of the trust to or for the benefit of the Principal Beneficiary in such amounts and at such periods and times as they shall think fit and in default thereof to accumulate the income.

(b) To pay or apply the capital of the trust to or for the benefit of the Principal Beneficiary in such amounts and at such periods and times as they shall think fit and in default thereof to accumulate the income.

2.3 In exercising the foregoing powers it shall be permissible for my trustees, at their absolute discretion:

(a) To purchase or to join with any other person or trustees in purchasing a property as a home for the Principal Beneficiary.

(b) To meet or to contribute towards the costs of any residential or other care or otherwise to discharge or assist with discharging the costs of caring for the Principal Beneficiary.

(c) To pay or contribute towards the costs or fees of any person or agency providing care or assistance to the Principal Beneficiary.

(d) To purchase any item of domestic or other assistance as might be required by the Principal Beneficiary.

(e) To pay for or towards any holiday or respite care for the Principal Beneficiary and notwithstanding that some other person might share in the benefit of such provision.

(f) To pay or donate money to any charity that is providing care or assistance to or towards the needs of the Principal Beneficiary.

(g) To pay for or towards the costs of a vehicle or for any transport for the benefit of the Principal Beneficiary.

(h) To pay for or towards the funeral costs of the Principal Beneficiary.

2.4 Subject to the exercise of the above discretions the capital and income of the trust shall be held for such of the Family Beneficiaries as my trustees might by deed appoint and in default of such appointment for [*name of charity*] [registered under Charity No.][2].

2.5 My trustees shall have powers by deed or deeds to permanently or temporarily to restrict all or any of the above trusts, powers and provisions[3].

1 This trust confers substantial discretion and flexibility but will not qualify for the favourable treatment under inheritance tax, nor for income and capital gains tax.

2 It is advisable to state both the charity's name and registered number if available. See **chapter 14** at paragraph **14.15**.

3 This power allows the trustees to restrict the trust so as to qualify for more favourable tax treatment.

FORM 18.2

Qualifying Trust for Section 89 and for Income / Capital Gains Tax[1]

1 My residue shall be divided into three equal shares as follows:

1.1 As to one third for [my son Jason] or if he does not survive me to such of his children as are alive at my death and reach the age of 18 years.

1.2 As to one third for [my daughter Alison], or if she does not survive me to such of her children as are alive at my death and reach the age of 18 years.

1.3 As to one third for the benefit of [my son Charles] as set out at clause [2] hereof.

AND I declare that if any person shall fail to acquire an interest under the above trusts then such share shall accrue to the other shares.

2 In this clause:

(a) 'The Principal Beneficiary' shall mean [Charles].

(b) 'The Family Beneficiaries' shall mean my children and grandchildren.

(c) 'The Trust Period' means the period ending 125 years after my death.

2.1 The share at 1.3 above shall be held by my Trustees UPON TRUST during the lifetime of the Principal Beneficiary:

(a) To pay or apply such of the income as my trustees think fit to or for the benefit of the Principal Beneficiary and subject thereto to accumulate the same.

(b) To pay or apply such of the capital of the trusts as my trustees think fit to or for the benefit of the Principal Beneficiary.

(c) To otherwise appoint the income and/or capital of the trust to or for the benefit of the Principal Beneficiary provided any such appointment shall ensure that (i) any income that is paid is applied for the benefit of the Principal Beneficiary and (ii) that any capital that is applied for the benefit of the Principal Beneficiary.

2.2 Subject to clause 2.1 the trust fund shall be held upon such trusts to or for the benefit of the Family Beneficiaries as my trustees shall not being fewer than two in number, appoint provided that (i) no appointment shall be made so as to prejudice any prior appointment or any previous payment of capital and income and (ii) no such appointment can be made after the end of the Trust Period and (iii) any such appointment shall cause the income and capital to vest within the Trust Period.

2.3 In default of the exercise of the power of appointment at clause 2.2 my trustees shall hold the trust fund for [*name of charity*] [registered under Charity No.][2].

2.4 My trustees shall have powers by deed or deeds to permanently or temporarily to restrict all or any of the above trusts, powers and provisions.

1 This trust will meet the requirements for a disabled trust under Inheritance Tax Act 1984 s 89 and as a qualifying trust for a vulnerable person under the income and capital gains tax legislation provided the beneficiary meets the requirements of a disabled person.

2 It is advisable to state both the charity's name and registered number if available. See **chapter 14** at paragraph **14.15.**

FORM 18.3

Qualifying Post Death Interest [and qualifying Trust for Income / Capital Gains Tax][1]

1 My residue shall be divided into three equal shares as follows:

1.1 As to one third for [my son Jason] or if he does not survive me to such of his children as are alive at my death and reach the age of 18 years.

1.2 As to one third for [my daughter Alison], or if she does not survive me to such of her children as are alive at my death and reach the age of 18 years.

1.3 As to one third for the benefit of [my son Charles] as set out at clause [2] hereof.

AND I declare that if any person shall fail to acquire an interest under the above trusts then such share shall accrue to the other shares.

2 In this clause:

(a) 'The Principal Beneficiary' shall mean [Charles].

(b) 'The Family Beneficiaries' shall mean my children and grandchildren.

(c) 'The Trust Period' means the period ending 125 years after my death.

2.1 The share at 1.3 above shall be held by my Trustees UPON TRUST during the lifetime of the Principal Beneficiary to pay the income to or for the benefit of the Principal Beneficiary.

2.2 My trustees shall have power at any time within the Trust period to pay or apply all or any part of the capital to or for the benefit of any of the Family Beneficiaries as they shall think fit [provided that during the lifetime of the Principal Beneficiary such power shall be exercised only to apply the capital for the benefit of the Principal Beneficiary].

2.3 After the death of the Principal Beneficiary the trust fund shall be held upon such trusts to or for the benefit of the Family Beneficiaries as my trustees shall not being fewer than two in number, appoint provided that (i) no appointment shall be made so as to prejudice any prior appointment or any previous payment of capital and income and (ii) no such appointment can be made after the end of the Trust Period and (iii) any such appointment shall cause the income and capital to vest within the Trust Period.

2.3 In default of the exercise of the power of appointment at clause 2.3 my trustees shall hold the trust fund for the Family Beneficiaries in equal shares and in default thereof for [*name of charity*] [registered under Charity No.][2].

2.4 My trustees shall have powers by deed or deeds to permanently or temporarily restrict all or any of the above trusts, powers and provisions.

1 This trust will meet the requirements for an immediate post death interest. If the words in square brackets are used it will also be a qualifying trust for a vulnerable person under the income and capital gains tax legislation provided the beneficiary meets the requirements of a disabled person.

2 It is advisable to state both the charity's name and registered number if available. See **chapter 14** at paragraph **14.15.**

19 Powers of Trustees

19.1 Personal representatives have wide powers given to them under statute and in many situations these statutory powers will be both sufficient and appropriate to enable the Will and any simple trusts created under it to be administered effectively. However, some circumstances will require these statutory powers to be either restricted or, more commonly, extended. The Will draftsman is therefore required to understand not only the current statutory powers but also when it is appropriate to make additions or restrictions to them and how to make such additions or restrictions.

19.2 This chapter summarises the effects of the most important statutory powers and duties as well as discussing some occasions where it might be appropriate to extend or restrict these powers and duties. The chapter contains practical precedents for extending or restricting these powers and duties where it is appropriate to do so. This chapter also includes a number of other non-statutory powers which can be included in the Will.

Powers of maintenance

19.3 Powers of maintenance are contained in s 31 of the Trustee Act 1925[1] which applies to all trusts created by Will unless a contrary intention is expressed in the Will[2]. The section enables trustees to pay or apply the income for or towards the maintenance, education or benefit of a minor who has an interest in the property generating the income. Income not paid or applied in this way is to be accumulated during the minority of the beneficiary and, thereafter, is payable to the beneficiary[3]. The power is subject to prior interests.

1 For the text of the Trustee Act 1925 s 31, see **appendix 34.2**.
2 Trustee Act 1925 s 69(2).
3 Trustee Act 1925 s 31(2). See **appendix 34.2**.

19.4 Previously it was often seen necessary to slightly broaden and/or clarify the trustees' powers with regard to s 31 to give the trustees the power to provide for maintenance whenever they see fit rather than merely 'as in all the circumstances appear reasonable'. This is no longer necessary as the Inheritance and Trustee Powers Act 2014 has made this change in the statute.

19.5 There is now no statutory restriction on accumulations[1] and so a further amendment to s 31 is possible to allow income to be accumulated throughout the continuation of the interest in question. This is most easily done by altering the age contingency in s 31(1)(ii) but many testators will not consider it necessary to do this and so the precedents in this book do not amend s 31 in this way as a matter of course.

1 See Perpetuities and Accumulations Act 2009 s 13. See the note at **16.19**.

19.6 Whenever minors are beneficiaries or may be beneficiaries it is advisable to include express provision for the trustees to accept a receipt from the beneficiary if over 16 years of age or a parent or guardian of the beneficiary if younger than 16[1]. There is provision under s 3(3) of the Children Act 1989 for a person with parental responsibility for a minor to give a good receipt on the minor's behalf but it is still advisable to include express provision in the Will so the trustees are aware of this power.

1 See **Form 19.1**.

Powers of advancement

19.7 Provisions for advancement are contained in s 32 of the Trustee Act 1925[1] and apply to all trusts created by Will unless a contrary intention is expressed in the Will[2]. Section 32 used to provide that trustees had the power to pay or apply up to one-half of the presumptive share of a beneficiary for the advancement or benefit of the beneficiary and it was very common for the draftsman to insert a clause extending this to cover the whole of the presumptive share. Following the enactment of the Inheritance and Trustees' Powers Act 2014 there is no longer any need for such a provision as s 32 has been amended to allow advancement of the entire presumptive share.

1 See **appendix 34.3**.
2 Trustee Act 1925 s 69(2).

19.8 The statutory power of advancement under the Trustee Act 1925 s 32 is not exercisable in favour of a life tenant. However, on occasion, it may be desirable for the trustees to be able to advance sums to the life tenant. This is typically where the surviving spouse or civil partner is left a life interest and the income from the residuary estate may be insufficient for their needs. It can be particularly useful where the surviving spouse or civil partner has to enter a nursing home and the fees of the nursing home exceed the income generated by the fund. If it is desired to give the power to advance money to the life tenant it is important that the power is to pay over capital and not the power to supplement income. If the power was drafted and used so as to supplement income the payments may be regarded as income in the hands of the life tenant and therefore subject to income tax. A clause giving the trustees the power to advance sums to the life tenant is contained at **Form 19.2**. A useful alternative option is the inclusion of a power for the trustees to make loans to the life tenant[1]. Loans to an impecunious life tenant may not be recoverable on his or her death and therefore should not be made by the trustees unless they have appropriate indemnities. Accordingly if it is desired to give the trustees the power to make loans to the life tenant consideration should be made to including an exoneration and indemnity clause such as in **Form 19.17**.

1 See **Form 19.3**.

Investment and management powers and duties

19.9 The Trustee Act 2000 contains wide powers of investment and management. The provisions of the Act cover powers in relation to the management of land[1], powers of investment[2], powers to delegate investment and investment-holding powers[3] and powers to charge[4]. With such wide-ranging powers it will often be unnecessary to extend these powers any further. However, in certain situations the extension of such powers may be desirable. Conversely, in other situations it may be desired to restrict the trustees' powers.

1 Dealt with in **chapter 11** at **11.9–11.11**. See also note at **19.31–19.38**.
2 Trustee Act 2000 ss 3–6, see **appendix 34.32–34.35**.
3 Trustee Act 2000 ss 11–26, see **appendix 34.38–34.53**.
4 Trustee Act 2000 ss 28–29, see **appendix 34.54–34.55**. Commentary on the power to charge appears at **8.27–8.31**.

19.10 The Trustee Act 2000 s 3 makes all kinds of investment (apart from equitable interests in land) authorised investments for trustees and personal representatives. This power is known as 'the general power of investment'[1]. Essentially, trustees have a power to make any kind of investment, including loans secured on land but otherwise excluding land (power to invest in which is dealt with separately) that trustees could make if they were absolutely entitled to the assets of the trust[2]. This is a very broad power which will not need to be extended in most circumstances. However, if lay trustees are to be appointed, consideration should be given to including an express power of investment to bring such power to the attention of the lay trustees. An example of such an express power is contained in **Form 19.5**. The statutory power of investment is in addition to any other powers conferred on the trustees but also subject to any restriction or exclusion imposed by the Will[3] meaning that a testator, if he or she so desires, can restrict the trustees' investment powers. Such restriction is rarely advisable. It is also arguably not needed to protect the trust as the trustees' general power of investment is subject to two express duties, the duty to have regard to standard investment criteria[4] and the duty to take advice[5]. Neither of these duties can be restricted and this may provide some comfort to a testator who is concerned that his trustees may invest unwisely.

1 Trustee Act 2000 s 3(2), see **appendix 34.32**.
2 Trustee Act 2000 s 3(1)–(3), see **appendix 34.32**.
3 Trustee Act 2000 s 6(1), see **appendix 34.35**.
4 Trustee Act 2000 s 4, see **appendix 34.33**.
5 Trustee Act 2000 s 5, see **appendix 34.34**.

19.11 In exercising their general power of investment (or indeed any investment power) trustees or personal representatives must have regard to 'the standard investment criteria'[1] which requires the trustees to consider the suitability of the investments to the trust and the need for diversification of investments if such is appropriate in the circumstances[2]. Having regard to the standard investment criteria is an ongoing duty and the trustees must periodically review the investments with reference to the standard investment criteria and consider whether the investments should be varied. No indication is given as to how often trustees must review the investment, but in the case of a large trust fund or one invested on the stock market at times of particular volatility or depression, frequent reviews might be required. Trustee Act 2000 s 4 makes it clear that the requirement of having regard to the standard investment criteria applies to all powers of investment, and that it is not capable of being excluded[3].

1 Trustee Act 2000 s 4(1), see **appendix 34.33**.

2 The precise wording is contained in Trustee Act 2000 s 4(3) which is contained at **appendix 34.33**.

3 Trustee Act 2000 s 6 applies to the general power of investment but does not appear to apply to the standard investment criteria of s 4, which are of general application. For Trustee Act 2000 s 6, see **appendix 34.35**.

19.12 The Trustees also have a duty to take advice when exercising their investment powers. Before exercising any investment power and when reviewing their investments, trustees must obtain and consider proper advice about the way in which, having regard to the standard investment criteria, their powers to invest or vary investments should be exercised[1]. Proper advice is the advice of a person who is reasonably believed by the trustees to be qualified to give it by his ability and practical experience of financial and other matters relating to the proposed investment[2]. They do not need to obtain such advice if they reasonably conclude that in all the circumstances it is unnecessary or inappropriate to do so[3]. As with the duty to have regard to the standard investment criteria the duty to take advice cannot be excluded[4].

1 Trustee Act 2000 s 5, see **appendix 34.34**.

2 Trustee Act 2000 s 5(4), see **appendix 34.34**.

3 Trustee Act 2000 s 5(3), see **appendix 34.34**.

4 Trustee Act 2000 s 6 applies to the general power of investment but does not appear to apply to the duty to take advice under s 5, which is of general application. For Trustee Act 2000 s 6, see **appendix 34.35**.

Power to insure

19.13 For obvious reasons trustees need the power to insure property against risks of loss and damage. However, the statutory powers given to trustees in relation to insurance are now extensive and is not anticipated there would be any need to make any express power to insure in the Will. Under the current statutory rules a trustee may insure any property subject to the trust against risks of loss or damage due to any event[1], and pay the premium out of any income or capital funds of the trust[2]. If the beneficiaries are of full age and capacity and are absolutely entitled to the property of the trust (ie the trustees hold the property on a bare trust) the beneficiaries can give a contrary direction to the trustees instructing them not to insure the property or to only insure on certain conditions[3]. If this is the case the trustees have no power to insure outside the wishes of the beneficiaries but would not be liable for any failure to insure in such circumstances.

1 Trustee Act 1925 s 19(1)(a), see **appendix 34.1**.

2 Trustee Act 1925 s 19(1)(b), (5), see **appendix 34.1**.

3 Trustee Act 1925 s 19(2), see **appendix 34.1**.

Power to borrow

19.14 The trustees have a statutory power to borrow under the Trustee Act 1925 s 16 but it is limited and does not permit unsecured borrowing or the borrowing to finance further investments or to continue to run a business. A power to borrow is also useful if the trustees require capital and have an investment which can only be realised at a disadvantage or under a penalty and it would be financially beneficial to borrow to avoid such a disadvantage or penalty. If it is thought that the trustees may need to borrow or it would be desirable for them to do so express provisions for this should be given[1].

1 **Form 19.6** is an example of a provision giving a power to borrow.

Powers and duties in relation to delegation

19.15 Some trustees will not have the time or knowledge to be able to personally exercise all their responsibilities and in many situations the testator would not wish their chosen trustees to personally bear all such responsibility. It is therefore important for the draftsman to understand the powers and duties in relation to delegation and to be able to advise the testator accordingly.

19.16 The Trustee Act 2000 confers on trustees and personal representatives a power to delegate their investment functions to investment managers and to vest trust assets in nominees[1]. The question which the Will draftsman must face is whether he should rely on the statutory powers or whether express provision should still be made. In most cases the statutory powers will probably be sufficient but occasionally forms of express power may be appropriate.

1 Trustee Act 2000 ss 11–26, see **appendix 34.38–34.53**.

19.17 The statutory power to delegate is broad and the trustees are able to authorise an agent to exercise any of their 'delegable functions'[1]. In relation to a non-charitable trust delegable functions are very broadly defined as all functions other than:

(a) any function relating to whether or in what way any assets of the trust should be distributed;
(b) any power to decide whether any fees or other payment due to be made out of the trust funds should be made out of income or capital;
(c) any power to appoint a person to be a trustee of the trust; or
(d) any power conferred by any other enactment or the trust instrument which permits the trustees to delegate any of their functions or to appoint a person to act as a nominee or custodian.

1 Trustee Act 2000 s 11(1), see **appendix 34.38**.

19.18 In relation to a charitable trust the delegable functions list is narrower and the only delegable functions are:

(a) any function consisting of carrying out a decision that the trustees have taken;
(b) any function relating to the investment of assets subject to the trust (including, in the case of land held as an investment, managing the land and creating or disposing of an interest in the land);
(c) any function relating to the raising of funds for the trust otherwise than by means of profits of a trade which is an integral part of carrying out the trust's charitable purpose;
(d) any other function prescribed by an order made by the Secretary of State.

19.19 In relation to their functions relating to the investment of assets[1], the acquisition of property[2] and the management of property[3] subject to the trust (the asset management functions) trustees may not authorise a person to act as their agent except by an agreement in or evidenced in writing[4] and may not do so unless they have prepared a statement in or evidenced in writing[5] as to how the asset management functions should be exercised (a policy statement)[6] and their agreement includes a term to the effect that the agent will comply with the policy statement[7].

1 Trustee Act 2000 s 15(5)(a), see **appendix 34.42**.
2 Trustee Act 2000 s 15(5)(b), see **appendix 34.42**.
3 Trustee Act 2000 s 15(5)(c), see **appendix 34.42**.
4 Trustee Act 2000 s 15(1), see **appendix 34.42**.

5 Trustee Act 2000 s 15(4), see **appendix 34.42**.
6 Trustee Act 2000 s 15(2)(a), see **appendix 34.42**.
7 Trustee Act 2000 s 15(2)(b), see **appendix 34.42**.

19.20 While the trustees do have extensive powers of delegation such power need not be of great concern to the beneficiaries as it does not necessarily result in less responsibility to the trust as agents to whom functions have been delegated are under the same duty in relation to the exercise of those functions as were the trustees themselves[1].

1 Trustee Act 2000 s 13(1), (2), see **appendix 34.40**.

19.21 There are a number of other restrictions on the delegation of powers designed to ensure that the interests of the beneficiaries and the trust are protected. Thus, in exercise of the power of delegation, trustees may authorise one or more of their number to exercise functions as their agent[1] but a function can only be delegated to more than one person if they are to exercise the power jointly (and not severally)[2]. Trustees may authorise an agent to receive remuneration[3] but, unless it is reasonably necessary, an agent may not be authorised to appoint a substitute[4], restrict his liability to the trustees or beneficiaries[5] or act in circumstances giving rise to a conflict of interest[6]. In addition a beneficiary cannot be appointed to exercise the functions of the trustees as their agent even if that beneficiary is also a trustee[7].

1 Trustee Act 2000 s 12(1), see **appendix 34.39**.
2 Trustee Act 2000 s 12(2), see **appendix 34.39**.
3 Trustee Act 2000 s 14(1), see see **appendix 34.41**. The trustees may remunerate agents out of the trust fund for services provided the terms of engagement include agreement for remuneration and the amount of the remuneration does not exceed what is reasonable in the circumstances: Trustee Act 2000 s 32, see **appendix 34.57**.
4 Trustee Act 2000 s 14(2), (3)(a), see **appendix 34.41**.
5 Trustee Act 2000 s 14(2), (3)(b), see **appendix 34.41**.
6 Trustee Act 2000 s 14(2), (3)(c), see **appendix 34.41**.
7 Trustee Act 2000 s 12(3), see **appendix 34.39**.

19.22 The powers to appoint agents under the Trustee Act 2000 are in addition to any powers conferred on the trustees elsewhere. This means that, if desired, the testator can give the trustees even wider powers of delegation in the Will or trust deed though it is unlikely to be necessary to do so. More common is the desire of testators to restrict the trustees' ability to delegate. These powers can be restricted or excluded by the Will or trust deed[1] but doing so can impose substantial personal burdens on the trustees and is not recommended unless clearly necessary in the circumstances.

1 Trustee Act 2000 s 26(b), see **appendix 34.53**.

Nominees and custodians

19.23 Trustees may appoint a person to act as their nominee in relation to the assets of the trust[1] and take such steps to secure that the assets are vested in the nominee as are necessary[2]. The appointment of a nominee must be in or evidenced in writing[3]. Trustees may also appoint[4] a person to undertake safe custody of the assets of the trust or of any documents or records concerning the assets (a custodian)[5]. The appointment of a custodian must also be in or evidenced in writing[6]. If the trustees invest in bearer securities they must appoint a person to act as custodian of the securities[7] unless the trust instrument permits them to invest in bearer securities without appointing a custodian[8].

1 Trustee Act 2000 s 16(1)(a), see **appendix 34.43**.
2 Trustee Act 2000 s 16(1)(b), see **appendix 34.43**.
3 Trustee Act 2000 s 16(2), see **appendix 34.43**.
4 Trustee Act 2000 s 17(1), see **appendix 34.44**.
5 Trustee Act 2000 s 17(2), see **appendix 34.44**.
6 Trustee Act 2000 s 17(3), see **appendix 34.44**.
7 Trustee Act 2000 s 18(1), see **appendix 34.45**.
8 Trustee Act 2000 s 18(2), see **appendix 34.45**.

19.24 Again there are certain limitations on the appointment of nominees and custodians which are designed to ensure that the interests of the beneficiaries and the trust are protected and this may provide some comfort to a concerned testator. Thus, a person may not be appointed as a nominee or custodian unless the person carries on a business which consists of or includes acting as a nominee or custodian[1], is a body corporate controlled by trustees[2] or is a body corporate recognised under s 9 of the Administration of Justice Act 1985[3]. Trustees may appoint one of their number if that one is a trust corporation[4] or two or more of their number if they are to act jointly[5]. The trustees may also appoint the same person to be nominee and custodian and their agent[6]. Trustees may authorise a nominee or custodian to receive remuneration[7] but, unless it is reasonably necessary, a nominee or custodian may not be authorised to appoint a substitute[8], restrict his liability to the trustees or beneficiaries[9] or act in circumstances giving rise to a conflict of interest[10].

1 Trustee Act 2000 s 19(1), (2)(a), see **appendix 34.46**.
2 Trustee Act 2000 s 19(1), (2)(b), see **appendix 34.46**. This is to be determined in accordance with the Corporation Tax Act 2010 s 1124.
3 Trustee Act 2000 s 19(1), (2)(c), see **appendix 34.46**.
4 Trustee Act 2000 s 19(5)(a), see **appendix 34.46**.
5 Trustee Act 2000 s 19(5)(b), see **appendix 34.46**.
6 Trustee Act 2000 s 19(6), (7), see **appendix 34.46**.
7 Trustee Act 2000 s 20(1), see **appendix 34.47**. The trustees may remunerate nominees and custodians out of the trust fund for services provided the terms of engagement include agreement for remuneration and the amount of the remuneration does not exceed what is reasonable in the circumstances: Trustee Act 2000 s 32, see **appendix 34.57**.
8 Trustee Act 2000 s 20(2), (3)(a), see **appendix 34.47**.
9 Trustee Act 2000 s 20(2), (3)(b), see **appendix 34.47**.
10 Trustee Act 2000 s 20(2), (3)(c), see **appendix 34.47**.

Review of and liability for agents, nominees and custodians

19.25 Testators, beneficiaries and, most importantly, trustees should remember that the appointment of agents, nominees and custodians does not absolve the trustees of their duties. This point may need to be re-emphasised by the draftsman to the testator who wishes to appoint family members only on the basis that they are able to hire others to do the day to day work. The appointment of agents, nominees and custodians does not mean the named trustees have nothing to do or are exempt from liability.

19.26 Thus, where trustees have authorised a person to exercise functions as their agent or appointed a person to act as their nominee or custodian then, while that person continues to act for the trust, the trustees must keep under review the arrangements by which the agent, nominee or custodian acts and how those arrangements are being put into effect[1] and, if appropriate, consider whether to exercise any power of intervention[2]. If the trustees consider that they need to exercise a power of intervention they must do so[3] and a failure to do so may lead to personal liability on behalf of the trustees.

1 Trustee Act 2000 ss 21 and 22(1)(a), see **appendix 34.48** and **34.49**.
2 Trustee Act 2000 s 22(1)(b), see **appendix 34.49**.
3 Trustee Act 2000 s 22(1)(c), see **appendix 34.49**.

19.27 Similarly, where an agent has been authorised to exercise asset management functions the trustees are under a duty to consider whether there is any need to revise or replace the policy statement[1] and must replace it if there is a need to do so[2]. Trustees are also under a duty to assess whether the policy statement is being complied with[3].

1 Trustee Act 2000 s 22(2)(a), see **appendix 34.49**.
2 Trustee Act 2000 s 22(2)(b), see **appendix 34.49**.
3 Trustee Act 2000 s 22(2)(c), see **appendix 34.49**.

19.28 Trustees are not liable for the act or defaults of agents, nominees or custodians unless they have failed to comply with their duty of care[1] and a failure by trustees to act within the limits of their powers in authorising a person to act as their agent or in appointing a nominee or custodian does not invalidate the authorisation or appointment[2].

1 Trustee Act 2000 s 23, see **appendix 34.50**.
2 Trustee Act 2000 s 24, see **appendix 34.51**.

19.29 If the testator wishes to provide maximum protection to his trustees with regard to delegation it is possible to insert a provision excluding the duty to review the acts of agents and nominees. An example of such clause is contained at **Form 19.16**.

Duty of care

19.30 The Trustee Act 2000 imposes a statutory duty of care[1] which applies (unless expressly excluded) to trustees or personal representatives when exercising their powers in relation to investment[2], acquisition of land[3], agents, nominees and custodians[4], compounding of liabilities[5], insurance[6], revisionary interests, valuations and audits[7].The duty of care requires that a trustee exercise such care and skill as is reasonable in the circumstances having regard in particular to any special knowledge or experience that he has or holds himself out as having[8]. If the trustee acts in the course of a business or profession he is also held to any special knowledge or experience that it is reasonable to expect of a person acting in the course of that kind of business or profession[9]. The statutory duty of care may be excluded or restricted by the Will[10]. A testator may wish to exclude it, particularly if he is appointing family or friends to be his executors and trustees and wishes to give them as much protection as possible. **Form 19.15** is an example of a provision excluding the statutory duty of care.

1 Trustee Act 2000 ss 1, 2 and Sch 1, see **appendix 34.30**, **34.31** and **34.60**.
2 Trustee Act 2000 Sch 1(1), see **appendix 34.60**.
3 Trustee Act 2000 Sch 1(2), see **appendix 34.60**.
4 Trustee Act 2000 Sch 1(3), see **appendix 34.60**.
5 Trustee Act 2000 Sch 1(4), see **appendix 34.60**.
6 Trustee Act 2000 Sch 1(5), see **appendix 34.60**.
7 Trustee Act 2000 Sch 1(6), see **appendix 34.60**.
8 Trustee Act 2000 s 1(1)(a), see **appendix 34.30**.
9 Trustee Act 2000 s 1(1)(b), see **appendix 34.30**.
10 Trustee Act 2000 Sch 1 para 7, see **appendix 34.60**.

Powers and duties in relation to trusts of land[1]

19.31 Where the trust property includes land, the trustees will have additional powers and duties imposed on them by the Trusts of Land and Appointment of Trustees Act 1996. As a result of this Act in every trust of land the trustees will have the power to postpone sale of the land at their discretion for an indefinite period[2] and this power applies even if the Will or trust deed says otherwise. There is, therefore, no need for the draftsman to include an express power to postpone sale in the Will.

1 See also **chapter 11** at **11.19–11.11**.
2 Trusts of Land and Appointment of Trustees Act 1996 s 4, see **appendix 34.17**.

19.32 Under the Trusts of Land and Appointment of Trustees Act 1996 s 6 the trustees are given all the powers of an absolute owner in relation to the land. This seemingly very broad provision is limited by the requirement that they only have such powers 'for the purposes of exercising their functions as trustees'[1]. Such powers can be restricted further by the Will or trust deed[2] but in most situations such a restriction is inappropriate. The trustees also have the power to convey the land subject to the trust to the beneficiaries if they are of full age and capacity and this power can be used against the wishes of the beneficiaries[3]. In some situations, especially when the concern is to protect the trustee for having to hold onto the property for a very long time, this will be a valuable power. However, in other situations such a power will not be appropriate and consideration should be given to restricting it[4]. In particular, if the property is to be held on trust for the benefit of an unincorporated association (eg a golf club) this power should be restricted because each individual member would be a beneficiary and if the trustees were to compel the property onto them it would be extremely complicated.

1 Trusts of Land and Appointment of Trustees Act 1996 s 6(1), see **appendix 34.19**.
2 Trusts of Land and Appointment of Trustees Act 1996 s 8, see **appendix 34.21**.
3 Trusts of Land and Appointment of Trustees Act 1996 s 6(2), see **appendix 34.19**.
4 **Form 19.13** is a form restricting this power.

19.33 The trustees also have the power to partition the land and provide for the payment of equality money. This is a useful power especially in the case of farming land where it is desired to keep the farm in sufficiently large parts to enable it to be workable or in a case where a testator wishes to treat his two sons equally but only has two properties and they are of different value. In such a case the properties could be left on trust for the sons and the trustees could give the large house to one son but require him to pay equality money to the other son to compensate him for getting the smaller house.

19.34 If two (or more) beneficiaries are entitled to occupy trust land the trustees can restrict the occupation of some of the beneficiaries and impose conditions (typically the payment of outgoings and/or an occupation rent) on the occupation of the property[1].

1 Trusts of Land and Appointment of Trustees Act 1996 s 13, see **appendix 34.27**.

19.35 Unlike powers under the Trustee Act 2000 the trustees have the power to delegate any of their powers as trustees of land to any of the beneficiaries who are of full age and beneficially entitled to an interest in possession[1]. If this happens the beneficiaries will owe the same duties and liabilities as the trustees[2]. The delegation can be revocable or irrevocable. Unless it is irrevocable the trustees must keep the delegation under review[3].

1 Trusts of Land and Appointment of Trustees Act 1996 s 9, see **appendix 34.22**.
2 Trusts of Land and Appointment of Trustees Act 1996 s 9(7), see **appendix 34.22**.
3 Trusts of Land and Appointment of Trustees Act 1996 s 9A(3), see **appendix 34.23**.

19.36 When exercising their powers in relation to the land the trustees must exercise a duty of care[1] which is of the same standard as the standard of care under the Trustee Act 2000[2]. Again such a duty can be restricted if it is desired to give extra protection to the trustees. An example of such a provision is at **Form 19.15**.

1 Trusts of Land and Appointment of Trustees Act 1996 s 6(9), see **appendix 34.19**.
2 See note at **19.30**.

19.37 Finally, s 11 of the Trusts of Land and Appointment of Trustees Act 1996 provides that the trustees of a trust of land have a duty to consult the beneficiaries when they are exercising their functions as trustees of land. The duty is to:

> '(a) so far as practicable, consult the beneficiaries of full age and beneficially entitled to an interest in possession in the land, and
> (b) so far as consistent with the general interest of the trust, give effect to the wishes of those beneficiaries, or (in case of dispute) of the majority (according to the value of their combined interests'.

19.38 The duty to consult adds considerably to the burdens and difficulties of trustees and in most circumstances it is advisable to exclude it. Not only does it place an extra administrative burden on the trustees but it also tends to encourage litigation as beneficiaries can get upset if they are not consulted when they believe they should be or if they are consulted but the trustees decide against their views. It is particularly advisable to exclude this duty if it is intended that the land should be sold and the proceeds divided amongst the beneficiaries. **Form 19.14** is an example of a provision excluding this duty. Of course, on occasion it will be important to retain this duty. In particular, if the trust provides for a right of residence for the surviving spouse most testators would wish for the spouse to be given the additional protection of being consulted by the trustees prior to them exercising any of their powers in relation to the land.

Miscellaneous additional powers

19.39 In addition to the statutory powers listed above there are a myriad of additional powers which can be given to trustees. It is not possible to list all the potential powers which could be used in any particular circumstances but some of the more common powers are worth briefly discussing.

Power to carry on the testator's business

19.40 Unless the trustees are given an express power to carry on the testator's business the trustees only have power to carry on the business so far as to enable it to be sold as a going concern. This is discussed more fully in **chapter 13** at **13.33–13.34** but there are numerous situations where it is desirable to give the trustees more extensive powers to carry on the testator's business. **Form 19.9** is an example of clause permitting the trustees to carry on the testator's business beyond the minimum needed to enable it to be sold as a going concern.

Power for the trustees to purchase trust assets

19.41 Unless there is an express power in the Will (or the consent of the court is obtained or all the beneficiaries are of full age and capacity and consent) a trustee cannot purchase trust assets. This is true even after he has ceased to be a trustee. In the case of professional trustees the inability to buy trust assets is unlikely to cause any problems. However, where the trustees are going to be friends or family members, consideration should be given to including express provision allowing the trustees (or a specified trustee) to purchase trust assets. Otherwise there is a risk that an asset with little monetary value but very significant emotional value for a trustee would have to be sold to other people when the trustee would be more than happy to pay market price (or more) for the asset. **Form 19.10** is an example of a clause permitting purchase of trust assets by trustees.

Power of appropriation

19.42 The power for a trustee to appropriate property to a beneficiary in satisfaction of a legacy or an interest in the testator's estate is a very valuable and useful power. The Administration of Estates Act 1925 s 41 gives the trustees the power to make such appropriation but this is conditional on obtaining the consent of the beneficiary in whose favour the appropriation is made. This is generally seen as an unwanted restriction on the power of appropriation and, unless the testator's specific circumstances require a limited power of appropriation it is recommended that the trustees be given a more extensive power of appropriation[1].

1 See **Form 19.11**.

STEP provisions

19.43 An increasing number of practitioners are choosing to incorporate the provisions of the Society of Trust and Estate Practitioners (STEP) in place of a long list of administrative powers and provisions. These provisions (now in their second edition) are available online on the STEP website[1] and consist of a series of Standard Provisions which contain many of the most commonly used administrative provisions in a Will including the most common powers given to trustees. The provisions also include a series of Special Provisions which, though they are not likely to be appropriate in every situation, will be suitable in many situations.

1 www.step.org.

19.44 The STEP provisions are a very valuable resource for any draftsman and consideration should be given to incorporating some or all of the provisions into the Will. The Standard Provisions or the Standard and Special Conditions can be incorporated by reference without setting out the provisions in full[1]. This is a very useful way of including necessary administrative provisions without producing an overly long Will which can often intimidate the testator. However, at the same time it must be emphasised that the use of the STEP provisions should not reduce the consideration of whether certain provisions are appropriate in the circumstances. A common cause of litigation is a busy draftsman who includes provisions from a standard form or precedent without due consideration as to whether each individual part of the standard form or precedent is appropriate or suitable in the circumstances.

The draftsman should therefore consider carefully whether it is appropriate to include each of the provisions within the STEP provisions before he collectively includes all of the STEP provisions in a single incorporation clause. He should also double check to ensure that there is no inconsistency between any of the STEP Provisions and any other clauses in the Will[2].

1 See **Form 19.18** for an example of a provision incorporating the STEP Standard Provisions and **Form 19.19** for an example of a provision incorporating the STEP Standard and Special Provisions.

2 For example STEP Standard Provision 4.16.2 contains provisions regarding a the failure of a gift to a charity and a conflicting provision could easily be contained in the clauses making the charitable gift.

PRECEDENTS

19.45

FORM 19.1

Minors – receipts

My Trustees shall have power to pay any money to which a beneficiary under 18 is entitled to his parent or guardian for his benefit or to the beneficiary himself once he has attained 16 and to rely upon the receipt then given by the parent or guardian or the minor himself.

FORM 19.2

Advancement in favour of life tenant[1]

My Trustees shall have power to pay or apply the whole or any part of the capital of [the trust fund] / [my residuary estate] for the benefit of [*name of life tenant*].

1 See note at **19.8**.

FORM 19.3

Loans to life tenant[1]

My Trustees shall have the power to make loans of capital to [*name of life tenant*[2]] which may be interest free, repayable on demand or repayable at a rate below the market rate.

1 See note at **19.8**.
2 Or the draftsman might substitute the words 'any beneficiary who is entitled to the income of the capital money'.

FORM 19.4

Introductory clause[1]

My Trustees shall have the following powers in addition to their powers under the general law:

[*Power to...*]

[*Power to...*]

[*Power to...*]

1 It is envisioned that this clause would be followed by a list of powers. Alternatively, each individual power can be prefaced with 'My trustees may' or 'My trustees shall have the power to'.

FORM 19.5

Investment[1]

My Trustees shall have the power to invest as if they were beneficially entitled and this power includes the right[2]:

(1) to invest in unsecured loans;

(2) to invest in other non-income producing assets including policies of life assurance;

(3) to purchase land anywhere in the world;

(4) to purchase an undivided share in land;

(5) to invest in land for the occupation or enjoyment of any beneficiary.

1 The object here is to give the personal representatives the widest possible powers in a way which enables lay trustees to understand that they have such powers.

2 These powers, in particular, ought to be included as an extension of the trustees' powers under the general law.

FORM 19.6

Borrowing[1]

My Trustees shall have the power to borrow money on such terms as they think fit including the giving of security[2] and to use it for any purpose for which the capital of my estate or these trusts may be used.

1 See note at **19.14**.

2 The express power to give security overcomes possible problems arising from the statutory limitations on trustees' borrowing powers.

FORM 19.7

Appointment of agents[1]

My Trustees shall have the power to delegate their powers of investment and management of trust property to an agent (including one of their number) on such terms including terms enabling the agent to charge remuneration, to appoint a substitute, to limit liability and to act in circumstances giving rise to a conflict of interest as my trustees think fit.

1 See note at **19.15–19.22**.

FORM 19.8

Use of nominees[1]

My Trustees shall have the power to appoint any person (including one of their number or a beneficiary) to act as their nominee and to take such steps as are necessary to vest any property in such person on such terms including terms enabling the agent to charge remuneration, to appoint a substitute, to limit liability and to act in circumstances giving rise to a conflict of interest as my trustees think fit.

1 See note at **19.23–19.24**.

FORM 19.9

Power to carry on testator's business[1]

My Trustees shall have the power to carry on my business ([known as (*name*)] *or* [of (*description of business*)]) carried on by me at my death for so long as they think fit and with the same powers as if they were beneficially entitled and in the exercise of this power my Trustees shall have the right to:

(i) form a company to carry on the business;

(ii) employ in the business any assets of my residuary estate[2];

(iii) be employed in the business and to retain for themselves any reasonable remuneration paid[3];

(iv) be directors of any such company and to retain for themselves any reasonable remuneration paid[3];

(v) be indemnified out of my residuary estate for any loss incurred[4].

1 See note at **19.40**. See also note at **13.33–13.34**.
2 This clause enables assets of the estate generally to be used in the business. Without this express authority, executors and trustees would be restricted to assets used by the testator himself in the business.
3 This clause is needed because of the general rule that a trustee may not profit from his office.
4 When trustees carry on a business under a power in a Will they are personally liable for any debts incurred. To prevent their right of indemnity being limited to assets used in the business an express right to resort to the whole of the residuary estate can be given but caution should be exercised in including this far-reaching power.

FORM 19.10

Purchase of trust assets by trustee[1]

My Trustees shall have the power to sell any asset of my residuary estate at its market value to ([any one or more of my Trustees] / [*named trustee*]) [provided that there is at least one other Trustee who is not purchasing any asset or assets from my residuary estate at the same time][2].

1 See note at **19.41**.
2 This proviso is intended as a safeguard where the testator considers it appropriate or necessary.

FORM 19.11

Appropriation[1]

Without the restrictions imposed by Administration of Estates Act 1925 s 41 my Trustees shall have the power:

(1) To appropriate to any beneficiary in satisfaction or partial satisfaction of the gift to him any asset forming part of my residuary estate and not subject to a specific gift.

(2) To appropriate as the assets or part of the assets of any trust created by this Will any asset forming part of my residuary estate and not subject to a specific gift.

1 See note at **19.42**.

FORM 19.12

Ancillary powers[1]

My Trustees shall have the power to do anything incidental to the powers which my Trustees have whether given by statute or under this Will.

1 This clause gives a measure of extra comfort in case there is a need for the trustees to do an act incidental to their express powers but such a power has not been expressly set out.

FORM 19.13

Restriction of power to convey land to beneficiaries[1]

My Trustees shall have no right to transfer land to the beneficiaries against their wishes and Trusts of Land and Appointment of Trustees Act 1996 s 6(2) shall not apply to the trusts of my Will.

1 See note at **19.32**.

FORM 19.14

Exclusion of duty to consult beneficiaries[1]

My Trustees shall be under no duty to consult with beneficiaries in exercising any of their functions relating to land subject to the trust and Trusts of Land and Appointment of Trustees Act 1996 s 11(1) shall not apply to the trusts of my Will.

1 See note at **19.37–19.38**.

FORM 19.15

Exclusion of duty of care[1]

My Trustees shall exercise their powers of investment and carry out their duties as trustees without regard to the statutory duty of care and Trustee Act 2000 s 1 shall not apply to the trusts of my Will.

1 See note at **19.30**.

FORM 19.16

Exclusion of duty to review acts of agents and nominees

My Trustees shall be under no duty to review the acts of agents, nominees and custodians appointed by them and Trustee Act 2000 s 22[1] shall not apply to the trusts of my Will.

1 See **appendix 34.49**.

FORM 19.17

Limitation of trustee liability

1. In the absence of an act or omission involving wilful fraud or dishonesty by the trustee in question none of my [lay][1] Trustees [(as defined by Trustee Act 2000 s 28)] shall be liable for any loss caused to my estate or any trust created under my Will or bound to take proceedings against a co-trustee for any breach of trust.

2. My [lay] Trustees shall be entitled to be indemnified out of the assets of my estate against all liabilities incurred in connection with the bona fide execution of their duties and powers.

1 If the limitation is intended to cover both lay and professional trustees then the words in square brackets should be removed. However, for obvious reasons the testator usually only wishes to restrict liability in relation to lay trustees who are much more likely to be friends or family members.

FORM 19.18

Incorporation of the STEP Standard Provisions[1]

The Standard Provisions of the Society of Trust and Estate Practitioners Second Edition shall apply to this Will and the trusts created under it.

1 See note at **19.43–19.44**.

FORM 19.19

Incorporation of all of the STEP Standard and Special Provisions[1]

The Standard Provisions and all of the Special Provisions of the Society of Trust and Estate Practitioners Second Edition shall apply to this Will and the trusts created under it.

1 See note at **19.43–19.44**.

FORM 19.20

Incorporation of the STEP Standard Provisions and selected Special Provisions[1]

The Standard Provisions and the following Special Provisions of the Society of Trust and Estate Practitioners Second Edition shall apply to this Will and the trusts created under it:

[insert Special Provisions intended to be included]…

1 See note at **19.43–19.44**.

20 Declarations

20.1 This section sets out a number of declaratory provisions which often appear at the end of a Will. The draftsman is advised to consult the declarations contained in this chapter as a matter of course at the end of drafting the Will to see if it is appropriate to include any of them in the particular circumstances. These declarations can be grouped together at the end of the Will either as successive clauses or grouped together as a single clause with each declaration used constituting a subclause of it. Where a declaration contained in this chapter is relevant to a particular clause it may be more appropriately included as a subclause of that particular clause rather than in a list of declarations at the end of the Will. Some of the particular declarations in this chapter are self-explanatory and the footnotes provide all the commentary needed. However, it is worth commenting on some of the areas covered by other declarations.

Intermediate income

20.2 When a gift is made under the Will there will almost certainly be a period of time between the date of death and the date the gift is transferred into the hands of the designated beneficiary. This may be a short period or, in the case of a legacy to a minor or a contingent legacy, it may be a considerable period of time. The question then arises whether the beneficiary should receive the income or interest created by the gift which relates to the period before the gift is in the hands of the beneficiary (the intermediate income). The rules relating to the application of intermediate income are complex and rules as to whether it is payable, from when and at what rate change depending on the type of legacy and class of beneficiary. It is therefore usually appropriate to provide that gifts other than those of the residuary estate shall not carry income or interest for one year after death to give the personal representatives time to administer the estate. **Form 20.2** is an example of such a provision. If a particular gift such as an annuity or priority legacy is to take effect from the date of death it should be excluded from this provision. Equally, if the object of a gift is to confer the right to intermediate income for inheritance purposes it should also be excluded from this provision. **Form 20.2** is drafted so as to provide for certain gifts to be excluded from this provision.

Legitimated, illegitimate, adopted and step-children

20.3 Legitimated children (children who were born illegitimate but were subsequently legitimated) are entitled to take any interest under a Will to which they would have been entitled to take had they been born legitimate[1]. The Family Law Reform Act 1987 ss 1 and 19[2] provides that references to a child or children in a disposition under a Will shall, in the absence of any evidence to the contrary, be presumed to include illegitimate children. Adopted children are also presumed to be treated as the child of the adopter unless the Will expresses a contrary intention[3]. Thus, if the testator wishes to exclude legitimated, illegitimate or adopted children (of himself or anybody else) he must make express provision doing so. **Form 20.10** is an example of a provision excluding such children from benefiting.

1 Legitimacy Act 1976 s 5, See **appendix 33.26**.
2 See **appendix 33.24–33.25**.
3 Adoption and Children Act 2002 s 67, see **appendix 33.28**.

20.4 The position is reversed with regard to step-children who are presumed not to fall within the definition of 'child' or 'children' in a Will and will, generally speaking, not benefit under such a gift. This presumption can be displaced by the circumstances and construction of the Will[1]. If the testator intends to benefit step-children it is therefore highly advisable to include an express declaration of this intention. This declaration can either be to include the entire class of step-children as if they were children of their step-parents[2] or merely to include specified step-children in their relevant class[3].

1 See for example *Upton v Jeans* (1895) 13 R 627.
2 See **Form 20.5.**
3 See **Form 20.6.**

Survivorship, lapse and accrual

20.5 Declarations on survivorship, lapse and accrual concern situations where the intended beneficiary dies before or shortly after the testator. In such a situation many testators may wish to provide for their gift to pass otherwise than in accordance with the default provisions.

20.6 Survivorship clauses require the beneficiary to survive the testator for a set period of time and if the beneficiary does not do so they are treated as predeceasing the testator. They are most often used in relation to residuary gifts and a full discussion of their benefits, risks and inheritance tax consequences is contained in **chapter 16** at **16.4–16.12**.

20.7 Where a Will contains a gift to a testator's child or remoter descendant of the testator and the beneficiary predeceases the testator leaving issue, the default provision is that the gift will take effect as a gift to the descendant beneficiary's issue[1]. This is subject to any contrary provision in the Will. Most testators will be content for this to occur but if the testator does not wish the descendant beneficiary's issue to take the beneficiary's share for whatever reason it will be necessary to include a provision excluding s 33 of the Wills Act 1837 and providing for such a gift to lapse on the death of the descendant beneficiary. This can be in the form of a general declaration[2] but it is usually better to include such a provision as a sub-clause of the clause making the gift to the descendant beneficiary as it will draw attention to such a gift and there is less chance of the provision being applicable to other gifts which the testator did not wish it to be applied to.

1 Wills Act 1837 s 33, see **appendix 33.14**.
2 See **Form 20.8**.

20.8 The object of an accrual clause is to avoid a partial intestacy where there is a gift to named persons equally or in fixed proportions. If one of the named persons dies before the testator and there is no contingency gift, their share will fall into residue (if it is a legacy) or will fall into intestacy (if it is a residuary gift). Accrual clauses provide that the share of the person predeceasing the testator does not fall into residue / intestacy but rather accrues to the other beneficiaries of the gift. Prima facie an accrual clause refers only to the original share and not to an augmented share which has already benefited from an earlier accrual and so additional words may need to be added to ensure that it also applies to an augmented share. **Form 20.9** contains two examples of suitable accrual clauses.

Satisfaction and ademption

20.9 The doctrines of satisfaction and ademption can operate to reduce the ultimate sum received by the beneficiary. The way these doctrines operate can often be a surprise to the testator and they should be explained to the testator prior to the execution of any Will.

20.10 The doctrine of satisfaction presumes that a legacy to a beneficiary will be in satisfaction or part satisfaction of a debt owed to the beneficiary. This means that if the testator owes the beneficiary £10,000 and leaves him a legacy of £5,000 the beneficiary is only entitled to a total of £10,000. If such satisfaction is not intended by the testator a form excluding the doctrine of satisfaction should be used[1] and the legacy will be in addition to any debt owed to the beneficiary. If the doctrine was excluded in the previous example the beneficiary would receive a total of £15,000 (a debt of £10,000 plus a legacy of £5,000).

1 See **Form 20.10**.

20.11 If a testator gives a legacy or a share of residue to one of his children and then, after making the Will, makes a substantial gift to the same child, the gift may be considered to have been as an advance against the child's testamentary benefit. This may result in the legacy or residuary share being adeemed or partly adeemed by the lifetime gift. In order to prevent such ademption a declaration such as that in **Form 20.11** can be used.

PRECEDENTS

20.12

FORM 20.1

Declaration that legacies are free of inheritance tax and other duties[1]

The legacies [*given by this Will*] [*at clauses* [ ] *to* [ ]] shall be paid free of inheritance tax and other taxes or duties payable as a result of my death.

1 See note at **10.5–10.7**.

FORM 20.2

Intermediate income[1]

1 Gifts made by this Will other than those of my residuary estate [and the gifts specified in subclause 2 below][2] shall not carry income or bear interest until the expiration of one year from my death and until then my Trustees may in their discretion:

1.1 accumulate the income and add it to the capital of my residuary estate;

1.2 apply it in accordance with their statutory or other powers;

1.3 pay it to the beneficiary of the asset from which the income arises.

[2 The gifts contained in [*insert clauses containing gifts which are intended to carry intermediate income*] shall be excluded from this provision][3].

1 See note at **20.2**.
2 These words should be included if there are certain gifts such as an annuity which are intended to carry intermediated income.
3 See footnote 2 above.

FORM 20.3

Declaration of exclusion[1]

No provision is hereby made for [*name*] [for the reasons set out in a letter signed by me and left with this my Will] [because I have given them a number of large lifetime gifts][2].

1 This declaration is used where the testator wishes to explain why a certain person who might otherwise have expected to inherit is excluded from benefit under the Will. It is usually used as a way of attempting to pre-empt an application under the Inheritance (Provision for Family and Dependants) Act 1975. See **chapter 2** at **2.31–2.45**.
2 It is usually inappropriate to set out the reasons in the Will itself as these may be scandalous and refused probate. However, where the reasons are not scandalous they may be set out in the Will.

FORM 20.4

Exclusion of illegitimate, legitimated and adopted children

For the purpose of ascertaining who is entitled to benefit under this Will:

(1) an illegitimate child shall not be treated as if he had been born legitimate and Family Law Reform Act 1987 ss 1 and 19[1] shall not apply;

(2) a legitimated child shall not be treated as if he had been born legitimate and Legitimacy Act 1976 s 5[2] shall not apply;

(3) an adopted child shall not be treated as the child of his adopter.

1 See **appendix 33.24** and **33.25**.
2 See **appendix 33.26**.

FORM 20.5

Inclusion of step-children as a class[1]

For the purpose of ascertaining who is entitled to benefit under this Will a step-child shall be treated as the child of his step-parent and references to 'child', 'children', 'grandchild', 'grandchildren' and 'issue' shall be construed accordingly.

1 See note at **20.4**.

FORM 20.6

Inclusion of specified step-children[1]

For the purpose of ascertaining who is entitled to benefit under this Will:

(i) [name of step-child] shall be considered as my child;

(ii) [name of step-grandchild] shall be considered to be a child of my [son] [daughter].

1 See note at **20.4**.

FORM 20.7

Survivorship[1]

Any beneficiary who [*does not survive me*] / [*is not proved to have survived me*] by [*insert survivorship* period] shall be treated as having died before me.

1 See note at **20.6**.

FORM 20.8

Lapse[1]

A gift to any of my children or remoter descendants shall lapse if the intended beneficiary dies before me and Wills Act 1837 s 33[2] shall not apply to the provisions of this Will.

1 See note at **20.7**.
2 See **appendix 33.14**.

FORM 20.9

Provision for proportional accrual[1]

If the trust of any share under this clause fails that share shall be added proportionally to the other shares and this provision shall apply to both an original share and an augmented share.

or

If any beneficiary named in this clause dies before me then the benefit he would have taken under this clause shall be shared proportionally by the beneficiaries named in this clause who survive me.

1 See note at **20.8**.

FORM 20.10

Excluding doctrine of satisfaction[1]

No gift in this Will is made in satisfaction or part satisfaction of any debt owed by me.

1 See note at **20.10**.

FORM 20.11

Excluding ademption[1]

No gift in this Will shall be adeemed in whole or in part by any gift made in my lifetime [*unless I expressly declare in writing at the relevant time that I intend the gift to be thereby adeemed*][2].

1 See note at **20.11**.
2 The additional words are advisable so to prevent the requirement to make a new Will if the testator subsequently decides to make a gift which is intended to adeem a beneficiary's share.

21 Attestation

21.1 The ordinary formalities[1] for a properly executed Will are laid down in s 9 of the Wills Act 1837[2]. Section 9 holds that no Will shall be valid unless:

(a) it is in writing, and signed by the testator, or by some other person in his presence and by his direction; and

(b) it appears that the testator intended by his signature to give effect to the will; and

(c) the signature is made or acknowledged by the testator in the presence of two or more witnesses present at the same time; and

(d) each witness either—

  (i) attests and signs the will; or

  (ii) acknowledges his signature;

in the presence of the testator.

1 Statutory Wills and the Wills of those on active service are exempt from the ordinary formalities.

2 See **appendix 33.3**.

21.2 The standard (and recommended) procedure is for the testator to sign the Will first in the presence of two witnesses and then for the two witnesses to sign in the presence of the testator and of one another. It is not necessary to strictly adhere to this recommended procedure. For example, the testator could acknowledge his signature in front of the witnesses who then sign or the witnesses could sign in the presence of the testator but not each other and the Will would still be validly attested. However, it is essential that whatever procedure is followed it complies with s 9. The requirements of s 9 are strict and a failure to follow them will result in the Will not being admitted to probate. This must be emphasised to the testator in the event that the draftsman is not supervising the attestation and the testator himself is arranging for the Will to be executed. There are, sadly, many cases of Wills which were clearly approved of by a testator of full capacity but refused probate on the basis that the formal requirements of s 9 were not followed. The case of *Re Colling*[1] is a classic example of such a case. There the testator signed his name in the presence of one witness who signed and then later the testator acknowledged his signature in the presence of the two witnesses and the second witness signed the Will. Even though the testator clearly approved the Will it was still held to be invalid because it failed to comply with s 9[2].

1 *Re Colling, Lawson v Von Winckler* [1972] 3 All ER 729.

2 To be valid in *Re Colling* the first witness would have had to sign again after the testator acknowledged his signature.

21.3 The draftsman should be careful to advise the testator as to the consequences of alterations made to the Will and how such alterations will be treated by the courts. Alterations made to a Will after its execution are invalid unless properly attested[1]. Unless there is evidence to the contrary, it is presumed that alterations have been made after execution. The initialling of alterations by the testator and witnesses is evidence that they were made before execution and the initialling of alterations made after execution will amount to re-execution if the attestation is good[2]. However, it is preferable to avoid the need to rely on any such evidence and, if at all possible, a new document containing the corrections should be the document executed. In the case of a draftsman supervising the execution of the testator's homemade Will or in cases of urgency, alterations may need to be made to the document but in most situations it should be simply a matter of the draftsman printing a new, updated document and having that document executed. If the document does have to be altered the draftsman should make a good note of the fact, content and attestation of the alteration and keep a copy of this on the Will file in case the alteration is later challenged.

1 Wills Act 1837 s 21, see **appendix 33.10**.
2 *Re Blewitt* (1880) 5 PD 116.

21.4 If the Will covers more than one page, as most Wills do, it is strongly advised (but not legally required) to number each page and to have each page signed by the testator. This will prevent any pages being added to or removed from the Will at a later date and will help have the Will admitted to probate even if the binding of the Will is later removed or becomes undone. Numbering and signing each page is also a requirement if the testator intends to make an International Will[1].

1 See **chapter 6** at **6.3–6.5**.

21.5 If the Will is executed under the supervision of a Will draftsman or some other person properly equipped and qualified to supervise execution and the qualified person gives evidence that s 9 was followed this will usually suffice to extinguish any claim that the Will was not properly executed.

21.6 Every Will should contain an attestation clause indicating that the statutory requirements have been carried out. If it contains such a clause and there are no other circumstances exciting suspicion this will usually be sufficient to obtain probate. If it does not contain a valid attestation clause an affidavit of due execution will be required before it will be granted probate. As it may not always be possible to tracc witnesses to give such an affidavit the importance of including a proper attestation clause cannot be overstated. An effective attestation clause can be drafted in a number of different ways and still be effective. The words used in **Form 21.1** were approved by the court in *Re Selby-Bigge*[1] and so will constitute an effective attestation clause. Additional words can be added to this clause but they serve no additional purpose.

1 [1950] 1 All ER 1009.

21.7 If the testator is blind or unable to read or write then a special attestation clause should be used instead of the standard clause. The reason for this is that the Non-Contentious Probate Rules 1987 rule 13 requires that:

> 'Before admitting to proof a Will which appears to have been signed by a blind or illiterate testator or by another person by a direction of the testator, or which for any other reason raises doubt as to the testator having had knowledge of the contents of the Will at the time of its execution, the district judge or registrar shall satisfy himself that the testator had such knowledge.'

Usually a special attestation clause will be sufficient to satisfy this requirement and the Will can then be duly admitted to probate. Examples of special attestation clauses are contained in **Forms 21.3**, **21.4** and **21.5**.

Witnesses

21.8 The draftsman should advise the testator as to which people are or are not suitable to be witnesses to the Will. This is especially true if the draftsman is not supervising the execution of the Will and the testator will be choosing who will witness the Will.

21.9 A blind person cannot be a valid witness to a Will. A person lacking sufficient mental capacity also cannot be a valid witness. The witnesses do not, however, have to be adults, provided that they are old enough to understand what they are doing and have sufficient mental capacity. However, for obvious reasons the use of adults is recommended. Though it will not necessarily invalidate the Will, it is undesirable to use as a witness any person who may prove to be unreliable or untraceable in the event that they are needed to give evidence as to due attestation.

21.10 The testator should also be advised that a beneficiary to a Will or a beneficiary's spouse or civil partner should not be a witness. While the use of a beneficiary or a beneficiary's spouse or civil partner as a witness will not invalidate the Will it will mean that the beneficiary will lose their gift or gifts under the Will[1]. However, this rule does not apply if the witness is an unnecessary witness (ie a third witness where there are two other valid witnesses)[2]. The rule also does not apply if the witness is not married or in a civil partnership with the beneficiary at the time of executing the Will but subsequently marries or enters into civil partnership with the beneficiary. The rule that a witness cannot obtain a benefit under the Will does not affect trustee charging clauses as the payment under such clauses is considered to be remuneration and not a gift[3]. Therefore, if such a professional acts as a witness to the Will he will not be prevented from charging fees under the professional charging clause.

1 Wills Act 1837 s 15, see **appendix 33.4**.
2 Wills Act 1968 s 1, see **appendix 33.18**.
3 Trustee Act 2000 ss 28(4) and 33(2)(a), see **appendix 34.54**.

21.11 While the category of potential witnesses is extremely broad, the ideal witness is a reliable adult who has legal experience or otherwise understands the requirements of the Wills Act 1837 and is likely to be easy to contact if needed in the future.

Draftsman's duty in relation to attestation

21.12 The duty in relation to the mechanics of attestation has been the subject of two partially inconsistent decisions of the High Court.

21.13 In *Gray & Ors v Richards Butler (a firm)*[1] Lloyd J held that a solicitor is under a duty to advise a testator on the proper procedure to be followed but found in that case that the solicitor's provision of 'most comprehensive' instructions for the execution of the Will was sufficient to ensure that his conduct did not fall short of that required of the reasonably competent solicitor.

1 [2000] WTLR 143.

21.14 Although not reported until 2000, *Gray v Richards Butler (a firm)*[1] was decided in 1997. Sadly, the decision was not cited to Longmore J in *Esterhuizen v Allied Dunbar Assurance plc*[2]. In *Esterhuizen*, Longmore J asked himself the question whether it was enough for a solicitor or a professional Will maker to provide comprehensive instructions for the execution of a Will and leave it at that. He answered that question in the negative. His words are important and should be noted by all practitioners[3]:

> 'The fact is that the process of signature and attestation is not completely straightforward and disaster may ensue if it is not correctly done. Any testator is entitled to expect reasonable assistance without having to ask expressly for it. It is in my judgment not enough just to leave written instructions with the testator. In ordinary circumstances just to leave written instructions and to do no more will not only be contrary to good practice but also in my view negligent.'

1 [2000] WTLR 143.
2 [1998] 2 FLR 668.
3 [1998] 2 FLR 668 at 677.

21.15 It is noted that in *Esterhuizen* the draftsman was not a solicitor but because he was offering a Will writing service the court held he must be held to the same standard as a solicitor

21.16 The view expressed in *Gray v Richards Butler* sets a lower standard than in *Esterhuizen* but in *Gray v Richards Butler* Lloyd J accepted that in circumstances in which the solicitor is not going to be present at that execution, the solicitor is under a duty to take proper care in advising the testator as to the procedure to be followed for the valid execution of his Will and that when the Will is returned to him after execution the solicitor is under a duty to examine it and consider whether it appears to be properly executed. If it is not then it is the solicitor's duty to raise the question with the testator in order to check that the Will has been properly executed or, if not, to advise him that it should be re-executed[1].

1 *Gray v Richards Butler (a firm)* [2000] WTLR 143, see at 157D–157E.

21.17 It is obviously desirable that the draftsman is present when the Will is executed in order to be able to provide guidance and assistance and to ensure that the requirements of Wills Act 1837 s 9 are complied with. It is advisable for every draftsman to offer such a service as a matter of course to all clients for whom the draftsman has drafted a Will. If the draftsman is governed by the Code of Practice for the Institute of Professional Willwriters the draftsman must offer such a service at no extra cost[1]. If the testator is to arrange for the execution of the Will themselves then under the Code the draftsman must provide written advice concerning the importance of correct attestation, the consequences of incorrect attestation and instructions on the correct attestation procedure. The Code also states that the draftsman must provide a service by post to check that the documents appear to have been attested properly and there must be no charge for such service.

1 Institute of Professional Willwriters, Code of Practice, clause 10.1.

21.18 The Law Society Wills and Inheritance Protocol[1] also requires a draftsman to offer a similar service. It requires[2] that the draftsman should offer the testator a choice between having the execution of the Will supervised by the draftsman and the testator arranging for the execution of the Will themselves with the draftsman providing full written instructions concerning execution. These instructions must include information on the choice of witnesses and the correct procedure for signing and witnessing the Will. Under the Protocol the draftsman must also offer to inspect the Will after unsupervised execution to check that formalities appear to have been complied with and to check that the witnesses are not beneficiaries or spouses or civil partners of beneficiaries. This service must be offered without additional charge. A similar check should be undertaken if the Will is returned to the draftsman for storage.

1 Publication date 3 July 2013.
2 Paragraph 14.

21.19 While not every draftsman will be formally required to comply with the Code of Practice for the Institute of Professional Willwriters or the Law Society Wills and Inheritance Protocol every draftsman is very strongly advised to take similar actions with regard to the execution of the Will. Following such procedures will offer protection to the draftsman and a failure to do so will leave the draftsman wide open to a negligence claim under the principles of *Gray v Richards Butler* and *Esterhuizen*.

PRECEDENTS

21.20

FORM 21.1

Standard form of testimonium and attestation clause

As Witness my hand this [--] day of [--------] 20[--]. [*Testator's Signature*]

Signed by the Testator in our presence and attested by us in the presence of the Testator and of each other.

[*Signatures, Addresses and Occupation of Witnesses*[1]]

1 The addresses and occupation of witnesses are not a legal requirement but they make it much easier to identify and, if needed, find the witnesses and therefore are a recommended addition.

FORM 21.2

Form of testimonium and attestation clause to a codicil

As Witness my hand this [--] day of [--------] 20[--]. [*Testator's Signature*]

Signed by the Testator as a codicil to [his/her] Will dated [*date of Will*] and attested by us in the presence of the Testator and of each other.

[*Signatures, Addresses and Occupation of Witnesses*[1]]

1 The addresses and occupation of witnesses are not a legal requirement but they make it much easier to identify and, if needed, find the witnesses and therefore are a recommended addition.

FORM 21.3

Where the testator is unable to read or write[1]

As Witness my hand this [--] day of [--------] 20[--]. [*Testator's Signature*]

The Testator being [blind]/[unable to read or write] this Will was read to the Testator and [he/she] stated that [he/she] understood it. At the direction[2] of the Testator it was then signed on the Testator's behalf by [*name of person signing for testator*][3] in the presence of the Testator and us and attested by us in the presence of the Testator and of [*name of person signing for testator*][4] and of each other.

[*Signatures, Addresses and Occupation of Witnesses*[5]]

1 See note at **21.7** for rules governing a blind or illiterate testator.
2 In the previous edition, this form used the word 'request', to which some district registries objected. Although other books of precedents continue to use request, this edition uses 'direction' which, it is understood, is preferred by probate registries.
3 It is possible for one of the witnesses to act as the signatory but it is the better practice for someone else to sign, in case the validity of the Will is questioned.
4 Strictly, the Will need not be attested in the signatory's presence but it is desirable and usually convenient that it should be.
5 The addresses and occupation of witnesses are not a legal requirement but they make it much easier to identify and, if needed, find the witnesses and therefore are a recommended addition.

FORM 21.4

Where the testator is able to sign but unable to read

As Witness my hand this [--] day of [--------] 20[--]. [*Testator's Mark*]

The Testator being unable to read, this Will was read to the Testator and [he/she] stated that [he/she] understood it. It was then signed by the Testator [*with his/her mark*] in our presence and attested by us in the presence of the Testator and in the presence of each other.

[*Signatures, Addresses and Occupation of Witnesses*[1]]

1 The addresses and occupation of witnesses are not a legal requirement but they make it much easier to identify and, if needed, find the witnesses and therefore are a recommended addition.

FORM 21.5

Testator is able to read but unable to sign his name – signed with mark[1]

As Witness my hand this [--] day of [--------] 20[--]. [*Testator's Mark*]

The Testator being [temporarily] unable to sign [his/her] name [*because of an injury to his hand*[2]] this Will was read by the Testator and was signed by the Testator with [his/her] mark in our presence and attested by us in the presence of the Testator and in the presence of each other.

[*Signatures, Addresses and Occupation of Witnesses*[3]]

1 Where the testator's incapacity is temporary, it is desirable that the reason for his incapacity is stated because, if the validity of the Will is disputed, it will be known that the testator was normally able to write. The same is true if the testator has only recently lost the ability to sign.

2 In the previous edition this form used the word 'request', to which some district registries objected. Although other books of precedents continue to use request, this edition uses 'direction' which, it is understood, is preferred by probate registries.

3 The addresses and occupation of witnesses are not a legal requirement but they make it much easier to identify and, if needed, find the witnesses and therefore are a recommended addition.

FORM 21.5

Testator is able to read but unable to sign his name – signed at his direction[1]

As Witness my hand this [--] day of [--------] 20[--]. [*Testator's Name*]

The Testator being [temporarily] unable to sign [his/her] name [*because of an injury to his hand*[2]] this Will was read by the Testator and at [his/her] direction[3] signed on [his/her] behalf by [*name of person signing for testator*][4] in the presence of the Testator and us and attested by us in the presence of the Testator and of [*name of person signing for Testator*][5] and of each other.

[*Signatures, Addresses and Occupation of Witnesses*[6]]

1 Where the testator's incapacity is temporary, it is desirable that the reason for his incapacity is stated because, if the validity of the Will is disputed, it will be known that the testator was normally able to write.

2 The same is true if the testator has only recently lost the ability to sign.

3 In the previous edition this form used the word 'request', to which some district registries objected. Although other books of precedents continue to use request, this edition uses 'direction' which, it is understood, is preferred by probate registries.

4 It is possible for one of the witnesses to act as the signatory but it is the better practice for someone else to sign, in case the validity of the Will is questioned.

5 Strictly, the Will need not be attested in the signatory's presence but it is desirable and usually convenient that it should be.

6 The addresses and occupation of witnesses are not a legal requirement but they make it much easier to identify and, if needed, find the witnesses and therefore are a recommended addition.

22 Inheritance Tax

22.1 This is not a book about inheritance tax, nor about inheritance tax mitigation. Effective inheritance tax mitigation requires lifetime planning and to commence with a Will is to start at the wrong end of the process. Nevertheless Wills must be drafted in the context of the burdens imposed by inheritance tax and proper Will drafting can avoid or reduce the impact of inheritance tax. The draftsman must, therefore, have a proper understanding of the impact and effect of inheritance tax.

22.2 The aim of this chapter is therefore to give the reader a basic understanding of the nature of inheritance tax and its effect upon Will drafting. The next chapter explains some of the more common techniques for drafting Wills to avoid or reduce inheritance tax. More thorough guidance and advice requires reference to a detailed work on inheritance tax.

An outline of inheritance tax

22.3 Inheritance tax is not a tax on inheritance. It is a tax on transfers of value[1] made by individuals that have the effect of reducing the value of their estates[2] with (i) an exemption for absolute lifetime transfers made more than seven years before their death[3] and (ii) a deemed transfer occurring on a person's death[4]. In addition it is a tax on transfers into or out of settlements, together with a 10 yearly charge upon those settlements[5].

1 Inheritance Tax Act 1984 ss 1 and 3.
2 Inheritance Tax Act 1984 s 3(1).
3 Inheritance Tax Act 1984 s 3A.
4 Inheritance Tax Act 1984 s 4.
5 Inheritance Tax Act 1984 ss 7, 64 and 65.

22.4 Inheritance tax on a lifetime transfer otherwise than into a settlement (ie a failed potentially exempt transfer (or PET) and upon a person's estate at death is taxed at 40%[1]. However, the first £325,000 is taxed at 0% and so is known as the nil rate band. This sum used to increase regularly (although not in line with price rises let alone the value of estates) but in recent years has remained frozen at £325,000. Lifetime transfers into settlements without qualifying interests in possession[2] are taxed at 20% but the total tax is affected by other lifetime transfers (and so the availability of the nil rate band) and so can increase if potentially exempt transfers fall into charge by the donor's death. Subsequent charges on settlements involve complex calculations but are (and have historically been) at relatively low levels that barely justify the difficulty in calculating the charge[3].

1 Inheritance Tax Act 1984 Sch 1.
2 See **22.13** below.
3 HMRC is currently consulting on a 'simplification' of the existing regime which has the appearance of being a means to increase the overall rates of charge (whilst in no way simplifying the rules).

Inheritance tax on death

22.5 The legislation deems there to occur on a person's death a transfer of the whole of the value of their estate[1]. This is a net transfer and so it is necessary to calculate the value of the whole of their assets and to then deduct from it their liabilities, including funeral expenses[2]. The net figure, together with any prior lifetime transfers that have fallen into charge, is subject to tax at 40% after deduction of the available nil rate band.

1 Inheritance Tax Act 1984 s 4.
2 Inheritance Tax Act 1984 s 5.

22.6 Certain assets are ignored for the purpose of calculating the value of a person's estate. At least where a person is UK domiciled (or deemed domiciled)[1] those assets are principally agricultural property or business property. Agricultural property essentially means agricultural land or property with a minimum period of occupation (of 2 years) or ownership (of 7 years) and only the agricultural value of the land or property is ignored[2]. Business property is intended to apply to businesses or business assets of an individual but ignoring assets owned by them as investments[3].

1 Inheritance Tax Act 1984 s 267.
2 Inheritance Tax Act 1984 ss 115–124B. See further **chapter 13** at **13.12–13.15**.
3 Inheritance Tax Act 1984 ss 103–114. See further **chapter 13** at **13.2–13.11**.

22.7 Certain transfers are also exempt from charge. The principal exemptions are to a person's spouse (or civil partner)[1] and to charity[2].

1 Inheritance Tax Act 1984 s 18.
2 Inheritance Tax Act 1984 s 23. See further **chapter 14**.

22.8 The net result is that the tax burden on death falls upon: (i) estates over the nil rate bands; (ii) that do not include (or do not include sufficient) agricultural or business assets; and (iii) which pass to persons other than spouses, civil partners or charities. It is unsurprising, therefore, that most inheritance tax mitigation, particularly that involving Wills, is aimed at reducing or avoiding taxation on gifts to children (or other non-exempt persons) and that such mitigation tends to be most effective when the estate includes some element of either excluded property or exempt person. Those techniques that are most common are discussed in more detail in the next chapter.

Inheritance tax on lifetime transfers

22.9 Lifetime transfers that are not immediately chargeable[1] are exempt from tax if the donor survives more than seven years[2]. In addition a form of taper relief applies provided the individual survives for more than three years[3]. As is the case for the deemed transfer on death, transfers of excluded assets or to exempt persons do not attract tax.

1 Transfers into settlements without qualifying interests in possession are immediately chargeable, Inheritance Tax Act 1984 ss 3 and 3A(2).
2 Inheritance Tax Act 1984 s 3A(4).
3 Inheritance Tax Act 1984 s 7(4).

22.10 If all gifts made more than seven years before death fell out of charge then all inheritance tax mitigation would focus upon giving away as much as possible as soon as possible. The consequence is that the inheritance tax legislation contains a number of provisions intended to prevent persons both giving away their cake and eating it, or in other words giving away assets whilst retaining the benefit or enjoyment of them. The most significant of those is that which applies to gifts with reservation of benefit[1]. This provides that an asset which is given away but which the donee does not enjoy, or where the donee's enjoyment is not wholly free of the donor's enjoyment, then the asset is treated as remaining within his estate (and so taxed on death or when the reservation of benefit ceases)[2]. This legislation has, over the years, proved relatively easy to avoid, leading to a series of amendments and eventually culminating in an entirely different tax, an income tax charge, known as the pre-owned asset tax[3].

1 Finance Act 1986 ss 102–102C.
2 Finance Act 1986 s 102(1).
3 See the Finance Act 1986 ss 102A, 102B, 102C and 102ZA. Pre-Owned Asset Tax was introduced in the Finance Act 2005. See note at **22.34–22.35** below.

22.11 The result of this is that most (but still not all) gifts that involve an asset the donor intends to continue to enjoy or benefit from are not effective for inheritance tax. The most significant consequence of that is that it tends to rule out planning with the family home outside of (i) certain permitted exceptions within the legislation[1] or (ii) the more imaginative or the more aggressive schemes that continue to be marketed.

1 See paragraph 6 of Sch 20 to the Finance Act 1986.

Settlements

22.12 Settlements are defined by the inheritance tax legislation to mean any disposition of property where the property is held in trust for persons in succession or for any person subject to any contingency or held by trustees on trust to accumulate the whole or any part of any income or charged or burdened with the payment of an annuity or other periodical payment payable for a life or for any other limited or terminable period[1].

1 Inheritance Tax Act 1984 s 43.

22.13 The legislation divides settlements into two kinds. The first are settlements that have a qualifying interest in possession and the second are those that do not. Settlements with a qualifying interest in possession are taxed as if they were part of the estate of the person with an interest in possession[1]. So a gift in a Will to Mary of a house for life will be taxed as a gift to her (and so exempt if she is a spouse) and on her death will be taxed together with the rest of her property. Settlements without a qualifying interest in possession are taxed as 'relevant property' with a 20% charge on lifetime transfers into the trust, a tax on any transfers from the settlement and a charge on every 10 year anniversary[2]. So in the above example, if the gift was made to Mary in the donor's lifetime her interest will not be qualifying and so the transfer will be immediately chargeable (even if she is a spouse) but will not be taxed as part of Mary's estate on her death.

1 Inheritance Tax Act 1984 s 49.
2 Inheritance Tax Act 1984 ss 7, 64 and 65.

22.14 Prior to 2006 any interest in possession was a qualifying life interest. So an entitlement to the income of the trust, whether for life or otherwise, whenever and however created was a qualifying interest in possession and meant that the trust was treated as forming part of that person's estate. Where such interests continue to exist they continue to be qualifying interests in possession[1]. However, after 2006 no new qualifying interests in possession can be created by a lifetime transfer. Only certain kinds of interests created by Will can be qualifying interests in possession. Those interests are:

(i) Immediate Post Death Interests[2]. These are interests in possession taking effect immediately after a person's death regardless of who the beneficiary is.
(ii) A Disabled Person's Interest[3]. This is an interest in favour of persons who are within the definition of disabled and where the trust restricts the payments of income and capital that are not made to them.

In addition, some interests created on the cessation of pre-2006 interests in possession can also qualify (so called transitional serial interests)[4].

1 For example, Inheritance Tax Act 1984 s 49(1A).
2 Inheritance Tax Act 1984 s 49A.
3 Inheritance Tax Act 1984 s 89B. See also **chapter 18**.
4 Inheritance Tax Act 1984 s 49B.

22.15 To add to the list of 'favoured' trusts, ie those trusts that are not fully subject to the relevant property regime, are trusts created by Will in favour of persons below the age of 18 and (to a lesser extent) under the age of 25[1]. Those trusts are considered in more detail in the next section.

1 Inheritance Tax Act 1984 ss 71A and 71D.

22.16 In drafting Wills, the principal question is whether or not the settlement created will be subject to the relevant property regime. The answer to that question essentially depends upon whether a qualifying life interest has been created or whether some other applicable exemption applies (eg that for young persons). If the settlement is within the regime then the applicable charges may be avoided if the property is below the nil rate band (at least until the 10 year anniversary) or if it is excluded property (principally agricultural or business relief property). In most other cases the relevant property regime is considered undesirable because of the regular charges and the administrative burden on calculating them. That said, sometimes the desirable flexibility of a wide discretionary trust is worth the cost of the charges imposed by the relevant property regime.

Age contingent gifts

22.17 A common form of testamentary provision is to gift a sum of money, or share of residue, to a child or children conditional upon their reaching a certain age. The concern of many testators is to ensure that individuals do not receive sums of money, particularly large sums of money, before they are mature enough to deal with them. For that reason the age that the beneficiary must attain is often greater than 18. The age of 25 years is common and testators do often ask for an even greater age.

22.18 Where the contingency is that of 18 and the testator dies before the children have reached that age then for inheritance tax purposes a settlement will arise as to such part of the trust as has not been vested because the interest is contingent[1]. The consequence, absent any other provision, would be that the settlement would be relevant property and would be taxed when the beneficiary becomes absolutely entitled on reaching the age of 18 or whenever the power to advance capital to the beneficiary is exercised[2]. However, Inheritance Tax Act s 71A provides that, provided a series of conditions are met, it will not be taxed as relevant property and tax will not be charged on either of those events. The effect is that such trusts are essentially free of inheritance tax. Such trusts are known as trusts for bereaved minors.

1 Inheritance Tax Act 1984 s 43(2).
2 Pursuant to the Trustee Act 1925 s 32 (as amended by the Inheritance and Trustees Powers Act 2014) trustees have power to apply capital to which a beneficiary is contingently entitled to or for their maintenance, education or benefit.

22.19 The conditions are that: (i) the provision is made in the Will of a parent (gifts from grandparents or others do not have this treatment); (ii) the beneficiary must become entitled to all of the capital and any of the accumulated income on becoming 18; (iii) any capital applied must be applied for the benefit of the beneficiary; and (iv) they must be entitled to all of the income arising or it must not be capable of being applied for the benefit of anyone else.

22.20 Where the condition is for an age greater than 18 but not greater than 25 then the above provisions will apply to the trust save that for the period of time between the age of 18 and 25 a form of relevant property taxation will apply[1]. The rate of taxation depends upon the period of time after the age of 18 at which the capital is paid or the beneficiary becomes entitled to it. The sums of money involved are small and even if none of the capital is paid or vested until the beneficiary reaches the age of 25 it cannot exceed 4.2%. Such trusts are known as 18–25 trusts.

1 Inheritance Tax Act 1984 s 71D.

22.21 Where the contingency is greater than 25, or where the conditions referred to above apply, then the trust will be taxed as a settlement without an interest in possession[1]. This is something of a trap for the unwary draftsman and must be carefully considered.

1 Not all contingent gifts will have non-qualifying interests in possession. For example, if a testator dies when the child is over 18 their entitlement will, subject to contrary provision in the Will, be to all of the income (Trustee Act 1925 s 31) so that their interest will be a qualifying immediate post death interest.

The spouse exemption

22.22 Transfers between spouses (or civil partners) are exempt from charge. The only exceptions to that are transfers from UK domiciled spouses to non-domiciled spouses which cannot exceed the limit of the nil rate band[1], currently £325,000. This is probably one of the most exploited exemptions in the legislation. Most obviously it means that a husband can freely give all of his assets to his wife and vice-versa. In addition, a bequest on trusts with a qualifying life interest in favour of a spouse is also exempt, so assets can be transferred *through* a spouse, and the termination of that interest in possession in the spouse's lifetime will be a potentially exempt transfer meaning that tax can in some cases be avoided entirely. This is considered in more detail in the next chapter[2].

1 Prior to 6 April 2013 the exemption was much more restrictive and was limited to the sum of £55,000.

2 See **23.17–23.19**.

Transferable nil rate bands

22.23 As set out above, whilst inheritance tax is taxed at the rate of 40% the first £325,000 is taxed at 0%. This is referred to as the nil rate band. Prior to October 2007 it was common to introduce into Wills a gift, often on trust, of a sum equal to the nil rate band with the remainder of the estate passing to the surviving spouse. That technique was used because without it the nil rate band was 'wasted'. Taking a simple example, where two spouses both had estates of £400,000 a gift by one of their whole estate to the other would lead to a charge to tax of £190,000 on the death of the second ((£800,000 – £325,000) × 0.4). If, however, the estate of the first spouse to die included a gift up to the nil rate band tax would only be £40,000 ((£400,000 – £325,000) + (£400,000 – £325,000) × 0.4), a saving of £150,000.

22.24 The necessity for this form of avoidance was largely negated by the introduction of transferable nil rate bands[1]. At its simplest this provides that where a spouse transfers the whole of his estate to his surviving spouse that spouse will have on his or her death, two available nil rate bands. In the event that a spouse partially uses their nil rate bands (eg by legacies to children or other non-exempt beneficiaries) then the second nil rate band available to the surviving spouse will be proportionately reduced.

1 By the Finance Act 2008 taking effect for deaths after 9 October 2007. See Inheritance Tax Act 1984 ss 8A–8C.

22.25 There will remain some cases where a nil rate band trust will be useful. For example, one spouse may already have a 'double' nil rate band available to them (having already survived a spouse) and it is not possible for them to have a third. And, of course, a gift on a discretionary trust that is not subject to any inheritance tax may itself be useful in providing what the testator wants. These possibilities are explored further in **chapter 23**.

Charities[1]

22.26 Transfers are exempt to the extent to which they are transfers to charities[2]. That is defined to mean gifts to charities or on trusts for the purposes of charity only. The definition of charity now includes charities within the European Union together with Iceland and Norway[3].

1 See further **chapter 14**.

2 Inheritance Tax Act 1984 s 23.

3 Finance Act 2010 s 30, Sch 6 Part 1.

22.27 As an incentive to charitable giving the applicable rate of inheritance tax is reduced by 4% where more than 10% of the estate is the subject of gifts to charity. This is discussed in greater detail in **chapter 14**.

The burden and allocation of inheritance tax

22.28 The general rule is that inheritance tax is a testamentary expense and so payable from the residue of the estate[1]. This is subject to any contrary provision in the Will.

1 Inheritance Tax Act 1984 s 211.

22.29 Where all beneficiaries are exempt no particular difficulty arises (as no tax is paid), nor when all are not exempt. However, where there is a mixture of exempt and non-exempt beneficiaries the statute provides how the tax is to be borne between them. In general terms, an exempt beneficiary should never bear the burden of any inheritance tax. More specifically:

- Where the residue is exempt (eg it goes wholly to a spouse) the tax must fall on the specific gifts. However, since specific gifts are (absence contrary provision) free of inheritance tax, this will usually require those gifts to be 'grossed up'. More tax will therefore be paid than if they had been expressly subject to tax.
- Where part of the residue is exempt and part non-exempt (eg a residue divided between spouse and two children) only the non-exempt part should bear inheritance tax.
- Where excluded property (eg agricultural or business property) is divided between an exempt and non-exempt residue the benefit of the relief is divided between all the residuary beneficiaries. It is therefore 'wasted' in respect of the exempt beneficiaries[1].

1 This is discussed further at **23.6–23.7**.

22.30 Where residue is divided between equally exempt and non-exempt beneficiaries the effect of the rules described above is for the exempt beneficiary to receive a greater sum than the non-exempt beneficiaries because their share will be free of tax. So, for example, where an estate of £1,000,000 is divided between three children and three charities the children will (ignoring the effect of the nil rate band) receive £300,000 (£500,000 less tax of £200,000) between them, whereas the charities will receive £500,000. In some instances testators prefer to ensure that each beneficiary will receive the same amount. It appears that it is possible to make such provision in a Will[1], but the effect is to 'gross up' the sums going to the non-exempt beneficiaries. So in the previous example the children and the charity will receive £125,000 with a total tax of £250,000. **Form 22.1** gives an example of a provision for the tax to be borne solely by the non-exempt beneficiaries while **Form 22.2** gives an example of a provision for the tax to be grossed up.

1 See *Re Ratcliffe (deceased)* [1999] STC 262 not following *Re Benham's Will Trusts* [1995] STC 210.

The foreign aspect

22.31 Where a person is domiciled in the United Kingdom the whole of their estate is subject to inheritance tax. Whether or not a person is domiciled in the UK depends upon the common law test of domicile but it is possible to be 'deemed domiciled' by being resident in the UK in the 17 of the last 20 years or by being domiciled in the UK within the last three years[1].

1 Inheritance Tax Act 1984 s 267.

22.32 Where a person is not domiciled in the UK their property situated outside of the United Kingdom is treated as 'excluded property' and exempt from inheritance tax[1]. The situs of assets can be a difficult issue and there is obviously a significant incentive to ensure that assets are not situated within the United Kingdom. That is one reason (among many) for non-domiciled individuals to place UK property within companies or trusts that are themselves not resident in the UK. For similar reasons, persons coming to the UK are often advised to place assets within trust prior to their becoming UK domiciled[2].

1 Inheritance Tax Act 1984 s 6.
2 Foreign property within a relevant property settlement will remain excluded property notwithstanding the domicile of the settlor later changing.

22.33 Gifts between UK domiciled spouses are exempt as are gifts between non-domiciled spouses. However, gifts by UK domiciled spouses to non-domiciled spouses are exempt only up to the sum of the nil rate band, currently £325,000[1].

1 Prior to 6 April 2013 the exemption was much more restrictive and was limited to the sum of £55,000.

Anti avoidance

22.34 There are a number of provisions of the inheritance tax legislation designed to avoid attempts to minimise the effect of that tax. Principal amongst them is the gift with reservation legislation, which treats gifts where the donor continues to enjoy the property, or where the donee does not enjoy that property to the exclusion of the donor, as remaining within the estate of the donor[1]. The legislation in its original form proved relatively easy to avoid and so was amended to catch a number of well-known arrangements[2]. Eventually, the Government tired of the game of 'cat and mouse' and introduced a wholly new charge to income tax, known as the pre-owned asset charge.

1 Finance Act 1986 ss 102–102C.
2 See Finance Act 1986 ss 102B, 102C and 102ZA.

22.35 The pre-owned asset charge is a charge to income tax[1]. It applies where a person has given away property, or has contributed in some way to property, which they occupy or otherwise continue to enjoy. It does not apply where that transaction is otherwise caught by the gift with reservation regime[2] but where it does not, it applies a charge to income tax based upon the benefit enjoyed by the individual. The individual has a choice to elect for the gifts with reservation legislation to apply or to continue to pay the charge to income tax whilst taking the benefit of the property falling outside of the estate[3].

1 Finance Act 2004 s 84 and Sch 15.
2 Finance Act 2004 Sch 15 s 11(5).
3 Finance Act 2004 Sch 15 s 21–23.

22.36 In addition to the above provisions the legislation includes provisions that deem certain transactions to be deemed as one (the Associated Operations provisions[1]) and which ignore certain liabilities, including liabilities that are secured upon excluded property[2]. The General Anti Abuse Rules also apply to inheritance tax[3] though it is yet to be seen how HMRC intends to operate and enforce those rules.

1 Inheritance Tax Act 1984 s 268.
2 Finance Act 1986 s 103.
3 Finance Act 2013 s 206.

PRECEDENTS

22.37

FORM 22.1

Provision for tax burden to be on non-exempt residue[1]

My residuary estate shall be divided equally between [ ], [ ] and [ ].

In order to determine their entitlement the residuary estate shall be divided into equal shares without making any deduction or allowance for the inheritance tax payable by reason of my death and attributable to my residuary estate and then reducing the shares that are not exempt from inheritance tax by the inheritance tax attributable to them.

1 As explained at **22.29–22.30** this is the 'default' provision and ensures that the total amount of inheritance tax is less.

FORM 22.2

Provision for residuary beneficiaries to receive equal amounts (with grossing up of non-exempt shares)[1]

My residuary estate shall be divided equally between [ ], [ ] and [ ] ('the residuary beneficiaries').

The entitlement of the residuary beneficiaries shall be determined by grossing up the shares of those who are not exempt from inheritance tax so that after making any deduction or allowance for the inheritance tax payable by reason of my death and attributable to my residuary estate the residuary beneficiaries shall receive equal shares so that net of inheritance tax the shares actually received by the residuary beneficiaries shall be of equal amounts whether or not any of them is exempt from inheritance tax.

1 As explained at **22.30** this provision appears to be effective but leads to grossing up and substantially more tax being paid.

23 Inheritance Tax Mitigation in Wills

23.1 There is only a limited amount of inheritance tax planning that can sensibly take place within a Will. Truly effective inheritance tax planning requires lifetime planning and consideration and a Will is only a small part of the process. Nevertheless, as this chapter explains there are steps that can be taken within a Will that can avoid or minimise the impact of Inheritance Tax upon an estate.

23.2 Most effective inheritance tax mitigation involving Wills involves the exploitation of the available reliefs or exemptions in inheritance tax together with ensuring that grossing up is avoided. For that reason this chapter considers: (i) the use of gifts of excluded property, particularly where the residue is exempt; (ii) gifts of the nil rate band; and (iii) means to take advantage of the spouse exemption. The use of short-term discretionary trusts is also discussed. It needs to be emphasised that these techniques are among the most common used and for more specialist planning a more specialist work should be consulted.

23.3 We discuss inheritance tax as it applies in particular circumstances in other places in this book. In particular, reference should be had to **chapters 17** and **18** on minors and disabled and vulnerable beneficiaries respectively.

Agricultural and business property[1]

23.4 Property consisting of a business or an interest in a business (including an interest in a partnership) together with the securities of an unquoted company which give the testator control of the business are wholly excluded from inheritance tax[2] provided: (i) the business does not consist wholly or mainly of dealing in securities, stocks or shares, land or buildings or making or holding investments[3] and (ii) the relevant ownership requirements are met[4]. There are some other forms of property that are subject to business relief at 50%[5]. In some cases the value of the business relief is reduced by the value of assets not required for the purposes of the business.

1 Reference should also be made to **chapter 13** where gifts of agricultural and business property and the available reliefs are discussed in some detail.

2 Inheritance Tax Act 1984 ss 104 and 105.

3 Inheritance Tax Act 1984 s 105(3).

4 A period of two years, but with provision for replacement property and property acquired from, for example, a spouse. See ss 106–109A.

5 Essentially, quoted shares and assets used for the purposes of a business but not owned by it, ss 104(1)(b) and 105(1)(cc), (d), (e).

23.5 The agricultural value of agricultural property is wholly excluded from inheritance tax provided the minimum period of ownership or occupation is met[1]. Agricultural property means:

> 'agricultural land or pasture and includes woodland and any building used in connection with the intensive rearing of livestock or fish if the woodland or building is occupied with agricultural land or pasture and the occupation is ancillary to that of the agricultural land or pasture; and also includes such cottages, farm buildings and farmhouses, together with the land occupied with them, as are of a character appropriate to the property.'[2]

It is only the agricultural value of land that is exempt, and so if a building (eg a home) has an element of non-agricultural value (such as its value as a home)[3] then that value is subject to inheritance tax.

1 Inheritance Tax Act 1984 ss 115 to 117. A minimum of two years' occupation or seven years' ownership with provisions for replacement property and property acquired from, for example, a spouse. See Inheritance Tax Act 1984 ss 117 to 121.

2 Inheritance Tax Act 1984 s 115(2). It is also necessary for the interest of the transferor to be that described in s 116(2) (essentially an entitlement to vacant possession or a letting under a modern Farm Business tenancy).

3 The agricultural value of agricultural property means its value if it were subject to a '*perpetual covenant prohibiting its use otherwise than as agricultural property*', s 115(3). So in the case of a house a value would need to be determined as if it could be occupied only for the purposes of agriculture together with its actual value. Only the former value would be exempt.

23.6 It is easy to waste the value of these exemptions, particularly if one or more residuary beneficiary is also exempt (such as a spouse). So agricultural property that passes with the residue of an estate divided between children and widow will reduce the value of the gift to the children but have no effect at all on the gift to the spouse (who receives their share free of tax in any case) and therefore the full value of the exemption will not be obtained. If, however, a specific gift had been made of the agricultural property, perhaps with the residue passing to the spouse alone[1] then the value of the exemption will be maximised.

1 The trusts referred to below at **23.17–23.19** could be used.

23.7 The key to the use of exempt property is, therefore, to include it within a specific gift, preferably to a non-exempt beneficiary. The simplest means to do this is to make a specific gift with reference to the property itself. At **Forms 23.1–23.3** we have given an example of a specific gift with reference to property that meets the description of agricultural or business property. **Chapter 13** and the accompanying forms should also be consulted to help maximise business and/or agricultural relief.

Avoiding grossing up

23.8 As well as ensuring that exemptions are maximised it is important to avoid increasing the amount of inheritance tax paid overall, at least unless that is intentional. Here there are two 'golden rules'. First, wherever the residue is wholly or partially exempt (usually because of gifts to a spouse or to a charity) specific gifts should bear their own inheritance tax. Since most legacies are assumed to be 'free of tax' this means including a specific provision that the gift bear its own tax[1]. Second, unless it is the very specific desire of the testator, the kind of provision that means that residuary beneficiaries receive the same amount of net estate whether or not they are exempt beneficiaries[2] should be avoided as this will cause complicated calculations and, ultimately, result in more tax being payable.

1 As in **Form 10.5**.
2 See **Form 22.1**. The form to avoid is at **Form 22.2**.

Transferable nil rate bands

23.9 Transferable nil rate bands apply only for spouses and civil partners from 9 October 2007. Where a spouse has died before 9 October 2007 the survivor can nonetheless take the first to die's unused nil rate band provided they die after 9 October 2007. In order to obtain the relief it is necessary for the personal representatives of the survivor to make a claim after their death.

23.10 The legislation process is that for the purposes of the statutory transferable nil rate band a person (the first to die) has unused nil-rate band on death if –

$$M > VT$$

where –

M is the maximum that could be transferred by the chargeable transfer made on death (under the Inheritance Tax Act 1984 s 4) on the person's death if it were to be wholly chargeable to tax at the rate of nil per cent; and

VT is the value actually transferred by that chargeable transfer (or nil if there is no such chargeable transfer).

Where a claim is made, the nil rate band maximum at the time of the survivor's death is to be treated for the purposes of the charge to tax on the death of the survivor as increased by the following percentage:

$$(E \div NRBMD) \times 100$$

Where –

E is the amount by which M is greater than VT in the case of the first to die; and

NRBMD is the nil rate band maximum at the time of the death of the first of the couple to die.

The term 'nil rate band maximum' is defined[1] to mean 'the amount shown in the second column in the first row of the Table in Schedule 1 to the Inheritance Tax Act 1984 (upper limit of portion of value charged at rate of nil per cent) and in the first column in the second row of that Table (lower limit of portion charged at next rate)'. This is the figure conventionally known as the nil rate band.

1 By the Inheritance Tax Act 1984 s 8A(7).

23.11 The effect of this is to mean that where a spouse left the whole of their estate to their surviving spouse then, assuming there were no failed potentially exempt transfers, they had a wholly unused nil rate band. On the death of the second spouse their (ie the survivor's) nil rate band will be increased by 100%. That will be so whatever the value of the nil rate band at the death of the first to die. On the other hand, where the nil rate band was partially used (eg by lifetime transfers or by legacies to children) then the percentage of that unused nil rate band will be applied to increase the surviving spouse's nil rate band. So if the nil rate band was only used as to half, the survivor's nil rate band will be increased by half.

23.12 The maximum increase to the nil rate band is 100%. So, whilst a person can rely upon more than one 'unused' nil rate band (for example where they have survived two spouses) they can only do so up to 100%. Neither can a survivor take advantage of their spouse's ability to claim an enhanced nil rate band (so where H marries W and W is a widower whose husband left all to her, it is not possible for H to make use of W's 'double nil rate' band, he can claim one).

23.13 It follows from this that there will still be circumstances where it is useful to include a gift of a nil rate band within a Will since otherwise the full extent of the available exemptions will not be received. In the above example of W, had she made a gift of the nil rate band upon trusts in her Will (and had she sufficient assets to fulfil this gift) then there would effectively be three nil rate bands available on H's death.

Nil rate band gifts

23.14 A gift of the nil rate band might be considered for a number of reasons. First, for the reasons explained above there may be circumstances where such a gift will still be of use in maximising the number of nil rate bands available. Second, a testator may consider making gifts up to the nil rate band, which are therefore tax free, and then gifting the residue to an exempt beneficiary, such as a charity.

23.15 Where this is relevant the testator has various options. The simplest gift is of the nil rate band to non-exempt beneficiaries (eg children) outright. However, for most modest estates a legacy of £325,000 (or £650,000 if two nil rate bands are possible) will leave little or no provision for the survivor. That is why in the days of the nil rate band discretionary trust various forms of trust were devised which (i) gave the nil rate band upon discretionary trusts to persons that included the children and the spouse and (ii) included provision that ensured the legacy was constituted by a loan or charge upon the matrimonial home allowing the survivor to benefit from the assets whilst ensuring they did not form part of their estate.

23.16 If the latter is considered desirable it is suggested that an earlier work is consulted and the old precedents dug out[1]. Otherwise, the options set out in the precedents section of this chapter are likely to be sufficient. They include a precedent for satisfying the nil rate band by promissory note[2].

1 See the Fifth edition at 15.30 et seq.
2 **Form 23.7**.

Life interests and exempt beneficiaries

23.17 A gift to an exempt beneficiary, such as a spouse, is exempt[1]. That is also the case where the gift is upon a life interest to the spouse taking effect immediately after the death of the deceased[2]. A subsequent termination of all or part of that life interest in favour of absolute interests will be a potentially exempt transfer by the spouse and therefore not subject to inheritance tax if the survivor survives for more than seven years (and taxed at a reduced rate if they survive three years). Moreover, if the whole estate is given to that spouse or on qualifying life interests in their favour, then the whole nil rate band will be unused so the survivor will have a double nil rate band available to them[3].

1 See note at **22.22**.

2 The life interest will qualify as an immediate post death interest and so will be treated as a gift of the whole of the property subject to the life interest to the surviving spouse.
3 See note at **22.23**.

23.18 So there is considerable scope for tax avoidance by making a residuary gift to a spouse upon terms that provide they are to have a life interest and which make it possible for that life interest to be terminated in respect of all or part of the trust[1].

1 See **Form 23.8**.

23.19 Some care is needed. To be effective for tax, the gift can be terminated at any time but it is important that there be at least some period during which the life interest has existed if the termination is not to be 'read back' under Inheritance Tax Act 1984 s 144(1). If implemented by way of deed of variation the spouse's interest must last at least two years[1] (and HMRC are suspicious of interests that last only a little longer)[2]. For such planning to be workable it needs to be possible for the survivor to be able to 'give up' on at least a substantial part of her spouse's estate. If claims for a lack of reasonable financial provision are to be avoided it is generally necessary to make the spouse one (but not the only one) of the trustees and to ensure that everyone is aware of – and willing to contemplate – the necessary tax planning.

1 Inheritance Tax Act 1984 s 142(4).
2 See Inheritance Tax Manual paragraph 35095.

Gifts to charities

23.20 In addition to charitable gifts being free from inheritance tax, if a testator leaves a certain percentage of his property to charity (or a registered Community Amateur Sports Club), then his estate may be able to claim a reduced rate of inheritance tax (36%) on the rest of his estate or on a particular component of his estate. This reduced rate and ways to maximise its use is discussed in more detail in **chapter 14** which deals specifically with charities and charitable gifts.

Short term discretionary trusts[1]

23.21 The Inheritance Tax Act 1984 s 144[2] permits dispositions made by trustees out of a discretionary trust less than two years after the testator's death to be read back into the Will. This has enabled Wills to be drafted with considerable flexibility giving an opportunity for the trustees to take stock before making a decision about the manner in which the estate should be distributed.

1 See **Form 23.9**.
2 Set out at **appendix 36.7**.

23.22 The trustees are able to appoint the capital among the beneficiaries so as to produce the best practical result in the circumstances which have emerged at the time of death or shortly afterwards. In theory the trustees are better placed to do this than the testator was because they know the value of the estate, the current inheritance tax rates and the foreseeable requirements of the widow and other beneficiaries. The short-term discretionary trust requires the trustees to exercise their discretion and bring the trust to an end within two years of the death so that the appointments of capital which they make will be treated as dispositions under the Will for inheritance tax purposes. This has disadvantages. It limits the trustees' scope and, for capital gains tax purposes, the recipient acquires the property appointed at its market value at the date of appointment and not at the date of death. There might also be a cash-flow problem during the administration of an estate in which inheritance tax must be paid at an early stage.

23.23 There will often be a strong case for an 'ordinary' discretionary trust[1] even though the discretion may well be exercised within the two-year period. Of course, whatever is appointed to the surviving spouse or civil partner will increase inheritance tax on his or her death whether or not an appointment is made within or outside the two years. Subject to the stance taken by HMRC, the surviving spouse or civil partner should ideally rely on benefits from the discretionary trust and not benefit from an appointment.

1 See **Form 16.18**.

PRECEDENTS

23.24

FORM 23.1

Specific Gift of Agricultural Property – simple form[1]

I GIVE all my share and interest in the farm and business known as [ABC Farm] to those of my children who survive me and attain 25 in equal shares.

1 Great care should always be taken to ensure that the interest in the farm is properly described. Is it held by a partnership, or through a company? See for example *Re Lewis's Will Trusts* [1984] 3 All ER 930 where the testator left a bequest of 'my freehold farms' when he actually owned three quarters of the shares in a company which owned the farm with the result that the gift failed.

FORM 23.2

Specific gift of Business Property together with the balance of the inheritance tax nil-rate band[1]

I GIVE my shares in [X Limited] if they qualify for 100% Business Relief [and the maximum amount which can be given to them under this clause without inheritance tax being payable] to those of my children who survive me and attain 25 in equal shares.

1 This is a form which makes it clear that the property attracting business relief is to form part of the nil rate band gift.

FORM 23.3

Specific Gift of Agricultural or Business Property – by reference to the available relief

I GIVE free of tax to those of my children who survive me and attain 25 in equal shares all of my assets:

(i) That are or would be reduced for the purposes of inheritance tax [by 100%][1] by reason of their meeting the definition of Relevant Business Property in section 105(1) of the Inheritance Tax Act 1984.

(ii) Whose agricultural value would or could be reduced [by 100%][2] by reason of their meeting the definition of Agricultural Property in section 115(2) of the Inheritance Tax Act 1984[3].

1 The words in square brackets would exclude assets that attract only 50% relief, including assets used within the business but not owned by it. To omit it, however, may mean that this gift will attract some taxation. Since it is expressed to be free of tax if the residue is exempt it would therefore have to be grossed up for the purposes of calculating inheritance tax.

2 There are relatively few instances of agricultural property not qualifying for 100% relief. The more limited relief (at 50%) applies in circumstances where the land is let on neither an Agricultural Holding or a Farm Business Tenancy and the owner is not entitled to vacant possession within 12 months. However, the words in square brackets may be desired for the reasons expressed above.

3 Note, as explained above (at **23.5**), it would still be possible for some part of the value of this gift to attract tax because of its non-agricultural value. Therefore, it is possible that some part of this gift could bear tax, with the resulting possibility of grossing up if the reside is exempt. The alternative is to make the gift subject to tax.

FORM 23.4

Gift to children of inheritance tax nil-rate band[1]

(1) I give the maximum amount which can be given to them under this clause without inheritance tax being payable[2] in equal shares to those of my[3] children who survive me [and attain [25]/[18]].

(2) If any of my children die before me his or her children [who attain 21][4] shall take equally the share which their parent would otherwise have inherited.

1 The use of the nil rate band clause has the advantage of avoiding the need to update the Will to accommodate the changes in banding but it has the disadvantage that any change may increase the amount of the legacy beyond that which the testator would wish and so care should be exercised in using a nil rate band clause instead of the current ceiling for the nil rate or a lesser sum. This is especially so where the size of the testator's estate is such as may not justify automatic increases in the legacy. See **Form 23.5** for a capped nil rate legacy.

2 This clause is intended to use the nil rate band. Where the testator has made no lifetime gifts which bite into the nil rate band, the gift under this clause will be the amount of the nil-rate band at the date of death. Where there have been gifts (including PETs) during the seven years preceding death, the legacy will be the amount of the nil rate band less the total of such gifts. The testator should be advised to consult his solicitor or Will draftsman if, at a later date, he contemplates making lifetime gifts because the consequences may require a review of this Will. Care should also be taken if the estate is likely to include agricultural or business property attracting relief at 100%. If so, the nil rate band gift defined by this clause will include all of that property perhaps leaving nothing in residue.

3 This clause refers expressly to the testator's own children as 'my children'. In circumstances in which the clause is used in one of two Wills for a married couple reference could be made to 'our' children. Where there is only one marriage and it is clear to whom the testator is referring the choice between 'my' and 'our' children will ordinarily pass without comment. Where there is more than one marriage the testator's children will always be included within 'my children'. Illegitimate children and adopted children will be included unless expressly excluded – Family Law Reform Act 1987 ss 1 and 19 and Adoption and Children Act 2002 s 67.

4 A gift at 25 will come within Inheritance Tax Act 1984 s 71D, see note at **22.20**.

FORM 23.5

Capped gift of inheritance tax nil-rate band to children[1]

(1) I give the maximum which can be given to them under this clause without inheritance tax becoming payable in respect of this gift [or (the sum of £]/[% of my estate]/[% of my Residue]/[£ increased by the percentage by which the latest available figure of the All Items Index of Retail Prices exceeds that last available before today]) if that is less in equal shares to those of my children who survive me [and attain [25]/[18]].

(2) If any of [my[2]] children dies before me, his or her children [who attain 21] shall take equally the share which their parent would otherwise have inherited.

1 See footnotes to the last precedent. The only difference between this form and the preceding form is the restriction on the gift.

2 See **Form 23.4** footnote 3.

FORM 23.6

Gift on discretionary trust of [capped] inheritance tax nil-rate band in favour of spouse and issue[1]

(1) I give the maximum which can be given to them under this clause without inheritance tax becoming payable in respect of this gift [[or the sum of £]/[% of my estate]/[% of my Residue]/[£ increased by the percentage by which the latest available figure of the All Items Index of Retail Prices exceeds that last available before today] if that is less] to my Trustees on the following trusts.

(2) In this clause the expression 'my beneficiaries' shall mean my spouse and my issue.

(3) My Trustees are to hold the assets of this clause or any other assets representing those assets or otherwise added to this trust ('the Trust Fund') for not more than 125 years ('the Trust Period') after my death to:

- (a) pay or apply the capital of the Trust Fund for the benefit of whichever of my beneficiaries my Trustees think fit;
- (b) pay or apply the income of the Trust Fund for the benefit of whichever of my beneficiaries my Trustees think fit or during the whole of the Trust Period to accumulate such income as is not so applied and to invest that income as an addition to the capital of the Trust Fund;
- (c) not later than 125 years after my death to end the trust by distributing the Trust Fund among whichever of my beneficiaries are then alive in equal shares;
- (d) if these trusts fail hold the Trust Fund on trust for whichever charity my Trustees think fit.

(3) My Trustees may:

- (a) invest or otherwise apply any part of the Trust Fund and vary investments and applications including by making loans [which may be interest-free or at less than a full market rate and may also be linked to the All Items Index of Retail Prices or its replacement] to any beneficiary;
- (b) make retentions to meet any taxes for which they may be liable and pay those taxes and any other expenses of the administration of the Trust Fund out of capital or income;
- (c) not except under subclause (3)(a) or on a distribution of the Trust Fund exercise their powers under this sub-clause so as to create an immediate post-death interest an interest under Inheritance Tax Act 1984 s 71A or 71D or any other interest in possession for a beneficiary.

1 If this gift is to be capped, the words in square brackets in (3)(a) should be included.

FORM 23.7

Clauses enabling use of a promissory note to satisfy the nil-rate band gift

(1) My Trustees may require [the Discretionary Trustees] to accept from them in full or partial satisfaction of [the Trust Fund] a promise on the part of my [wife]/[husband]/[civil partner] to pay [the Trust Fund] on demand or a charge of any part of my Residue with payment when demanded of all or part of [the Trust Fund].

(2) The promise or charge may include whatever terms my Trustees think fit including terms:

(a) relating to the provision of fixed or floating security;

(b) requiring the payment of interest; and

(c) making the sum payable linked to the All Items Index of Retail Prices or any other index.

(3) [The Discretionary Trustees]:

(a) may refrain from calling in or exercising any rights in relation to any sum the subject of the promise or charge for as long as they think fit;

(b) will not be liable for any loss which may occur through the exercise of any power under this clause if my Trustees are unable to make payment in full or any security given becomes inadequate.

(4) The powers given under this clause are exercisable even though [the Discretionary Trustees] and my Trustees are one and the same provided that my [wife]/[husband]/[civil partner] must not be the only trustee in either case.

FORM 23.8

Residue on life interests to spouse – power for the trustee to terminate within the lifetime of the spouse[1]

(1) I give the residue of my estate after the payment of testamentary, funeral and administration expenses to be held by [and [ ] ("my Residuary Trustees") on the following trusts.

(2) My Residuary Trustees are to hold the residuary estate on trust:

(i) Subject to clause (4) below to pay the income thereof to my wife for her life.

(ii) On the termination of the interests at (i) above in equal shares for such of my children as survive me in equal shares provided that if any child or children should die before me leaving children such share as they would have inherited under this clause shall be divided equally between their children.

(3) Notwithstanding the entitlement of my wife to the income of residue my Residuary Trustees (being not less than two in number or a trust corporation) shall have power at their absolute discretion to:

(i) At any time during the life of my wife by deed revoke all or any part of her entitlement to the income with the effect that the capital over which that entitlement existed shall be held upon the trusts at clause 2(ii).

(ii) Apply for the benefit of any person absolutely or contingently entitled thereto the whole or part of the income from any capital to which he is or may become entitled.

(iii) Apply for the benefit of any beneficiary absolutely or contingently entitled thereto the whole or part of the capital to which he is or may become entitled.

1 See note at **23.17–23.19.**

FORM 23.9

Short Term Discretionary Trusts for the benefit of spouse and issue[1]

(1) I give the residue of my estate after the payment of testamentary, funeral and administration expenses to be held by my Trustees on the following trusts.

(2) In this clause the following expressions shall have the following meanings:

(i) 'my beneficiaries' shall mean my spouse and my issue.

(ii) 'The Trust Period' shall mean the period of 125 years after my death.

(3) My Trustees are to hold the residuary estate on such trusts to or for the benefit of my beneficaries as they shall by deed or deeds appoint at any time within the period of two years after my death (but no sooner than three months after my death)[2].

(4) Such appointment may be in any term or terms whatsoever PROVIDED THAT:

(i) Such appointment must cause the trust to end or the interests in the capital of the Trust Fund to be vested within the Trust Period and shall not permit any further appointment or appointments in breach of this rule.

(ii) No appointment shall prejudice or affect any prior appointment or other payment.

(5) In default of any such appointment the residue of my estate shall be held equally for those of my spouse and my children as survive me in equal shares.

1 See note at **23.21**.

2 An appointment made within three months will not be 'read back' for the purposes of the Inheritance Tax Act 1984 s 144(1).

24 Complete Wills

24.1 As in previous editions, the Complete Wills are divided into five common situations, the purpose and effect of each of which is described where they occur. In this edition each of these cases is considered in a separate chapter. The five situations are:

- single adults (**chapter 25**);
- married couples or civil partners with no children (**chapter 26**);
- married couples or civil partners with children (**chapter 27**);
- unmarried couples with children (**chapter 28**); and
- second marriages or civil partnerships (**chapter 29**).

24.2 In addition to those five categories, this chapter sets out two examples of non-dispositive Will forms and two examples of a codicil. The two non-dispositive 'complete' Wills are provided to illustrate how the essential elements of each should appear without the complication of dispositive provisions interfering. As in the previous edition, one of these incorporates the standard provisions of the Society of Trust and Estate Practitioners[1] (STEP) while the other does not. Both do the same job but in different ways. These forms (**Forms 24.1** and **24.2**) show that incorporation of the STEP standard provisions provides a useful shorthand for Will draftsmen but, as pointed out at **19.44**, if a practitioner is to incorporate the STEP standard provisions, no additional powers should be incorporated without exercising great care. Thus, it would be inappropriate to include express provision for trustee charging and exoneration when those matters are already dealt with by the standard provisions. However, the Will draftsman should also take care in including non-administrative powers (such as powers of maintenance and advancement). This is because the STEP provisions contain a mix of dispositive and administrative powers.

1 The STEP standard provisions are available online at www.step.org, as is the clause recommended by STEP for the incorporation of the STEP standard provisions.

24.3 There are disadvantages in using the STEP standard provisions. Not all practitioners are familiar with their terms and it is all too easy to incorporate terms which might conflict with those expressly set out in the Will. There is the further problem that incorporation of powers by reference can lead to uncertainty (real or imagined) as to what powers are in fact available. Lay trustees in particular prefer to see their powers clearly set out in the Will than to have to look elsewhere to discover what they can and cannot do. This is, of course, true both of the STEP provisions and a reliance on statute and the general law.

24.4 As in the previous edition, the Will's date appears at the end. There is then less chance of the date being overlooked if it is inserted immediately before the signatures are made on the same page. The testator ought to have read through the Will and be happy with it. If it is desired **Form 4.2** contains an opening to a Will which contains the date at the start rather than the end.

24.5 While the Wills contained in this chapter and in the subsequent five chapters can be seen as largely 'complete' Wills with all the necessary provisions as to opening, dispositive provisions, administrative provisions and attestation it is emphasised that these should only be used as a guideline and must be amended and altered to reflect the personal circumstances and wishes of the testator. In particular, while the precedents may contain lists of trustee powers which are likely to be suitable to the circumstances these powers should be considered carefully to ensure they are appropriate in the circumstances and do not need to be removed or added to.

PRECEDENTS

24.6

Non-dispositive Will forms

Form 24.1 Non-dispositive clauses of complete Will incorporating STEP provisions

Form 24.2 Non-dispositive clauses of complete Will in the longer form

Codicil

Form 24.3 Codicil

Form 24.4 Codicil revoking nil rate band legacy

FORM 24.1

Non-dispositive clauses of complete Will incorporating STEP provisions[1]

I, [*full name*] of [*home address*] revoke all earlier Wills and declare this to be my last Will.

1. I appoint as my executor my [wife/husband/civil partner] [*name*] of [*address*] but if [he/she] is unable or unwilling to act or if [he/she] dies before proving my Will I appoint as my executors those of my children who survive me.

2. I appoint as my trustees those of my executors who obtain probate of this Will and in this Will the expression 'my Trustees' means (as the context requires) those of my executors who obtained probate and the trustees for the time being of any trust arising under this Will.

3. I give the following legacies free of inheritance tax:

   [(a) …

   [(b) …]

4. I give the rest of my property to my Trustees to hold my estate on trust for sale with power to postpone sale to pay executorship expenses and debts including mortgages secured on real or leasehold property and any inheritance tax in respect of property passing under this Will or which becomes payable because of my death on any lifetime transfer by me or payable because of my death on property in which I hold a beneficial interest as joint tenant.

5. My Trustees shall hold the residue of my estate ('my residuary estate') on trust … [*Insert dispositive provisions here*].

6. [The Standard Provisions of the Society of Trust and Estate Practitioners Second Edition shall apply to this Will and the trusts created under it][2].

As Witness my hand this [--] day of [--------] 20[--]. [*Testator's Signature*]

Signed by the Testator in our presence and attested by us in the presence of the Testator and of each other.

[*Signatures, Addresses and Occupation of Witnesses*]

1 This form does not actually do anything other than appoint executors/trustees and give the estate to them to hold on the trusts of clause 4. It is merely an example.

2 If desired this clause could be amended to include some or all of the Special Provisions as well as the Standard Provisions. See **Form 19.20**.

FORM 24.2

Non-dispositive clauses of complete Will in the longer form[1]

I, [*full name*] of [*home address*] revoke all earlier Wills and declare this to be my last Will.

1. I appoint as my executor my [wife/husband/civil partner] [*name*] of [*address*] but if [he/she] is unable or unwilling to act or if [he/she] dies before proving my Will I appoint as my executors those of my children who survive me.

2. I appoint as my trustees those of my executors who obtain probate of this Will and in this Will the expression 'my Trustees' means (as the context requires) those of my executors who obtained probate and the trustees for the time being of any trust arising under this Will.

3. I give the following legacies free of inheritance tax:

   [(a) …

   [(b) …].

4. I give the rest of my property to my Trustees to hold my estate on trust for sale with power to postpone sale to pay executorship expenses and debts including mortgages secured on real or leasehold property and any inheritance tax in respect of property passing under this Will or which becomes payable because of my death on any lifetime transfer by me or payable because of my death on property in which I hold a beneficial interest as joint tenant.

5. My Trustees shall hold the residue of my estate ('my residuary estate') on trust … [*Insert dispositive provisions here*].

6. My Trustees shall have power[2]:

   (1) to apply for the benefit of any beneficiary who has a contingent interest the whole or any part of the income from any capital to which he may become entitled;

   (2) during the whole of the period in which a beneficiary has a contingent interest to accumulate such income as is not so applied and to invest that income as an addition to the capital of the share to which that beneficiary is entitled;

   (3) to pay or apply for the benefit of any beneficiary who has a contingent interest the whole or any part of the capital to which he may become entitled;

   (4) to pay any money to which a beneficiary under eighteen is entitled to his parent or guardian for his benefit or to the beneficiary himself once he has attained sixteen and to rely upon the receipt then given by the parent or guardian or the minor himself.

7. My Trustees shall have the following powers in addition to their powers under the general law[3]:

   (1) Power to invest as if they were beneficially entitled and this power includes the right:

      (a) to invest in unsecured loans;

      (b) to invest in other non-income producing assets including policies of life assurance;

      (c) to purchase land anywhere in the world;

      (d) to purchase an undivided share in land;

      (e) to invest in land for the occupation or enjoyment of any beneficiary.

   (2) Power to delegate their powers of investment and management of trust property to an agent (including one of their number) on such terms including terms enabling the agent to charge remuneration, to appoint a substitute, to limit liability and to act in circumstances giving rise to a conflict of interest as my Trustees think fit.

   (3) Power to appoint any person (including one of their number or a beneficiary) to act as their nominee and to take such steps as are necessary to vest any property in such person on such terms including terms enabling the agent to charge remuneration, to appoint a substitute, to limit liability and to act in circumstances giving rise to a conflict of interest as my Trustees think fit.

   (4) Power to make loans of capital to a beneficiary which may be interest free, repayable on demand or repayable at a rate below the market rate.

   (5) Power to borrow money on such terms as they think fit including the giving of security and to use it for any purpose for which the capital of my estate may be used.

   (6) Power without the restrictions imposed by Administration of Estates Act 1925 s 41:

      (a) To appropriate to any beneficiary in satisfaction or partial satisfaction of the gift to him any asset forming part of my residuary estate and not subject to a specific gift.

      (b) To appropriate as the assets or part of the assets of any trust created by this Will any asset forming part of my residuary estate and not subject to a specific gift.

8. (1) My Trustees shall exercise their powers of investment and carry out their duties as trustees without regard to the statutory duty of care and the Trustee Act 2000 s 1 shall not apply to the trusts of my Will[4].

   (2) My Trustees shall be under no duty to review the acts of agents, nominees and custodians appointed by them and Trustee Act 2000 s 22 shall not apply to the trusts of my Will[5].

   (3) Section 11 Trusts of Land and Appointment of Trustees Act 1996 (consultation with beneficiaries) shall not apply[6].

(4) In the absence of proof of dishonesty or the wilful commission of an act known to be a breach of trust none of my Trustees shall be liable for any loss or bound to take proceedings against a co-trustee for any breach of trust.

(5) My Trustees shall be entitled to be indemnified out of the assets of my estate against all liabilities incurred in connection with the bona fide execution of their duties and powers.

As Witness my hand this [--] day of [--------] 20[--]. [*Testator's Signature*]

Signed by the Testator in our presence and attested by us in the presence of the Testator and of each other.

[*Signatures, Addresses and Occupation of Witnesses*]

1 This form does not actually do anything other than appoint executors/trustees and give the estate to them to hold on the trusts of clause 4. It is merely an example.

2 All of these powers are used by way of example and in each situation it may or may not be appropriate to include any individual power. For a general discussion of trustees' powers see **chapter 19**.

3 See footnote 2 above.

4 See note at **19.30**.

5 See note at **19.15–19.29**.

6 See note at **19.38**.

FORM 24.3

Codicil

I, [*full name*] of [*home address*] make this [*first*] Codicil to my Will dated [*date*].

1. I REVOKE [AB]'s appointment as one of my Executors and Trustees and appoint [EF] in his place to act jointly with my other Executors and Trustees.

2. In Clause [4] of my Will the gift of '£[x]' is to be replaced by '£[y] increased by the percentage by which the latest available figure of the All Items Index of Retail Prices exceeds that last available before today'[1].

3. In all other respects I confirm my Will.

As Witness my hand this [--] day of [--------] 20[--]. [*Testator's Signature*]

Signed by the Testator in our presence and attested by us in the presence of the Testator and of each other.

[*Signatures, Addresses and Occupation of Witnesses*]

1 This is, of course, only an example.

FORM 24.4

Codicil revoking nil rate band legacy

I, [*full name*] of [*home address*] make this [*first*] Codicil to my Will dated [*date*].

1. I revoke Clause […] of my Will by which I give to my trustees [the maximum which can be given to them under that clause without inheritance tax becoming payable in respect of the gift] to hold on the discretionary trusts set out in that clause[1].

2. In all other respects I confirm my Will.

As Witness my hand this [--] day of [--------] 20[--]. [*Testator's Signature*]

Signed by the Testator in our presence and attested by us in the presence of the Testator and of each other.

[*Signatures, Addresses and Occupation of Witnesses*]

1 This is, of course, only an example. In this example the testator revokes the nil rate band discretionary trust created by his Will. This is appropriate where the residue passes to the spouse and a nil rate band trust was inserted in each Will for inheritance tax saving purposes. This ensures that the nil rate band is not used up (other than in respect of other pecuniary legacies) so that the unused nil rate band will be available to augment the testator's spouse's nil rate band on his or her death.

25 Single adults

25.1 The single adult might be a bachelor, a spinster, a widow, a widower or one half of an unmarried or homosexual couple who have not married or formed a civil partnership. Each of these situations is different but the appropriate Will is often very similar whichever category a person falls into. Most intend to make provision for another adult or for other adults including, for example, their siblings, and many wish to include gifts in favour of charity. Every single adult should be reminded that unless their Will indicates that it is made in contemplation of marriage (or civil partnership) it will be revoked by the marriage (or civil partnership). **Forms 25.1** to **25.4** cater for single adults and require no further explanation.

PRECEDENTS

25.2

Wills for single adults

Form 25.1 Single adult leaving everything to a single adult who is appointed executor

Form 25.2 Single adult leaving everything to a single adult who is appointed executor with gift over on beneficiary predeceasing testator

Form 25.3 Will giving residue to nephews and nieces with funeral arrangement, specific gifts and legacies

Form 25.4 Will of widow or widower in favour of children with specific and pecuniary legacies

FORM 25.1

Will of single adult leaving everything to a single adult who is appointed executor[1]

I, [*full name*] of [*home address*] revoke all earlier Wills and declare this to be my last Will.

[This Will is made expecting to [*marry*] [*form a civil partnership*] with [*name*] and is not to be revoked by this [*marriage*]/[*civil partnership*] taking place.][2]

1. I appoint [AB] of [*address*] as my sole executor [but if [he]/[she] is unable or unwilling to act or if [he]/[she] dies before proving my Will I appoint [CD] of [*address*] as my executor][3].
2. I GIVE all my real and personal property to [AB] absolutely [if [he]/[she] survives me by 30 days and if [he]/[she] does not survive me by 30 days my executor shall apply the whole of my estate for whatever charitable purposes my executor thinks fit][4].

As Witness my hand this [--] day of [--------] 20[--]. [*Testator's Signature*]

Signed by the Testator in our presence and attested by us in the presence of the Testator and of each other.

[*Signatures, Addresses and Occupation of Witnesses*]

1 It is unwise for the testator to give the whole of his estate to a single beneficiary without some long-stop provision. There is the possibility of including a survivorship condition with a general gift over to charity by using the words in square brackets at the end of clause 2.

2 Unless the Will is made in expectation of marriage/civil partnership it will be revoked by any subsequent marriage or civil partnership. If the single adult is in a long-term relationship this point needs to be emphasised and it may be that the single adult wishes to put in such a clause to cater for a future marriage. See note at **4.7**.

3 If there are children then usually all the children or none should be appointed executors. It can be divisive to do otherwise unless a child has asked or agreed not to act. In the case of a large family, the three eldest children can be appointed jointly with the other spouse with the fourth child being

substituted for the first to die on the second death. In the case of a single adult with no children the formula adopted in this form is common.

4 Unless the specific circumstances of the testator require it a Will in such simple terms does not really need the inclusion of express powers whether set out in the Will or incorporated by reference. If powers are desired the 'Standard Provisions of the Society of Trust and Estate Practitioners' (2nd edition) are likely to be suitable and could be incorporated. Alternatively the powers set out in clauses 6 to 8 of **Form 24.2** could be incorporated but many of them are quite unnecessary in this situation.

FORM 25.2

Will of single adult leaving everything to a single adult who is appointed executor with gift over only on beneficiary predeceasing testator[1]

I, [*full name*] of [*home address*] revoke all earlier Wills and declare this to be my last Will.

[This Will is made expecting to [*marry*] [*form a civil partnership*] with [*name*] and is not to be revoked by this [*marriage*]/[*civil partnership*] taking place.][2]

1. I appoint [AB] of [*address*] as my sole executor [but if [he]/[she] is unable or unwilling to act or if [he]/[she] dies before proving my Will I appoint [CD] of [*address*] as my executor].

2. I give all my real and personal property to [AB] absolutely if [he]/[she] survives me[3].

3. If the gift made by clause 2 of this Will fails I give all my real and personal property to [CD] if [he]/[she] survives me[4].

4. If the gift made by clause 3 of this Will also fails I give all my real and personal property to my personal representatives for whatever charitable purposes they think fit[5].

As Witness my hand this [--] day of [--------] 20[--]. [*Testator's Signature*]

Signed by the Testator in our presence and attested by us in the presence of the Testator and of each other.

[*Signatures, Addresses and Occupation of Witnesses*]

1 It is unwise for the testator to give the whole of his estate to a single beneficiary without some long-stop provision.

2 Unless the Will is made in expectation of marriage/civil partnership it will be revoked by any subsequent marriage or civil partnership. If the single adult is in a long-term relationship this point needs to be emphasised and it may be that the single adult wishes to put in such a clause to cater for a future marriage. See note at **4.7**.

3 This form could include a survivorship condition by including here the words 'by [30 days]/[six months]' (see **16.4–16.12**). Where a testator intends to leave the whole of his estate to an individual there is usually no requirement.

4 See footnote 3 above.

5 There is no point in directing that the executor is to decide in these circumstances because the executor [CD] will be dead. As to powers, see footnote 3 to the previous form.

FORM 25.3

Will giving residue to nephews and nieces with funeral arrangement, specific gifts and legacies

I, [*full name*] of [*home address*] revoke all earlier Wills and declare this to be my last Will.

1. I appoint as my executors my nephew [AB] and my niece [CD] and in this Will the expression 'my Trustees' means (as the context requires) my executors and the trustees for the time being of any trust arising under this Will.

2. I wish my funeral service to be held at [ ]. [I direct that my funeral shall be undertaken by [ ] of [*address*] with whom I have deposited money for my funeral expenses [*under plan number #*].][1]

3. I give my jewellery and articles of personal use or adornment to my niece [CD].

4. I give to my Trustees all other personal chattels as defined by the Administration of Estates Act 1925 s 55(1)(x) to be distributed among those of my nephews and nieces who survive me as my Trustees shall think fit and without imposing any binding obligation I direct that my Trustees shall endeavour to share them (as nearly as possible) equally having regard to their nature and value[2].

5. I give:

   (1) £[ ] to my goddaughter [MN];

   (2) £1,000 to [*name of charity*] [registered under Charity No.] ('the charity'). The receipt of a person who [is] [appears to be] a proper officer of the charity shall be a full discharge to my Trustees[3].

6. I give all the rest of my property to my Trustees to hold my estate on trust for sale with power to postpone sale to pay executorship expenses and debts including mortgages secured on real or leasehold property and any inheritance tax in respect of property passing under this Will or which becomes payable because of my death on any lifetime transfer by me or payable because of my death on property in which I hold a beneficial interest as joint tenant.

7. My Trustees shall hold the residue of my estate on trust for those of my nephews and nieces who survive me in equal shares.

[8. *Powers*[4]]

As Witness my hand this [--] day of [--------] 20[--]. *[Testator's Signature]*

Signed by the Testator in our presence and attested by us in the presence of the Testator and of each other.

[Signatures, Addresses and Occupation of Witnesses

1 See notes at **chapter 7** regarding funeral wishes.
2 This is taken from **Form 12.18**. See the note at **12.9–12.11**. A gift in these terms does not include

a gift over into residue. If the trustees cannot distribute the chattels in specie they will have to sell and divide the proceeds of sale.

3 This is an example of a simple pecuniary legacy to a single charity taken from **Form 14.3**. Further examples of charitable legacies are contained in **chapter 14**.

4 In a simple case such as that contemplated by this Will then unless the specific circumstances of the testator require it there is no compelling reason to set out express dispositive and administrative powers. This is so even where one or more of the nephews or nieces may be a minor for in such a case the statutory powers under the Trustee Act 1925 and Trustee Act 2000 ought to suffice but there is likely to be little harm in taking in either the STEP standard provisions by incorporation (as in **Form 24.1**) or express powers (as in clauses 6 to 8 of **Form 24.2**).

FORM 25.4

Will of widow or widower in favour of children or their spouses or, alternatively, the grandchildren with specific and pecuniary legacies

I, [*full name*] of [*home address*] revoke all earlier Wills and declare this to be my last Will

1. I appoint as my executors and trustees my son [AB] and my daughter [CD] and in this Will the expression 'my Trustees' means (as the context requires) my executors and the trustees for the time being of any trust arising under this Will.

2. I give to my nephew the Georgian table which is kept in my study and which has belonged to members of my family for over 167[1] years.

3. I give the following legacies:

    (1) £1,000 to each of my grandchildren living at my death [who attains the age of 21 years][2];

    (2) £10,000 to my sister [FG];

    (3) £500 each to:

        (a) [LN] of [*address*];

        (b) [PQ] of [address];

        (c) [RS] of [address].

    (4) £[ ] to [*name of charity*] [registered under Charity No.] ('the charity'). It is my wish without creating a binding obligation on the charity that this gift is used for [*(its projects in Ethiopia) (its education work with girls) (its research into bowel cancer)*]. The receipt of a person who [is] [appears to be] a proper officer of the charity shall be a full discharge to my Trustees. If for whatever reason the charity has ceased to exist or is otherwise unidentifiable and this gift is liable to fail for this reason this gift shall not fail but take effect as a gift to my Trustees who shall divide the gift in such shares as they see fit and pay it to the charity or charities which they in their sole discretion consider most nearly fulfils the objects I intended to benefit[3].

4. I give all the rest of my property to my Trustees to hold my estate on trust for sale with power to postpone sale to pay executorship expenses and debts including mortgages secured on real or leasehold property

and any inheritance tax in respect of property passing under this Will or which becomes payable because of my death on any lifetime transfer by me or payable because of my death on property in which I hold a beneficial interest as joint tenant.

5. My Trustees shall hold the residue of my estate on trust for those of my children who survive me in equal shares and if any of my children dies before me [his or her spouse [or civil partner][4]] / [his or her children shall take equally [upon attaining 21] the share which their parent would otherwise have inherited] shall take the share of my estate which my deceased child would otherwise have inherited.

6. My Trustees shall have power[5]:

   (1) to apply for the benefit of any beneficiary who has a contingent interest the whole or any part of the income from any capital to which he may become entitled;

   (2) during the whole of the period in which a beneficiary has a contingent interest to accumulate such income as is not so applied and to invest that income as an addition to the capital of the share to which that beneficiary is entitled[6];

   (3) to pay or apply for the benefit of any beneficiary who has a contingent interest the whole or any part of the capital to which he may become entitled;

   (4) to pay any money to which a beneficiary under eighteen is entitled to his parent or guardian for his benefit or to the beneficiary himself once he has attained sixteen and to rely upon the receipt then given by the parent or guardian or the minor himself.

7. My Trustees shall have the following powers in addition to their powers under the general law:

   (1) Power to invest as if they were beneficially entitled and this power includes the right:

      (a) to invest in unsecured loans;

      (b) to invest in other non-income producing assets including policies of life assurance;

      (c) to purchase land anywhere in the world;

      (d) to purchase an undivided share in land;

      (e) to invest in land for the occupation or enjoyment of any beneficiary.

   (2) Power to delegate their powers of investment and management of trust property to an agent (including one of their number) on such terms including terms enabling the agent to charge remuneration, to appoint a substitute, to limit liability and to act in circumstances giving rise to a conflict of interest as my Trustees think fit.

   (3) Power to appoint any person (including one of their number or a beneficiary) to act as their nominee and to take such steps as are necessary to vest any property in such person on such terms including terms enabling the agent to charge remuneration, to

appoint a substitute, to limit liability and to act in circumstances giving rise to a conflict of interest as my Trustees think fit.

(4) Power to make loans of capital to a beneficiary which may be interest free, repayable on demand or repayable at a rate below the market rate.

(5) Power to borrow money on such terms as they think fit including the giving of security and to use it for any purpose for which the capital of my estate may be used.

(6) Power without the restrictions imposed by the Administration of Estates Act 1925 s 41:

(a) To appropriate to any beneficiary in satisfaction or partial satisfaction of the gift to him any asset forming part of my residuary estate and not subject to a specific gift.

(b) To appropriate as the assets or part of the assets of any trust created by this Will any asset forming part of my residuary estate and not subject to a specific gift.

8. (1) My Trustees shall exercise their powers of investment and carry out their duties as trustees without regard to the statutory duty of care and the Trustee Act 2000 s 1 shall not apply to the trusts of my Will.

(2) My Trustees shall be under no duty to review the acts of agents, nominees and custodians appointed by them and the Trustee Act 2000 s 22 shall not apply to the trusts of my Will.

(3) Section 11 of the Trusts of Land and Appointment of Trustees Act 1996 (consultation with beneficiaries) shall not apply.

(4) In the absence of an act or omission involving wilful fraud or dishonesty by the trustee in question none of my [lay][7] Trustees [(as defined by the Trustee Act 2000 s 28)] shall be liable for any loss caused to my estate or any trust created under my Will or bound to take proceedings against a co-trustee for any breach of trust.

(5) My Trustees shall be entitled to be indemnified out of the assets of my estate against all liabilities incurred in connection with the bona fide execution of their duties and powers.

As Witness my hand this [--] day of [--------] 20[--]. [*Testator's Signature*]

Signed by the Testator in our presence and attested by us in the presence of the Testator and of each other.

[*Signatures, Addresses and Occupation of Witnesses*]

1 In keeping with tradition this table has aged in accordance with this book. In the previous edition this table was in the family for 167 years and prior to that, 159 years. It has not been moved since the first (or possibly second) edition of this book. Long may it continue in family ownership!

2 The use of an age contingency at 21 years in both clause 3(1) and clause 5 is no longer necessary as an upper limit because the Perpetuities and Accumulations Act 2009 has introduced a single perpetuity period of 125 years. In the case of clause 3(1) this could never have been a problem provided that the legacies were payable only to those living at the testator's death (which is obviously the most sensible approach). The residuary gift at clause 5 is absolute and immediate in the first instance and, once again, it only contemplates a gift over to grandchildren in existence at the date of the testator's death. Most testators will want to delay the vesting in possession of

a grandchild's interest in a legacy or in residue to a point at which that grandchild might have developed sufficient maturity to cope with the gift. The selection of 21 years as the appropriate age is arbitrary but popular. This does mean, however, that the trustees will have to hold on to a fund to satisfy the gift when the grandchild attains the specified age.

3 This clause is adapted from **Form 14.5**. Further examples of charitable legacies are contained in **chapter 14**.

4 Where civil partners are intended to be included an express inclusion is required since 'spouse' does not include 'civil partner'.

5 These powers at clauses 6 to 8 are taken from **Form 24.2**.

6 The Perpetuities and Accumulations Act 2009 has removed the statutory restrictions on accumulations so that this power may be expressed even if the specified age in clause 5 is an age in excess of 21 years.

7 If the limitation is intended to cover both lay and professional trustees then the words in square brackets should be removed. However, for obvious reasons the testator usually only wishes to restrict liability in relation to lay trustees who are much more likely to be friends or family members.

26 Wills for Married Couples or Civil Partners with no Children

26.1 The case of a married couple or civil partners with no children is similar to that of an individual in many respects. There is usually one principal adult beneficiary (the spouse or civil partner) and then there may be additional pecuniary legacies or substitutional gifts in favour of siblings, friends and charity. If the whole of the estate of the first to die is left to the survivor the nil rate band of the first to die will be unused and the survivor will be entitled to a nil rate band enhanced by 100%. This is more fully discussed in **chapters 22**[1] and **23**[2]. **Forms 26.1** and **26.2** cater for married couples and civil partners with no children but **Forms 25.1–25.4** could easily be adapted to cater for this situation.

1 See notes at **22.23–22.25**.
2 See notes at **23.9–23.19**.

PRECEDENTS

26.2

Wills for married couples or civil partners with no children

Form 26.1 Will in favour of surviving spouse or civil partner with substitutional gift to brothers, sisters, brothers-in-law and sisters-in-law

Form 26.2 Will leaving spouse or civil partner life interest in the entire estate with remainder to brothers, sisters, brothers-in-law and sisters-in-law

FORM 26.1

Will in favour of surviving spouse or civil partner with substitutional gift to brothers, sisters, brothers-in-law and sisters-in-law

I, [*full name*] of [*home address*] revoke all earlier Wills and declare this to be my last Will.

1. I appoint my [wife]/[husband]/[civil partner] [AB] as my sole [executrix]/[executor] or if [she]/[he] is unable or unwilling to act or dies before proving my Will I appoint my brother [JC] and my sister-in-law [VL] as my executors and trustees.

2. If [she]/[he] survives me I give the whole of my estate to my [wife]/[husband]/[civil partner] absolutely[1].

3. If the gift at clause 2 fails then I give all my property to my Trustees to hold my estate on trust for sale with power to postpone sale to pay executorship expenses and debts including mortgages secured on real or leasehold property and any inheritance tax in respect of property passing under this Will or which becomes payable because of my death on any lifetime transfer by me or payable because of my death on property in which I hold a beneficial interest as joint tenant. My Trustees shall hold the residue of my estate:

   (1) As to one half for those of my brothers and sisters who survive me in equal shares and if any of them dies before me his or her children shall take per stirpes the share of my estate which their parent would otherwise have inherited;

   (2) As to the other half for those of my [wife's]/[husband's]/[civil partner's] brothers and sisters who survive me in equal shares and if any of them dies before me his or her children shall take per stirpes the share of my estate which their parent would otherwise have inherited.

[4. *Powers*[2]]

As Witness my hand this [--] day of [--------] 20[--]. [*Testator's Signature*]

Signed by the Testator in our presence and attested by us in the presence of the Testator and of each other.

[*Signatures, Addresses and Occupation of Witnesses*]

1 The inclusion of a survivorship condition is now likely to be of no effect or even detrimental where the gift is in favour of a surviving spouse because of the transferability of the nil rate band (discussed in **chapter 22** and **chapter 23**). However, if the survivor's Will is not in reciprocal terms or the surviving spouse has an enhanced nil rate band by virtue of a previous marriage there will be some justification for including the survivorship condition. In the previous edition the survivorship condition appears in the following terms:

'If [she]/[he] survives me by [30 days]/[six months] I give the whole of my estate to my [wife]/[husband]/[civil partner] absolutely'.

2 In a simple case such as that contemplated by this Will then unless the special circumstances of the testator require it there is no compelling reason to set out express dispositive and administrative powers. However, where the primary beneficiaries under clause 3 die, the nephews and nieces (or nephews-in-law and nieces-in-law) might include minors. In such a case the statutory powers under the Trustee Act 1925 and the Trustee Act 2000 ought to suffice but there is likely to be little harm in taking in either the STEP standard provisions by incorporation (as in **Form 24.1**), or express powers (as in **Form 24.2**).

FORM 26.2

Will leaving spouse or civil partner life interest in the entire estate with remainder to brothers, sisters, brothers-in-law and sisters-in-law[1]

I, [*full name*] of [*home address*] revoke all earlier Wills and declare this to be my last Will.

1. (1) I appoint my [wife]/[husband]/[civil partner] [AB] and the partners at my death in the firm of [ ] ('the Firm') as my executors and trustees and in this Will the expression 'my Trustees' means (as the context requires) my executors and the trustees for the time being of any trust arising under this Will.

(2) In this clause:

(a) The expression 'the Firm' means not only [*name*] but any other firm which at my death has succeeded to and carries on its practice including a firm which has been incorporated or has formed a limited liability partnership; and

(b) The expression 'partners' means the persons commonly described as partners in the Firm including salaried partners and, in the case of an incorporated practice or limited liability partnership, the directors, members and beneficial owners of any share of the Firm.

(3) I wish my [wife]/[husband]/[civil partner] and not more than [one] of the partners in the Firm to apply for probate of this Will.

(4) If my [wife]/[husband]/[civil partner] is unable or unwilling to act or dies before proving my Will I appoint my brother [JC] as executor in her place to act with the partners in the Firm.

(5) Any of my Trustees who is a solicitor may charge fees for work done by him or his firm (whether or not the work is of a professional nature) on the same basis as if he were not one of my Trustees but employed to carry out the work on their behalf.

2. I give to my [wife]/[husband]/[civil partner] my personal chattels as defined by the Administration of Estates Act 1925 s 55(1)(x)[2].

3. If my [wife]/[husband]/[civil partner] does not survive me[3] I give legacies of £500 to each of my nephews and nieces and to each of the nephews and nieces of my [wife]/[husband]/[civil partner].

4. I give the rest of my property to my Trustees to hold my estate on trust for sale with power to postpone sale to pay executorship expenses and debts including mortgages secured on real or leasehold property and any inheritance tax in respect of property passing under this Will or which becomes payable because of my death on any lifetime transfer by me or payable because of my death on property in which I hold a beneficial interest as joint tenant.

5. My Trustees shall hold the residue of my estate ('my residuary estate') on trust to pay the income from my residuary estate to my [wife]/[husband]/[civil partner] during [her]/[his] lifetime with power to pay or apply the whole or any part of the capital of my residuary estate for the benefit of my [wife]/[husband]/[civil partner][4] and subject to any exercise of that power after [her]/[his] death:

   (1) as to one half of my residuary estate in equal shares to those of my brothers and sisters who survive me in equal shares and if any of them dies before me his or her children shall take per stirpes the share of my estate which their parent would otherwise have inherited[5];

   (2) as to the other half of my estate to those of my [wife's]/[husband's]/[civil partner's] brothers and sisters who survive me in equal shares and if any of them dies before me his or her children shall take per stirpes the share of my estate which their parent would otherwise have inherited[6].

6. My Trustees shall have power[7]:

   (1) to apply for the benefit of any beneficiary who has a contingent interest the whole or any part of the income from any capital to which he may become entitled;

   (2) during the whole of the period in which a beneficiary has a contingent interest to accumulate such income as is not so applied and to invest that income as an addition to the capital of the share to which that beneficiary is entitled;

   (3) to pay or apply for the benefit of any beneficiary who has a contingent interest the whole or any part of the capital to which he may become entitled;

   (4) to pay any money to which a beneficiary under eighteen is entitled to his parent or guardian for his benefit or to the beneficiary himself once he has attained sixteen and to rely upon the receipt then given by the parent or guardian or the minor himself.

7. My Trustees shall have the following powers in addition to their powers under the general law:

   (1) Power to invest as if they were beneficially entitled and this power includes the right:

      (a) to invest in unsecured loans;

(b) to invest in other non-income producing assets including policies of life assurance;

(c) to purchase land anywhere in the world;

(d) to purchase an undivided share in land;

(e) to invest in land for the occupation or enjoyment of any beneficiary.

(2) Power to delegate their powers of investment and management of trust property to an agent (including one of their number) on such terms including terms enabling the agent to charge remuneration, to appoint a substitute, to limit liability and to act in circumstances giving rise to a conflict of interest as my Trustees think fit.

(3) Power to appoint any person (including one of their number or a beneficiary) to act as their nominee and to take such steps as are necessary to vest any property in such person on such terms including terms enabling the agent to charge remuneration, to appoint a substitute, to limit liability and to act in circumstances giving rise to a conflict of interest as my Trustees think fit.

(4) Power to make loans of capital to a beneficiary which may be interest free, repayable on demand or repayable at a rate below the market rate.

(5) Power to borrow money on such terms as they think fit including the giving of security and to use it for any purpose for which the capital of my estate may be used.

(6) Power without the restrictions imposed by the Administration of Estates Act 1925 s 41:

(a) To appropriate to any beneficiary in satisfaction or partial satisfaction of the gift to him any asset forming part of my residuary estate and not subject to a specific gift.

(b) To appropriate as the assets or part of the assets of any trust created by this Will any asset forming part of my residuary estate and not subject to a specific gift.

8. (1) My Trustees shall exercise their powers of investment and carry out their duties as trustees without regard to the statutory duty of care and the Trustee Act 2000 s 1 shall not apply to the trusts of my Will.

(2) My Trustees shall be under no duty to review the acts of agents, nominees and custodians appointed by them and the Trustee Act 2000 s 22 shall not apply to the trusts of my Will.

(3) Section 11 of the Trusts of Land and Appointment of Trustees Act 1996 (consultation with beneficiaries) shall not apply.

(4) My Trustees shall be entitled to be indemnified out of the assets of my estate against all liabilities incurred in connection with the bona fide execution of their duties and powers.

As Witness my hand this [--] day of [--------] 20[--]. [*Testator's Signature*]

Signed by the Testator in our presence and attested by us in the presence of the Testator and of each other.

[*Signatures, Addresses and Occupation of Witnesses*]

1 This Will is not suitable for the younger couple. Binding a young widow, widower or surviving civil partner to a life interest can be overly wasteful and complex. It might also lead to a claim under the Inheritance (Provision for Family and Dependants) Act 1975.

2 It is unwise to settle chattels. They deteriorate over time, require maintenance and their upkeep necessitates expense. See note at **12.2**.

3 This gift is made without a survivorship condition in order to avoid double payment but that is only a concern where the Wills are in reciprocal or mirror terms. As to survivorship conditions generally see **16.4–16.12**. The inclusion of a survivorship condition can have a detrimental effect for inheritance tax purposes between spouses, as to which see **chapter 22** and **chapter 23**.

4 Note that this clause includes an express power to pay or apply capital to the life tenant. This could be important if a capital outlay is needed in connection with the provision of assisted accommodation. The gift of a life interest is an immediate post-death interest within the Inheritance Tax Act 1984 s 49A, as added by the Finance Act 2006.

5 In this case the brothers and sisters living at the death of the testator have been chosen but the gift could be limited to those living at the death of the surviving spouse with an increased risk of a partial intestacy.

6 See footnote 5 above.

7 This form deserves full powers. Presuming there are no exceptional circumstances the STEP Standard Provisions could be incorporated in place of clauses 6 to 8. See **chapter 19** for a discussion of the most common statutory and other powers and when they might or might not be appropriate.

27 Wills for Married Couples or Civil Partners with Children

Married couples or civil partners with children

27.1 For most couples with children the overriding requirement is to make provision for the surviving spouse and those children who are not self-sufficient. They are often greatly concerned about the possibility of their both being killed in a common calamity leaving minor children surviving them. In many cases the mitigation of inheritance tax is of little or no significance. Despite these concerns clients rarely contemplate the appointment of guardians without prompting but invariably accept that such an appointment is highly desirable if both are to die while they have a child under 18[1].

1 See **chapter 9** for a full discussion on guardians.

27.2 Couples should be encouraged to discuss the provisions of their Wills with each other and their solicitor or Will draftsman so as to ensure that the provisions are in harmony. Where the assets are vested in the husband he often has to be reminded that, while his wife has 'nothing to leave', the whole of his estate will constitute her intestacy if she were to die shortly after him. It goes without saying that almost invariably (taking no account of the moral issue) it is undesirable for the total assets of a married couple or civil partners to be vested entirely in one or other of them.

27.3 It is a truism to say that the particular circumstance of the client will govern the precise terms of his Will. In the case of married couples and civil partners the variety of possible situations is broader and more subtle. What is a sensible provision for a married man or woman in their early thirties will be quite different from that of the same man or woman in their early seventies. There are, however, certain family situations which are commonly encountered by the practitioner and possible approaches which may be applicable to them are considered below.

Couples with adult children

27.4 In the case of a married couple (neither of whom have previously been widowed) with adult children who have no claims to dependency on their parents, there are three popular forms of Will.

(1) In most cases the most appropriate provision will be for each party to give the whole of his or her estate to the other with a gift over to the children equally in the event of the spouse or (where appropriate) civil partner predeceasing the testator. **Forms 27.1** and **27.2** are examples.

(2) An alternative is to give the survivor a life interest. Assuming it takes effect immediately after the death of the testator it will qualify as an immediate post-death interest in possession, and as gifts to a spouse/civil partner are exempt there is no tax on the first death. It also has the advantage that the nil rate band is not used where it is left to the surviving spouse or civil partner who then benefits from an augmented nil rate band on his or her death. **Form 27.3** is an example.

(3) A further alternative (which saw a rapid decline in popularity after the introduction of a transferable nil rate band between spouses and civil partners) is to give the inheritance tax free band direct to the children. This was only ever appropriate where the joint assets would result in inheritance tax being payable on the second death and it was thought that half the joint assets would provide adequately for the surviving spouse. The same considerations as to the size of the estate still apply but, in an inversion of previous thinking, a gift of the nil rate band to the children is now considered wasteful although this will not necessarily be the case if, for example, the survivor remarries and is widowed again[1]. **Forms 27.4** and **27.5** are examples.

1 See further the notes at **23.9–23.13**.

Couples with minor children

27.5 Another common situation is that of a married couple with children, all of whom are under 18 and in full-time education. Particularly in the case of a younger couple, both husband and wife may be content that the whole of their estate should pass to the survivor and be confident that the survivor will make proper provision for the dependent children, but they may be concerned about what would happen if they both die while the children are not self-sufficient.

27.6 Prior to the Finance Act 2006 this book suggested that, notwithstanding the privileged inheritance tax treatment of accumulation and maintenance trusts, a discretionary trust ought to be preferred. This is because the traditional class gift to the children with powers of advancement is somewhat inflexible whereas a discretionary trust for the children with a distribution of the unallocated funds once the reason for the discretionary trust has ceased to exist provides rather more flexibility. In the new inheritance tax environment the pendulum swung first in favour of fully discretionary trusts for the children and then, because of the introduction of the transferrable nil rate band, towards making no provision for the children whatever. In circumstances in which there is a desire to make provision for children which overrides the advantages inherent in a transferable nil rate band between spouses, the fully discretionary trust is now the most sensible solution. The privileged treatment of old accumulation and maintenance trusts has been phased out and the potential for creating new trusts along these lines is now limited to trusts for bereaved minors (which must vest at 18) and 18 – 25 trusts[1] (which must vest at 25). The vast majority of parents will not want substantial sums to vest in their children when they are as young as 18 and many will take the view – particularly in the economic climate in which young people currently live – that it is a little early for sums to vest in their children at 25 when they might be both immature and debt-ridden. Most will lean in favour of fully discretionary trusts under which trustees will be able to make sums available to children in full-time education without them being in charge of it.

1 See **chapter 22** at **22.17–22.21**.

27.7 There is much sense in this because the needs of the children during their formative years will vary and, if their parents are alive, they will accommodate those needs as seems best at the time without necessarily treating the children equally. Thus, the object of the discretionary trust is, so far as practicable, to provide for the children in the same way as their parents would have done if they had been alive. It follows that they must have complete confidence in the trustees appointed. **Forms 27.2**, **27.4** and **27.5** are examples creating such trusts.

Pensions

27.8 Where one spouse (usually the husband) enjoys a substantial salary and is in pensionable employment, inheritance tax may be a relevant consideration on the first death, particularly if a large sum will be payable from his pension fund if he dies before reaching pensionable age. It is then worthwhile considering the terms of the pension scheme, which often provide that a lump sum payment on death may be paid to dependents of the deceased at the discretion of the trustees of the pension fund. It is usual to invite the employee to nominate his preferred beneficiary or beneficiaries. The lump sum payment falls outside the scope of inheritance tax, and it may be a waste of a tax-free sum for all of this sum to pass to the surviving spouse (who is an exempt beneficiary). A nomination of the death benefit in favour of the children, coupled with a Will-making provision for the surviving spouse is more tax advantageous than providing for the children by Will with the pension lump sum being paid over to the surviving spouse. On the other hand, if the pension fund is needed by the surviving spouse, it may be possible for the nomination to be in favour of the trustees of a discretionary trust for spouse and children created by the testator during his lifetime (with nominal assets).

Remarriage or the formation of a (new) civil partnership

27.9 The practitioner frequently has to face the delicate problem posed by the testator who is anxious that the surviving spouse should have ample provision for his or her needs but is apprehensive that the survivor will remarry or form a (new) civil partnership and their children will be deprived of what the testator considers to be their lawful inheritance. Remarriage amongst the elderly is an increasingly common occurrence and the fear that children may be disinherited is genuine[1]. Often the problem is essentially one of human relationships and is incapable of being satisfactorily resolved by a legal formula. A provision relating to remarriage or the creation of a civil partnership may well be ineffective because the current morals of society do not inhibit cohabitation. At the same time, a provision in the Will relating to cohabitation could well prove offensive to the testator's spouse or civil partner or even to the testator himself as well as being difficult, in most certain circumstances, to establish or enforce. Both provisions might also be seen as an invitation for the surviving spouse to challenge the provision made by commencing proceedings under the Inheritance (Provision for Family and Dependants) Act 1975.

1 A further problem is that those entering into a second marriage easily forget (if they ever understood) that marriage revokes a Will.

27.10 The only obvious solution available involves the use of a life interest – which ought to be an immediate post-death interest. Especially in the current economic climate, to provide a satisfactory income, however, the estate or fund supporting the life interest needs to be substantial and so the solution to one problem creates another. There may be a potentially large inheritance tax liability saved up for the future although the introduction of transferable nil rate bands between spouses and civil partners has mitigated this problem to some extent. Further, the lifetime termination of an immediate post-death interest will be treated as a gift by the life tenant for gift with reservation purposes which can seriously reduce the flexibility of this structure. If the estate is not very large, a life interest in the matrimonial home with an absolute gift of income-producing assets may be the acceptable compromise. If the estate is sufficiently large, a gift to the children of a sum equal to the inheritance tax free band with a gift of the residue to the survivor may provide a solution, as it gives partial protection against the children being disinherited and simultaneously constitutes a form of inheritance tax planning, albeit one that does not give the surviving spouse the right to an augmented nil rate band so stores up an inheritance tax problem for the future. There is no entirely satisfactory solution to the problem. **Form 27.4** makes provision for a discretionary trust leaving the spouse a life interest in residue. **Form 27.6** provides another solution.

Drafting points where trusts are created

27.11 Where a trust is created, the reasons should, of course, be explained to the client, as should the extended powers of the trustees. There are pitfalls in the creation of trusts which can entrap even the experienced Will draftsman if he is not on his guard. This is not the place for a dissertation on the law relating to trusts but it is appropriate to remind the draftsman of certain important considerations.

(1) The need to draft with care the provisions relating to class gifts. Remember that a gift which confers a vested interest on the beneficiaries will have different consequences from one which confers a contingent interest.
(2) The significance of the 'immediate post-death interest'.
(3) The risk of a partial intestacy where there is a residuary gift to a number of persons in equal shares with no provision as to what should happen to the share of a beneficiary who dies before the testator[1].
(4) The consequences of the provisions of Wills Act 1837 s 33 in respect of a gift to a child or remoter issue of the testator when the beneficiary fails to survive him.

Prior to 6 April 2010 when the Perpetuities and Accumulations Act 2009 came into force, the Will draftsman had to take care to avoid offending the rule against perpetuities, particularly in the case of contingent gifts to grandchildren. It was also important to bear in mind the necessity of limiting the right to accumulate income to 21 years from the testator's death. The Perpetuities and Accumulations Act 2009 has introduced a single perpetuity period of 125 years which severely limits the risk of new trusts offending that rule (there is, in any event, a wait and see provision). The Act has also removed the statutory restrictions on accumulations altogether.

1 See **Forms 16.5**, **16.6** and **20.9** for provisions whereby the risk of partial intestacy is reduced by accruing the gift to any surviving beneficiaries.

PRECEDENTS

27.12

Wills for married couples or civil partners with children

Form 27.1 Will of married adult with adult children leaving everything to spouse with substitutional gift to children

Form 27.2 Will leaving everything to spouse or civil partner creating discretionary trust for children if spouse or civil partner has predeceased

Form 27.3 Will of married adult with adult children leaving everything to spouse for life with gift of remainder to children

Form 27.4 Will creating capped 21-year nil rate band discretionary trust with residue to spouse or civil partner

Form 27.5 Will creating nil rate band discretionary trust with residue to spouse or civil partner for life

Form 27.6 Will creating trust for a disabled child with residue to the testator's spouse or civil partner

Form 27.7 Will giving testator's interest in residence to children with residue to spouse or civil partner

Form 27.8 Will for previously married testator whose spouse has an enhanced nil rate band creating nil rate band discretionary trust with residue to spouse or civil partner absolutely. Will including promissory note provisions

FORM 27.1

Will of married adult with adult children leaving everything to spouse or civil partner with substitutional gift to children[1]

I, [*full name*] of [*home address*] revoke all earlier Wills and declare this to be my last Will.

1. I appoint my [wife]/[husband]/[civil partner]/[*name*] as my sole [executrix]/[executor] but if [she]/[he] is unable or unwilling to act or if [she]/[he] dies before proving my Will I appoint my children [*name*] and [*name*] as my executors[2].

2. I appoint as my trustees those of my executors who obtain probate of this Will and in this Will the expression 'my Trustees' means (as the context requires) those of my executors who obtained probate and the trustees for the time being of any trust arising under this Will.

3. I give all my property to my [wife]/[husband/civil partner] absolutely if [she]/[he] survives me[3] but if this gift fails the remaining clauses of my Will shall take effect.

[4. If I am the sole surviving parent with parental responsibility for my children then I appoint [*name*] of [*address*] and [*name*] of [*address*] as guardians of any of my children under eighteen[4].]

5. I give all my property to my Trustees to hold my estate on trust for sale with power to postpone sale to pay executorship expenses and debts including mortgages secured on real or leasehold property and any inheritance tax in respect of property passing under this Will or which becomes payable because of my death on any lifetime transfer by me or payable because of my death on property in which I hold a beneficial interest as joint tenant.

6. My Trustees shall hold the residue ('my residuary estate') for those of my children who survive me [and attain the age of 25 years[5]] in equal shares.

[7. If any of my children does not attain the age of 25 years then his or her children who survive him or her and attain the age of 25 years shall take in equal shares per stirpes the share which he or she would otherwise have taken[6].]

8. My Trustees shall have power[7]:

   (1) to apply for the benefit of any beneficiary who is has a contingent interest the whole or any part of the income from any capital to which he may become entitled;

   (2) during the whole of the period in which a beneficiary has a contingent interest to accumulate such income as is not so applied and to invest that income as an addition to the capital of the share to which that beneficiary is entitled[7];

   (3) to pay or apply for the benefit of any beneficiary who has a contingent interest the whole or any part of the capital to which he may become entitled;

   (4) to pay any money to which a beneficiary under eighteen is entitled to his parent or guardian for his benefit or to the beneficiary himself once he has attained sixteen and to rely upon the receipt then given by the parent or guardian or the minor himself.

9. My Trustees shall have the following powers in addition to their powers under the general law:

   (1) Power to invest as if they were beneficially entitled and this power includes the right:

      (a) to invest in unsecured loans;

      (b) to invest in other non-income producing assets including policies of life assurance;

      (c) to purchase land anywhere in the world;

      (d) to purchase an undivided share in land;

      (e) to invest in land for the occupation or enjoyment of any beneficiary.

   (2) Power to delegate their powers of investment and management of trust property to an agent (including one of their number) on such terms including terms enabling the agent to charge remuneration, to appoint a substitute, to limit liability and to act in circumstances giving rise to a conflict of interest as my Trustees think fit.

(3) Power to appoint any person (including one of their number or a beneficiary) to act as their nominee and to take such steps as are necessary to vest any property in such person on such terms including terms enabling the agent to charge remuneration, to appoint a substitute, to limit liability and to act in circumstances giving rise to a conflict of interest as my Trustees think fit.

(4) Power to make loans of capital to a beneficiary which may be interest free, repayable on demand or repayable at a rate below the market rate.

(5) Power to borrow money on such terms as they think fit including the giving of security and to use it for any purpose for which the capital of my estate may be used.

(6) Power without the restrictions imposed by the Administration of Estates Act 1925 s 41:

(a) To appropriate to any beneficiary in satisfaction or partial satisfaction of the gift to him any asset forming part of my residuary estate and not subject to a specific gift.

(b) To appropriate as the assets or part of the assets of any trust created by this Will any asset forming part of my residuary estate and not subject to a specific gift.

10. (1) My Trustees shall exercise their powers of investment and carry out their duties as trustees without regard to the statutory duty of care and the Trustee Act 2000 s 1 shall not apply to the trusts of my Will.

(2) My Trustees shall be under no duty to review the acts of agents, nominees and custodians appointed by them and the Trustee Act 2000 s 22 shall not apply to the trusts of my Will.

(3) Section 11 of the Trusts of Land and Appointment of Trustees Act 1996 (consultation with beneficiaries) shall not apply.

(4) In the absence of an act or omission involving wilful fraud or dishonesty by the trustee in question none of my [lay][8] Trustees [(as defined by the Trustee Act 2000 s 28)] shall be liable for any loss caused to my estate or any trust created under my Will or bound to take proceedings against a co-trustee for any breach of trust

(5) My Trustees shall be entitled to be indemnified out of the assets of my estate against all liabilities incurred in connection with the bona fide execution of their duties and powers[9].

As Witness my hand this [--] day of [--------] 20[--]. [*Testator's Signature*]

Signed by the Testator in our presence and attested by us in the presence of the Testator and of each other.

[*Signatures, Addresses and Occupation of Witnesses*]

1 This Will is also suitable for testators with minor children.
2 It is not appropriate to appoint the children if they are not adults.
3 The inclusion of a survivorship condition is now likely to be of no effect or even detrimental where the gift is in favour of a surviving spouse because of the transferability of the nil rate band (discussed in **chapter 22** and **chapter 23**). However, if the survivor's Will is not in reciprocal

terms or the surviving spouse has an enhanced nil rate band by virtue of a previous marriage there will be some justification for including the survivorship condition. In the previous edition the survivorship condition appears in the following terms:

'If [she]/[he] survives me by [30 days]/[six months] I give the whole of my estate to my [wife]/[husband]/[civil partner] absolutely'.

4 For commentary on this see **chapter 9**. This clause is, of course, unnecessary if the children are adults.

5 If the words in square brackets at the end of clause 6 are not included the whole of clause 7 should also be left out of account. These words (at the end of clause 6) settle property for bereaved minors at the age of 25 bringing the provision within s 71D: see **chapter 22** at **22.17–22.20**. Grandchildren taking by substitution are not bereaved minors.

6 See footnote 5.

7 These are the powers as set out in **Form 24.2**. The particular circumstances of the testator may require some alteration to some of the powers.

8 If the limitation is intended to cover both lay and professional trustees then the words in square brackets should be removed. However, for obvious reasons the testator usually only wishes to restrict liability in relation to lay trustees who are much more likely to be friends or family members.

9 In previous editions the age specified here was 21 years in order to avoid the need to rely on the 'wait and see rule' for perpetuity purposes. Now that there is only one perpetuity period of 125 years, this is not a serious risk so the testator is able to specify an age of 25 years for both children and grandchildren.

The Perpetuities and Accumulations Act 2009 has removed the statutory restrictions on accumulations (see note at **16.19**) so that this power may be expressed, as in this form, to be of indefinite duration although it will, of course, expire with the trust at the end of the perpetuity period.

FORM 27.2

Will leaving everything to spouse or civil partner creating discretionary trust for children if spouse or civil partner has predeceased[1]

I, [*full name*] of [*home address*] revoke all earlier Wills and declare this to be my last Will.

1. If my [wife]/[husband]/[civil partner] survives me[2] I appoint [him]/[her] as my sole [executrix]/[executor] and I give the whole of my estate to my [wife]/[husband]/[civil partner] but if this gift fails the following provisions will apply.

2. (1) I appoint the partners at my death in the firm of [ ] ('the Firm') as my executors and trustees and in this Will the expression 'my Trustees' means (as the context requires) my executors and the trustees for the time being of any trust arising under this Will.

(2) In this clause:

(a) The expression 'the Firm' means not only [*name*] but any other firm which at my death has succeeded to and carries on its practice including a firm which has been incorporated or has formed a limited liability partnership; and

(b) The expression 'partners' means the persons commonly described as partners in the Firm including salaried partners and, in the case of an incorporated practice or limited liability partnership, the directors, members and beneficial owners of any share of the Firm.

(3) Any of my Trustees who is a solicitor may charge fees for work done by him or his firm (whether or not the work is of a professional nature) on the same basis as if he were not one of my Trustees but employed to carry out the work on their behalf.

3. If I am the sole surviving parent with parental responsibility for my children then I appoint [*name*] of [*address*] and [*name*] of [*address*] as guardians of any of my children under eighteen[3].

4. I give all my property to my Trustees to hold my estate on trust for sale with power to postpone sale to pay executorship expenses and debts including mortgages secured on real or leasehold property and any inheritance tax in respect of property passing under this Will or which becomes payable because of my death on any lifetime transfer by me or payable because of my death on property in which I hold a beneficial interest as joint tenant.

5. (1) In this clause[4]:

(a) 'the Trust Fund' means my residuary estate.

(b) 'my Beneficiaries' include my children and remoter issue and any spouse [civil partner[5]] widow widower [former civil partner[6]] of my children and remoter issue.

(2) My Trustees shall hold the Trust Fund upon the following trusts:

(a) For not more than 125 years from my death (which is the perpetuity period for these trusts) to apply the capital of the Trust Fund for the benefit of such of my Beneficiaries as my Trustees think fit.

(b) To apply the income of the Trust Fund for the benefit of such of my Beneficiaries as my Trustees think fit or to accumulate the whole or any part of it as an addition to the capital of the Trust Fund.

(c) Within 125 years of my death to end these trusts by distributing the Trust Fund among such of my Beneficiaries as my Trustees think fit.

(d) To exercise their discretionary powers over capital or income when and how they think fit without having to make payments to or for the benefit of all my Beneficiaries or to ensure equality among those who have benefited.

(3) My Trustees shall have the powers appearing in the following clauses in addition to their powers under the general law[7].

6. My Trustees shall have power:

(1) to apply for the benefit of any beneficiary who is has a contingent interest the whole or any part of the income from any capital to which he may become entitled;

(2) to pay or apply for the benefit of any beneficiary who has a contingent interest the whole or any part of the capital to which he may become entitled;

(3) to pay any money to which a beneficiary under eighteen is entitled to his parent or guardian for his benefit or to the beneficiary himself once he has attained sixteen and to rely upon the receipt then given by the parent or guardian or the minor himself.

7. My Trustees shall have the following powers in addition to their powers under the general law:

(1) Power to invest as if they were beneficially entitled and this power includes the right:

(a) to invest in unsecured loans;

(b) to invest in other non-income producing assets including policies of life assurance;

(c) to purchase land anywhere in the world;

(d) to purchase an undivided share in land;

(e) to invest in land for the occupation or enjoyment of any beneficiary.

(2) Power to delegate their powers of investment and management of trust property to an agent (including one of their number) on such terms including terms enabling the agent to charge remuneration, to appoint a substitute, to limit liability and to act in circumstances giving rise to a conflict of interest as my Trustees think fit.

(3) Power to appoint any person (including one of their number or a beneficiary) to act as their nominee and to take such steps as are necessary to vest any property in such person on such terms including terms enabling the agent to charge remuneration, to appoint a substitute, to limit liability and to act in circumstances giving rise to a conflict of interest as my Trustees think fit.

(4) Power to make loans of capital to a beneficiary which may be interest free, repayable on demand or repayable at a rate below the market rate.

(5) Power to borrow money on such terms as they think fit including the giving of security and to use it for any purpose for which the capital of my estate may be used.

(6) Power without the restrictions imposed by the Administration of Estates Act 1925 s 41:

(a) To appropriate to any beneficiary in satisfaction or partial satisfaction of the gift to him any asset forming part of my residuary estate and not subject to a specific gift.

(b) To appropriate as the assets or part of the assets of any trust created by this Will any asset forming part of my residuary estate and not subject to a specific gift.

8. (1) My Trustees shall exercise their powers of investment and carry out their duties as trustees without regard to the statutory duty of care and the Trustee Act 2000 s 1 shall not apply to the trusts of my Will.

(2) My Trustees shall be under no duty to review the acts of agents, nominees and custodians appointed by them and the Trustee Act 2000 s 22 shall not apply to the trusts of my Will.

(3) Section 11 of the Trusts of Land and Appointment of Trustees Act 1996 (consultation with beneficiaries) shall not apply.

(4) My [lay] Trustees shall be entitled to be indemnified out of the assets of my estate against all liabilities incurred in connection with the bona fide execution of their duties and powers.

As Witness my hand this [--] day of [--------] 20[--]. [*Testator's Signature*]

Signed by the Testator in our presence and attested by us in the presence of the Testator and of each other.

[*Signatures, Addresses and Occupation of Witnesses*]

1 This form is suitable for a married couple or for civil partners of fairly modest means with younger children whose circumstances are likely to vary over time. It is intended that reciprocal Wills should be made in this form. In the first instance the surviving spouse has care of the children and receives the whole of the deceased's estate but the survivor appoints guardians and creates a discretionary trust of the whole of his or her estate for the benefit of the children.

2 The inclusion of a survivorship condition is now likely to be of no effect or even detrimental where the gift is in favour of a surviving spouse because of the transferability of the nil rate band (discussed in **chapter 22** and **chapter 23**). However, if the survivor's Will is not in reciprocal terms or the surviving spouse has an enhanced nil rate band by virtue of a previous marriage there will be some justification for including the survivorship condition. In the previous edition the survivorship condition appears in the following terms:

'If [she]/[he] survives me by [30 days]/[six months] I give the whole of my estate to my [wife]/[husband]/[civil partner] absolutely'.

3 For commentary on this see **chapter 9**. This clause is, of course, unnecessary if the children are adults.

4 For a brief commentary on the use of discretionary trusts see **chapter 16** at **16.28–16.29** and **chapter 23** at **23.21–23.23**. Although this discretionary trust has a perpetuity period of 125 years it should be explained to the testator that it can be wound up at any time before then and so need not last until the end of the period.

5 If it is intended to include civil partners this must be done so expressly as 'spouse' will not include a civil partner.

6 See footnote 5.

7 The particular circumstances of the testator may require some alteration to some of the powers.

FORM 27.3

Will of married adult with adult children leaving everything to spouse or civil partner for life with gift of remainder to children[1]

I, [*full name*] of [*home address*] revoke all earlier Wills and declare this to be my last Will.

1. (1) I appoint my [wife]/[husband]/[civil partner] [AB] and the partners at my death in the firm of [ ] ('the Firm') as my executors and trustees and in this Will the expression 'my Trustees' means (as the context requires) my executors and the trustees for the time being of any trust arising under this Will.

(2) In this clause:

(a) The expression 'the Firm' means not only [*name*] but any other firm which at my death has succeeded to and carries on its practice including a firm which has been incorporated or has formed a limited liability partnership; and

(b) The expression 'partners' means the persons commonly described as partners in the Firm including salaried partners and, in the case of an incorporated practice or limited liability partnership, the directors, members and beneficial owners of any share of the Firm.

(3) I wish my [wife]/[husband]/[civil partner] and not more than [one] of the partners in the Firm to apply for probate of this Will.

(4) If my [wife]/[husband]/[civil partner] is unable or unwilling to act or dies before proving my Will I appoint my brother [CD] as executor in [his]/[her] place to act with the partners in the Firm.

(5) Any of my Trustees who is a solicitor may charge fees for work done by him or his firm (whether or not the work is of a professional nature) on the same basis as if he were not one of my Trustees but employed to carry out the work on their behalf.

2. I give to my [wife]/[husband]/[civil partner] my personal chattels as defined by the Administration of Estates Act 1925 s 55(1)(x)[2].

3. I give all the rest of my property to my Trustees to hold my estate on trust for sale with power to postpone sale to pay executorship expenses and debts including mortgages secured on real or leasehold property and any inheritance tax in respect of property passing under this Will or which becomes payable because of my death on any lifetime transfer by me or payable because of my death on property in which I hold a beneficial interest as joint tenant.

4. My Trustees shall hold the residue of my estate ('my residuary estate') on trust to pay the income from my residuary estate to my [wife]/[husband]/[civil partner] during [her]/[his] lifetime with power to pay or apply the whole or any part of the capital of my residuary estate for the benefit of my [wife]/[husband]/[civil partner][3] and subject to any exercise of that power after [her]/[his] death to hold the capital and income of my residuary estate in equal shares to those of my children by my [wife]/[husband] who survive me in equal shares and if any of them dies before me his or her children shall take per stirpes the share of my estate which their parent would otherwise have inherited.

5. My Trustees shall have power[4]:

(1) to apply for the benefit of any beneficiary who is has a contingent interest the whole or any part of the income from any capital to which he may become entitled;

(2) during the whole of the period in which a beneficiary has a contingent interest to accumulate such income as is not so applied and to invest that income as an addition to the capital of the share to which that beneficiary is entitled[5];

(3) to pay or apply for the benefit of any beneficiary who has a contingent interest the whole or any part of the capital to which he may become entitled;

(4) to pay any money to which a beneficiary under eighteen is entitled to his parent or guardian for his benefit or to the beneficiary himself once he has attained sixteen and to rely upon the receipt then given by the parent or guardian or the minor himself.

6. My Trustees shall have the following powers in addition to their powers under the general law:

(1) Power to invest as if they were beneficially entitled and this power includes the right:

(a) to invest in unsecured loans;

(b) to invest in other non-income producing assets including policies of life assurance;

(c) to purchase land anywhere in the world;

(d) to purchase an undivided share in land;

(e) to invest in land for the occupation or enjoyment of any beneficiary.

(2) Power to delegate their powers of investment and management of trust property to an agent (including one of their number) on such terms including terms enabling the agent to charge remuneration, to appoint a substitute, to limit liability and to act in circumstances giving rise to a conflict of interest as my Trustees think fit.

(3) Power to appoint any person (including one of their number or a beneficiary) to act as their nominee and to take such steps as are necessary to vest any property in such person on such terms including terms enabling the agent to charge remuneration, to appoint a substitute, to limit liability and to act in circumstances giving rise to a conflict of interest as my Trustees think fit.

(4) Power to make loans of capital to a beneficiary which may be interest free, repayable on demand or repayable at a rate below the market rate.

(5) Power to borrow money on such terms as they think fit including the giving of security and to use it for any purpose for which the capital of my estate may be used.

(6) Power without the restrictions imposed by Administration of Estates Act 1925 s 41:

(a) To appropriate to any beneficiary in satisfaction or partial satisfaction of the gift to him any asset forming part of my residuary estate and not subject to a specific gift.

(b) To appropriate as the assets or part of the assets of any trust created by this Will any asset forming part of my residuary estate and not subject to a specific gift.

7. (1) My Trustees shall exercise their powers of investment and carry out their duties as trustees without regard to the statutory duty of

care and the Trustee Act 2000 s 1 shall not apply to the trusts of my Will.

(2) My Trustees shall be under no duty to review the acts of agents, nominees and custodians appointed by them and the Trustee Act 2000 s 22 shall not apply to the trusts of my Will.

(3) Section 11 of the Trusts of Land and Appointment of Trustees Act 1996 (consultation with beneficiaries) shall not apply.

(4) In the absence of an act or omission involving wilful fraud or dishonesty by the trustee in question none of my [lay] Trustees [(as defined by the Trustee Act 2000 s 28)] shall be liable for any loss caused to my estate or any trust created under my Will or bound to take proceedings against a co-trustee for any breach of trust[6].

(5) My [lay] Trustees shall be entitled to be indemnified out of the assets of my estate against all liabilities incurred in connection with the bona fide execution of their duties and powers.

As Witness my hand this [--] day of [--------] 20[--]. [*Testator's Signature*]

Signed by the Testator in our presence and attested by us in the presence of the Testator and of each other.

[*Signatures, Addresses and Occupation of Witnesses*]

1 This Will is not suitable for the younger couple. Binding a young widow, widower or surviving civil partner to a life interest can be overly wasteful and complex. It might also lead to a claim under the Inheritance (Provision for Family and Dependants) Act 1975.

2 It is unwise to settle chattels. They deteriorate over time, require maintenance and their upkeep necessitates expense. See note at **12.2**.

3 Note that this clause includes an express power to pay or apply capital to the life tenant. This could be important if a capital outlay is needed in connection with the provision of assisted accommodation. The gift of a life interest is an immediate post-death interest within the Inheritance Tax Act 1984 s 49A, as added by the Finance Act 2006.

4 This form deserves full powers. Presuming there are no exceptional circumstances the STEP Standard Provisions could be incorporated in place of clauses 5 to 7. See **chapter 19** for a discussion of the most common statutory and other powers and when they might or might not be appropriate.

5 The Perpetuities and Accumulations Act 2009 has removed the statutory restrictions on accumulations (see note at **16.19**) so that this power may be expressed without making reference to the previous limit on the duration of a power to accumulate income.

6 If the limitation is intended to cover both lay and professional trustees then the words in square brackets should be removed. However, for obvious reasons the testator usually only wishes to restrict liability in relation to lay trustees who are much more likely to be friends or family members.

FORM 27.4

Will creating capped 21-year capped nil rate band discretionary trust with residue to spouse or civil partner[1]

I, [*full name*] of [*home address*] revoke all earlier Wills and declare this to be my last Will.

1. (1) I appoint as my executors the partners at my death in the firm of [ ] ('the Firm').

(2) In this clause:

(a) The expression 'the Firm' means not only [*name*] but any other firm which at my death has succeeded to and carries on its practice including a firm which has been incorporated or has formed a limited liability partnership; and

(b) The expression 'partners' means the persons commonly described as partners in the Firm including salaried partners and, in the case of an incorporated practice or limited liability partnership, the directors, members and beneficial owners of any share of the Firm.

(3) I wish not more than [two] of the partners in the Firm to apply for probate of this Will.

(4) Any of my executors who is a solicitor may charge fees for work done by him or his firm (whether or not the work is of a professional nature) on the same basis as if he were not one of my executors but employed to carry out the work on their behalf.

(5) I appoint as my trustees those of my executors who obtain probate of this Will and in this Will the expression 'my Trustees' means (as the context requires) those of my executors who obtained probate and the trustees for the time being of any trust arising under this Will.

2. I give £1,000 to each of my nephews and nieces [living at my death]/[who attains the age of 21 years][2];

3. I give to my Trustees on the trust set out in clause 4 assets equal in value to the maximum which at my death can be given to them on these trusts without inheritance tax becoming payable in respect of this gift or the sum of £250,000 if less[3].

4. (1) In this clause:

(a) 'the Trust Fund' means the assets at any particular time held by my Trustees on the trust set out in subclause 4(2);

(b) 'my Beneficiaries' are:

(i) my [wife]/[husband]/[civil partner],

(ii) my children,

(iii) the spouse [or civil partner] of any of my children,

(iv) the issue of any of my children.

(2) My Trustees shall hold the Trust Fund on the following trust:

(a) For not more than 21 years after my death:

(i) to apply the capital of the Trust Fund for the benefit of such of my Beneficiaries as my Trustees think fit,

(ii) to apply the income of the Trust Fund for the benefit of such of my Beneficiaries as my Trustees think fit or to accumulate the whole or any part of it as an addition to the capital of the Trust Fund.

(b) Not later than 21 years after my death to end this trust by distributing the Trust Fund among such of my Beneficiaries as my Trustees think fit;

(c) My Trustees may exercise their discretionary powers when and how they think fit and need not make payments to or for the benefit of all my Beneficiaries nor ensure equality among those who have benefited.

(3) My Trustees shall have the following powers:

(a) To constitute the Trust Fund by appropriating to it such of my assets as they think fit;

(b) To retain or sell any of the assets constituting the Trust Fund;

(c) To invest as if they were beneficially entitled and this power includes the right to invest in:

(i) unsecured interest free loans,

(ii) other non-income producing assets including policies of life assurance (with power to pay premiums out of income or capital).

(d) To hold investments in the name of such person or body as they think fit;

(e) To borrow money on such terms as they think fit including the giving of security and to use it for any purpose for which the capital of the Trust Fund may be used;

(f) To use the income or capital of the Trust Fund for or towards the cost of maintaining or improving any property forming part of the Trust Fund;

(g) To do anything incidental to the powers they have whether given by statute or under this Will.

5. My Trustees shall hold the rest of my estate on trust for sale with power to postpone sale to pay executorship expenses and debts including mortgages secured on real or leasehold property and any inheritance tax in respect of property passing under this Will or which becomes payable because of my death on any lifetime transfer by me or payable because of my death on property in which I hold a beneficial interest as joint tenant.

6. My Trustees shall hold the residue ('my residuary estate') on the following trusts:

(1) To pay my residuary estate to my [wife]/[husband]/[civil partner] if [she]/[he] survives me[4];

(2) If my [wife]/[husband]/[civil [partner] does not survive me to divide my residuary estate among those of [my]/[our][5] children who survive me and attain the age of 25 years in equal shares;

(3) If any of [my]/[our][6] children die before us the share of our estate which he or she would otherwise have inherited shall be taken as to one half by his or her spouse [or civil partner][7] and as to one half equally by those of his or her children who survive me;

(4) If there is no surviving spouse [or civil partner][8] of any of [my]/[our][9] children who dies before me then his or her children shall take equally the whole of the share which their parent would otherwise have inherited;

(5) If any of [my]/[our][10] children dies before me leaving no children his or her spouse [or civil partner][11] shall take the share of my estate which he or she would otherwise have inherited.

[*For powers take in clauses 6, 7 and 8 of* ***Form 27.2***]

As Witness my hand this [--] day of [--------] 20[--]. [*Testator's Signature*]

Signed by the Testator in our presence and attested by us in the presence of the Testator and of each other.

[*Signatures, Addresses and Occupation of Witnesses*]

1 This Will is suitable for a relatively wealthy couple with young children. The discretionary trust is capped at 21 years because there is likely to be a distribution of the whole fund within that time either to the surviving spouse or to the children. In many cases a distribution to the spouse within two years will be the most satisfactory option since, unless the spouse is left particularly well off without having recourse to the discretionary fund, there is little point in leaving it in place. In addition, it should be remembered that this precedent 'wastes' part of the nil rate band of the first to die so that the survivor will not be entitled to the maximum enhanced nil rate band on death.

2 In previous editions the age specified here was 21 years in order to avoid the need to rely on the 'wait and see rule' for perpetuity purposes. Now that there is only one perpetuity period of 125 years this is not a serious risk so the testator is able to specify a greater age although 21 years is often considered the maximum suitable age for receipt of a modest legacy. The class-closing rules limit this gift to those grandchildren living at the testator's death but there is no harm in including an express provision to that effect.

3 There are a number of points to bear in mind in relation to this gift. It does not take advantage of the transferable nil rate band between spouses or civil partners but is not entirely inheritance tax inefficient either. It is quite simply not a purely inheritance tax-driven gift: first the sum given is capped at a level below the nil rate band and, secondly, the discretionary trust takes effect even if the testator is the second to die. In most cases there is little point in or desire to include a discretionary trust of this sort in the Will of the second to die (see the next form) but where the circumstances of the family are in flux a testator might wish to leave property on discretionary trust with guidance being provided by a letter of wishes which might be varied from time to time without the need to make a new Will on a regular basis.

The capped figure could be index-linked by using the following formula:

> 'I give the lesser of £250,000 increased by the percentage by which the latest available figure of the All Items Index of Retail Prices at my death exceeds that last available before today and the maximum amount (after taking Relief into account) which can be given without inheritance tax being payable …'

The discretionary trust in this case is limited in duration to 21 years but a different period (up to 125 years) could be employed.

It is important to note that if the testator's estate contains business or agricultural property this uncapped gift could be very valuable. See note at **13.2–13.15**.

4 There is little point in providing an extended survivorship period where the nil rate band has almost been exhausted.

5 A gift to 'our children' has been held to refer to all children of all marriages of both spouses: *Re Zehr* [1944] 2 DLR 670; but as a matter of construction it may be limited to the children of the marriage, thus excluding children from a previous relationship. Legitimated, illegitimate and adopted children are presumed to inherit under a provision for children unless otherwise indicated but step-children will not. If the testator wishes to alter any of these presumptions express provisions needs to be made. See notes at **20.3–20.4** and accompanying forms.

6 See footnote 5.

7 If it is intended to include civil partners this must be done so expressly as 'spouse' will not include a civil partner.

8 See footnote 7 above.
9 See footnote 5 above.
10 See footnote 5 above.
11 See footnote 7 above.

FORM 27.5

Will creating nil rate band discretionary trust with residue to spouse or civil partner for life[1]

I, [*full name*] of [*home address*] revoke all earlier Wills and declare this to be my last Will.

[1. *Appointment of executors as in clause 1 of* ***Form 27.4***.]

2. If my [wife]/[husband]/[civil partner] survives me by [30 days]/[six months][2] I give to my Trustees on the trust set out in clause 4 assets equal in value to the maximum which at my death can be given to them on my death without inheritance tax becoming payable in respect thereof[3].

3. If I am the sole surviving parent with parental responsibility for my children then I appoint [*name*] of [*address*] and [*name*] of [*address*] as guardians of any of my children under eighteen[4].

4. I give to my Trustees on the trust set out in clause 5 assets equal in value to the maximum which at my death can be given to them on these trusts without inheritance tax becoming payable in respect of this gift[5].

5. (1) In this clause:

   (a) 'the Trust Fund' means the assets at any particular time held by my Trustees on the trust set out in subclause 5(2);

   (b) 'my Beneficiaries' are:

      (i) my [wife]/[husband]/[civil partner],

      (ii) my children,

      (iii) the spouse [or civil partner] of any of my children,

      (iv) the issue of any of my children.

   (2) My Trustees shall hold the Trust Fund upon the following trusts:

   (a) For not more than 125 years from my death (which is the perpetuity period for these trusts) to apply the capital of the Trust Fund for the benefit of such of my Beneficiaries as my Trustees think fit;

   (b) To apply the income of the Trust Fund for the benefit of such of my Beneficiaries as my Trustees think fit or to accumulate the whole or any part of it as an addition to the capital of the Trust Fund;

   (c) Within 125 years of my death to end these trusts by distributing the Trust Fund among such of my Beneficiaries as my Trustees think fit;

(d) To exercise their discretionary powers over capital or income when and how they think fit without having to make payments to or for the benefit of all my Beneficiaries or to ensure equality among those who have benefited.

(3) My Trustees shall have the powers appearing in the following clauses in addition to their powers under the general law[6]:

(a) To constitute the Trust Fund by appropriating to it such of my assets as they think fit;

(b) To retain or sell any of the assets constituting the Trust Fund;

(c) To invest as if they were beneficially entitled and this power includes the right to invest in:

(i) unsecured interest free loans,

(ii) other non-income producing assets including policies of life assurance (with power to pay premiums out of income or capital).

(d) To hold investments in the name of such person or body as they think fit;

(e) To borrow money on such terms as they think fit including the giving of security and to use it for any purpose for which the capital of the Trust Fund may be used;

(f) To use the income or capital of the Trust Fund for or towards the cost of maintaining or improving any property forming part of the Trust Fund;

(g) To do anything incidental to the powers they have whether given by statute or under this Will.

6. My Trustees shall hold the rest of my estate on trust for sale with power to postpone sale to pay executorship expenses and debts including mortgages secured on real or leasehold property and any inheritance tax in respect of property passing under this Will or which becomes payable because of my death on any lifetime transfer by me or payable because of my death on property in which I hold a beneficial interest as joint tenant.

7. My Trustees shall hold the residue of my estate ('my residuary estate') on trust to pay the income from my residuary estate to my [wife]/[husband]/[civil partner] during [her]/[his] lifetime with power to pay or apply the whole or any part of the capital of my residuary estate for the benefit of my [wife]/[husband]/[civil partner][7] and subject to any exercise of that power after [her]/[his] death:

(1) to divide my residuary estate among those of [my]/[our][8] children who survive me and attain the age of 25 years in equal shares;

(2) if any of [my]/[our][9] children die before us the share of our estate which he or she would otherwise have inherited shall be taken as to one half by his or her spouse [or civil partner][10] and as to one half equally per stirpes by those of his or her children who survive me;

(3) if there is no surviving spouse [or civil partner][11] of any of [my]/[our][12] children who dies before me then his or her children shall take equally per stirpes the whole of the share which their parent would otherwise have inherited;

(4) if any of [my]/[our][13] children dies before me leaving no children his or her spouse [or civil partner][14] shall take the share of my estate which he would otherwise have inherited.

[*For powers take in clauses 6, 7 and 8 of* ***Form 27.2***]

As Witness my hand this [--] day of [--------] 20[--]. [*Testator's Signature*]

Signed by the Testator in our presence and attested by us in the presence of the Testator and of each other.

[*Signatures, Addresses and Occupation of Witnesses*]

1 This Will was previously recommended for a relatively wealthy couple with young children but makes use of the nil rate band of the first to die so that the transferable nil rate band will be lost between the spouses. It is therefore less inheritance tax efficient than was previously the case but may be considered useful where the wealth of the couple is such that the nil rate band is not especially significant or where the couple accept the possibility that the survivor might well remarry.

2 Unlike the nil rate band gift in the previous form this one only takes effect on the death of the first spouse to die.

3 It should be remembered that if there is business or agricultural property in the estate this uncapped gift could be very valuable indeed.

4 See **chapter 9** for further discussion regarding the appointment of guardians.

5 It is important to note that if the testator's estate contains business or agricultural property this uncapped gift could be very valuable. See note at **13.2–13.15**.

6 The particular circumstances of the testator may require some alteration to some of the powers.

7 Note that this clause includes an express power to pay or apply capital to the life tenant.

8 A gift to 'our children' has been held to refer to all children of all marriages of both spouses: *Re Zehr* [1944] 2 DLR 670; but as a matter of construction it may be limited to the children of the marriage, thus excluding children from a previous relationship. Legitimated, illegitimate and adopted children are presumed to inherit under a provision for children unless otherwise indicated but step-children will not. If the testator wishes to alter any of these presumptions express provisions needs to be made. See note at **20.3–20.4** and accompanying forms.

9 See footnote 8 above.

10 If it is intended to include civil partners this must be done so expressly as 'spouse' will not include a civil partner.

11 See footnote 10 above.

12 See footnote 7 above.

13 See footnote 8 above.

14 See footnote 10 above.

FORM 27.6

Will creating trust for a disabled child with residue to the testator's spouse or civil partner[1]

I, [*full name*] of [*home address*] revoke all earlier Wills and declare this to be my last Will.

1. I appoint my [wife]/[husband]/[civil partner] [*name*] and my children [AB] and [CD] as my executors and if my [wife]/[husband]/[civil partner] is unable or unwilling to act or dies before proving my Will I appoint my son [EF] to be an additional executor in [her]/[his] place.

2. I appoint as my trustees those of my executors who obtain probate of this Will and in this Will the expression 'my Trustees' means (as the context requires) those of my executors who obtained probate and the trustees for the time being of any trust arising under this Will.

3. If I am the sole surviving parent with parental responsibility for my children then I appoint [*name*] of [*address*] and [*name*] of [*address*] as guardians of any of my children under eighteen[2].

4. I give to my Trustees the sum of £[ ] to be held by my Trustees on the following trusts:

   (1) In this clause:

      (a) 'the Trust Fund' means the assets at any particular time held by my Trustees on the trusts of this clause;

      (b) 'the Primary Beneficiary' means my [son/daughter] [*name of disabled child*];

      (c) 'my other Beneficiaries' are:

         (i) my [wife]/[husband]/[civil partner],

         (ii) my children other than the Primary Beneficiary,

         (iii) my grandchildren.

   (2) My Trustees shall hold the Trust Fund on the following trusts:

      (a) During the lifetime of the Primary Beneficiary:

         (i) to apply the capital of the Trust Fund for the benefit of the Primary Beneficiary and my other Beneficiaries as my Trustees think fit so long as not less than half of any capital appointed is applied for the benefit of the Primary Beneficiary;

         (ii) to accumulate the whole or any part of the income arising from the Trust Fund as an addition to the capital of the Trust Fund and to apply any income not accumulated solely for the benefit of the Primary Beneficiary.

      (b) After the death of the Primary Beneficiary:

         (i) to apply the capital of the Trust Fund for the benefit of such of my other Beneficiaries as my Trustees think fit,

         (ii) to apply the income of the Trust Fund for the benefit of such of my other Beneficiaries as my Trustees think fit or to accumulate the whole or any part of it,

         (iii) within 12 months of the Primary Beneficiary's death to end these trusts by distributing the Trust Fund among such of my other Beneficiaries as my Trustees think fit.

   (3) My Trustees shall have the following powers:

      (a) To retain or sell any of the assets constituting the Trust Fund;

      (b) To invest as if they were beneficially entitled and this power includes the right to invest in non-income producing assets including policies of life assurance;

(c) To hold investments in the name of such person or body as they think fit;

(d) To borrow money on such terms as they think fit and to use it for any purpose for which the capital of the Trust Fund may be used;

(e) In exercising the statutory power of appointing new trustees to appoint a professional person and give him the right to charge for work done by him or his firm;

(f) To make retentions for any taxes for which they may be liable;

(g) To appropriate to the Trust Fund any asset forming part of my residuary estate;

(h) To do anything incidental to the powers which my Trustees have whether given by statute or under these trusts.

5. My Trustees shall hold the rest of my estate on trust for sale with power to postpone sale to pay executorship expenses and debts including mortgages secured on real or leasehold property and any inheritance tax in respect of property passing under this Will or which becomes payable because of my death on any lifetime transfer by me or payable because of my death on property in which I hold a beneficial interest as joint tenant.

6. My Trustees shall hold the residue ('my residuary estate') on the following trusts:

(1) To pay my residuary estate to my [wife]/[husband]/[civil partner] if [she]/[he] survives me;

(2) If my [wife]/[husband]/[civil partner] does not survive me to divide my residuary estate among those of [my]/[our][3] children who survive me in equal shares;

(3) If any of [my]/[our][4] children dies before me his or her children shall take equally the share which their parent would otherwise have inherited.

[*For powers take in clauses 6, 7 and 8 of* ***Form 27.2***]

As Witness my hand this [--] day of [--------] 20[--]. [*Testator's Signature*]

Signed by the Testator in our presence and attested by us in the presence of the Testator and of each other.

[*Signatures, Addresses and Occupation of Witnesses*]

1 For notes on providing for disabled and vulnerable beneficiaries in general see **chapter 18**.

A trust for a disabled person created during the lifetime of the settlor has inheritance tax and capital gains tax advantages but a trust created by Will has no inheritance tax advantage. A disabled person is defined in the Inheritance Tax Act 1984 s 89(4). Stated shortly, he is a person who, because of mental disorder, is incapable of managing his affairs or a person in receipt of disability living allowance or an attendance allowance or would have been in receipt of those allowances in the manner prescribed by the Inheritance Tax Act 1984 s 89(5) and (6). The trustees of a settlement created by Will can obtain the capital gains tax exemption available to individuals (instead of the one-half allowed to trustees) if:

(i) the disability of the beneficiary existed during the relevant year of assessment,
(ii) under the trust not less than half the capital of the trust fund which is applied is applied for the benefit of the disabled person, and
(iii) that person is entitled to not less than half of the income arising from the trust fund or no such income may be applied for the benefit of any other person.

The object of a trust for the disabled is to preserve the state benefits received by the disabled person but to make available income and, if necessary, capital to supplement those benefits. A discretionary trust is usually preferred to granting the disabled person a life interest in the trust fund. The terms of the trust, in effect, create a discretionary trust during the lifetime of the disabled person with a gift over on his death. The trust fund may be a specific sum which is settled by the testator or the whole or part of the residue.

Unless the trust fund is substantial it will be preferable in many cases to use an ordinary discretionary trust although both actual and deemed interests in possession may qualify as disabled person's interests under the Inheritance Tax Act 1984 s 89B(1) introduced by the Finance Act 2006.

2 For commentary on this see **chapter 9**. This clause is, of course, unnecessary if the children are adults.

3 A gift to 'our children' has been held to refer to all children of all marriages of both spouses: *Re Zehr* [1944] 2 DLR 670; but as a matter of construction it may be limited to the children of the marriage, thus excluding children from a previous relationship. Legitimated, illegitimate and adopted children are presumed to inherit under a provision for children unless otherwise indicated but step-children will not. If the testator wishes to alter any of these presumptions express provisions needs to be made. See note at **20.3–20.4** and accompanying forms.

4 See footnote 3.

FORM 27.7

Will giving testator's interest in residence to children with residue to spouse or civil partner[1]

I, [*full name*] of [*home address*] revoke all earlier Wills and declare this to be my last Will.

1. I appoint my [wife]/[husband]/[civil partner] [*name*] and my children [AB] and [CD] as my executors.

2. I appoint as my trustees those of my executors who obtain probate of this Will and in this Will the expression 'my Trustees' means (as the context requires) those of my executors who obtained probate and the trustees for the time being of any trust arising under this Will.

3. I give in equal shares to those of my children who survive me my share and beneficial interest in the house known as [ ] or the house that constitutes the home of my [wife]/[husband]/[civil partner] and me at my death.

4. If my [wife]/[husband]/[civil partner] survives me I give the rest of my estate to [him]/[her].

5. If my [wife]/[husband]/[civil partner] does not survive me I give the rest of my estate in equal shares to those of my children who survive me and if any of them dies before me his or her children shall take the share of my estate which their parent would otherwise have inherited.

As Witness my hand this [--] day of [--------] 20[--]. [*Testator's Signature*]

Signed by the Testator in our presence and attested by us in the presence of the Testator and of each other.

[*Signatures, Addresses and Occupation of Witnesses*]

1 This is a useful vehicle for the older couple in, say, a case in which the survivor might have to be moved to a nursing home in the future and face having their interest in the matrimonial home charged with the nursing fees. It is not a Will for those whose principal aim is to minimise inheritance tax although if the surviving spouse does not survive for very long, the loss of a transferable nil rate band need not be serious. It is not suitable for couples with young children and so does not include an appointment of guardians.

FORM 27.8

Will for previously married testator whose spouse has an enhanced nil rate band creating nil rate band discretionary trust with residue to spouse or civil partner absolutely. Will including promissory note provisions[1]

I, [*full name*] of [*home address*] revoke all earlier Wills and declare this to be my last Will.

[1. *Appointment of executors as in clause 1 of* ***Form 27.4***.[2]]

2. If my [wife]/[husband]/civil partner] survives me[3] I give to my Trustees on the trust set out in clause 4 assets equal in value to the maximum which at my death can be given to them without inheritance tax becoming payable in respect thereof[4].

3. If I am the sole surviving parent with parental responsibility for my children then I appoint [*name*] of [*address*] and [*name*] of [*address*] as guardians of any of my children under eighteen[5].

4. In this clause:

    (a) 'the Trust Fund' means the assets at any particular time held by the Discretionary Trustees on the trust set out in subclause 4(2) subject to the powers set out in subclauses 4(3) and 4(4);

    (b) 'my Beneficiaries' are:

        (i) my [wife]/[husband]/[civil partner],

        (ii) my children,

        (iii) the spouse [or civil partner] of any of my children,

        (iv) the issue of any of my children.

    (c) 'the Discretionary Trustees' means the trustees for the time being of the Trust Fund.

(2) My Trustees shall hold the Trust Fund on the following trust:

    (a) For not more than 21 years after my death:

        (i) to apply the capital of the Trust Fund for the benefit of such of my Beneficiaries as my Trustees think fit,

        (ii) to apply the income of the Trust Fund for the benefit of such of my Beneficiaries as my Trustees think fit or to accumulate the whole or any part of it,

(b) Not later than 21 years after my death to end this trust by distributing the Trust Fund among such of my Beneficiaries as my Trustees think fit;

(c) My Trustees may exercise their discretionary powers when and how they think fit and need not make payments to or for the benefit of all my Beneficiaries nor ensure equality among those who have benefited.

(3) My Trustees shall have the following powers:

(a) To constitute the Trust Fund by appropriating to it such of my assets as they think fit;

(b) To retain or sell any of the assets constituting the Trust Fund;

(c) To invest as if they were beneficially entitled and this power includes the right to invest in:

(i) unsecured interest free loans,

(ii) other non-income producing assets including policies of life assurance (with power to pay premiums out of income or capital).

(d) To hold investments in the name of such person or body as they think fit;

(e) To borrow money on such terms as they think fit including the giving of security and to use it for any purpose for which the capital of the Trust Fund may be used;

(f) To use the income or capital of the Trust Fund for or towards the cost of maintaining or improving any property forming part of the Trust Fund;

(g) To do anything incidental to the powers they have whether given by statute or under this Will.

(4) My Trustees may require the Discretionary Trustees to accept from them in full or partial satisfaction of the Trust Fund a promise on the part of my [wife]/[husband]/[civil partner] to pay the Trust Fund on demand or a charge of any part of my Residue with payment when demanded of all or part of the Trust Fund[6].

(a) The promise or charge may include whatever terms my Trustees think fit including terms:

(i) relating to the provision of fixed or floating security,

(ii) requiring the payment of interest, and

(iii) making the sum payable linked to the All Items Index of Retail Prices or any other index.

(b) The Discretionary Trustees:

(i) may refrain from calling in or exercising any rights in relation to any sum the subject of the promise or charge for as long as they think fit,

(ii) will not be liable for any loss which may occur through the exercise of any power under this clause if my Trustees are unable to make payment in full or any security given becomes inadequate.

(c) The powers given under this clause are exercisable even though the Discretionary Trustees and my Trustees are one and the same provided that my [wife]/[husband]/[civil partner] must not be the only trustee in either case.

[5. *Administration trusts of residue as in clause 6 of* ***Form 27.5***.]

6. My Trustees shall hold the residue ('my residuary estate') on the following trusts:

(1) To pay my residuary estate to my [wife]/[husband]/[civil partner] if [she]/[he] survives me;

(2) If my [wife]/[husband]/[civil partner] does not survive me to divide my residuary estate among those of [my]/[our][7] children who survive me and attain the age of 25 years in equal shares;

(3) If any of [my]/[our][8] children die before us the share of our estate which he or she would otherwise have inherited shall be taken as to one half by his or her spouse [or civil partner] and as to one half equally by those of his or her children who survive me;

(4) If there is no surviving spouse [or civil partner] of any of [my]/[our][9] children who dies before me then his or her children shall take equally the whole of the share which their parent would otherwise have inherited;

(5) If any of [my]/[our][10] children dies before me leaving no children his or her spouse [or civil partner] shall take the share of my estate which he or she would otherwise have inherited.

[*For powers take in clauses 6, 7 and 8 of* ***Form 27.2***]

As Witness my hand this [--] day of [--------] 20[--]. [*Testator's Signature*]

Signed by the Testator in our presence and attested by us in the presence of the Testator and of each other.

[*Signatures, Addresses and Occupation of Witnesses*]

1 This Will is principally driven by an interest in inheritance tax planning where the other spouse already has an enhanced nil rate band as a result of previously being widowed. The intention is to employ the promissory note scheme described in **chapter 15**.

2 The surviving spouse should not be a sole trustee.

3 Unlike the nil rate band gift in the previous form this one only takes effect on the death of the first spouse to die.

4 It is important to note that if the testator's estate contains business or agricultural property this uncapped gift could be very valuable. See note at **13.2–13.15**.

5 For commentary on this see **chapter 9**. This clause is, of course, unnecessary if the children are adults.

6 See note at **23.15–23.16**.

7 A gift to 'our children' has been held to refer to all children of all marriages of both spouses: *Re Zehr* [1944] 2 DLR 670; but as a matter of construction it may be limited to the children

of the marriage, thus excluding children from a previous relationship. Legitimated, illegitimate and adopted children are presumed to inherit under a provision for children unless otherwise indicated but step-children will not. If the testator wishes to alter any of these presumptions express provisions needs to be made. See note at **20.3–20.4**.

8 See footnote 7 above.

9 See footnote 7 above.

10 See footnote 7 above.

28 Unmarried Couples with Children

28.1 The concerns of unmarried couples are similar to those of married couples (although there is less opportunity for inheritance tax mitigation). The provision of life interests and rights of residence are often favoured. **Forms 28.1** and **28.2** cater exclusively for unmarried couples but the earlier forms relating to married couples can be adapted with little difficulty. Each unmarried couple should be reminded that unless their Will indicates that it is made in contemplation of marriage (or civil partnership) it will be revoked by a marriage (or civil partnership).

PRECEDENTS

28.2

Wills for unmarried couples with children

Form 28.1 Legacies; residue equally between children and partner

Form 28.2 Will providing for right of residence and legacy for partner with residue to children

FORM 28.1

Legacies; residue equally between children and partner[1]

I, [*full name*] of [*home address*] revoke all earlier Wills and declare this to be my last Will.

[This Will is made expecting to [*marry*] [*form a civil partnership*] with [*name*] and is not to be revoked by this [*marriage*]/[*civil partnership*] taking place.] [2]

1. (1) I appoint as my executors the partners at my death in the firm of [   ] ('the Firm').

   (2) In this clause:

   (a) The expression 'the Firm' means not only [*name*] but any other firm which at my death has succeeded to and carries on its practice including a firm which has been incorporated or has formed a limited liability partnership; and

   (b) The expression 'partners' means the persons commonly described as partners in the Firm including salaried partners and, in the case of an incorporated practice or limited liability partnership, the directors, members and beneficial owners of any share of the Firm.

   (3) I wish not more than [two] of the partners in the Firm to apply for probate of this Will.

   (4) Any of my Trustees who is a solicitor may charge fees for work done by him or his firm (whether or not the work is of a professional nature) on the same basis as if he were not one of my Trustees but employed to carry out the work on their behalf.

2. I appoint as my trustees those of my executors who obtain probate of this Will and in this Will the expression 'my Trustees' means (as the context requires) those of my executors who obtained probate and the trustees for the time being of any trust arising under this Will.

3. If I am the sole surviving parent with parental responsibility for my children then I appoint [*name*] of [*address*] and [*name*] of [*address*] as guardians of any of my children under eighteen[3].

4. I give to [LL] my personal chattels as defined by the Administration of Estates Act 1925 s 55(1)(x)[4].

5. I give my [stamp collection] to my friend [AB].

6. I give legacies of £5,000 each to my friends:

   [CD] of

   [EF] of

   [GH] of

7. My Trustees shall hold the rest of my estate on trust for sale with power to postpone sale to pay executorship expenses and debts including mortgages secured on real or leasehold property and any inheritance tax in respect of property passing under this Will or which becomes payable because of my death on any lifetime transfer by me or payable because of my death on property in which I hold a beneficial interest as joint tenant.

8. My Trustees shall hold the residue ('my residuary estate') on the following trusts:

   (1) To pay one half of the residue to [LL] who has been my partner for over 25 years;

   (2) To divide the other half of the residue equally among such of [my]/[our][5] children as survive me in equal shares;

   (3) If any of [my]/[our][6] children die before us the share of our estate which he or she would otherwise have inherited shall be taken as to one half by his or her spouse [or civil partner[7]] and as to one half equally by those of his or her children who survive me;

   (4) If there is no surviving spouse [or civil partner] of any of [my]/[our][8] children who dies before me then his or her children shall take equally the whole of the share which their parent would otherwise have inherited;

   (5) If any of [my]/[our][9] children dies before me leaving no children his or her spouse [or civil partner[10]] shall take the share of my estate which he or she would otherwise have inherited.

9. My Trustees shall have power[11]:

   (1) to apply for the benefit of any beneficiary who has a contingent interest the whole or any part of the income from any capital to which he may become entitled;

   (2) during the whole of the period in which a beneficiary has a contingent interest to accumulate such income as is not so applied and to invest that income as an addition to the capital of the share to which that beneficiary is entitled;

   (3) to pay or apply for the benefit of any beneficiary who has a contingent interest the whole or any part of the capital to which he may become entitled;

   (4) to pay any money to which a beneficiary under eighteen is entitled to his parent or guardian for his benefit or to the beneficiary himself once he has attained sixteen and to rely upon the receipt then given by the parent or guardian or the minor himself.

10. My Trustees shall have the following powers in addition to their powers under the general law:

(1) Power to invest as if they were beneficially entitled and this power includes the right:

(a) to invest in unsecured loans;

(b) to invest in other non-income producing assets including policies of life assurance;

(c) to purchase land anywhere in the world;

(d) to purchase an undivided share in land;

(e) to invest in land for the occupation or enjoyment of any beneficiary.

(2) Power to delegate their powers of investment and management of trust property to an agent (including one of their number) on such terms including terms enabling the agent to charge remuneration, to appoint a substitute, to limit liability and to act in circumstances giving rise to a conflict of interest as my Trustees think fit.

(3) Power to appoint any person (including one of their number or a beneficiary) to act as their nominee and to take such steps as are necessary to vest any property in such person on such terms including terms enabling the agent to charge remuneration, to appoint a substitute, to limit liability and to act in circumstances giving rise to a conflict of interest as my Trustees think fit.

(4) Power to make loans of capital to a beneficiary which may be interest free, repayable on demand or repayable at a rate below the market rate.

(5) Power to borrow money on such terms as they think fit including the giving of security and to use it for any purpose for which the capital of my estate may be used.

(6) Power without the restrictions imposed by the Administration of Estates Act 1925 s 41:

(a) To appropriate to any beneficiary in satisfaction or partial satisfaction of the gift to him any asset forming part of my residuary estate and not subject to a specific gift;

(b) To appropriate as the assets or part of the assets of any trust created by this Will any asset forming part of my residuary estate and not subject to a specific gift.

11. (1) My Trustees shall exercise their powers of investment and carry out their duties as trustees without regard to the statutory duty of care and the Trustee Act 2000 s 1 shall not apply to the trusts of my Will.

(2) My Trustees shall be under no duty to review the acts of agents, nominees and custodians appointed by them and the Trustee Act 2000 s 22 shall not apply to the trusts of my Will.

(3) Section 11 of the Trusts of Land and Appointment of Trustees Act 1996 (consultation with beneficiaries) shall not apply.

[(4) In the absence of proof of dishonesty or the wilful commission of an act known to be a breach of trust none of my Trustees shall be liable for any loss or bound to take proceedings against a co-trustee for any breach of trust.

(5) My Trustees shall be entitled to be indemnified out of the assets of my estate against all liabilities incurred in connection with the bona fide execution of their duties and powers.][12]

As Witness my hand this [--] day of [--------] 20[--]. [*Testator's Signature*]

Signed by the Testator in our presence and attested by us in the presence of the Testator and of each other.

[*Signatures, Addresses and Occupation of Witnesses*]

1 This Will, for the unmarried couple ([LL] being the partner), simply splits residue between the partner and the children. It is an easy solution but not necessarily one which is morally justifiable.

2 Unless the Will is made in expectation of marriage/civil partnership it will be revoked by any subsequent marriage or civil partnership. If the single adult is in a long-term relationship this point needs to be emphasised and it may be that the single adult wishes to put in such a clause to cater for a future marriage. See note at **4.7**.

3 The question of the parental responsibility of the survivor may need investigation. For example, if the surviving partner does not have parental responsibility, the testator may wish to appoint them. See further **chapter 9**.

4 This express gift is not essential but may be seen as desirable.

5 A gift to 'our children' has been held to refer to all children of all marriages of both spouses: *Re Zehr* [1944] 2 DLR 670; but as a matter of construction it may be limited to the children of the marriage, thus excluding children from a previous relationship. Legitimated, illegitimate and adopted children are presumed to inherit under a provision for children unless otherwise indicated but step-children will not. If the testator wishes to alter any of these presumptions express provisions needs to be made. See note at **20.3–20.4** and accompanying forms. It is particularly important, in the context of unmarried couples (where it is possible that only one name appears on a child's birth certificate), to ensure that the beneficiaries are described accurately. Clause 8(2) could be adapted to read '… our children [*name*], [*name*] and [*name*] …' in order to avoid uncertainty.

6 If it is intended to include civil partners this must be done so expressly as 'spouse' will not include a civil partner.

7 See footnote 6 above.

8 See footnote 5 above.

9 See footnote 5 above.

10 See footnote 6 above.

11 This form deserves full powers. Presuming there are no exceptional circumstances the STEP Standard Provisions could be incorporated in place of clauses 5 to 7. See **chapter 19** for a discussion of the most common statutory and other powers and when they might or might not be appropriate.

12 As this Will does not appoint any lay trustees it is unnecessary to include these provisions giving additional protection to the professional trustees.

FORM 28.2

Will providing for right of residence and legacy for partner with residue to children[1]

I, [*full name*] of [*home address*] revoke all earlier Wills and declare this to be my last Will.

[This Will is made expecting to [*marry*] [*form a civil partnership*] with [*name*] and is not to be revoked by this [*marriage*]/[*civil partnership*] taking place.][2]

1. (1) I appoint as my executors the partners at my death in the firm of [ ] ('the Firm').

(2) In this clause:

(a) The expression 'the Firm' means not only [*name*] but any other firm which at my death has succeeded to and carries on its practice including a firm which has been incorporated or has formed a limited liability partnership; and

(b) The expression 'partners' means the persons commonly described as partners in the Firm including salaried partners and, in the case of an incorporated practice or limited liability partnership, the directors, members and beneficial owners of any share of the Firm.

(3) I wish not more than [two] of the partners in the Firm to apply for probate of this Will.

(4) Any of my Trustees who is a solicitor may charge fees for work done by him or his firm (whether or not the work is of a professional nature) on the same basis as if he were not one of my Trustees but employed to carry out the work on their behalf.

2. I appoint as my trustees those of my executors who obtain probate of this Will and in this Will the expression 'my Trustees' means (as the context requires) those of my executors who obtained probate and the trustees for the time being of any trust arising under this Will.

3. If I am the sole surviving parent with parental responsibility for my children then I appoint [*name*] of [*address*] and [*name*] of [*address*] as guardians of any of my children under eighteen[3].

4. I give to [LL] my personal chattels as defined by the Administration of Estates Act 1925 s 55(1)(x)[4].

5. I give the property that constitutes my principal private residence at my death ('the House') to my Trustees on trust on the following terms[5]:

(1) My Trustees shall permit [LL] ('the Occupant') to live in the House free of charge so long as [she]/[he] wishes.

(2) While the Occupant is living in the House my Trustees shall not sell it without [her]/[his] consent.

(3) When the Occupant has ceased to live in the House my Trustees shall hold it as part of my residuary estate.

(4) At the Occupant's request my Trustees may sell the House and buy another to be held on trust [for sale] on the same terms as the House.

(5) In purchasing a replacement in accordance with the previous power my Trustees may join with any person in purchasing an undivided share of land.

6. I give [LL] the sum of [£250,000].

7. My Trustees shall hold the rest of my estate on trust for sale with power to postpone sale to pay executorship expenses and debts including

mortgages secured on real or leasehold property and any inheritance tax in respect of property passing under this Will or which becomes payable because of my death on any lifetime transfer by me or payable because of my death on property in which I hold a beneficial interest as joint tenant.

8. My Trustees shall hold the residue on trust for such of [my]/[our][6] children as survive me in equal shares.

[*For powers take in clauses 9, 10 and 11 of* ***Form 28.1***]

As Witness my hand this [--] day of [--------] 20[--]. [*Testator's Signature*]

Signed by the Testator in our presence and attested by us in the presence of the Testator and of each other.

[*Signatures, Addresses and Occupation of Witnesses*]

1 This Will makes provision for the unmarried partner by way of a right of residence and a substantial gift. Inheritance tax planning is not a concern for this couple: there will be an inheritance tax charge on the death of the testator and probably on the death of the surviving partner. If they want to minimise inheritance tax and are able to do so they should get married/form a civil partnership.

2 Unless the Will is made in expectation of marriage/civil partnership it will be revoked by any subsequent marriage or civil partnership. If the single adult is in a long-term relationship this point needs to be emphasised and it may be that the single adult wishes to put in such a clause to cater for a future marriage. See note at **4.7**.

3 The question of the parental responsibility of the survivor may need investigation. For example, if the surviving partner does not have parental responsibility, the testator may wish to appoint them. See further **chapter 9**.

4 This express gift is not essential but may be seen as desirable.

5 For a discussion of the grant of rights of residence by Will see **11.19–11.21**.

6 A gift to 'our children' has been held to refer to all children of all marriages of both spouses: *Re Zehr* [1944] 2 DLR 670; but as a matter of construction it may be limited to the children of the marriage, thus excluding children from a previous relationship. Legitimated, illegitimate and adopted children are presumed to inherit under a provision for children unless otherwise indicated but step-children will not. If the testator wishes to alter any of these presumptions express provisions needs to be made. See note at **20.3–20.4** and accompanying forms. It is particularly important, in the context of unmarried couples (where it is possible that only one name appears on a child's birth certificate), to ensure that the beneficiaries are described accurately. Clause 8(2) could be adapted to read '... our children [*name*], [*name*] and [*name*] ...' in order to avoid uncertainty.

29 Second Marriages or Civil Partnerships

29.1 Where the testator has remarried or formed a new civil partnership and there are children of the first marriage or civil partnership specific difficulties arise. Usually these difficulties come from the testator's desire to provide for his current spouse/civil partner (and their children) but at the same time ensuring that the children from the first marriage are given their 'fair share' of his estate. This can be a particularly difficult area because, while many second spouses/civil partners will have a good relationship with the children from the first marriage, sometimes there can be terrible animosity between the children and the second spouse/civil partner. This increases the risk of litigation if there is any slight ambiguity in the Will. Second marriages are also a fruitful source of litigation under the Inheritance (Provision for Family and Dependants) Act 1975 with both the children of the first marriage and the spouse/civil partner of the second marriage often being applicants.

29.2 The draftsman should also be careful in cases of second marriages to ascertain how the first marriage ended. A marriage which ended with the death of the former spouse may result in the testator being entitled to an enhanced nil rate band on his death[1]. This will depend upon the disposition of the estate of the former spouse (which ought to be investigated while there is still an opportunity to do so). Where the testator is entitled to an enhanced nil rate band adequate provision might be made for the children of the first marriage by means of a nil rate band gift as in **Forms 27.5** or **27.8**. It is, however, up to the personal representatives of the testator to claim the enhanced nil rate band. Enlarging a nil rate band gift at the expense of residue is contrary to the interests of the surviving second spouse and so, in such cases, it would not be wise to appoint the second spouse as one of the executors because of the conflict that would naturally arise.

1 See **chapter 22** at **22.23–22.25** and **chapter 23** at **23.9–23.13**.

PRECEDENTS

29.3

Wills where there is a second marriage or civil partnership

Form 29.1 Will giving legacies to children of first marriage and residue to spouse or civil partner

Form 29.2 Will giving residence to surviving spouse or civil partner with half residue to spouse and half residue to children of first marriage or civil partnership

Form 29.3 Will giving right of residence to surviving spouse or civil partner with half residue to spouse and half residue to children of first marriage

Form 29.4 Will giving right of residence and life interest in residue to surviving spouse or civil partner; remainder to children

Form 29.5 Two-thirds to wife or civil partner; one-third to in-laws

FORM 29.1

Will in favour of testator's second spouse with legacies to children of first marriage[1]

I, [*full name*] of [*home address*] revoke all earlier Wills and declare this to be my last Will.

1. I appoint my [wife]/[husband]/[civil partner] [*name*] to be my [executrix]/[executor] but if my [wife]/[husband]/[civil partner] is unable or unwilling to act or dies before proving my Will I appoint as my executors those of my children who survive me but it is my wish that not more than two of them obtain probate of my Will.
2. I give legacies of £5,000 to each of my[2] children.
3. If my [wife]/[husband]/[civil partner] does not survive me I appoint [*name*] of [*address*] and [*name*] of [*address*] as guardians of any of my children under eighteen[3].
4. If my [wife]/[husband]/[civil partner] survives me[4] I give the rest of my estate to [him]/[her]. If the gift made by this clause fails I give the rest of my estate to those of my[5] children who survive me in equal shares.
5. A gift to any of my children shall lapse if he or she dies before me and the Wills Act 1837 s 33 shall not apply to the provisions of this Will.

As Witness my hand this [--] day of [--------] 20[--]. [*Testator's Signature*]

Signed by the Testator in our presence and attested by us in the presence of the Testator and of each other.

[*Signatures, Addresses and Occupation of Witnesses*]

1 This Will, for the less wealthy testator, makes only limited provision for the children.

2 A gift to 'our children' has been held to refer to all children of all marriages of both spouses: *Re Zehr* [1944] 2 DLR 670; but as a matter of construction it may be limited to the children of the

marriage, thus excluding children from a previous relationship. Where the family relationships include step-children it is more precise to refer to 'my children and step-children'. If the testator does not intend to include step-children or illegitimate children who might subsequently come out of the woodwork the description should be 'my children by my [wife]/[husband]', although if the testator has children by a previous relationship words will then have to be used to include them. In such a case it might be better to name them.

3 Only the survivor should appoint guardians but the question of the parental responsibility of the survivor may need investigation. For example, if the wife/husband/civil partner does not have parental responsibility, they should be appointed as guardian. See further **chapter 9**.

4 The inclusion of a survivorship condition is now likely to be of no effect or even detrimental where the gift is in favour of a surviving spouse because of the transferability of the nil rate band (discussed in **chapter 22** and **chapter 23**). However, if the survivor's Will is not in reciprocal terms or the surviving spouse has an enhanced nil rate band by virtue of a previous marriage there will be some justification for including the survivorship condition. In the previous edition the survivorship condition appears in the following terms:

> 'If [she]/[he] survives me by [30 days]/[six months] I give the whole of my estate to my [wife]/[husband]/[civil partner] absolutely'.

5 See footnote 2.

FORM 29.2

Will giving residence to surviving spouse with half residue to spouse or civil partner and half residue to children of first marriage or civil partnership

I, [*full name*] of [*home address*] revoke all earlier Wills and declare this to be my last Will.

1. I appoint my [wife]/[husband]/[civil partner] [*name*] and my children [AB] and [CD] as my executors.
2. I appoint as my trustees those of my executors who obtain probate of this Will and in this Will the expression 'my Trustees' means (as the context requires) those of my executors who obtained probate and the trustees for the time being of any trust arising under this Will.
3. If I am the sole surviving parent with parental responsibility for my children then I appoint [*name*] of [*address*] and [*name*] of [*address*] as guardians of any of my children under eighteen[1].
4. If [she]/[he] survives me by [30 days]/[six months] I give to my [wife]/[husband]/[civil partner] the house that constitutes at my death our matrimonial home.
5. My Trustees shall hold the rest of my estate on trust for sale with power to postpone sale to pay executorship expenses and debts including mortgages secured on real or leasehold property and any inheritance tax in respect of property passing under this Will or which becomes payable because of my death on any lifetime transfer by me or payable because of my death on property in which I hold a beneficial interest as joint tenant.
6. My Trustees shall hold the residue ('my residuary estate') on the following trusts:

   (1) As to one half of my residuary estate for my [wife]/[husband]/[civil partner] if [she]/[he] survives me by [30 days]/[six months] but if my [wife]/[husband] does not survive me by [30 days]/[six months] my Trustees shall hold this half of my residuary estate upon the trusts of subclause 6(2) of my Will;

(2) As to the other half of my residuary estate to those of my children [and stepchildren][2] who survive me in equal shares and if any of them dies before me his or her children shall take the share of my estate which their parent would otherwise have inherited.

7. My Trustees shall have power[3]:

(1) to apply for the benefit of any beneficiary who is has a contingent interest the whole or any part of the income from any capital to which he may become entitled;

(2) during the whole of the period in which a beneficiary has a contingent interest to accumulate such income as is not so applied and to invest that income as an addition to the capital of the share to which that beneficiary is entitled;

(3) to pay or apply for the benefit of any beneficiary who has a contingent interest the whole or any part of the capital to which he may become entitled;

(4) to pay any money to which a beneficiary under eighteen is entitled to his parent or guardian for his benefit or to the beneficiary himself once he has attained sixteen and to rely upon the receipt then given by the parent or guardian or the minor himself.

8. My Trustees shall have the following powers in addition to their powers under the general law:

(1) Power to invest as if they were beneficially entitled and this power includes the right:

(a) to invest in unsecured loans;

(b) to invest in other non-income producing assets including policies of life assurance;

(c) to purchase land anywhere in the world;

(d) to purchase an undivided share in land;

(e) to invest in land for the occupation or enjoyment of any beneficiary.

(2) Power to delegate their powers of investment and management of trust property to an agent (including one of their number) on such terms including terms enabling the agent to charge remuneration, to appoint a substitute, to limit liability and to act in circumstances giving rise to a conflict of interest as my Trustees think fit.

(3) Power to appoint any person (including one of their number or a beneficiary) to act as their nominee and to take such steps as are necessary to vest any property in such person on such terms including terms enabling the agent to charge remuneration, to appoint a substitute, to limit liability and to act in circumstances giving rise to a conflict of interest as my Trustees think fit.

(4) Power to make loans of capital to a beneficiary which may be interest free, repayable on demand or repayable at a rate below the market rate.

(5) Power to borrow money on such terms as they think fit including the giving of security and to use it for any purpose for which the capital of my estate may be used.

(6) Power without the restrictions imposed by the Administration of Estates Act 1925 s 41:

(a) To appropriate to any beneficiary in satisfaction or partial satisfaction of the gift to him any asset forming part of my residuary estate and not subject to a specific gift;

(b) To appropriate as the assets or part of the assets of any trust created by this Will any asset forming part of my residuary estate and not subject to a specific gift.

9. (1) My Trustees shall exercise their powers of investment and carry out their duties as trustees without regard to the statutory duty of care and the Trustee Act 2000 s 1 shall not apply to the trusts of my Will.

(2) My Trustees shall be under no duty to review the acts of agents, nominees and custodians appointed by them and the Trustee Act 2000 s 22 shall not apply to the trusts of my Will.

(3) Section 11 of the Trusts of Land and Appointment of Trustees Act 1996 (consultation with beneficiaries) shall not apply.

(4) In the absence of proof of dishonesty or the wilful commission of an act known to be a breach of trust none of my [lay][4] Trustees shall be liable for any loss or bound to take proceedings against a co-trustee for any breach of trust.

(5) My [lay] Trustees shall be entitled to be indemnified out of the assets of my estate against all liabilities incurred in connection with the bona fide execution of their duties and powers.

As Witness my hand this [--] day of [--------] 20[--]. [*Testator's Signature*]

Signed by the Testator in our presence and attested by us in the presence of the Testator and of each other.

[*Signatures, Addresses and Occupation of Witnesses*]

1 This clause presupposes that the children of the first marriage are adults or that the former spouse is responsible for appointing guardians etc. If it is desired that appointments should be made in respect of the children of both marriages but that different appointments are desired in respect of each class of child then the clause needs to be split so that one set of guardians is appointed in respect of the children of the first marriage and another appointed in respect of children of the second marriage. **Form 9.5** is an example of such a clause.

2 See footnote 2 to **Form 29.2**.

3 This form deserves full powers. Presuming there are no exceptional circumstances the STEP Standard Provisions could be incorporated in place of clauses 7 to 9. See **chapter 19** for a discussion of the most common statutory and other powers and when they might or might not be appropriate.

4 If the limitation is intended to cover both lay and professional trustees then the words in square brackets should be removed. However, for obvious reasons the testator usually only wishes to restrict liability in relation to lay trustees who are much more likely to be friends or family members.

FORM 29.3

Will giving right of residence to surviving spouse with half residue to spouse or civil partner and half residue to children of first marriage[1]

I, [*full name*] of [*home address*] revoke all earlier Wills and declare this to be my last Will.

1. I appoint my [wife]/[husband]/[civil partner] [*name*] and my children [AB] and [CD] as my executors.

2. I appoint as my trustees those of my executors who obtain probate of this Will and in this Will the expression 'my Trustees' means (as the context requires) those of my executors who obtained probate and the trustees for the time being of any trust arising under this Will.

3. If my [wife]/[husband]/[civil partner] does not survive me I appoint [*name*] of [*address*] and [*name*] of [*address*] as guardians of any of my children under eighteen[2].

4. I give the property that constitutes my principal private residence at my death ('the House') to my Trustees on trust on the following terms[3]:

   (1) My Trustees shall permit my [wife]/[husband]/[civil partner] to live in the House free of charge so long as [she]/[he] wishes.

   (2) While my [wife]/[husband]/[civil partner] is living in the House my Trustees shall not sell it without [her]/[his] consent.

   (3) When my [wife]/[husband]/[civil partner] has ceased to live in the House my Trustees shall hold it as part of my residuary estate.

   (4) At my [wife]/[husband]/[civil partner]'s request my Trustees may sell the House and buy another to be held on trust [for sale] on the same terms as the House.

   (5) In purchasing a replacement in accordance with the previous power my Trustees may join with any person in purchasing an undivided share of land.

5. I give to my [wife]/[husband]/[civil partner] my personal chattels as defined by the Administration of Estates Act 1925 s 55(1)(x)[4].

6. My Trustees shall hold the rest of my estate on trust for sale with power to postpone sale to pay executorship expenses and debts including mortgages secured on real or leasehold property and any inheritance tax in respect of property passing under this Will or which becomes payable because of my death on any lifetime transfer by me or payable because of my death on property in which I hold a beneficial interest as joint tenant.

7. My Trustees shall hold the residue ('my residuary estate') on the following trusts:

   (1) As to one half of my residuary estate for my [wife]/[husband]/[civil partner] if [she]/[he] survives me but if my [wife]/[husband]/[civil partner] does not survive me my Trustees shall hold this half of my residuary estate upon the trusts of subclause 7(2) of my Will;

(2) As to the other half of my residuary estate to those of our[5] children who survive me in equal shares and if any of them dies before me his or her children shall take the share of my estate which their parent would otherwise have inherited.

[*For powers take in clauses 7, 8 and 9 except 9(3) (exclusion of consultation with occupying beneficiary) of* ***Form 29.2***]

As Witness my hand this [--] day of [--------] 20[--]. [*Testator's Signature*]

Signed by the Testator in our presence and attested by us in the presence of the Testator and of each other.

[*Signatures, Addresses and Occupation of Witnesses*]

1 A variation on the previous form giving only a right of residence and half the residue to the spouse.

2 See footnote 1 to **Form 29.2**.

3 For a discussion of the grant of rights of residence by Will see **11.19–11.21**. Instead of a gift of 'the house' the testator could give 'my beneficial share and interest in the house' with the remainder of the clause unchanged. This will cater for the situation in which the testator and another own as tenants in common but it should be noted that the Will will not override the interests of the co-owner.

4 Often a desirable thing to do in these family circumstances rather than having the chattels pass under residue.

5 See footnote 2 to **Form 29.1**.

FORM 29.4

Will giving right of residence and life interest in residue to surviving spouse or civil partner with remainder to children of first marriage[1]

I, [*full name*] of [*home address*] revoke all earlier Wills and declare this to be my last Will.

1. I appoint my [wife]/[husband]/[civil partner] [*name*] and my children [AB] and [CD] as my executors.

2. I appoint as my trustees those of my executors who obtain probate of this Will and in this Will the expression 'my Trustees' means (as the context requires) those of my executors who obtained probate and the trustees for the time being of any trust arising under this Will.

3. I give the property that constitutes my principal private residence at my death ('the House') to my Trustees on trust on the following terms[2]:

   (1) My Trustees shall permit my [wife]/[husband]/[civil partner] to live in the House free of charge so long as [she]/[he] wishes.

   (2) While my [wife]/[husband]/[civil partner] is living in the House my Trustees shall not sell it without [her]/[his] consent.

   (3) When my [wife]/[husband]/[civil partner] has ceased to live in the House my Trustees shall hold it upon trust for my children in equal shares.

   (4) At my [wife]/[husband]/[civil partner]'s request my Trustees may sell the House and buy another to be held on trust [for sale] on the same terms as the House.

(5) In purchasing a replacement in accordance with the previous power my Trustees may join with any person in purchasing an undivided share of land.

4. I give to [wife]/[husband]/[civil partner] my personal chattels as defined by the Administration of Estates Act 1925 s 55(1)(x)[3].

5. My Trustees shall hold the rest of my estate on trust for sale with power to postpone sale to pay executorship expenses and debts including mortgages secured on real or leasehold property and any inheritance tax in respect of property passing under this Will or which becomes payable because of my death on any lifetime transfer by me or payable because of my death on property in which I hold a beneficial interest as joint tenant.

6. My Trustees shall hold the residue of my estate ('my residuary estate') on trust to pay the income from my residuary estate to my [wife]/[husband]/[civil partner] during [her]/[his] lifetime with power to pay or apply the whole or any part of the capital of my residuary estate for the benefit of my [wife]/[husband]/[civil partner][4] and subject to any exercise of that power after [her]/[his] death for my[5] children in equal shares.

[*Adapt clauses 7, 8 and 9 (except 9(3) (exclusion of consultation with occupying beneficiary)) of* ***Form 29.2***]

As Witness my hand this [--] day of [--------] 20[--]. [*Testator's Signature*]

Signed by the Testator in our presence and attested by us in the presence of the Testator and of each other.

[*Signatures, Addresses and Occupation of Witnesses*]

1 Another variation, this time only giving the spouse a right of residence and a life interest in the residue. This is suitable for the older couple.

2 For a discussion of the grant of rights of residence by Will see **11.19–11.21**. Instead of a gift of 'the house' the testator could give 'my beneficial share and interest in the house' with the remainder of the clause unchanged. This will cater for the situation in which the testator and another own as tenants in common but it should be noted that the Will will not override the interests of the co-owner.

3 Often a desirable thing to do in these family circumstances. Since the spouse/civil partner takes a life interest in residue a separate gift of chattels ought to be included. The testator may also want to include specific legacies of items of sentimental value to the children of his first marriage.

4 Note that this clause includes an express power to pay or apply capital to the life tenant.

5 See footnote 2 to **Form 29.1**.

FORM 29.5

Will sharing estate between the testator's second spouse or civil partner and the brothers and sisters of the first spouse or civil partner[1]

I, [*full name*] of [*home address*] revoke all earlier Wills and declare this to be my last Will.

1. I appoint my [wife]/[husband]/[civil partner] [*name*] to be my [executrix]/[executor] but if my [wife]/[husband]/[civil partner] is unable or unwilling to act or dies before proving my Will I appoint [my brother-in-law] [*name*] to be my executor.

2. I appoint as my trustees those of my executors who obtain probate of this Will and in this Will the expression 'my Trustees' means (as the context requires) those of my executors who obtained probate and the trustees for the time being of any trust arising under this Will.

3. If my [wife]/[husband]/[civil partner] does not survive me I give the whole of my estate to the brothers and sisters of my late [wife]/[husband]/[civil partner] who survive me in equal shares.

4. If my [wife]/[husband]/[civil partner] survives me I give two-thirds of my net estate to my [wife]/[husband]/[civil partner] absolutely and the remaining one-third of my estate shall be shared equally by those of the brothers and sisters of my late [wife]/[husband]/[civil partner] [*name of first spouse or civil partner*] who survive me.

As Witness my hand this [--] day of [--------] 20[--]. [*Testator's Signature*]

Signed by the Testator in our presence and attested by us in the presence of the Testator and of each other.

[*Signatures, Addresses and Occupation of Witnesses*]

1 This Will is suitable for a childless testator with an ongoing relationship with the relatives of their previous spouse.

30 Wills in the Court of Protection

Introduction

30.1 Where a person lacks the capacity to create a Will they cannot do so[1]. However, it is common for circumstances to arise where despite the incapacity it is necessary or desirable that a new Will or codicil be executed. In those circumstances it is possible to apply to the Court of Protection for an Order authorising some other person to execute a Will on behalf of the incapacitated individual. This chapter explores the jurisdiction to make such a Will together with the factors taken into account by the Court in deciding whether a Will is in a person's best interests. It also sets out the procedure for making an application and the process for executing the Will.

1 For the test for capacity to make a Will see **chapter 2** at **2.9–2.23**.

The jurisdiction

30.2 The Mental Capacity Act 2005 created a new jurisdiction to act on behalf of a person to make a decision which that person lacks the capacity to make. In doing so, the Act introduced a new approach to issues of mental incapacity. Whereas before the question was whether a person lacked the capacity to manage their property and affairs[1], the question under the statute is decision specific, so that the question is whether the person is able to make the particular decision.

1 Under Part VII of the Mental Health Act 1983.

30.3 In applying the statute the following principles apply[1]:

(i) A person must be assumed to have capacity unless it is established that he lacks capacity;
(ii) A person is not to be treated as unable to make a decision unless all practicable steps to help him to do so have been taken without success;
(iii) A person is not to be treated as unable to make a decision merely because he makes an unwise decision;
(iv) An act done, or decision made, under the Act for or on behalf of a person who lacks capacity must be done, or made, in his best interests;
(v) Before the act is done, or decision is made, regard must be had to whether the purpose for which it is needed can be as effectively achieved in a way that is less restrictive of the person's rights and freedoms.

1 Mental Capacity Act 2005 s 1.

30.4 For the purposes of the statute, a person lacks capacity in respect of a particular matter if at the material time he is unable to make a decision for himself in relation to the matter because of an impairment of, or a disturbance in the functioning of, the mind or brain[1]. It does not matter whether the impairment is permanent or temporary[2]. A lack of capacity cannot be established merely by reference to: (a) a person's age or appearance, or (b) a condition of his, or an aspect of his behaviour, which might lead others to make unjustified assumptions about his capacity[3].

1 Mental Capacity Act 2005 s 2(1).
2 Mental Capacity Act 2005 s 2(2).
3 Mental Capacity Act 2005 s 2(3).

30.5 A person is unable to make a decision for himself if he is unable: (a) to understand the information relevant to the decision; (b) to retain that information; (c) to use and weigh that information as part of the process of making the decision; or (d) to communicate his decisions (whether by talking, using sign language or any other means)[1]. A person is not to be regarded as unable to understand the information relevant to a decision if he is able to understand an explanation of it given to him in a way that is appropriate to his circumstances (using simple languages, visual aids or any other means)[2]. The fact that a person is able to retain the information relevant to a decision for a short period only does not prevent him from being regarded as able to make the decision[3]. The information relevant to a decision includes information about the reasonably foreseeable consequences of (a) deciding one way or another; or (b) failing to make the decision[4].

1 Mental Capacity Act 2005 s 3(1).
2 Mental Capacity Act 2005 s 3(2).
3 Mental Capacity Act 2005 s 3(3).
4 Mental Capacity Act 2005 s 3(4).

30.6 All decisions taken must be taken in the best interests of the person on whose behalf the decision is being made[1]. The Act sets out a structured decision making process that must be followed in determining a person's best interests. So, in determining for the purposes of the Act what is in a person's best interests, the person making the determination must not make it merely on the basis of (a) the person's age or appearance; or (b) a condition of his or an aspect of his behaviour, which might lead others to make unjustified assumptions about what might be in his best interests[2]. The person making the determination must consider all the relevant circumstances and, in particular, take the following steps[3]:

(a) He must consider (i) whether it is likely that the person will at some time have capacity in relation to the matter in question, and (ii) if it appears likely that he will, when that is likely to be.

(b) He must, so far as reasonably practicable, permit and encourage the person to participate, or to improve his ability to participate, as fully as possible in any act done for him and any decision affecting him.

(c) Where the determination relates to life-sustaining treatment he must not, in considering whether the treatment is in the best interests of the person concerned, be motivated by a desire to bring about his death.

(d) He must consider, so far as reasonably ascertainable – (i) the person's past and present wishes and feelings (and, in particular, any relevant written statement made by him when he had capacity), (ii) the beliefs and values that would be likely to influence his decision if he had capacity, and (iii) the other factors that he would be likely to consider if he were able to do so.

(e) He must take into account, if it is practicable and appropriate to consult them, the views of (i) anyone named by the person as someone to be consulted on the latter in questions or on matters of that kind, (ii) anyone engaged in caring for the person or interested in his welfare, (iii) any donee of a lasting power of attorney granted by the persons, and any deputy appointed for the person by the court, as to what would be in the person's best interests and, in particular, as to the matters mentioned in (d) above.

1 Mental Capacity Act 2005 s 1(5).
2 Mental Capacity Act 2005 s 4(1).
3 Mental Capacity Act 2005 s 4(2)–(7).

30.7 Pursuant to the Act there are lengthy Codes of Practice that provide guidance on the operation of the Act and how best to act for or in the interests of a person who lacks capacity. It is a duty of any person acting in relation to a person who lacks capacity as an attorney, deputy, in a professional capacity or for remuneration that they have regard to any relevant code and the provisions of such codes, must be taken into account (if relevant) by any court[1].

1 Mental Capacity Act 2005 s 42. The section specifies other capacities which are not relevant here.

Statutory Wills and codicils

30.8 The statute authorises the Court to make a decision regarding an individual who lacks the capacity to make that decision in respect of either their personal welfare or their property and affairs[1]. In respect of the latter, the powers extend expressly to the execution of a Will (and implicitly a codicil)[2]. The power cannot be exercised by a deputy (and an attorney has no such authority) and so the decision can only be one made by the Court[3].

1 Mental Capacity Act 2005 s 16(1).
2 Mental Capacity Act 2005 s 18(1)(i).
3 Mental Capacity Act 2005 s 16(2).

30.9 No statutory Will can be made for a person under the age of 18[1].

1 Mental Capacity Act 2005 s 18(2).

30.10 The Will may make any provision (whether by disposing of property or by exercising a power or otherwise) which could be made by a Will executed by the person who lacks capacity[1].

1 Mental Capacity Act 2005 Sch 2, para 2.

Best interests in statutory Wills and codicils

30.11 In deciding whether to make a statutory Will, and if so then the terms of that statutory Will, the Court must act in the best interests of the individual concerned[1]. Since the Mental Capacity Act 2005 came into force there have now been a number of decisions made as to how the question of best interests is considered and determined in the context of a statutory Will and these provide considerable assistance in determining whether the Court is likely to order that a Will or codicil be executed and in what terms[2].

1 Mental Capacity Act 2005 s 1(5).
2 See *Re P* [2009] EWHC 163; *Re M* [2009] EWHC 2525; *Re D* [2010] EWHC 2159; *Re G (TJ)* [2010] EWHC 3005 and *NT v FS* [2013] EWHC 684.

30.12 Decisions made under the previous legislation, such as the Mental Health Act 1983, must be ignored[1]. The predominate approach under that legislation was to make a 'substituted judgment' for the person concerned[2]. Such an approach requires the Court to consider what the particular individual would themselves do, assuming them to not be incapacitated, to have received proper advice and to be acting rationally. The Mental Capacity Act 2005 has replaced that approach with a consideration of what is in the person's best interests together with a structured decision making process that must be used to make that determination.

1 *Re P* [2009] EWHC 163.
2 For example, see *Re D(J)* [1982] Ch 237.

30.13 The structured decision making process is set out in s 4 of the Act and is referred to above[1]. It requires the person (or the Court) making the determination to not make the decision merely on the basis of the person's age or appearance, or a condition of his or an aspect of his behaviour which might lead others to make unjustified assumptions about what might be in his best interests[2]. It then requires the decision maker to consider all the relevant circumstance and in particular to take the steps set out above[3]. That includes a consideration of the individual's own past and present wishes and feelings, the beliefs and values which might be likely to influence the decision they might make and the consideration of the views of persons caring for the individual, or appointed as attorney or deputy for that person.

1 See **30.6** above.
2 Mental Capacity Act 2005 s 4(1).
3 Mental Capacity Act 2005 s 4(2). See **30.6** above.

30.14 The consideration of a person's best interests involves weighing up the various factors specified by the Act as relevant to be considered. Since the Act requires the Court to consider 'all the relevant circumstances' that will necessarily include a number of different factors. The Act lays down no hierarchy between these factors and all must be taken into account. However, the weight attaching to each factor will vary in each case and it may well be the case that one factor will be of 'magnetic importance' in influencing or determining the outcome of an application[1].

1 See *Re M* [2009] EWHC 2525.

30.15 A consideration that is frequently of significant importance in the context of an application for a statutory Will is the person's past or present wishes and feelings. That may include wishes they have expressed at the time of the application (albeit whilst incapacitated) or wishes they have previously expressed. In many cases that will include their previous history of testamentary provision. A court will usually require significant persuasion to depart significantly from a prior history of Will giving and it will often be necessary to demonstrate some particular reason for such a change.

30.16 A factor that has proved controversial is that of wanting to ensure that the individual is shown as having done the 'right thing'. This was referred to as a factor of importance in the cases of *Re P*[1] and *Re M*[2]. However, subsequent cases have doubted this approach (the Court, after all, is making the provision, not the individual)[3]. It is suggested that this is simply one factor whose relevance will vary from case to case.

1 [2009] EWHC 163.
2 [2009] EWHC 2525.
3 For example, *Re G(TJ) and Re JC* [2012] WTLR 121.

30.17 Cases fairly often arise where it is apparent that unless a new Will is made for an individual there will be a dispute after their death as to the validity of previous Wills. In such circumstances it is possible to apply to the Court of Protection for an Order authorising a new Will. The Court will consider the importance of preventing such a dispute as a reason for ordering a new Will. However, the Court is not equipped to determine the outcome of such a dispute and so will limit its consideration to what the terms of such a new Will should be, rather than which of the earlier Wills is valid[1].

1 See *Re D* [2010] EWHC 2159.

Procedure

30.18 An application for a statutory Will will usually be made by a person with the control or management of the individual's property and affairs, by a person affected by an existing Will or codicil or by a person who might be expected to benefit under such a Will but does not. Where applications are made by such persons then no permission is required to make the application. Where the application is made by any other person it is necessary to obtain the Court's permission to make the application. Assuming that permission is not required, then the application will usually be made by way of new proceedings (rather than an application within existing proceedings).

30.19 In order to make any application to the Court of Protection a multiplicity of standardised forms are required. For an application for a statutory Will in new proceedings, forms COP1 and COP1A must be completed. In addition it is necessary to complete COP3. This form establishes that the individual lacks the capacity to make the particular decision. Evidence of this is usually provided by the opinion of a medical expert who has had recent contact with the individual or who has examined the person for that purpose.

30.20 Together with the COP1, COP1A and COP3 it is usually necessary to provide evidence explaining the nature and purpose of the application. Evidence by way of witness statement must be provided on, or attached to, COP24.

30.21 The critical factor in any application is ensuring that the Court, together with the other parties, have sufficient information upon which to base the decision. The absence of such information will lead to the application being delayed or even dismissed. The key requirements for the application are set out in Court of Protection Practice Direction 9F and this should be referred to when making any application. Paragraph 6 of the Practice Direction states that for any application the following information must be provided (in the form of a witness statement including documents exhibited as necessary):

(a) A draft of the proposed Will or codicil.
(b) A copy of any existing Wills or codicils.
(c) Consents to act by proposed executors.
(d) Details of the individual's family, preferably in the form of a family tree, including details of the full name and date of birth of each person included in the family tree.
(e) A schedule showing details of the individual's current assets, with up to date valuations.
(f) A schedule showing the estimated net yearly income and spending of the person.

(g) A statement showing the individual's needs, both current and future estimates, and his general circumstances.
(h) If the individual is living in National Health Service Accommodation, information on whether he may be discharged to local authority accommodation, to other fee-paying accommodation or to his own home.
(i) If the applicant considers it relevant, full details of the resources of any proposed beneficiary, and details of any likely changes if the application is successful.
(j) Details of any capital gains tax, inheritance tax or income tax which may be chargeable in respect of the subject matter of the application.
(k) An explanation of the effect, if any, that the proposed changes, will have on the individual's circumstances, preferably in the form of a 'before and after' schedule of assets and income.
(l) If appropriate, a statement of whether any land would be affected by the proposed Will or settlement and if so, details of its location and title number, if applicable.
(m) Where the application is for a settlement of property or for the variation of an existing settlement or trust, a draft of the proposed deed, plus one copy.
(n) A copy of any registered enduring power of attorney or lasting power of attorney.
(o) Confirmation that the individual is a resident of England or Wales; and
(p) An up to date report of the individual's present medical condition, life expectancy, likelihood of requiring increased expenditure in the foreseeable future and testamentary capacity.

30.22 In the COP1 form it is necessary to specify who should be made parties to any application and who should be notified of the application. It is mandatory to make as a party (or respondent) to the application:
(a) any beneficiary under an existing Will or codicil who is likely to be materially or adversely affected by the application;
(b) any beneficiary under a proposed Will or codicil who is likely to be materially or adversely affected by the application; and
(c) any prospective beneficiary under the individual's intestacy where there is no existing Will.

It is possible to notify persons who might be interested in some other way in the application without making them full respondents to it.

30.23 In most cases the Court will also join the individual themselves as a party to the proceedings and, where a litigation friend is required, invite the Official Solicitor to act as litigation friend. The Official Solicitor is an important party to such proceedings. The office of the Official Solicitor acts both as someone independent of the proceedings and with great experience of similar proceedings. Their view is therefore always relevant and important and can often sway the Court in the decision that it makes. In large or significant applications where it is clear that the Official Solicitor will become involved it may be useful to discuss the proposed proceedings with the office of the Official Solicitor even before issuing the application.

30.24 The application is made once the Court issues the application form. Together with the application form the applicant must file all the evidence and documents upon which he intends to rely as well as the order for permission (if this was required) and the COP3. Following issue, the application form (and accompanying documents) must be served on the respondents together with a form for acknowledging service and any persons to be notified of the application form must be notified.

30.25 The process from this point depends upon the approach of any other parties, including the Official Solicitor. If the matter is to be contested, evidence will be filed and directions will be given for a determination, either at a full attended hearing or on paper. If the matter is not contested it will nevertheless be necessary to satisfy the Court that the order should be made although this may be done at a telephone hearing or on paper, rather than at a full attended hearing.

Executing the Will or codicil

30.26 The Order the Court will make is for an identified person to execute a Will or codicil in the form scheduled to the Order on behalf of the incapacitated person. The Will or codicil is therefore executed by that person as if they were the incapacitated person. There is no need or reason to include the incapacitated person in the process. Once executed the Will or codicil will stand as their Will and will (depending upon its terms) have the effect of revoking and replacing previous Wills and codicils.

30.27 The process of execution is the same as that for any other Will. Thus, the nominated person must attest the Will in the presence of two witnesses who must themselves sign the Will in the presence of the nominated person.

PRECEDENTS

30.28

FORM 30.1

Commencement of statutory Will/codicil

I, [*incapacitated person*] acting by [*nominated person*] of [*address*] the person authorised in that behalf by an Order dated [ ] (the 'Order') made under the Mental Capacity Act 2005 declare this to be my Will dated [ ].

FORM 30.2

Attestation clause for a statutory Will/codicil

As Witness the hand of [*name of testator*] acting by [*name of the nominated person*] this [--] day of [--------] 20[--]. [*Testator's Name*] [*Nominated Person's Signature*]

Signed by the said [*incapacitated person*] (acting by the said [*nominated person*]) and by the said [*nominated person*] with his own name (pursuant to the Order) in our presence and attested by us in the presence of the said [*nominated person*].

[*Signatures, Addresses and Occupation of Witnesses*]

Sealed with the official seal of the Court of Protection on this [--] day of [--------] 20[--][1]

1 The Will must be sealed with the official seal of the Court of Protection.

31 Variations after Death

31.1 The testator does not necessarily have the final say in the distribution of his or her estate. Even if the Will and all its provisions are valid the distribution of the testator's estate can be varied after the testator's death to provide for a different distribution of the assets. Altering the distribution of the assets can be done either through a disclaimer or a variation provided that the person who is entitled to the assets under the Will consents to the giving up of part or all of their entitlement. Variations and disclaimers are usually used in relation to Wills but apply equally to entitlements under the intestacy provisions as well.

31.2 There are a number of reasons why a beneficiary may wish to give up part or all of their entitlement. It may be that the gift is onerous or the beneficiary does not need or want the asset or that they agree to give up some interest as a way of settling a probate dispute. However, variations and disclaimers are most commonly used to help save tax because, provided the requirements of the legislation are satisfied, the variation or disclaimer will take effect as if the dispositions effected by it were made by the deceased thus potentially saving inheritance tax and capital gains tax.

31.3 To take advantage of the provisions for saving inheritance tax[1] and capital gains tax[2], the variation or disclaimer must be in writing and made within two years of the death by the persons who benefit or would benefit under the dispositions affected.

1 Inheritance Tax Act 1984 s 142(1), see **appendix 36.5**.
2 Taxation of Chargeable Gains Act 1992 s 62(6), see **appendix 36.10**.

31.4 A variation or disclaimer is only effective both as a matter of general law and fiscally if made by all of the persons who benefit or would benefit under the dispositions affected. If any of them is not of full age and mental capacity then they cannot join in. In an appropriate case the court, exercising the special jurisdiction of the Variation of Trusts Act 1958, might approve a variation on behalf of persons who are not of full age and mental capacity but it has no power to compel persons who are able to consent to do so. This is true even if the variation would result in a better position for all of the relevant parties.

31.5 If additional inheritance tax will be payable (eg if an exempt beneficiary is disclaiming or varying in favour of a non-exempt beneficiary) the personal representatives must be parties to the variation or disclaimer unless they hold insufficient assets to pay that tax. The property which is the subject of the variation or disclaimer will then be treated for inheritance tax and capital gains tax purposes as if it passed to the recipient under the Will or intestacy of the deceased. There will be no transfer of value for the purpose of inheritance tax and no capital gains tax charge will arise.

31.6 Inheritance Tax Act 1984 s 142(1) does not apply to a variation or disclaimer made for any consideration in money or money's worth, other than consideration consisting of the making of another variation or disclaimer in relation to the testator's estate[1]. Usually it should be clear whether or not consideration is being provided for the variation or disclaimer but there may be some difficult situations which need to be approached carefully. For example, it is best if the prospective recipient does not agree to pay all the costs of the variation or disclaimer as this, in theory, could be classified as consideration for the variation or disclaimer.

1 Inheritance Tax Act 1984 s 142(3), see **appendix 36.5**.

31.7 There is no income tax equivalent of the Inheritance Tax Act 1984 s 142. This means that if one of the parties to a variation gives up an interest under the Will or intestacy and the variation settles that interest this will be considered a settlement of which that party is settlor. Therefore, if any of the property or related property in the settlement will or may be payable or applicable to or for the benefit of the varying beneficiary's spouse or civil partner the income will be taxed as his under the Income Tax (Trading and Other Income) Act 2005 ss 624 and 625. If his minor children or step-children (who are not married or in a civil partnership) benefit (although he does not) the income will still be taxed as his under s 629. This position is only true with regard to variations and not disclaimers as HMRC accepts that under a disclaimer the property was never owned by the disclaiming beneficiary. Accordingly, if this situation occurred but the beneficiary giving up the interest used a disclaimer rather than a variation then they would not be treated as a settlor and not taxed as such for the purposes of income tax.

Disclaimer

31.8 A beneficiary may disclaim a benefit obtained by Will, under intestacy or by survivorship. If the beneficiary disclaims he is treated as having never owned the property. If the beneficiary disclaims an interest under a Will or intestacy then, unless a contrary intention appears in the Will (if there is one), they are treated as having predeceased the testator[1]. This means that if a beneficiary is a child of the testator and the beneficiary disclaims a gift in the Will then the Wills Act 1837 s 33[2] will operate (in the absence of any contrary intention in the Will) so that the gift is held for the beneficiary's issue.

Unlike a variation a gift may not be disclaimed in part so that, if a Will contains a gift of £5,000, the beneficiary cannot disclaim £2,000 of it. He must disclaim it in its entirety or not at all. If, however, there are two separate gifts in the Will it is possible for the same beneficiary to disclaim one and retain the other. Similarly, it is thought that a beneficiary under intestacy may only disclaim the whole or none of his entitlement. A gift cannot be disclaimed after it has been accepted by the beneficiary, for example, by paying into his bank account a cheque which he has received from the executors in satisfaction or on account of his benefit under the Will. Accordingly, a beneficiary who is considering disclaiming should refrain from accepting the gift pending that decision.

1 Administration of Estates Act 1925 ss 33A (Wills) and 46A (intestacy), inserted by the Estates of Deceased Persons (Forfeiture Rule and Law of Succession) Act 2011.
2 See **appendix 33.14**.

31.9 A disclaimer can be made through informal acts (eg refusal to accept the gift) or simple writing but it is usually (and most advisedly) made by deed. It does not require to be stamped or contain any statement for the Inheritance Tax Act 1984 s 142(1) and the Taxation of Chargeable Gains Act 1992 s 62(6) to apply. An example of a disclaimer is at **Form 31.1**.

Deed of variation

31.10 A Deed of Variation can relate to property passing under the deceased's Will, his intestacy or by survivorship. If the statutory requirements are complied with, the property to which the variation relates will pass to the beneficiary receiving it under the variation as if he had been entitled under the Will or intestacy. In the case of a variation affecting property passing by survivorship the deceased's half share in the property will be treated as part of his estate and not passing to the surviving joint owner. The variation will not be treated as a transfer of value between the original and the substituted beneficiary. Unlike a disclaimer it is possible for a beneficiary to only vary part of a gift and to keep the rest of the gift. See **Form 31.2** for an example where the beneficiary retains an interest in part of the gift.

31.11 If a variation is to be effective for inheritance tax and capital gains tax purposes the instrument (usually a deed) must also contain a statement that the Inheritance Tax Act 1984 s 142(1) and Taxation of Chargeable Gains Act 1992 s 62(6) are intended to take effect. Once such a statement is made it cannot be revoked. The forms in this chapter all contain such a statement.

31.12 Where a variation results in the payment of additional inheritance tax any of the parties or the personal representatives must, within six months after the day on which the instrument is made, deliver a copy to HMRC and notify it of the amount of the additional tax[1]. There is otherwise an obligation to report variations to HMRC.

1 Inheritance Tax Act 1984 s 218A.

31.13 If the variation will result in additional inheritance tax being payable the personal representatives must be parties unless they hold insufficient assets to pay that additional tax. If no additional tax is payable the only person who must be a party to a variation is the beneficiary who is giving up the interest. However, for practical reasons it is usually advisable for the personal representatives and the substituted beneficiary to also be parties to the deed. There will be situations, however, where the inclusion of the substituted beneficiaries will not be desirable or possible; for example if the Deed of Variation is in favour of a minor beneficiary.

31.14 Unlike a disclaimer, a Deed of Variation can be concluded after the property to which it relates has been distributed to the original beneficiary. This is not recommended but can sometimes be necessary. In particular, where one party has already received the property but there is an ongoing dispute, a Deed of Variation may be the best way to agree to end the dispute.

31.15 Deeds of Variation ceased to be subject to stamp duty following the Stamp Duty (Exempt Instruments) Regulations 1987, SI 1987/516 provided that they were certified under category M of the Regulations. The Regulations remain in force but, for practical purposes, stamp duty has been abolished and replaced with stamp duty land tax except in relation to stock or marketable securities. HMRC had previously advised that, except in the highly unusual case of a variation actually amounting to a stock transfer form (which should continue to be certified), no stamp duty certificate is required in the Deed of Variation[1]. The stock transfer form should incorporate a certificate instead. However, the position is still not entirely certain because the *Inheritance Tax Manual*[2] now states that the appropriate certificate (usually category M) should be included if the parties are relying on the instrument to reduce the liability to inheritance tax. A cautious draftsman should therefore continue to include such a certificate in order to avoid any potential liability in this regard.

1 See Capital Taxes Office *IHT Newsletter*, August 2004.
2 Inheritance Tax Manual paragraph 35060 (*Has Stamp Duty exemption been claimed?*).

31.16 Following the enactment of the Finance Act 2003 s 49 variations carried out within two years of death for no consideration in money or money's worth other than the making of a variation of another disposition are exempt from charge to stamp duty land tax under Sch 3 para 4. It is not necessary to include any certificate or statement to that effect in the deed itself.

31.17 It is possible to have more than one variation in respect of the same estate but not in respect of the same property in the same estate[1]. A Deed of Variation cannot be the subject of a further variation within the Inheritance Tax Act 1984 s 142. It is always sensible to try to include all variations in one document if at all possible although failure to do so is less likely to excite the interest of HMRC now that tax neutral or tax saving variations no longer need to be reported. It is, of course, possible to have a variation followed by one (or more) disclaimers.

1 *Russell v IRC* [1988] STC 195.

31.18 There are a number of different precedents contained in the forms at the end of this chapter. It is difficult to supply a precedent of general application because there are so many possible alternatives even when the deceased has died intestate. Deeds of Variation, though often quite straightforward should not be settled by the inexperienced or by anyone without giving the deed and its ramifications careful thought. This is particularly important because if the Declaration of Variation does not achieve its intentions it is not possible, for inheritance tax purposes, to correct it by making another variation of the same property. However, in an appropriate case rectification[1] may be a possible solution to a badly drafted variation.

1 As in *Martin v Nicholsan* [2005] WTLR 175.

PRECEDENTS

31.19

FORM 31.1

Deed of Disclaimer[1]

This Deed of Disclaimer dated [*insert date*] is made by [*name*] of [*address*] ('the Beneficiary')

1.1 [*Name*] ('the Testator') died on [*date*] [and probate of his Will was granted to [*name(s)*] ('the Executors') by the [Principal]/[District] Probate Registry on [*date*]][2].

1.2 By his Will the Testator gave [*specified gift(s) disclaimed*] ('the Gift(s)') to the Beneficiary.

2.1 By this deed the Beneficiary disclaims the Gift(s) in [its]/[their] entirety.

2.2 The Beneficiary has not entered into possession of the Gift(s) nor done anything which would constitute an acceptance of the Gift(s)[3].

Signed as a Deed by [*the Beneficiary*]

in the presence of:

1 It is recommended that any disclaimer be made by deed for certainty. However, it is not strictly necessary. See note at **31.9**.

2 A disclaimer can be effected before a grant of probate has been obtained. In such a case the words included in square parenthesis here should be omitted.

3 Entering into possession or accepting the gifts (even temporarily) would mean no disclaimer is possible. See note at **31.8**.

FORM 31.2

Simple Deed of Variation

THIS DEED OF VARIATION is made this [*insert date*] BY [*names and addresses of Executors*] ('the Executors') [*name and address of Original Beneficiary*] ('the Donor') [*name and address of donee*] ('the Donee')[1].

Recitals:

1.1 [*Name of testator*] of [*address*] ('the Testator') died on [*date of death*] having made his last Will dated [*date of Will*] ('the Will') by which he appointed the Executors to be his Executors and Trustees.

1.2 The Executors [obtained]/[intend to apply for][2] a grant of Probate out of the [Principal]/[District] Probate Registry [on [*date of grant*]]/[shortly following execution of this deed][2].

1.3 By clause [X] of the Will the Testator gave the whole of his residuary estate to the Donor absolutely[3].

1.4 The Donor has a [nephew][3] ('the Donee') [*name and address of nephew*][3].

1.5 The Donor and the Executors wish to vary the disposition of the Testator's estate effected by his Will for the benefit of the Donee in the following manner.

Operative Variation:

2.1 The parties to this deed vary the disposition of the Testator's estate effected by his Will as follows:

2.1.1 The Will shall be varied and the Testator's estate administered as if from the death of the Testator clause [X] of the Will had provided that the Testator's residuary estate should be held by the Executors on trust for the Donor and the Donee in equal shares absolutely.

2.1.2 In accordance with Section 142(2) of the Inheritance Tax Act 1984 and Section 62(7) of the Taxation of Chargeable Gains Act 1992 the parties hereto make a statement that they intend that the provisions of Section 142(1) of the Inheritance Tax Act 1984 and of Section 62(6) of the Taxation of Chargeable Gains Act 1992 shall apply in relation to the variation effected by this deed to the intent that such variation shall be treated as if it were made by the Testator for the purposes of inheritance tax and capital gains tax[4].

[**Stamp Duty Certificate:**

2.2 The parties certify that this instrument falls within Category M in the Schedule to the Stamp Duty (Exempt Instruments) Regulations 1987.][5]

IN WITNESS whereof the parties hereto have executed these presents as their deed the day and year first above written

SIGNED and DELIVERED as a deed by the said

[*name of first Executor*][6] in the presence of:

SIGNED and DELIVERED as a deed by the said

[*name of second Executor*][6] in the presence of:

SIGNED and DELIVERED as a deed by the said

[*name of Donor*] in the presence of:

SIGNED and DELIVERED as a deed by the said

[*name of Donee*][6] in the presence of:

1 The donee does not normally need to be a party but is commonly included. The executors also do not need to be a party unless additional tax is payable. However, again it is common practice to include them and, in most situations, is to be recommended.

2 A grant is not a prerequisite although an intention to obtain a grant ought to be recited if it has not been obtained.

3 These are, of course, only examples.

4 See **31.11**.

5 See **31.15**.

6 See footnote 1 above. The donee and executors may not need to be parties to the deed but if possible it is usually advisable if they are included.

FORM 31.3

Deed of Variation – longer alternative

THIS DEED OF VARIATION is made this [*insert date*] BY [*names and addresses of Executors*] ('the Executors') [*name and address of Original Beneficiary*] ('the Donor') and [*names and addresses of Trustees*] ('the Trustees')[1].

Recitals:

1.1 [*Name of testator*] of [*address*] ('the Testator') died on [*date of death*] having made his last Will dated [*date of Will*] ('the Will') by which he appointed the Executors to be his Executors and Trustees.

1.2 The Executors [obtained]/[intend to apply for][2] a grant of Probate out of the [Principal]/[District] Probate Registry [on [*date of grant*]]/ [shortly following execution of this deed][2].

1.3 In the events which have occurred the Testator gave the whole of his estate to the Donor absolutely[3].

1.4 The Donor and the Executors wish to vary the disposition of the Testator's estate effected by his Will for the benefit of the persons described below in the following manner.

Operative Variation:

2.1 The parties to this deed vary the disposition of the Testator's estate effected by his Will as follows:

2.1.1 The Will shall be varied and the Testator's estate administered as if from his death the Testator had given the whole of his estate to the Trustees to hold on the trusts set out in the Schedule hereto.

2.1.2 In accordance with Section 142(2) of the Inheritance Tax Act 1984 and Section 62(7) of the Taxation of Chargeable Gains Act 1992 the parties hereto make a statement that they intend that the provisions of Section 142(1) of the Inheritance Tax Act 1984 and of Section 62(6) of the Taxation of Chargeable Gains Act 1992 shall apply in relation to the variation effected by this deed to the intent that such variation shall be treated as if it were made by the Testator for the purposes of inheritance tax and capital gains tax[4].

[**Stamp Duty Certificate:**

2.2 The parties certify that this instrument falls within Category M in the Schedule to the Stamp Duty (Exempt Instruments) Regulations 1987.][5]

IN WITNESS whereof the parties hereto have executed these presents as their deed the day and year first above written.

SCHEDULE

[Terms of substitute provisions]

SIGNED and DELIVERED etc[6].

1 The intended ultimate donees do not need to be parties where the gift is to trustees. In the sort of case contemplated by this deed there might well be only one executor who could also be the donor.
2 A grant is not a prerequisite although an intention to obtain a grant ought to be recited if it has not been obtained.
3 This is only an example but the most common case in which a substitute Will is to be written is that in which the whole estate is left to one beneficiary.
4 See **31.11**.
5 See **31.15.**
6 See **Form 31.2** for provisions as regard signatures and witnesses.

FORM 31.4

Deed of Variation – Double Death Variation[1]

THIS DEED OF VARIATION is made this [*insert date*] BY [*names and addresses of Executors*] ('the Executors') [*names and addresses of Administrators of Original Beneficiary*] ('the Administrators') [*name and address of the Donor*] ('the Donor') and [*names and addresses of Trustees*] ('the Trustees')[2].

Recitals:

1.1 [*Name of testator*] of [*address*] ('the Testator') died on [*date of death*] having made his last Will dated [*date of Will*] ('the Will') by which he appointed the Executors to be his Executors and Trustees.

1.2 The Executors [obtained]/[intend to apply for][3] a grant of Probate out of the [Principal]/[District] Probate Registry [on [*date of grant*]]/[shortly following execution of this deed][3].

1.3 By clause [X] of his Will the Testator gave the whole of his estate to the [*name of the Original Beneficiary*] ('the Original Beneficiary') absolutely[4].

1.4 The Original Beneficiary died on [*date of death*] intestate without issue[4].

1.5 Letters of administration to the estate of the Original Beneficiary were issued out of the [Principal]/[District] Probate Registry on [*date of grant*] to the Administrators.

1.6 Under the rules relating to intestacy under the Administration of Estates Act 1925 the Original Beneficiary's estate is held for the Donor absolutely[4].

1.7 The Donor the Administrators the Executors and the Trustees wish to vary the disposition of the Testator's estate effected by his Will in the following manner.

Operative Variation:

2.1 The parties to this deed vary the disposition of the Testator's estate effected by his Will as follows:

2.1.1 The Will shall be varied and the Testator's estate administered as if from his death the Testator had given the whole of his estate to the Trustees to hold on the trusts set out in the Schedule hereto.

2.1.2 In accordance with Section 142(2) of the Inheritance Tax Act 1984 and Section 62(7) of the Taxation of Chargeable Gains Act 1992 the parties hereto make a statement that they intend that the provisions of Section 142(1) of the Inheritance Tax Act 1984 and of Section 62(6) of the Taxation of Chargeable Gains Act 1992 shall apply in relation to the variation effected by this deed to the intent that such variation shall be treated as if it were made by the Testator for the purposes of inheritance tax and capital gains tax[5].

[**Stamp Duty Certificate:**

2.2 The parties certify that this instrument falls within Category M in the Schedule to the Stamp Duty (Exempt Instruments) Regulations 1987.][6]

IN WITNESS whereof the parties hereto have executed these presents as their deed the day and year first above written.

SCHEDULE

[*Terms of substitute provisions*]

SIGNED and DELIVERED etc[7].

1 This is an example of a variation where the original beneficiary has died within two years of the testator's death and the Deed of Variation is being used to alter the provisions distributing the estate of the original testator.
2 The intended ultimate donees do not need to be parties. The trustees stand in their place.
3 A grant is not a prerequisite although an intention to obtain a grant ought to be recited if it has not been obtained.
4 This is only an example.
5 See **31.11**.
6 See **31.15**.
7 See **Form 31.2** for provisions as regard signatures and witnesses.

FORM 31.5

Deed of Variation – Widow with Enhanced Nil Rate Band[1]

THIS DEED OF VARIATION is made this [*insert date*] BY [*names and addresses of Executors*] ('the Executors') [*name and address of the widow*] ('the Widow') and [*names and addresses of testator's children*] ('the Children')[2].

Recitals:

1.1 [*Name of testator*] of [*address*] ('the Testator') died on [*date of death*] having made his last Will dated [*date of Will*] ('the Will') by which he appointed the Executors to be his Executors and Trustees.

1.2 [The Executors [obtained]/[intend to apply for] a grant of Probate out of the [Principal]/[District] Probate Registry [on [*date of grant*]]/ [shortly following execution of this deed][3].

1.3 In the events which have occurred the Testator gave the whole of his estate to the Widow absolutely[4].

1.4 The Widow the Executors and the Children wish to vary the disposition of the Testator's estate effected by his Will in the following manner.

Operative Variation:

2.1 The parties to this deed vary the disposition of the Testator's estate effected by his Will as follows:

2.1.1 The Will shall be varied and the Testator's estate administered as if from his death the Testator had given by his Will a pecuniary legacy of [£325,000[5]]/[the maximum amount which could be given without any inheritance tax being payable[6]] to the Children in equal shares and given the whole of the residue of his estate to the Widow absolutely.

2.1.2 In accordance with Section 142(2) of the Inheritance Tax Act 1984 and Section 62(7) of the Taxation of Chargeable Gains Act 1992 the parties hereto make a statement that they intend that the provisions of Section 142(1) of the Inheritance Tax Act 1984 and of Section 62(6) of the Taxation of Chargeable Gains Act 1992 shall apply in relation to the variation effected by this deed to the intent that such variation shall be treated as if it were made by the Testator for the purposes of inheritance tax and capital gains tax[7].

[**Stamp Duty Certificate:**

2.2 The parties certify that this instrument falls within Category M in the Schedule to the Stamp Duty (Exempt Instruments) Regulations 1987.][8]

IN WITNESS whereof the parties hereto have executed these presents as their deed the day and year first above written.

SCHEDULE

[*Terms of substitute provisions*]

SIGNED and DELIVERED etc[9].

1 This form is drafted on the basis of a widow who has an enhanced nil rate band from a previous marriage and wishes to maximise the use of her enhanced nil rate band. It could easily be adapted to provide for a widower instead of a widow or for a surviving civil partner.

2 The intended donees (the children) do not need to be parties but they are usually included. If they are not parties they will need to be defined elsewhere in the deed.

3 A grant is not a prerequisite although an intention to obtain a grant ought to be recited if it has not been obtained.

4 This is only an example but it is probably the most common case.
5 This is the current nil rate band. The variation should refer to the nil rate band at the date of death.
6 In the case of post-death variations where the sum available is known the deed need only specify a pecuniary legacy as in the first alternative. Where, however, there remains uncertainty as to the value of lifetime gifts or legacies to non-exempt beneficiaries and the like, it is more sensible to include an ambulatory provision defining the nil rate gift since the sum available free of inheritance tax will not be known at the date of the variation and the second alternative should be chosen.
7 See **31.11**.
8 See **31.15**.
9 See **Form 31.2** for provisions as regard signatures and witnesses.

FORM 31.6

Deed of Variation – intestacy, simple form

THIS DEED OF VARIATION is made this [*insert date*] BY [*names and addresses of Administrators*] ('the Administrators') [*name and address of Original Beneficiary*] ('the Donor') and [*names and addresses of Trustees*] ('the Trustees')[1].

Recitals:

1.1 [*Name of deceased*] of [*address*] ('the Intestate') died on [*date of death*] survived by his sister, the Donor.

1.2 Letters of administration to the estate of the Original Beneficiary were issued out of the [Principal]/[District] Probate Registry on [*date of issue*] to the Administrators[2].

1.3 Under the rules relating to intestacy under the Administration of Estates Act 1925 the Original Beneficiary's estate is held for the Donor absolutely[3].

1.4 The Donor the Administrators and the Trustees wish to vary the disposition of the Intestate's estate effected by his intestacy in the following manner.

Operative Variation:

2.1 The parties to this deed vary the disposition of the Intestate's estate effected by his intestacy as follows:

2.1.1 The Will shall be varied and the Intestate's estate administered from the date of his death as if after the payment of all debts, taxes and other administration expenses he had given a legacy of £20,000 to the Donor absolutely and given the residue of his estate to the Trustees to hold on the trusts set out in the Schedule hereto[4].

2.1.2 In accordance with Section 142(2) of the Inheritance Tax Act 1984 and Section 62(7) of the Taxation of Chargeable Gains Act 1992 the parties hereto make a statement that they intend that the provisions of Section 142(1) of the Inheritance Tax Act 1984 and of Section 62(6) of the Taxation of Chargeable Gains Act 1992 shall apply in relation to the variation effected by this deed to the intent that such variation shall be treated as if it were made by the Intestate for the purposes of inheritance tax and capital gains tax[5].

[**Stamp Duty Certificate:**

2.2 The parties certify that this instrument falls within Category M in the Schedule to the Stamp Duty (Exempt Instruments) Regulations 1987.][6]

IN WITNESS whereof the parties hereto have executed these presents as their deed the day and year first above written.

SCHEDULE

[*Terms of substitute provisions*]

SIGNED and DELIVERED etc[7].

1 The intended donees do not need to be parties. The trustees stand in their place.
2 A grant is not a prerequisite although an intention to obtain a grant ought to be recited if it has not been obtained.
3 This is only an example.
4 In this example the donor has held back £20,000 for herself but wishes to vary the disposition of the remainder of the estate. This cannot be done by way of disclaimer.
5 See **31.11**.
6 See **31.15**.
7 See **Form 31.2** for provisions as regard signatures and witnesses.

FORM 31.7

Deed of Variation – where some of the property passes by survivorship

THIS DEED OF VARIATION is made this [*insert date*] BY [*names and addresses of Administrators*] ('the Administrators') [*name and address of surviving joint tenant*] ('the Donor') and [*name and address of Donee*] ('the Donee')[1].

Recitals:

1.1 [*Name of deceased*] of [*address*] ('the Deceased') died on [*date of death*] survived by the Donor.

1.2 Prior to the death of the Deceased the matrimonial home at [*address of matrimonial home*] ('the Property') was vested in the joint names of the Deceased and the Donor as beneficial joint tenants[2].

1.3 Under the law of survivorship the legal estate and the Deceased's severable share and interest in the Property passed to the Donor by survivorship.

1.4 Letters of administration to the estate of the Deceased were issued out of the [Principal]/[District] Probate Registry on [*date of issue*] to the Administrators.

1.5 Under the rules relating to intestacy under the Administration of Estates Act 1925 the Deceased's estate is held for the Donor absolutely[3].

1.6 The Donor the Administrators and the Donee wish to vary the disposition of the severable share of the Deceased in the Property which passed to the Donee by survivorship in the following manner.

Operative Variation:

2.1 The parties to this deed vary the disposition of the Property effected by the Deceased's death by right of survivorship as follows:

2.1.1 It shall be deemed and the Deceased's estate shall be administered as if the joint tenancy in equity of the Deceased and the Donor in the Property had been severed immediately before the death of the Deceased.

2.1.2 The severable share in equity deemed to be held by the Deceased in the Property immediately before his death shall be treated as having devolved on the Donee (instead of to the Donor under the law of survivorship) as if the Deceased had made a will to that effect with the result that the Donor holds the Property upon trust for the Donor and the Donee as tenants in common in equal shares[4].

2.1.3 In accordance with Section 142(2) of the Inheritance Tax Act 1984 and Section 62(7) of the Taxation of Chargeable Gains Act 1992 the parties hereto make a statement that they intend that the provisions of Section 142(1) of the Inheritance Tax Act 1984 and of Section 62(6) of the Taxation of Chargeable Gains Act 1992 shall apply in relation to the variation effected by this deed to the intent that such variation shall be treated as if it were made by the Deceased for the purposes of inheritance tax and capital gains tax[5].

[**Stamp Duty Certificate:**

2.2 The parties certify that this instrument falls within Category M in the Schedule to the Stamp Duty (Exempt Instruments) Regulations 1987.[6]]

IN WITNESS whereof the parties hereto have executed these presents as their deed the day and year first above written.

SCHEDULE

[*Terms of substitute provisions*]

SIGNED and DELIVERED etc[7].

1 The intended donees do not need to be parties.
2 This presupposes that the property comprises the matrimonial home but other property such as an interest in joint bank accounts could be specified. If there are a number of assets it might be better to list the joint assets in a schedule.
3 This is only an example but probably the most common case encountered in practice.

4 In this example the severable share is simply held by the donor and a particular donee for themselves as tenants in common in equity. As an alternative, the severable share could be given to trustees to hold on the trusts set out in a schedule or given to the executors to hold on the trusts of the Will.

5 See **31.11**.

6 See **31.15**.

7 See **Form 31.2** for provisions as regard signatures and witnesses.

32 Letters and Other Support Materials

32.1 Communication with the testator does not begin and end with the drafting of the Will provisions. A draftsman is often required to have fairly extensive communications with the testator from the initial contact through the drafting process until long after the Will has been made. This chapter is intended to give some assistance to some of the other communications with the client which the draftsman may be required to do either during or after the preparation of the Will provisions.

32.2 While this book is mainly concerned with the substantive provisions of the Will itself and the advice which a draftsman might have to give in relation to any particular provision, guidance has also been provided in relation to taking instructions[1], attestation[2] and general overarching considerations regarding Wills[3]. A failure to take due care with regard to any of these areas may leave the draftsman open to a negligence claim just as much as if the draftsman makes an error in relation to the drafting to the provisions of the Will. The same is true with regard to the letters and other support material contained in this chapter. Just as a draftsman should never include a provision in a Will without due consideration as to whether it is appropriate in the circumstances, equally a draftsman should not use any of the letters and other supporting material in this chapter without due consideration as to whether they are appropriate in the circumstances.

1 See **chapter 3**.
2 See **chapter 21**.
3 See **chapter 2**.

Letter enclosing Wills for completion

32.3 For commentary on a Will draftsman's duty in relation to attestation see **21.12–21.18**.

Dear [ ]

RE: Your Will

We enclose your Will for you to complete if you are happy with it. If you do not understand any part of it or would like it changed in any way before you sign and execute it please get in touch with us as soon as possible. We remind you that the Will is not valid until it has been signed and witnessed properly.

We emphasise that it is extremely important that the Will is signed and witnessed correctly. The rules regarding this are very strict and if you do not comply with them there is a real danger your Will will not be valid. [As we discussed at our last meeting] [We/we] are happy to supervise the signing and witnessing of your Will to help ensure it is done correctly. If you wish to make use of this service please contact us.

If you are going to sign and execute the Will yourself you will need two witnesses to your signature. A witness cannot be blind. A witness must also **not** be a person who will (or may) receive a gift or benefit under your Will and must also **not** be the husband, wife or civil partner of anybody who will (or may) receive a gift or benefit under your Will. Each witness should be over 18 and of full mental capacity. They should also be reliable people.

The two witnesses should be present and paying attention throughout the signing of the Will. When you and the two witnesses are present please follow the following steps:

1. Initial each page of the Will.
2. On the last page of the Will date the Will in your usual handwriting.
3. On the last page sign your usual signature in the place indicated. **The two witnesses must see you do this**. It is very important that you sign **before** the witnesses sign.
4. The witness should then sign their usual signatures and add their names and occupations where indicated. **You must see the witnesses sign the Will**.
5. The witnesses should then also initial each page.

We offer a free service to check the signatures of the Will to see if there are any obvious problems. Please send the Will to us if you wish us to undertake this service.

[As discussed we]/[We] are also happy to store your Will for you. Please contact us if you wish us to store the Will. We would, of course, provide you with copies if you desired. In any event, wherever you chose to store the Will you should ensure that those who are to deal with the administration of your estate will be able to locate your Will after your death.

We emphasise that it is vital that nothing is ever attached to the Will and that no amendments are made to the Will. If you become unhappy with the Will or any provision of it and wish to change it please contact us or another suitable organisation or person to execute a formal codicil or a new Will.

Finally, we remind you that a Will is not a 'once and for all' document. Changing circumstances may make your new Will inappropriate or even invalid. For this reason we advise making a new Will after important life events such as births, deaths, adoptions, marriages, divorces, buying of houses and moving countries. We also recommend the regular reviewing of your Will in any event to ensure it remains suitable despite any changes in the law or in your personal circumstances.

Yours sincerely,

Letter about a life interest trust

32.4 An explanation of what a life interest trust is and how it works should be done in a face to face meeting where it is easier to explain and to answer any questions the testator may have. However, even if the testator indicates that he wishes to make a life interest trust at that meeting the draftsman may wish to follow this up with a letter.

In any event, the contents of this letter can provide a good outline to give to the testator in a face to face meeting about what a life interest trust is and how it would work.

Dear [ ]

After taking advice you have decided to include a gift to [ ] 'the Life Tenant') on trust for life. The asset(s) in which you intend to give the Life Tenant a life interest in [is/are] [ ] ('the Trust Property'). The effect of this gift is that the Life Tenant will be entitled to receive the income produced by the Trust Property but will not be entitled to be paid the capital. After the Life Tenant dies the Trust Property will be held for [ ] ('the Remaindermen'). Thus, both the Life Tenant and the Remaindermen will have an interest in the Trust Property. In order to ensure that the interests of both the Life Tenant and the Remaindermen are protected it is important that there are trustees who are able to balance both interests. For this reason you may wish to consider appointing at least one professional trustee (eg a solicitor).

The trustees will hold the Trust Property on trust to pay income to the Life Tenant. They also have a power to pay capital to the Remaindermen[1]. If they do this it will diminish the fund from which income is produced for the Life Tenant and so the Life Tenant has to consent to any such payment[2]. In other respects the trustees are expected to weigh the interests of all parties in the balance before making investments or otherwise deal with the Trust Property.

Administration of a trust can sometimes be expensive and professional trustees will charge for their time and services. Annual accounts and tax returns have to be completed and tax has to be paid on trust income. Inheritance and capital gains tax might also have to be paid from time to time. Further, trustees can be expected to take legal, accountancy and investment advice when necessary or appropriate and the costs of this advice will be paid from the trust fund.

However, for the reasons discussed with you, it is desirable that you should make provision for the Life Tenant in this way and the likely expense is justified in order to make the provision which you intend to make.

If you have any further queries about this trust or if you no longer wish to include such a trust in your Will please let us know as soon as possible. [In the meantime we will proceed with drafting the rest of your Will in accordance with your instructions.][3]

Yours sincerely

1 Presuming, of course, the terms of the relevant clause so provide.
2 Presuming, of course, the terms of the relevant clause so provide.
3 This assumes that there had been a previous meeting where the testator had given instructions for a Will to be drafted and this letter is merely confirming the position as regards the life interest trust. Other circumstances may require different conclusions to the letter.

Letter about a discretionary trust

32.5 An explanation of what a discretionary trust is and how it would work should be done in a face to face meeting where it is easier to explain and to answer any questions the testator may have. However, even if the testator indicates that he wishes to make a discretionary trust at that meeting a draftsman may wish to follow this up with a letter.

In any event, the contents of this letter can provide a good outline to give to the testator in a face to face meeting about what a discretionary trust is and how it would work.

Dear [ ]

After taking advice you have decided to include a discretionary trust in your Will. This means that the property within the discretionary trust is given to your trustees who will hold it on trust for the beneficiaries of the trust. The trustees will have a discretion as to which beneficiaries to give the trust property to and in what percentages. No beneficiary will have any absolute right to receive income or capital or to control the trustees and each individual beneficiary could, in theory at least, receive no funds.

A big advantage of the discretionary trust is its flexibility. If the circumstances of any beneficiary changes and they require more or less money from the trust fund the trustees can manage the trust so as to reflect this.

It is advisable to write a letter about your wishes for the trust's future to your trustees so that they have guidance as to how you wish the capital and income of the trust fund to be used. However, such a letter expressing your wishes will **not** be binding on the trustees. They will be entitled to ignore it and may well be obliged to do so if the circumstances envisaged by you have changed. It is therefore absolutely crucial that you should have the fullest confidence in your trustees.

Administration of a trust can sometimes be expensive and professional trustees will charge for their time and services. Annual accounts and tax returns have to be completed and tax has to be paid on trust income. Inheritance and capital gains tax might also have to be paid from time to time. Trustees can be expected to take legal, accountancy and investment advice when necessary or appropriate and the cost of this advice will be paid by the trust fund.

However, for the reasons discussed with you the expense is justified in order to make the provision you wish to make.

If you have any further queries about this trust or if you no longer wish to include such a trust in your Will please let us know as soon as possible. [In the meantime we will proceed with drafting the rest of your Will in accordance with your instructions.][1]

Yours sincerely

1 This assumes that there had been a previous meeting where the testator had given instructions for a Will to be drafted and this letter is merely confirming the position as regards the life interest trust. Other circumstances may require different conclusions to the letter.

Notice of severance

32.6 Severance of a joint tenancy is discussed in **Chapter 2** at **2.12–2.13**. As mentioned there, the most common (and most advisable) method of severing a joint tenancy in equity is by a notice given by one joint owner to the other. The following is an adequate form for such a notice of severance but it is by no means unique. The form below contemplates that one joint tenant will sign and give notice of severance and the other will then sign to acknowledge receipt. The second signature is not strictly necessary as severance can be done unilaterally and without consent[1].

However, the presence of both signatures helps to avoid future disputes that may not be predictable at the time.

Often the two joint tenants will be husband and wife and will be making Wills together. If this is the case the notice can be explained to both of them and 'given' by one to the other in the presence of the draftsman. However, there are situations in which the joint tenants are not both making Wills at the same time and/or where relations are hostile. Where relations between the joint tenants are hostile a joint tenant who wishes to sever might not want to exacerbate an already difficult relationship by giving notice of severance. However, there is no way around this and notice must be given if it is to be effective.

In hostile situations service is usually effected by post and this is recommended for all cases in which the joint tenants are not present before the solicitor or Will draftsman. The use of ordinary post is inadvisable because if the recipient subsequently denies receipt the severance will not be presumed. The proper course is to send the notice of severance by registered post. If the notice is not returned undelivered it will be deemed to have been served by Law of Property Act 1925 s 196(4). This is so even where the addressee never sees the notice, even if that is because the sender intercepts it after delivery[2]. A record of the posting should be kept so that disputes about severance do not subsequently arise.

After severance an application can be made to the Land Registry in order to enter a restriction on the title to the property preventing disposal by a sole proprietor.

NOTICE OF SEVERANCE OF JOINT TENANCY

To: [*name of receiving joint tenant*]

I give you notice to sever the joint tenancy in equity of [all of the property] [the following property [ ]] which we have previously owned as joint tenants at law and in equity.

Dated [ ]

....

(joint tenant serving notice)

RECEIVED this Notice on [ ]

....

(joint tenant receiving notice)

1 Law of Property Act 1925 s 36(2).
2 *Kinch v Bullard* [1998] 4 All ER 650.

Promissory note

32.7 Promissory note schemes are much less popular than previously with the advent of the transferable nil rate band. Nevertheless, as explained in **chapter 23**, there are occasions where a nil rate band gift might be desirable and hence a promissory note might be used. An example of a Will allowing a promissory note is provided at **Form 27.8**.

PROMISSORY NOTE

(Address of surviving spouse or Trustees of residue)

To: [*(names of nil rate band beneficiaries)*] [*(executors' names)* (as Executors of YZ Deceased)]

[I *(surviving spouse's full names)*]/[We *(executors' full names)* as Trustees of YZ's *(date)* Will] promise to pay you:

1. on demand [£ [1]] increased by the percentage by which the latest figure of the All Items Index of Retail Prices published by the Office for National Statistics or its successor available before the date of repayment exceeds that last available before today.
2. interest at the annual rate of 1% payable annually in arrear and taking into account any fluctuations in the debt during the year.

DATED [ ]

EITHER

....

[*(name of surviving spouse)*]

OR

....

....

....

[YZ's Executors as Trustees of his Will]

1 Insert amount of legacy as provided for the Will.

Appointment ending a short term discretionary trust within two years of death

32.8 Short term discretionary trusts and their advantages and disadvantages are discussed in **chapter 23** at **23.21–23.33**. The below Deed of Appointment should be suitable to bring to an end the short term discretionary trust set up in **form 23.9**.

THIS DEED OF APPOINTMENT is made the [ ] day of [*month*] [*year*]

BY [*names and addresses of Trustees*] ('the Trustees')

Recitals:

1.1 [*Name of testator*] of [*address*] ('the Testator') died on [*date of death*] having made [his] last Will dated [*date of Will*] ('the Will').

1.2 By clause [X] of the Will the Testator gave to the Trustees to hold on the discretionary trusts described in that clause.

1.3 [*Name*] is the [Widow][1] of the Testator and is one of the persons named as beneficiary of the trusts of clause [X] of the Will.

1.4 The Trustees are the persons appointed trustees of the trusts of clause [X].

1.5 The Trustees desire that the trusts of clause [X] be brought to an end and the whole of the trust property be appointed to [*Name of Widow*] absolutely.

Operative provisions:

2.1 The Trustees in exercise of the power of appointment given to them by clause [X] of the Will and each and every other power them enabling by this Deed appoint the property subject to the trusts of clause [X] of the Will to [*Name of Widow*] absolutely.

IN WITNESS whereof the parties hereto have executed these presents as their deed the day and year first above written

SIGNED and DELIVERED as a deed by the said

[*name of first Trustee*] in the presence of:

SIGNED and DELIVERED as a deed by the said

[*name of second Trustee*] in the presence of[2]:

1 This deed is based on a husband testator setting up a discretionary trust of which the wife is a beneficiary. However, it could be easily adapted for the reverse situation.

2 Continue if there are more than two trustees.

Appendix

PART 1: ATTESTATION, CONSTRUCTION AND INTERPRETATION

WILLS ACT 1837		
s 1	Meaning of certain words in this Act	**33.1**
s 7	No will of a person under age valid	**33.2**
s 9	Signing and attestation of wills	**33.3**
s 15	Gifts to an attesting witness, or his or her wife or husband, to be void	**33.4**
s 18	Wills to be revoked by marriage, except in certain cases	**33.5**
s 18A	Effect of dissolution or annulment of marriage on wills	**33.6**
s 18B	Wills to be revoked by civil partnership, except in certain cases	**33.7**
s 18C	Effect of dissolution or annulment of civil partnership on wills	**33.8**
s 20	No will to be revoked otherwise than as aforesaid or by another will or codicil, or by destruction thereof	**33.9**
s 21	No alteration in a will after execution except in certain cases, shall have any effect unless executed as a will	**33.10**
s 22	No revoked will shall be revived otherwise than by re-execution or a codicil, etc.	**33.11**
s 24	Wills shall be construed, as to the estate comprised, to speak from the death of the testator	**33.12**
s 29	The words "die without issue", or "die without leaving issue", shall be construed to mean die without issue living at the death	**33.13**
s 33	Gifts to children or other issue who leave issue living at the testator's death shall not lapse	**33.14**
LAW OF PROPERTY ACT 1925		
s 184	Presumption of survivorship in regard to claims to property	**33.15**
ADMINISTRATION OF ESTATES ACT 1925		
s 35	Charges on property of deceased to be paid primarily out of the property charged	**33.16**
s 55	Definitions	**33.17**
WILLS ACT 1968		
s 1	Restriction of operation of Wills Act 1837	**33.18**
ADMINISTRATION OF JUSTICE ACT 1982		
s 20	Rectification	**33.19**
s 21	Interpretation of wills—general rules as to evidence	**33.20**
MENTAL CAPACITY ACT 2005		
s 16	Powers to make decisions and appoint deputies: general	**33.21**
s 18	Section 16 powers: property and affairs	**33.22**
Sch 2	Property and affairs: supplementary provisions	**33.23**

FAMILY LAW REFORM ACT 1987
s 1 General principle **33.24**
s 19 Dispositions of property **33.25**
LEGITIMACY ACT 1976
s 5 Rights of legitimated persons and others to take interests in property **33.26**
ADOPTION AND CHILDREN ACT 2002
s 66 Meaning of adoption in Chapter 4 **33.27**
s 67 Status conferred by adoption **33.28**
s 68 Adoptive relatives **33.29**
s 69 Rules of interpretation for instruments concerning property **33.30**
s 70 Dispositions depending on date of birth **33.31**
s 72 Protection of trustees and personal representatives **33.32**
s 73 Meaning of disposition **33.33**

PART 2: POWERS

TRUSTEE ACT 1925
s 19 Power to insure **34.1**
s 31 Power to apply income for maintenance and to accumulate surplus income during a minority **34.2**
s 32 Power of advancement **34.3**
s 33 Protective trusts **34.4**
PERPETUITIES AND ACCUMULATIONS ACT 1964
s 1 Power to specify perpetuity period **34.5**
PERPETUITIES AND ACCUMULATIONS ACT 2009
s 1 Application of the rule **34.6**
s 5 Perpetuity period **34.7**
s 6 Start of perpetuity period **34.8**
s 7 Wait and see rule **34.9**
s 8 Exclusion of class of members to avoid remoteness **34.10**
s 11 Powers of appointment **34.11**
s 15 Application of this Act **34.12**
s 20 Interpretation **34.13**
TRUSTS OF LAND AND APPOINTMENT OF TRUSTEES ACT 1996
s 1 Meaning of "trust of land" **34.14**
s 2 Trusts in place of settlements **34.15**
s 3 Abolition of doctrine of conversion **34.16**
s 4 Express trusts for sale as trusts of land **34.17**
s 5 Implied trusts for sale as trusts of land **34.18**
s 6 General powers of trustees **34.19**
s 7 Partition by trustees **34.20**
s 8 Exclusion and restriction of powers **34.21**
s 9 Delegation by trustees **34.22**
s 9A Duties of trustees in connection with delegation etc. **34.23**
s 10 Consents **34.24**
s 11 Consultation with beneficiaries **34.25**
s 12 The right to occupy **34.26**
s 13 Exclusion and restriction of right to occupy **34.27**
s 18 Application of part to personal representatives **34.28**
SCHEDULES
Sch 1 Provisions consequential on section 2 **34.29**

TRUSTEE ACT 2000

PART I THE DUTY OF CARE

s 1	The duty of care	**34.30**
s 2	Application of duty of care	**34.31**

PART II INVESTMENT

s 3	General power of investment	**34.32**
s 4	Standard investment criteria	**34.33**
s 5	Advice	**34.34**
s 6	Restriction or exclusion of this part etc.	**34.35**

PART III ACQUISITION OF LAND

s 8	Power to acquire freehold and leasehold land	**34.36**
s 9	Restriction or exclusion of this part etc.	**34.37**

PART IV AGENTS, NOMINEES AND CUSTODIANS AGENTS

s 11	Power to employ agents	**34.38**
s 12	Persons who may act as agents	**34.39**
s 13	Linked functions etc.	**34.40**
s 14	Terms of agency	**34.41**
s 15	Asset management: special restrictions	**34.42**

NOMINEES AND CUSTODIANS

s 16	Power to appoint nominees	**34.43**
s 17	Power to appoint custodians	**34.44**
s 18	Investment in bearer securities	**34.45**
s 19	Persons who may be appointed as nominees or custodians	**34.46**
s 20	Terms of appointment of nominees and custodians	**34.47**

REVIEW OF AND LIABILITY FOR AGENTS, NOMINEES AND CUSTODIANS ETC

s 21	Application of sections 22 and 23	**34.48**
s 22	Review of agents, nominees and custodians etc.	**34.49**
s 23	Liability for agents, nominees and custodians etc.	**34.50**

SUPPLEMENTARY

s 24	Effect of trustees exceeding their powers	**34.51**
s 25	Sole trustees	**34.52**
s 26	Restriction or exclusion of this part etc.	**34.53**

PART V REMUNERATION

s 28	Trustee's entitlement to payment under trust instrument	**34.54**
s 29	Remuneration of certain trustees	**34.55**
s 31	Trustees' expenses	**34.56**
s 32	Remuneration and expenses of agents, nominees and custodians	**34.57**

PART VI MISCELLANEOUS AND SUPPLEMENTARY

s 35	Personal representatives	**34.58**
s 39	Interpretation	**34.59**

SCHEDULE 1 Application of duty of care **34.60**

PART 3: INTESTACY RULES

ADMINISTRATION OF ESTATES ACT 1925

s 46	Succession to real and personal estate on intestacy	**35.1**
s 47	Statutory trusts in favour of issue and other classes of relatives of intestate	**35.2**
s 47A	Right of surviving spouse to have his own life interest redeemed	**35.3**

PART 4: INHERITANCE TAX AND CAPITAL GAINS TAX

INHERITANCE TAX ACT 1984
s 8A Transfer of unused nil-rate band between spouses and civil partners **36.1**
s 8B Claims under section 8A **36.2**
s 8C Section 8A and subsequent charges **36.3**
FINANCE ACT 2008
s 10 Sch 4 Inheritance Tax: Transfer of Nil-rate Band etc. **36.4**
INHERITANCE TAX ACT 1984
s 142 Alteration of dispositions taking effect on death **36.5**
s 143 Compliance with testator's request **36.6**
s 144 Distribution etc. from property settled by will **36.7**
Inland Revenue statement of practice 10/79 **36.8**
Inland Revenue press release 6 August 1975 **36.9**
TAXATION OF CHARGEABLE GAINS ACT 1992
s 62 Death: general provisions **36.10**

Appendix Part 1: Attestation, Construction and Interpretation

WILLS ACT 1837 ss 1, 7, 9, 15, 18, 18A, 24 and 33

1 Meaning of certain words in this Act

33.1 … the words and expressions herein-after mentioned, which in their ordinary signification have a more confined or a different meaning, shall in this Act, except where the nature of the provision or the context of the Act shall exclude such construction, be interpreted as follows; (that is to say,) the word "will" shall extend to a testament, and to a codicil, and to an appointment by will or by writing in the nature of a will in exercise of a power, [and also to an appointment by will of a guardian of a child][1], [and also to an appointment by will of a representative under section 4 of the Human Tissue Act 2004,][2] …[3] and to any other testamentary disposition; and the words "real estate" shall extend to manors, advowsons, messuages, lands, tithes, rents, and hereditaments, …[3] whether corporeal, incorporeal, or personal, …[4] and to any estate, right, or interest (other than a chattel interest) therein; and the words "personal estate" shall extend to leasehold estates and other chattels real, and also to monies, shares of government and other funds, securities for money (not being real estates), debts, choses in action, rights, credits, goods, and all other property whatsoever which by law devolves upon the executor or administrator, and to any share or interest therein; and every word importing the singular number only shall extend and be applied to several persons or things as well as one person or thing; and every word importing the masculine gender only shall extend and be applied to a female as well as a male[5].

1 The words in square brackets were substituted by the Children Act 1989 s 108(5), Sch 13 para 1 with effect from 14 October 1991.

2 The words in square brackets were inserted by the Human Tissue Act 2004 s 56, Sch 6 para 1 with effect from 1 September 2006.

3 The words omitted were repealed by the Statute Law (Repeals) Act 1969 s 1, Schedule Pt III with effect from 1 January 1970.

4 The words omitted were repealed by the Trusts of Land and Appointment of Trustees Act 1996 s 25(2), Sch 4 with effect from 1 January 1997.

5 Other words omitted were repealed by the Statute Law Revision Act 1893.

7 No Will of a person under age valid

33.2 … no will made by any person under the age of [eighteen years][1] shall be valid[2].

1 Words in square brackets substituted by the Family Law Reform Act 1969 s 3(1)(*a*) with effect from 1 January 1970.
2 Words omitted were repealed by the Statute Law Revision (No 2) Act 1888.

9 Signing and attestation of Wills[1]

33.3 No will shall be valid unless—
(*a*) it is in writing, and signed by the testator, or by some other person in his presence and by his direction; and
(*b*) it appears that the testator intended by his signature to give effect to the Will; and
(*c*) the signature is made or acknowledged by the testator in the presence of two or more witnesses present at the same time; and
(*d*) each witness either—
(i) attests and signs the Will; or
(ii) acknowledges his signature,
in the presence of the testator (but not necessarily in the presence of any other witness),
but no form of attestation shall be necessary.

1 This section was substituted by the Administration of Justice Act 1982 s 17 with effect from 1 January 1983.

15 Gifts to an attesting witness, or his or her wife or husband, to be void[1]

33.4 ... if any person shall attest the execution of any Will to whom or to whose wife or husband any beneficial devise, legacy, estate, interest, gift, or appointment, of or affecting any real or personal estate (other than and except charges and directions for the payment of any debt or debts), shall be thereby given or made, such devise, legacy, estate, interest, gift, or appointment shall, so far only as concerns such person attesting the execution of such Will, or the wife or husband of such person, or any person claiming under such person or wife or husband, be utterly null and void, and such person so attesting shall be admitted as a witness to prove the execution of such Will, or to prove the validity or invalidity thereof, notwithstanding such devise, legacy, estate, interest, gift, or appointment mentioned in such Will[2].

1 See Wills Act 1968 s 1 for exception.
2 Words omitted were repealed by the Statute Law Revision (No 2) Act 1888. This section applies in relation to the attestation of a Will by a person to whose civil partner there is given or made any such disposition as is here described as it applies in relation to a person to whose spouse is given or made any such disposition: Civil Partnership Act 2004 s 71, Sch 4 para 3.

18 Wills to be revoked by marriage, except in certain cases[1]

33.5 (1) Subject to subsections (2) to (4) below, a Will shall be revoked by the testator's marriage.

(2) A disposition in a Will in exercise of a power of appointment shall take effect notwithstanding the testator's subsequent marriage unless the property so appointed would in default of appointment pass to his personal representatives.

(3) Where it appears from a Will that at the time it was made the testator was expecting to be married to a particular person and that he intended that the Will should not be revoked by the marriage, the Will shall not be revoked by his marriage to that person.

(4) Where it appears from a Will that at the time it was made the testator was expecting to be married to a particular person and that he intended that a disposition in the Will should not be revoked by his marriage to that person—

(*a*) that disposition shall take effect notwithstanding the marriage; and

(*b*) any other disposition in the Will shall take effect also, unless it appears from the Will that the testator intended the disposition to be revoked by the marriage.

1 This section was substituted by the Administration of Justice Act 1982 s 18(1) with effect from 1 January 1983.

18A Effect of dissolution or annulment of marriage on Wills[1]

33.6 (1) Where, after a testator has made a Will, a decree of a court [of civil jurisdiction in England and Wales][2] dissolves or annuls his marriage [or his marriage is dissolved or annulled and the divorce or annulment is entitled to recognition in England and Wales by virtue of Part II of the Family Law Act 1986][3],—

[(*a*) provisions of the Will Appointing executors or trustees or conferring a power of appointment, if they appoint or confer the power on the former spouse, shall take effect as if the former spouse had died on the date on which the marriage is dissolved or annulled, and

(*b*) any property which, or an interest in which, is devised or bequeathed to the former spouse shall pass as if the former spouse had died on that date, except in so far as a contrary intention appears by the Will.][4]

(2) Subsection (1)(*b*) above is without prejudice to any right of the former spouse to apply for financial provision under the Inheritance (Provision for Family and Dependants) Act 1975[5].

1 This section was inserted by the Administration of Justice Act 1982 s 18(2) with effect from 1 January 1983.

2 The words in square brackets were inserted by the Family Law Act 1986 s 53(*a*) with effect from 4 April 1988.

3 The words in square brackets were substituted by the Family Law Act 1986 s 53(*b*) with effect from 4 April 1988.

4 Paragraphs (*a*) and (*b*) were substituted by the Law Rcform Succession Act 1995 s 3(1) with effect from 8 November 1995.

5 The original subsection (3) was repealed by the Law Reform Succession Act 1995 s 5, Schedule with effect from 8 November 1995.

18B Will to be revoked by civil partnership[1]

33.7 (1) Subject to subsections (2) to (6), a will is revoked by the formation of a civil partnership between the testator and another person.

(2) A disposition in a will in exercise of a power of appointment takes effect despite the formation of a subsequent civil partnership between the testator and another person unless the property so appointed would in default of appointment pass to the testator's personal representatives.

(3) If it appears from a will—

(*a*) that at the time it was made the testator was expecting to form a civil partnership with a particular person, and

(*b*) that he intended that the will should not be revoked by the formation of the civil partnership,
the will is not revoked by its formation.

(4) Subsections (5) and (6) apply if it appears from a will—
(*a*) that at the time it was made the testator was expecting to form a civil partnership with a particular person, and
(*b*) that he intended that a disposition in the will should not be revoked by the formation of the civil partnership.

(5) The disposition takes effect despite the formation of the civil partnership.

(6) Any other disposition in the will also takes effect, unless it appears from the will that the testator intended the disposition to be revoked by the formation of the civil partnership.

1 This section was inserted by the Civil Partnership Act 2004 s 71, Sch 4 paras 1, 2 with effect from 5 December 2005.

18C Effect of dissolution or annulment of civil partnership on wills[1]

33.8 (1) This section applies if, after a testator has made a will—
(*a*) a court of civil jurisdiction in England and Wales dissolves his civil partnership or makes a nullity order in respect of it, or
(*b*) his civil partnership is dissolved or annulled and the dissolution or annulment is entitled to recognition in England and Wales by virtue of Chapter 3 of Part 5 of the Civil Partnership Act 2004.

(2) Except in so far as a contrary intention appears by the will—
(*a*) provisions of the will appointing executors or trustees or conferring a power of appointment, if they appoint or confer the power on the former civil partner, take effect as if the former civil partner had died on the date on which the civil partnership is dissolved or annulled, and
(*b*) any property which, or an interest in which, is devised or bequeathed to the former civil partner shall pass as if the former civil partner had died on that date.

(3) Subsection (2)(*b*) does not affect any right of the former civil partner to apply for financial provision under the Inheritance (Provision for Family and Dependants) Act 1975.

1 This section was inserted by the Civil Partnership Act 2004 s 71, Sch 4 paras 1, 2 with effect from 5 December 2005.

20 No will to be revoked otherwise than as aforesaid or by another will or codicil, or by destruction thereof

33.9 … no will or codicil, or any part thereof, shall be revoked otherwise than as aforesaid, or by another will or codicil executed in manner herein-before required, or by some writing declaring an intention to revoke the same and executed in the manner in which a will is herein-before required to be executed, or by the burning, tearing, or otherwise destroying the same by the testator, or by some person in his presence and by his direction, with the intention of revoking the same.

21 No alteration in a will after execution except in certain cases, shall have any effect unless executed as a will

33.10 … no obliteration, interlineation, or other alteration made in any will after the execution thereof shall be valid or have any effect, except so far as the words or effect of the will before such alteration shall not be apparent, unless such alteration shall be executed in like manner as herein-before is required for the execution of the will; but the will, with such alteration as part thereof, shall be deemed to be duly executed if the signature of the testator and the subscription of the witnesses be made in the margin or on some other part of the will opposite or near to such alteration, or at the foot or end of or opposite to a memorandum referring to such alteration, and written at the end or some other part of the will.

22 No revoked will shall be revived otherwise than by re-execution or a codicil, etc

33.11 … no will or codicil, or any part thereof, which shall be in any manner revoked, shall be revived otherwise than by the re-execution thereof or by a codicil executed in manner herein-before required and showing an intention to revive the same; and when any will or codicil which shall be partly revoked, and afterwards wholly revoked, shall be revived, such revival shall not extend to so much thereof as shall have been revoked before the revocation of the whole thereof, unless an intention to the contrary shall be shown.

24 Wills shall be construed, as to the estate comprised, to speak from the death of the testator

33.12 … every Will shall be construed, with reference to the real estate and personal estate comprised in it, to speak and take effect as if it had been executed immediately before the death of the testator, unless a contrary intention shall appear by the Will[1].

1 Words omitted were repealed by the Statute Law Revision (No 2) Act 1888.

29 The words "die without issue", or "die without leaving issue", shall be construed to mean die without issue living at the death

33.13 … in any devise or bequest of real or personal estate the words "die without issue," or "die without leaving issue," or "have no issue," or any other words which may import either a want or failure of issue of any person in his lifetime or at the time of his death, or an indefinite failure of his issue, shall be construed to mean a want or failure of issue in the lifetime or at the time of the death of such person, and not an indefinite failure of his issue, unless a contrary intention shall appear by the will, by reason of such person having a prior estate tail, or of a preceding gift, being, without any implication arising from such words, a limitation of an estate tail to such person or issue, or otherwise: Provided, that this Act shall not extend to cases where such words as aforesaid import if no issue described in a preceding gift shall be born, or if there shall be no issue who shall live to attain the age or otherwise answer the description required for obtaining a vested estate by a preceding gift to such issue.

33 Gifts to children or other issue who leave issue living at the testator's death shall not lapse[1]

33.14 (1) Where—
(*a*) a Will contains a devise or bequest to a child or remoter descendant of the testator; and
(*b*) the intended beneficiary dies before the testator, leaving issue; and
(*c*) issue of the intended beneficiary are living at the testator's death,

then, unless a contrary intention appears by the Will, the devise or bequest shall take effect as a devise or bequest to the issue living at the testator's death.

(2) Where—
(*a*) a Will contains a devise or bequest to a class of person consisting of children or remoter descendants of the testator; and
(*b*) a member of the class dies before the testator, leaving issue, and
(*c*) issue of that member are living at the testator's death,

then, unless a contrary intention appears by the Will, the devise or bequest shall take effect as if the class included the issue of its deceased member living at the testator's death.

(3) Issue shall take under this section through all degrees, according to their stock, in equal shares if more than one, any gift or share which their parent would have taken and so that [(subject to section 33A)][2] no issue shall take whose parent is living at the testator's death and that no issue shall take whose parent is living at the testator's death and so capable of taking.

(4) For the purposes of this section—
(*a*) the illegitimacy of any person is to be disregarded; and
(*b*) a person conceived before the testator's death and born living thereafter is to be taken to have been living at the testator's death.

1 This section was substituted by the Administration of Justice Act 1982 s 19 with effect from 1 January 1983.
2 The words in square brackets were inserted by the Estates of Deceased Persons (Forfeiture Rule and Law of Succession) Act 2011 s 2(1), (3) with effect from 1 February 2012.

LAW OF PROPERTY ACT 1925 s 184

184 Presumption of survivorship in regard to claims to property

33.15 In all cases where, after the commencement of this Act, two or more persons have died in circumstances rendering it uncertain which of them survived the other or others, such deaths shall (subject to any order of the court), for all purposes affecting the title to property, be presumed to have occurred in order of seniority, and accordingly the younger shall be deemed to have survived the elder.

ADMINISTRATION OF ESTATES ACT 1925 ss 35 and 55

35 Charges on property of deceased to be paid primarily out of the property charged

33.16 (1) Where a person dies possessed of, or entitled to, or, under a general power of appointment (including the statutory power to dispose of entailed interests) by his will disposes of, an interest in property, which at the time of his death is charged with the payment of money, whether by way of legal mortgage, equitable charge or otherwise (including a lien for unpaid purchase money), and the deceased has not by will deed or other document signified a contrary or other intention, the interest so charged, shall as between the different persons claiming through the deceased, be primarily liable for the payment of the charge; and every part of the said interest, according to its value, shall bear a proportionate part of the charge on the whole thereof.

(2) Such contrary or other intention shall not be deemed to be signified—
(*a*) by a general direction for the payment of debts or of all the debts of the testator out of his personal estate, or his residuary real and personal estate, or his residuary real estate; or
(*b*) by a charge of debts upon any such estate;

unless such intention is further signified by words expressly or by necessary implication referring to all or some part of the charge.

(3) Nothing in this section affects the right of a person entitled to the charge to obtain payment or satisfaction thereof either out of the other assets of the deceased or otherwise.

55 DEFINITIONS

33.17 In this Act, unless the context otherwise requires, the following expressions have the meanings hereby assigned to them respectively, that is to say—

(1)—
(i) "Administration" means, with reference to the real and personal estate of a deceased person, letters of administration whether general or limited, or with the will annexed or otherwise;
(ii) "Administrator" means a person to whom administration is granted;
(iii) "Conveyance" includes a mortgage, charge by way of legal mortgage, lease, assent, vesting, declaration, vesting instrument, disclaimer, release and every other assurance of property or of an interest therein by any instrument, except a will, and convey has a corresponding meaning, and disposition includes a conveyance also a devise bequest and an appointment of property contained in a will, and dispose of has a corresponding meaning;
[(iiiA) "the County Court limit", in relation to any enactment contained in this Act, means the amount for the time being specified by an Order in Council under section 145 of the County Courts Act 1984 as the county court limit for the purposes of that enactment (or, where no such Order in Council has been made, the corresponding limit specified by Order in Council under section 192 of the County Courts Act 1959);][1]

(iv) "the Court" means the High Court and also the county court, where that court has jurisdiction …[2];

(v) "Income" includes rents and profits;

(vi) "Intestate" includes a person who leaves a will but dies intestate as to some beneficial interest in his real or personal estate;

[(via) "Land" has the same meaning as in the Law of Property Act 1925;][3]

(vii) "Legal estates" mean the estates charges and interests in or over land (subsisting or created at law) which are by statute authorised to subsist or to be created at law; and equitable interests mean all other interests and charges in or over land …[4];

(viii) …[5];

(ix) "Pecuniary legacy" includes an annuity, a general legacy, a demonstrative legacy so far as it is not discharged out of the designated property, and any other general direction by a testator for the payment of money, including all death duties free from which any devise, bequest, or payment is made to take effect;

[(x) "Personal chattels" means tangible movable property, other than any such property which–

Consists of money or securities for money, or

was used at the death of the intestate solely or mainly for business purposes, or

was held at the death of the intestate solely as an investment;][6]

(xi) "Personal representative" means the executor, original or by representation, or administrator for the time being of a deceased person, and as regards any liability for the payment of death duties includes any person who takes possession of or intermeddles with the property of a deceased person without the authority of the personal representatives or the court, and executor includes a person deemed to be appointed executor as respects settled land;

(xii) "Possession" includes the receipt of rents and profits or the right to receive the same, if any;

(xiii) "Prescribed" means prescribed by rules of court …[7];

(xiv) "Probate" means the probate of a will;

(xv) …[8]

(xvi) …[9]

(xvii) "Property" includes a thing in action and any interest in real or personal property;

(xviii) "Purchaser" means a lessee, mortgagee, or other person who in good faith acquires an interest in property for valuable consideration, also an intending purchaser and valuable consideration includes marriage [and formation of a civil partnership][10], but does not include a nominal consideration in money;

(xix) "Real estate" save as provided in Part IV of this Act means real estate, including chattels real, which by virtue of Part I of this Act devolves on the personal representative of a deceased person;

(xx) "Representation" means the probate of a will and administration, and the expression taking out representation refers to the obtaining of the probate of a will or of the grant of administration;

(xxi) "Rent" includes a rent service or a rentcharge, or other rent, toll, duty, or annual or periodical payment in money or moneys worth, issuing out of or charged upon land, but does not include mortgage interest; and rentcharge includes a fee farm rent;

(xxii) …[11]

(xxiii) "Securities" include stocks, funds, or shares;

(xxiv) "Tenant for life", "statutory owner", ...[12] "settled land", "settlement", "trustees of the settlement", "term of years absolute", "death duties", and "legal mortgage", have the same meanings as in the Settled Land Act 1925, and "entailed interest" and "charge by way of legal mortgage" have the same meanings as in the Law of Property Act 1925;

(xxv) "Treasury solicitor" means the solicitor for the affairs of His Majesty's Treasury, and includes the solicitor for the affairs of the Duchy of Lancaster;

(xxvi) "Trust corporation" means the public trustee or a corporation either appointed by the court in any particular case to be a trustee or entitled by rules made under subsection (3) of section four of the Public Trustee Act 1906, to act as custodian trustee;

(xxvii) ...[13]

(xxviii) "Will" includes codicil.

(2) References to a child or issue living at the death of any person include child or issue en ventre sa mère at the death.

(3) References to the estate of a deceased person include property over which the deceased exercises a general power of appointment (including the statutory power to dispose of entailed interests) by his will.

1 Paragraph (iiiA) was inserted by the County Courts Act 1984 s 148(1), Sch 2 para 15 with effect from 1 August 1984.
2 The word omitted was repealed by the Courts Act 1971 s 56(4), Sch 11 Pt II with effect from 1 October 1971.
3 Paragraph (via) was inserted by the Trusts of Land and Appointment of Trustees Act 1996 s 25(1), Sch 3 para 6(1), (5) with effect from 1 January 1997.
4 The words omitted were repealed by the Trusts of Land and Appointment of Trustees Act 1996 s 25(2), Sch 4 with effect from 1 January 1997.
5 Paragraph (viii) was repealed by the Mental Capacity Act 2005 s 67(1), (2), Sch 6 para 5(1), (3), Sch 7 with effect from 1 October 2007.
6 Paragraph (x) was substituted by the Inheritance and Trustees' Powers Act 2014 s 3(1) with effect from 1 October 2014.
7 The words omitted were repealed by the Senior Courts Act 1981 s 152(4), Sch 7 with effect from 22 July 2004.
8 Paragraph (xv) was repealed by the Law of Property (Miscellaneous Provisions) Act 1994 s 21(2), Sch 2 with effect from 15 February 1995.
9 Paragraph (xvi) was repealed by the Senior Courts Act 1981 s 152(4), Sch 7 with effect from 22 July 2004.
10 The words in square brackets were inserted by the Civil Partnership Act 2004 s 71, Sch 4 para 12 with effect from 5 December 2005.
11 Paragraph (xxii) was repealed by the Senior Courts Act 1981 s 152(4), Sch 7 with effect from 22 July 2004.
12 The word omitted was repealed by the Trusts of Land and Appointment of Trustees Act 1996 s 25(2), Sch 4 with effect from 1 January 1997.
13 Paragraph (xxvii) was repealed by the Trusts of Land and Appointment of Trustees Act 1996 s 25(2), Sch 4 with effect from 1 January 1997.

WILLS ACT 1968 s 1

1 Restriction of operation of Wills Act 1837 s 15

33.18 (1) For the purposes of section 15 of the Wills Act 1837 (avoidance of gifts to attesting witnesses and their spouses) the attestation of a Will by a person to whom or to whose spouse there is given or made any such disposition as is described in that section shall be disregarded if the Will is duly executed without his attestation and without that of any other such person.

(2) This section applies to the Will of any person dying after the passing of this Act, whether executed before or after the passing of this Act[1].

1 This section applies in relation to the attestation of a Will by a person to whose civil partner there is given or made any such disposition as is here described as it applies in relation to a person to whose spouse is given or made any such disposition: Civil Partnership Act 2004 s 71, Sch 4 para 3.

ADMINISTRATION OF JUSTICE ACT 1982 ss 20 and 21

20 Rectification

33.19 (1) If a court is satisfied that a Will is so expressed that it fails to carry out the testator's intentions, in consequence—

(*a*) of a clerical error; or

(*b*) of a failure to understand his instructions,

it may order that the Will shall be rectified so as to carry out his intentions.

(2) An application for an order under this section shall not, except with the permission of the court, be made after the end of the period of six months from the date on which representation with respect to the estate of the deceased is first taken out.

(3) The provisions of this section shall not render the personal representatives of a deceased person liable for having distributed any part of the estate of the deceased, after the end of the period of six months from the date on which representation with respect to the estate of the deceased is first taken out, on the ground that they ought to have taken into account the possibility that the court might permit the making of an application for an order under this section after the end of that period; but this subsection shall not prejudice any power to recover, by reason of the making of an order under this section, any part of the estate so distributed.

[(4) The following are to be left out of account when considering for the purposes of this section when representation with respect to the estate of a deceased person was first taken out—

(*a*) a grant limited to settled land or to trust property,

(*b*) any other grant that does not permit any of the estate to be distributed,

(*c*) a grant limited to real estate or to personal estate, unless a grant limited to the remainder of the estate has previously been made or is made at the same time,

(*d*) a grant, or its equivalent, made outside the United Kingdom (but see subsection (5)).

(5) A grant sealed under section 2 of the Colonial Probates Act 1892 counts as a grant made in the United Kingdom for the purposes of subsection (4), but is to be taken as dated on the date of sealing.][1]

1 Subsections (4) and (5) were substituted for sub-s (4) by the Inheritance and Trustees' Powers Act 2014 s 7, Sch 3, para 3 with effect from 1 October 2014.

21 Interpretation of wills—general rules as to evidence

33.20 (1) This section applies to a Will—

(*a*) in so far as any part of it is meaningless;

(*b*) in so far as the language used in any part of it is ambiguous on the face of it;

(*c*) in so far as evidence, other than evidence of the testator's intention, shows that the language used in any part of it is ambiguous in the light of surrounding circumstances.

(2) In so far as this section applies to a will extrinsic evidence, including evidence of the testator's intention, may be admitted to assist in its interpretation.

MENTAL CAPACITY ACT 2005 ss 16, 18 and Sch 2 paras 1 to 4

16 Powers to make decisions and appoint deputies: general

33.21 (1) This section applies if a person ("P") lacks capacity in relation to a matter or matters concerning—

. . .

(*b*) P's property and affairs.

(2) The court may—

(*a*) by making an order, make the decision or decisions on P's behalf in relation to the matter or matters, or

(*b*) appoint a person (a "deputy") to make decisions on P's behalf in relation to the matter or matters.

(3) The powers of the court under this section are subject to the provisions of this Act and, in particular, to sections 1 (the principles) and 4 (best interests).

. . .

18 Section 16 powers: property and affairs

33.22 (1) The powers under section 16 as respects P's property and affairs extend in particular to—

. . .

(j) the execution for P of a will;

. . .

(2) No will may be made under subsection (1)(i) at a time when P has not reached 18.

. . .

(4) Schedule 2 supplements the provisions of this section.

SCHEDULE 2
PROPERTY AND AFFAIRS: SUPPLEMENTARY PROVISIONS

Wills: general

33.23 1

Paragraphs 2 to 4 apply in relation to the execution of a will, by virtue of section 18, on behalf of P

Provision that may be made in will

2

The will may make any provision (whether by disposing of property or exercising a power or otherwise) which could be made by a will executed by P if he had capacity to make it.

Wills: requirements relating to execution

3

(1) Sub-paragraph (2) applies if under section 16 the court makes an order or gives directions requiring or authorising a person ("the authorised person") to execute a will on behalf of P.

(2) Any will executed in pursuance of the order or direction—
(*a*) must state that it is signed by P acting by the authorised person,
(*b*) must be signed by the authorised person with the name of P and his own name, in the presence of two or more witnesses present at the same time,
(*c*) must be attested and subscribed by those witnesses in the presence of the authorised person, and
(*d*) must be sealed with the official seal of the court.

Wills: effect of execution

4

(1) This paragraph applies where a will is executed in accordance with paragraph 3.

(2) The Wills Act 1837 has effect in relation to the will as if it were signed by P by his own hand, except that—
(*a*) section 9 of the 1837 Act (requirements as to signing and attestation) does not apply, and
(*b*) in the subsequent provisions of the 1837 Act any reference to execution in the manner required by the previous provisions is to be read as a reference to execution in accordance with paragraph 3.

(3) The will has the same effect for all purposes as if—
(*a*) P had had the capacity to make a valid will, and
(*b*) the will had been executed by him in the manner required by the 1837 Act.

(4) But sub-paragraph (3) does not have effect in relation to the will—
(*a*) in so far as it disposes of immovable property outside England and Wales, or
(*b*) in so far as it relates to any other property or matter if, when the will is executed—
  (i) P is domiciled outside England and Wales, and
  (ii) the condition in sub-paragraph (5) is met.

(5) The condition is that, under the law of P's domicile, any question of his testamentary capacity would fall to be determined in accordance with the law of a place outside England and Wales.

FAMILY LAW REFORM ACT 1987 ss 1 and 19

Part I
General Principle

1 General principle

33.24 (1) In this Act and enactments passed and instruments made after the coming into force of this section, references (however expressed) to any relationship between two persons shall, unless the contrary intention appears, be construed without regard to whether or not the father and mother of either of them, or the father and mother of any person through whom the relationship is deduced, have or had been married to each other at any time.

(2) In this Act and enactments passed after the coming into force of this section, unless the contrary intention appears—
(*a*) references to a person whose father and mother were married to each other at the time of his birth include; and
(*b*) references to a person whose father and mother were not married to each other at the time of his birth do not include, references to any person to whom subsection (3) below applies, and cognate references shall be construed accordingly.

(3) This subsection applies to any person who—
(*a*) is treated as legitimate by virtue of section 1 of the Legitimacy Act 1976;
(*b*) is a legitimated person within the meaning of section 10 of that Act;
[(*ba*) has a parent by virtue of section 42 of the Human Fertilisation and Embryology Act 2008 (which relates to treatment provided to a woman who is at the time of treatment [married to a woman or][1] a party to a civil partnership or, in certain circumstances, a void [marriage or][1] civil partnership);
(*bb*) has a parent by virtue of section 43 of that Act (which relates to treatment provided to woman who agrees that second woman to be parent) who—
(i) is [married to or][1] the civil partner of the child's mother at the time of the child's birth, or
(ii) was [married to or][1] the civil partner of the child's mother at any time during the period beginning with the time mentioned in section 43(*b*) of that Act and ending with the child's birth;][2]
[(*c*) is an adopted person within the meaning of Chapter 4 of Part 1 of the Adoption of Children Act 2002][3]; or
(*d*) is otherwise treated in law as legitimate.

(4) For the purpose of construing references falling within subsection (2) above, the time of a person's birth shall be taken to include any time during the period beginning with—
(*a*) the insemination resulting in his birth; or
(*b*) where there was no such insemination, his conception,
and (in either case) ending with his birth.

[(5) A child whose parents are parties to a void civil partnership shall, subject to subsection (6), be treated as falling within subsection (3)(bb) if at the time when the parties registered as civil partners of each other both or either of the parties reasonably believed that the civil partnership was valid.

(6) Subsection (5) applies only where the woman who is a parent by virtue of section 43 was domiciled in England and Wales at the time of the birth or, if she died before the birth, was so domiciled immediately before her death.

(7) Subsection (5) applies even though the belief that the civil partnership was valid was due to a mistake as to law.

(8) It shall be presumed for the purposes of subsection (5), unless the contrary is shown, that one of the parties to a void civil partnership reasonably believed at the time of the formation of the civil partnership that the civil partnership was valid.][4]

1 The words in square brackets were inserted by the Marriage (Same Sex Couples) Act 2013 (Consequential and Contrary Provisions and Scotland) Order 2014, SI 2014/560, art 2, Sch 1 para 19 with effect from 13 March 2014.

2 Paragraphs (*ba*) and (*bb*) were inserted by the Human Fertilisation and Embryology Act 2008 ss 56, Sch 6 paras 24(1), (2) with effect from 6 April 2009.

3 Paragraph (*c*) was substituted by the Adoption and Children Act 2002 s 139(1), Sch 3 paras 50, 51 with effect from 30 December 2005.

4 Subsections (5), (6), (7) and (8) were inserted by the Human Fertilisation and Embryology Act 2008 ss 56, Sch 6 paras 24(1), (3) with effect from 6 April 2009.

19 Dispositions of property

33.25 (1) In the following dispositions, namely—

(*a*) dispositions inter vivos made on or after the date on which this section comes into force; and

(*b*) dispositions by will or codicil where the will or codicil is made on or after that date,

references (whether express or implied) to any relationship between two persons shall be construed in accordance with section 1 above.

(2) It is hereby declared that the use, without more, of the word "heir" or "heirs" or any expression [purporting to create][1] an entailed interest in real or personal property does not show a contrary intention for the purposes of section 1 as applied by subsection (1) above.

(3) In relation to the dispositions mentioned in subsection (1) above, section 33 of the Trustee Act 1925 (which specifies the trust implied by a direction that income is to be held on protective trusts for the benefit of any person) shall have effect as if any reference (however expressed) to any relationship between two persons were construed in accordance with section 1 above.

(4) Where under any disposition of real or personal property, any interest in such property is limited (whether subject to any preceding limitation or charge or not) in such a way that it would, apart from this section, devolve (as nearly as the law permits) along with a dignity or title of honour, then—

(*a*) whether or not the disposition contains an express reference to the dignity or title of honour; and

(*b*) whether or not the property or some interest in the property may in some event become severed from it,

nothing in this section shall operate to sever the property or any interest in it from the dignity or title, but the property or interest shall devolve in all respects as if this section had not been enacted.

(5) This section is without prejudice to section 42 of the Adoption Act 1976 [or section 69 of the Adoption and Children Act 2002][2] (construction of dispositions in cases of adoption).

(6) In this section "disposition" means a disposition, including an oral disposition, of real or personal property whether inter vivos or by will or codicil.

(7) notwithstanding any rule of law, a disposition made by will or codicil executed before the date on which this section comes into force shall not be treated for the purposes of this section as made on or after that date by reason only that the will or codicil is confirmed by a codicil executed on or after that date.

1 The words in square brackets were substituted by the Trusts of Land and Appointment of Trustees Act 1996 s 25(1), Sch 3 para 25 with effect from 1 January 1997.

2 The words in square brackets were inserted by the Adoption and Children Act 2002 s 139(1), Sch 3 paras 50, 52 with effect from 30 December 2005.

Legitimacy Act 1976 s 5

5 Rights of legitimated persons and others to take interests in property

33.26 (1) Subject to any contrary indication, the rules of construction contained in this section apply to any instrument other than an existing instrument, so far as the instrument contains a disposition of property.

(2) For the purposes of this section, provisions of the law of intestate succession applicable to the estate of a deceased person shall be treated as if contained in an instrument executed by him (while of full capacity) immediately before his death.

(3) A legitimated person, and any other person, shall be entitled to take any interest as if the legitimated person had been born legitimate.

(4) A disposition which depends on the date of birth of a child or children of the parent or parents shall be construed as if—
(*a*) a legitimated child had been born on the date of legitimation,
(*b*) two or more legitimated children legitimated on the same date had been born on that date in the order of their actual births,
but this does not affect any reference to the age of a child.

(5) Examples of phrases in wills on which subsection (4) above can operate are—
1. Children of A "living at my death or born afterwards".
2. Children of A "living at my death or born afterwards before any one of such children for the time being in existence attains a vested interest, and who attain the age of 21 years".
3. As in example 1 or 2, but referring to grandchildren of A, instead of children of A.
4. A for life "until he has a child" and then to his child or children.

Note. Subsection (4) above will not affect the reference to the age of 21 years in example 2.

(6) If an illegitimate person or a person adopted by one of his natural parents dies, or has died before the commencement of this Act, and—
(*a*) after his death his parents marry or have married; and
(*b*) the deceased would, if living at the time of the marriage, have become a legitimated person,

this section shall apply for the construction of the instrument so far as it relates to the taking of interests by, or in succession to, his spouse, children and remoter issue as if he had been legitimated by virtue of the marriage.

(7) In this section "instrument" includes a private Act settling property, but not any other enactment.

ADOPTION AND CHILDREN ACT 2002 ss 66 to 70, 72 and 73

Status of Adopted Children

66 Meaning of adoption in Chapter 4

33.27 (1) In this Chapter "adoption" means—
(*a*) adoption by an adoption order or a Scottish or Northern Irish adoption order,
(*b*) adoption by an order made in the Isle of Man or any of the Channel Islands,
(*c*) an adoption effected under the law of a Convention country outside the British Islands, and certified in pursuance of Article 23(1) of the Convention (referred to in this Act as a "Convention adoption"),
(*d*) an overseas adoption, or
(*e*) an adoption recognised by the law of England and Wales and effected under the law of any other country;

and related expressions are to be interpreted accordingly.

(2) But references in this Chapter to adoption do not include an adoption effected before the day on which this Chapter comes into force (referred to in this Chapter as "the appointed day").

(3) Any reference in an enactment to an adopted person within the meaning of this Chapter includes a reference to an adopted child within the meaning of Part 4 of the Adoption Act 1976 (c 36).

67 Status conferred by adoption

33.28 (1) An adopted person is to be treated in law as if born as the child of the adopters or adopter.

(2) An adopted person is the legitimate child of the adopters or adopter and, if adopted by—
(*a*) a couple, or
(*b*) one of a couple under section 51(2),

is to be treated as the child of the relationship of the couple in question.

(3) An adopted person—
(*a*) if adopted by one of a couple under section 51(2), is to be treated in law as not being the child of any person other than the adopter and the other one of the couple, and
(*b*) in any other case, is to be treated in law, subject to subsection (4), as not being the child of any person other than the adopters or adopter;

but this subsection does not affect any reference in this Act to a person's natural parent or to any other natural relationship.

(4) In the case of a person adopted by one of the person's natural parents as sole adoptive parent, subsection (3)(*b*) has no effect as respects entitlement to property depending on relationship to that parent, or as respects anything else depending on that relationship.

(5) This section has effect from the date of the adoption.

(6) Subject to the provisions of this Chapter and Schedule 4, this section—
(*a*) applies for the interpretation of enactments or instruments passed or made before as well as after the adoption, and so applies subject to any contrary indication, and
(*b*) has effect as respects things done, or events occurring, on or after the adoption.

68 Adoptive relatives

33.29 (1) A relationship existing by virtue of section 67 may be referred to as an adoptive relationship, and—
(*a*) an adopter may be referred to as an adoptive parent or (as the case may be) as an adoptive father or adoptive mother,
(*b*) any other relative of any degree under an adoptive relationship may be referred to as an adoptive relative of that degree.

(2) Subsection (1) does not affect the interpretation of any reference, not qualified by the word "adoptive", to a relationship.

(3) A reference (however expressed) to the adoptive mother and father of a child adopted by—
(*a*) a couple of the same sex, or
(*b*) a partner of the child's parent, where the couple are of the same sex,
is to be read as a reference to the child's adoptive parents.

69 Rules of interpretation for instruments concerning property

33.30 (1) The rules of interpretation contained in this section apply (subject to any contrary indication and to Schedule 4) to any instrument so far as it contains a disposition of property.

(2) In applying section 67(1) and (2) to a disposition which depends on the date of birth of a child or children of the adoptive parent or parents, the disposition is to be interpreted as if—
(*a*) the adopted person had been born on the date of adoption,
(*b*) two or more people adopted on the same date had been born on that date in the order of their actual births;

but this does not affect any reference to a person's age.

(3) Examples of phrases in wills on which subsection (2) can operate are—
1 Children of A "living at my death or born afterwards".
2 Children of A "living at my death or born afterwards before any one of such children for the time being in existence attains a vested interest and who attain the age of 21 years".

3 As in example 1 or 2, but referring to grandchildren of A instead of children of A.

4 A for life "until he has a child", and then to his child or children.

Note Subsection (2) will not affect the reference to the age of 21 years in example 2.

(4) Section 67(3) does not prejudice—

(*a*) any qualifying interest, ...[1]

(*b*) any interest expectant (whether immediately or not) upon a qualifying interest[, or

(*c*) any contingent interest (other than a contingent interest in remainder) which the adopted person has immediately before the adoption in the estate of a deceased parent, whether testate or intestate.][2]

"Qualifying interest" means an interest vested in possession in the adopted person before the adoption.

(5) Where it is necessary to determine for the purposes of a disposition of property effected by an instrument whether a woman can have a child—

(*a*) it must be presumed that once a woman has attained the age of 55 years she will not adopt a person after execution of the instrument, and

(*b*) if she does so, then (in spite of section 67) that person is not to be treated as her child or (if she does so as one of a couple) as the child of the other one of the couple for the purposes of the instrument.

(6) In this section, "instrument" includes a private Act settling property, but not any other enactment.

1 Word omitted was repealed by the Inheritance and Trustees' Powers Act 2014 s 4(1)(*a*) with effect from 1 October 2014.

2 Words in square brackets were inserted by the Inheritance and Trustees' Powers Act 2014 s 4(1)(*b*) with effect from 1 October 2014.

70 Dispositions depending on date of birth

33.31 (1) Where a disposition depends on the date of birth of a person who was born illegitimate and who is adopted by one of the natural parents as sole adoptive parent, section 69(2) does not affect entitlement by virtue of Part 3 of the Family Law Reform Act 1987 (dispositions of property).

(2) Subsection (1) applies for example where—

(*a*) a testator dies in 2001 bequeathing a legacy to his eldest grandchild living at a specified time,

(*b*) his unmarried daughter has a child in 2002 who is the first grandchild,

(*c*) his married son has a child in 2003,

(*d*) subsequently his unmarried daughter adopts her child as sole adoptive parent.

In that example the status of the daughter's child as the eldest grandchild of the testator is not affected by the events described in paragraphs (*c*) and (*d*).

72 Protection of trustees and personal representatives

33.32 (1) A trustee or personal representative is not under a duty, by virtue of the law relating to trusts or the administration of estates, to enquire, before conveying or distributing any property, whether any adoption has been effected or revoked if that fact could affect entitlement to the property.

(2) A trustee or personal representative is not liable to any person by reason of a conveyance or distribution of the property made without regard to any such fact if he has not received notice of the fact before the conveyance or distribution.

(3) This section does not prejudice the right of a person to follow the property, or any property representing it, into the hands of another person, other than a purchaser, who has received it.

73 Meaning of disposition

33.33 (1) This section applies for the purposes of this Chapter.

(2) A disposition includes the conferring of a power of appointment and any other disposition of an interest in or right over property; and in this subsection a power of appointment includes any discretionary power to transfer a beneficial interest in property without the furnishing of valuable consideration.

(3) This Chapter applies to an oral disposition as if contained in an instrument made when the disposition was made.

(4) The date of death of a testator is the date at which a will or codicil is to be regarded as made.

(5) The provisions of the law of intestate succession applicable to the estate of a deceased person are to be treated as if contained in an instrument executed by him (while of full capacity) immediately before his death.

Appendix Part 2: Powers

TRUSTEE ACT 1925 ss 19, 31 and 32

19 Power to insure[1]

34.1 (1) A trustee may—
(*a*) insure any property which is subject to the trust against risks of loss or damage due to any event, and
(*b*) pay the premiums out of the trust funds.

(2) In the case of property held on a bare trust, the power to insure is subject to any direction given by the beneficiary or each of the beneficiaries—
(*a*) that any property specified in the direction is not to be insured,
(*b*) that any property specified in the direction is not to be insured except on such conditions as may be so specified.

(3) Property is held on a bare trust if it is held on trust for—
(*a*) a beneficiary who is of full age and capacity and absolutely entitled to the property subject to the trust, or
(*b*) beneficiaries each of whom is of full age and capacity and who (taken together) are absolutely entitled to the property subject to the trust.

(4) If a direction under subsection (2) of this section is given, the power to insure, so far as it is subject to the direction, ceases to be a delegable function for the purposes of section 11 of the Trustee Act 2000 (power to employ agents).

(5) In this section "trust funds" means any income or capital funds of the trust.

1 This section was substituted by the Trustee Act 2000 s 34(1) with effect from 1 February 2001.

31 Power to apply income for maintenance and to accumulate surplus income during a minority

34.2 (1) Where any property is held by trustees in trust for any person for any interest whatsoever, whether vested or contingent, then, subject to any prior interests or charges affecting that property—
(i) during the infancy of any such person, if his interest so long continues, the trustees may, at their sole discretion, pay to his parent or guardian, if any, or otherwise apply for or towards his maintenance, education, or benefit, the

whole or such part, if any, of the income of that property [as the trustees may think fit][1] whether or not there is—

(*a*) any other fund applicable to the same purpose, or

(*b*) any person bound by law to provide for his maintenance or education, and

(ii) if such person on attaining the age of [eighteen years][2] has not a vested interest in such income, the trustees shall thenceforth pay the income of that property and of any accretion thereto under subsection (2) of this section to him, until he either attains a vested interest therein or dies, or until failure of his interest:

. . .[3]

(2) During the infancy of any such person, if his interest so long continues, the trustees shall accumulate all the residue of that income [by investing it, and any profits from so investing it][4] from time to time in authorised investments, and shall hold those accumulations as follows:—

(i) If any such person—

(*a*) attains the age of [eighteen years][2], or marries under that age [or forms a civil partnership under that age][5], and his interest in such income during his infancy[, or until his marriage or his formation of a civil partnership,][6] is a vested interest; or

(*b*) on attaining the age of [eighteen years][2] or on marriage[, or formation of a civil partnership,][7] under that age becomes entitled to the property from which such income arose in fee simple, absolute or determinable, or absolutely, or for an entailed interest;

the trustees shall hold the accumulations in trust for such person absolutely, but without prejudice to any provision with respect thereto contained in any settlement by him made under any statutory powers during his infancy, and so that the receipt of such person after marriage [or formation of a civil partnership][8], and though still an infant, shall be a good discharge; and

(ii) In any other case the trustees shall, notwithstanding that such person had a vested interest in such income, hold the accumulations as an accretion to the capital of the property from which such accumulations arose, and as one fund with such capital for all purposes, and so that, if such property is settled land, such accumulations shall be held upon the same trusts as if the same were capital money arising therefrom;

but the trustees may, at any time during the infancy of such person if his interest so long continues, apply those accumulations, or any part thereof, as if they were income arising in the then current year.

(3) This section applies in the case of a contingent interest only if the limitation or trust carries the intermediate income of the property, but it applies to a future or contingent legacy by the parent of, or a person standing in loco parentis to, the legatee, if and for such period as, under the general law, the legacy carries interest for the maintenance of the legatee, and in any such case as last aforesaid the rate of interest shall (if the income available is sufficient, and subject to any rules of court to the contrary) be five pounds per centum per annum.

(4) This section applies to a vested annuity in like manner as if the annuity were the income of property held by trustees in trust to pay the income thereof to the annuitant for the same period for which the annuity is payable, save that in any case accumulations made during the infancy of the annuitant shall be held in trust for the annuitant or his personal representatives absolutely.

(5) This section does not apply where the instrument, if any, under which the interest arises came into operation before the commencement of this Act.

1 The words in square brackets were substituted by the Inheritance and Trustees' Powers Act 2014 s 8(*a*) with effect from 1 October 2014.
2 The words in square brackets were substituted by the Family Law Reform Act 1969 s 1(3), Sch 1 Pt I with effect from 1 January 1970.
3 The words omitted were repealed by the Inheritance and Trustees' Powers Act 2014 s 8(*b*) with effect from 1 October 2014.
4 The words in square brackets were substituted by the Trustee Act 2000 s 40(1), Sch 2 para 25 with effect from 1 February 2001.
5 The words in square brackets were inserted by the Civil Partnership Act 2004 s 261(1), Sch 27 para 5(1), (2)(*a*) with effect from 5 December 2005.
6 The words in square brackets were substituted by the Civil Partnership Act 2004 s 261(1), Sch 27 para 5(1), (2)(*b*) with effect from 5 December 2005.
7 The words in square brackets were inserted by the Civil Partnership Act 2004 s 261(1), Sch 27 para 5(1), (3) with effect from 5 December 2005.
8 The words in square brackets were inserted by the Civil Partnership Act 2004 s 261(1), Sch 27 para 5(1), (5) with effect from 5 December 2005.

32 Power of advancement

34.3 (1) Trustees may at any time or times pay or apply any capital money subject to a trust, [or transfer or apply any other property forming part of the capital of the trust property,][1] for the advancement or benefit, in such manner as they may, in their absolute discretion, think fit, of any person entitled to the capital of the trust property or of any share thereof, whether absolutely or contingently on his attaining any specified age or on the occurrence of any other event, or subject to a gift over on his death under any specified age or on the occurrence of any other event, and whether in possession or in remainder or reversion, and such payment[, transfer][1] or application may be made notwithstanding that the interest of such person is liable to be defeated by the exercise of a power of appointment or revocation, or to be diminished by the increase of the class to which he belongs:

Provided that—

(*a*) [property (including any money) so paid, transferred or applied for the advancement or benefit of any person must not, altogether, represent more than][2] …[3] the presumptive or vested share or interest of that person in the trust property, and

(*b*) if that person is or becomes absolutely and indefeasibly entitled to a share in the trust property [the money or other property so paid, transferred or applied][2] shall be brought into account as part of such share, and

(*c*) no such payment[, transfer][1] or application shall be made so as to prejudice any person entitled to any prior life or other interest, whether vested or contingent, in the money [or other property paid, transferred][2] or applied unless such person is in existence and of full age and consents in writing to such payment[, transfer][1] or application.

[(1A) In exercise of the foregoing power trustees may pay, transfer or apply money or other property on the basis (express or implied) that it shall be treated as a proportionate part of the capital out of which it was paid, transferred or applied, for the purpose of bringing it into account in accordance with proviso (*b*) to subsection (1) of this section.][1]

[(2) This section does not apply to capital money arising under the Settled Land Act, 1925.][4]

(3) This section does not apply to trusts constituted or created before the commencement of this Act.

1 The words in square brackets were inserted by the Inheritance and Trustees' Powers Act 2014 s 9(1), (2), (5)(*a*), (6) with effect from 1 October 2014.
2 The words in square brackets were substituted by the Inheritance and Trustees' Powers Act 2014 s 9(1), (3)(*a*), (4), (5)(*b*) with effect from 1 October 2014.
3 The words omitted were repealed by the Inheritance and Trustees' Powers Act 2014 s 9(1), (3)(*b*) with effect from 1 October 2014.
4 Subsection (2) was substituted by the Trusts of Land and Appointment of Trustees Act 1996 s 25(1), Sch 3 para 3(1), (8) with effect from 1 January 1997.

33 Protective trusts

34.4 (1) Where any income, including an annuity or other periodical income payment, is directed to be held on protective trusts for the benefit of any person (in this section called "the principal beneficiary") for the period of his life or for any less period, then, during that period (in this section called the "trust period") the said income shall, without prejudice to any prior interest, be held on the following trusts, namely:—

(i) Upon trust for the principal beneficiary during the trust period or until he, whether before or after the termination of any prior interest, does or attempts to do or suffers any act or thing, or until any event happens, other than an advance under any statutory or express power, whereby, if the said income were payable during the trust period to the principal beneficiary absolutely during that period, he would be deprived of the right to receive the same or any part thereof, in any of which cases, as well as on the termination of the trust period, whichever first happens, this trust of the said income shall fail or determine;

(ii) If the trust aforesaid fails or determines during the subsistence of the trust period, then, during the residue of that period, the said income shall be held upon trust for the application thereof for the maintenance or support, or otherwise for the benefit, of all or any one or more exclusively of the other or others of the following persons (that is to say)—
  (*a*) the principal beneficiary and his or her [spouse or civil partner][1], if any, and his or her children or more remote issue, if any, or
  (*b*) if there is no [spouse or civil partner][1] or issue of the principal beneficiary in existence, the principal beneficiary and the persons who would, if he were actually dead, be entitled to the trust property or the income thereof or to the annuity fund, if any, or arrears of the annuity, as the case may be,

as the trustees in their absolute discretion, without being liable to account for the exercise of such discretion, think fit.

(2) This section does not apply to trusts coming into operation before the commencement of this Act, and has effect subject to any variation of the implied trusts aforesaid contained in the instrument creating the trust.

(3) Nothing in this section operates to validate any trust which would, if contained in the instrument creating the trust, be liable to be set aside.

[(4) In relation to the dispositions mentioned in section 19(1) of the Family Law Reform Act 1987, this section shall have effect as if any reference (however expressed) to any relationship between two persons were construed in accordance with section 1 of that Act.][2]

1 The words in square brackets were substituted by the Civil Partnership Act 2004 s 261(1), Sch 27 para 6 with effect from 5 December 2005.

2 Subsection (4) was inserted by the Family Law Reform Act 1987 s 33(1), Sch 2 para 2 with effect from 4 April 1988.

PERPETUITIES AND ACCUMULATIONS ACT 1964 s 1

1 Power to specify perpetuity period

34.5 (1) Subject to section 9(2) of this Act and subsection (2) below, where the instrument by which any disposition is made so provides, the perpetuity period applicable to the disposition under the rule against perpetuities, instead of being of any other duration, shall be of a duration equal to such number of years not exceeding eighty as is specified in that behalf in the instrument.

(2) Subsection (1) above shall not have effect where the disposition is made in exercise of a special power of appointment, but where a period is specified under that subsection in the instrument creating such a power the period shall apply in relation to any disposition under the power as it applies in relation to the power itself.

PERPETUITIES AND ACCUMULATIONS ACT 2009 ss 1, 5 to 8, 11, 15 and 20

Application of rule against perpetuities

1 Application of the rule

34.6 (1) The rule against perpetuities applies (and applies only) as provided by this section.

(2) If an instrument limits property in trust so as to create successive estates or interests the rule applies to each of the estates or interests.

(3) If an instrument limits property in trust so as to create an estate or interest which is subject to a condition precedent and which is not one of successive estates or interests, the rule applies to the estate or interest.

(4) If an instrument limits property in trust so as to create an estate or interest subject to a condition subsequent the rule applies to—
(*a*) any right of re-entry exercisable if the condition is broken, or
(*b*) any equivalent right exercisable in the case of property other than land if the condition is broken.

(5) If an instrument which is a will limits personal property so as to create successive interests under the doctrine of executory bequests, the rule applies to each of the interests.

(6) If an instrument creates a power of appointment the rule applies to the power.

(7) For the purposes of subsection (2) an estate or interest includes an estate or interest—

(*a*) which arises under a right of reverter on the determination of a determinable fee simple, or

(*b*) which arises under a resulting trust on the determination of a determinable interest.

(8) This section has effect subject to the exceptions made by section 2 and to any exceptions made under section 3.

(9) In section 4(3) of the Law of Property Act 1925 (c 20) (rights of entry affecting a legal estate) omit the words from "but" to the end.

Perpetuity period

5 Perpetuity period

34.7 (1) The perpetuity period is 125 years (and no other period).

(2) Subsection (1) applies whether or not the instrument referred to in section 1(2) to (6) specifies a perpetuity period; and a specification of a perpetuity period in that instrument is ineffective.

Perpetuities: miscellaneous

6 Start of perpetuity period

34.8 (1) The perpetuity period starts when the instrument referred to in section 1(2) to (6) takes effect; but this is subject to subsections (2) and (3).

(2) If section 1(2), (3) or (4) applies and the instrument is made in the exercise of a special power of appointment the perpetuity period starts when the instrument creating the power takes effect; but this is subject to subsection (3).

(3) If section 1(2), (3) or (4) applies and—

(*a*) the instrument nominates benefits under a relevant pension scheme, or

(*b*) the instrument is made in the exercise of a power of advancement arising under a relevant pension scheme,

the perpetuity period starts when the member concerned became a member of the scheme.

(4) The member concerned is the member in respect of whose interest in the scheme the instrument is made.

7 Wait and see rule

34.9 (1) Subsection (2) applies if (apart from this section and section 8) an estate or interest would be void on the ground that it might not become vested until too remote a time.

(2) In such a case—
(*a*) until such time (if any) as it becomes established that the vesting must occur (if at all) after the end of the perpetuity period the estate or interest must be treated as if it were not subject to the rule against perpetuities, and
(*b*) if it becomes so established, that does not affect the validity of anything previously done (whether by way of advancement, application of intermediate income or otherwise) in relation to the estate or interest.

(3) Subsection (4) applies if (apart from this section) any of the following would be void on the ground that it might be exercised at too remote a time—
(*a*) a right of re-entry exercisable if a condition subsequent is broken,
(*b*) an equivalent right exercisable in the case of property other than land if a condition subsequent is broken,
(*c*) a special power of appointment.

(4) In such a case—
(*a*) the right or power must be treated as regards any exercise of it within the perpetuity period as if it were not subject to the rule against perpetuities, and
(*b*) the right or power must be treated as void for remoteness only if and so far as it is not fully exercised within the perpetuity period.

(5) Subsection (6) applies if (apart from this section) a general power of appointment would be void on the ground that it might not become exercisable until too remote a time.

(6) Until such time (if any) as it becomes established that the power will not be exercisable within the perpetuity period, it must be treated as if it were not subject to the rule against perpetuities.

8 Exclusion of class members to avoid remoteness

34.10 (1) This section applies if—
(*a*) it is apparent at the time an instrument takes effect or becomes apparent at a later time that (apart from this section) the inclusion of certain persons as members of a class would cause an estate or interest to be treated as void for remoteness, and
(*b*) those persons are potential members of the class or unborn persons who at birth would become members or potential members of the class.

(2) From the time it is or becomes so apparent those persons must be treated for all the purposes of the instrument as excluded from the class unless their exclusion would exhaust the class.

(3) If this section applies in relation to an estate or interest to which section 7 applies, this section does not affect the validity of anything previously done (whether by way of advancement, application of intermediate income or otherwise) in relation to the estate or interest.

(4) For the purposes of this section—
(*a*) a person is a member of a class if in that person's case all the conditions identifying a member of the class are satisfied, and
(*b*) a person is a potential member of a class if in that person's case some only of those conditions are satisfied but there is a possibility that the remainder will in time be satisfied.

11 Powers of appointment

34.11 …

(3) Subsection (4) applies to a power of appointment exercisable by will (whether or not it is also exercisable otherwise than by will).

(4) For the purposes of the rule against perpetuities the power is a special power unless—
(*a*) the instrument creating it expresses it to be exercisable by one person only, and
(*b*) that person could exercise it so as to transfer to that person's personal representatives the whole of the estate or interest to which it relates.

(5) Subsection (6) applies to a power of appointment exercisable by will or otherwise.

(6) If for the purposes of the rule against perpetuities the power would be a special power under one but not both of subsections (2) and (4), for the purposes of the rule it is a special power.

Application of statutory provisions

15 Application of this Act

34.12 (1) Sections 1, 2, 4 to 11, 13 and 14 apply in relation to an instrument taking effect on or after the commencement day, except that—
(*a*) those sections do not apply in relation to a will executed before that day, and
(*b*) those sections apply in relation to an instrument made in the exercise of a special power of appointment only if the instrument creating the power takes effect on or after that day.

(2) Section 12 applies (except as provided by subsection (3)) in relation to—
(*a*) a will executed before the commencement day (whether or not it takes effect before that day),
(*b*) an instrument, other than a will, taking effect before that day.

(3) Section 12 does not apply if—
(*a*) the terms of the trust were exhausted before the commencement day, or
(*b*) before that day the property became held on trust for charitable purposes by way of a final disposition of the property.

(4) The commencement day is the day appointed under section 22(2).

20 Interpretation

34.13 …

(6) An instrument which is a will takes effect at the testator's death.

(7) A reference to a will includes a reference to a codicil.

TRUSTS OF LAND AND APPOINTMENT OF TRUSTEES ACT 1996 ss 1 to 13, 18 and Sch 1

PART I
TRUSTS OF LAND

1 MEANING OF "TRUST OF LAND"

34.14 (1) In this Act—
(*a*) "trust of land" means (subject to subsection (3)) any trust of property which consists of or includes land, and
(*b*) "trustees of land" means trustees of a trust of land.

(2) The reference in subsection (1)(*a*) to a trust—
(*a*) is to any description of trust (whether express, implied, resulting or constructive), including a trust for sale and a bare trust, and
(*b*) includes a trust created, or arising, before the commencement of this Act.

(3) The reference to land in subsection (1)(*a*) does not include land which (despite section 2) is settled land or which is land to which the Universities and College Estates Act 1925 applies.

2 TRUSTS IN PLACE OF SETTLEMENTS

34.15 (1) No settlement created after the commencement of this Act is a settlement for the purposes of the Settled Land Act 1925; and no settlement shall be deemed to be made under that Act after that commencement.

(2) Subsection (1) does not apply to a settlement created on the occasion of an alteration in any interest in, or of a person becoming entitled under, a settlement which—
(*a*) is in existence at the commencement of this Act, or
(*b*) derives from a settlement within paragraph (*a*) or this paragraph.

(3) But a settlement created as mentioned in subsection (2) is not a settlement for the purposes of the Settled Land Act 1925 if provision to the effect that it is not is made in the instrument, or any of the instruments, by which it is created.

(4) Where at any time after the commencement of this Act there is in the case of any settlement which is a settlement for the purposes of the Settled Land Act 1925 no relevant property which is, or is deemed to be, subject to the settlement, the settlement permanently ceases at that time to be a settlement for the purposes of that Act.

In this subsection "relevant property" means land and personal chattels to which section 67(1) of the Settled Land Act 1925 (heirlooms) applies.

(5) No land held on charitable, ecclesiastical or public trusts shall be or be deemed to be settled land after the commencement of this Act, even if it was or was deemed to be settled land before that commencement.

(6) Schedule 1 has effect to make provision consequential on this section (including provision to impose a trust in circumstances in which, apart from this section, there would be a settlement for the purposes of the Settled Land Act 1925 (and there would not otherwise be a trust)).

3 ABOLITION OF DOCTRINE OF CONVERSION

34.16 (1) Where land is held by trustees subject to a trust for sale, the land is not to be regarded as personal property; and where personal property, is subject to a trust for sale in order that the trustees may acquire land, the personal property is not to be regarded as land.

(2) Subsection (1) does not apply to a trust created by a will if the testator died before the commencement of this Act.

(3) Subject to that, subsection (1) applies to a trust whether it is created, or arises, before or after that commencement.

4 EXPRESS TRUSTS FOR SALE AS TRUSTS OF LAND

34.17 (1) In the case of every trust for sale of land created by a disposition there is to be implied, despite any provision to the contrary made by the disposition, a power for the trustees to postpone sale of the land; and the trustees are not liable in any way for postponing sale of the land, in the exercise of their discretion, for an indefinite period.

(2) Subsection (1) applies to a trust whether it is created, or arises, before or after the commencement of this Act.

(3) Subsection (1) does not affect any liability incurred by trustees before that commencement.

5 IMPLIED TRUSTS FOR SALE AS TRUSTS OF LAND

34.18 (1) Schedule 2 has effect in relation to statutory provisions which impose a trust for sale of land in certain circumstances so that in those circumstances there is instead a trust of the land (without a duty to sell).

(2) Section 1 of the Settled Land Act 1925 does not apply to land held on any trust arising by virtue of that Schedule (so that any such land is subject to a trust of land).

6 GENERAL POWERS OF TRUSTEES

34.19 (1) For the purpose of exercising their functions as trustees, the trustees of land have in relation to the land subject to the trust all the powers of an absolute owner.

(2) Where in the case of any land subject to a trust of land each of the beneficiaries interested in the land is a person of full age and capacity who is absolutely entitled to the land, the powers conferred on the trustees by subsection (1) include the power to convey the land to the beneficiaries even though they have not required the trustees to do so; and where land is conveyed by virtue of this subsection—

(*a*) the beneficiaries shall do whatever is necessary to secure that it vests in them, and

(*b*) if they fail to do so, the court may make an order requiring them to do so.

(3) The trustees of land have power to [acquire land under the power conferred by section 8 of the Trustee Act 2000][1].

(4) ...[2]

(5) In exercising the powers conferred by this section trustees shall have regard to the rights of the beneficiaries.

(6) The powers conferred by this section shall not be exercised in contravention of, or of any order made in pursuance of, any other enactment or any rule of law or equity.

(7) The reference in subsection (6) to an order includes an order of any court or of the [Charity Commission][3].

(8) Where any enactment other than this section confers on trustees authority to act subject to any restriction, limitation or condition, trustees of land may not exercise the powers conferred by this section to do any act which they are prevented from doing under the other enactment by reason of the restriction, limitation or condition.

[(9) The duty of care under section 1 of the Trustee Act 2000 applies to trustees of land when exercising the powers conferred by this section.][4]

1 The words in square brackets were substituted by the Trustee Act 2000 s 40(1), Sch 2 para 45(1) with effect from 1 February 2001.
2 Subsection (4) was repealed by the Trustee Act 2000 s 40(1), (3), Sch 2 para 45(2), Sch 4 Pt II with effect from 1 February 2001.
3 The words in square brackets were substituted by the Charities Act 2006 s 75(1), Sch 8 para 182 with effect from 27 February 2007.
4 Subsection (9) was inserted by the Trustee Act 2000 s 40(1), Sch 2 para 45(3) with effect from 1 February 2001.

7 PARTITION BY TRUSTEES

34.20 (1) The trustees of land may, where beneficiaries of full age are absolutely entitled in undivided shares to land subject to the trust, partition the land, or any part of it, and provide (by way of mortgage or otherwise) for the payment of any equality money.

(2) The trustees shall give effect to any such partition by conveying the partitioned land in severalty (whether or not subject to any legal mortgage created for raising equality money), either absolutely or in trust, in accordance with the rights of those beneficiaries.

(3) Before exercising their powers under subsection (2) the trustees shall obtain the consent of each of those beneficiaries.

(4) Where a share in the land is affected by an incumbrance, the trustees may either give effect to it or provide for its discharge from the property allotted to that share as they think fit.

(5) If a share in the land is absolutely vested in a minor, subsections (1) to (4) apply as if he were of full age, except that the trustees may act on his behalf and retain land or other property representing his share in trust for him.

[(6) Subsection (1) is subject to sections 21 (part-unit: interests) and 22 (part-unit: charging) of the Commonhold and Leasehold Reform Act 2002.][1]

1 Subsection (6) was inserted by the Commonhold and Leasehold Reform Act 2002 s 68, Sch 5 para 8 with effect from 27 September 2004.

8 EXCLUSION AND RESTRICTION OF POWERS

34.21 (1) Sections 6 and 7 do not apply in the case of a trust of land created by a disposition in so far as provision to the effect that they do not apply is made by the disposition.

(2) If the disposition creating such a trust makes provision requiring any consent to be obtained to the exercise of any power conferred by sections 6 or 7, the power may not be exercised without that consent.

(3) Subsection (1) does not apply in the case of charitable, ecclesiastical or public trusts.

(4) Subsections (1) and (2) have effect subject to any enactment which prohibits or restricts the effect of provision of the description mentioned in them.

9 DELEGATION BY TRUSTEES

34.22 (1) The trustees of land may, by power of attorney, delegate to any beneficiary or beneficiaries of full age and beneficially entitled to an interest in possession in land subject to the trust any of their functions as trustees which relate to the land.

(2) Where trustees purport to delegate to a person by a power of attorney under subsection (1) functions relating to any land and another person in good faith deals with him in relation to the land, he shall be presumed in favour of that other person to have been a person to whom the functions could be delegated unless that other person has knowledge at the time of the transaction that he was not such a person.

And it shall be conclusively presumed in favour of any purchaser whose interest depends on the validity of that transaction that that other person dealt in good faith and did not have such knowledge if that other person makes a statutory declaration to that effect before or within three months after the completion of the purchase.

(3) A power of attorney under subsection (1) shall be given by all the trustees jointly and (unless expressed to be irrevocable and to be given by way of security) may be revoked by any one or more of them; and such a power is revoked by the appointment as a trustee of a person other than those by whom it is given (though not by any of those persons dying or otherwise ceasing to be a trustee).

(4) Where a beneficiary to whom functions are delegated by a power of attorney under subsection (1) ceases to be a person beneficially entitled to an interest in possession in land subject to the trust—
(*a*) if the functions are delegated to him alone, the power is revoked,
(*b*) if the functions are delegated to him and to other beneficiaries to be exercised by them jointly (but not separately), the power is revoked if each of the other beneficiaries ceases to be so entitled (but otherwise functions exercisable in accordance with the power are so exercisable by the remaining beneficiary or beneficiaries), and
(*c*) if the functions are delegated to him and to other beneficiaries to be exercised by them separately (or either separately or jointly), the power is revoked in so far as it relates to him.

(5) A delegation under subsection (1) may be for any period or indefinite.

(6) A power of attorney under subsection (1) cannot be [an enduring power of attorney or lasting power of attorney within the meaning of the Mental Capacity Act 2005][1].

(7) Beneficiaries to whom functions have been delegated under subsection (1) are, in relation to the exercise of the functions, in the same position as trustees (with the same duties and liabilities); but such beneficiaries shall not be regarded as trustees for any other purposes (including, in particular, the purposes of any enactment permitting the delegation of functions by trustees or imposing requirements relating to the payment of capital money).

(8) ...[2]

(9) Neither this section nor the repeal by this Act of section 29 of the Law of Property Act 1925 (which is superseded by this section) affects the operation after the commencement of this Act of any delegation effected before that commencement.

1 The words in square brackets were substituted by the Mental Capacity Act 2005 s 67(1), Sch 6 para 42(1), (2) with effect from 1 October 2007.

2 Subsection (8) was repealed by the Trustee Act 2000 s 40(1), (3), Sch 2 para 46, Sch 4 Pt II with effect from 1 February 2001.

9A DUTIES OF TRUSTEES IN CONNECTION WITH DELEGATION ETC[1]

34.23 (1) The duty of care under section 1 of the Trustee Act 2000 applies to trustees of land in deciding whether to delegate any of their functions under section 9.

(2) Subsection (3) applies if the trustees of land
(*a*) delegate any of their functions under section 9, and
(*b*) the delegation is not irrevocable.

(3) While the delegation continues, the trustees
(*a*) must keep the delegation under review,
(*b*) if the circumstances make it appropriate to do so, must consider whether there is a need to exercise any power of intervention that they have, and
(*c*) if they consider that there is a need to exercise such a power, must do so.

(4) "Power of intervention" includes
(*a*) a power to give directions to the beneficiary,
(*b*) a power to revoke the delegation.

(5) The duty of care under section 1 of the 2000 Act applies to trustees in carrying out any duty under subsection (3).

(6) A trustee of land is not liable for any act or default of the beneficiary, or beneficiaries, unless the trustee fails to comply with the duty of care in deciding to delegate any of the trustees' functions under section 9 or in carrying out any duty under subsection (3).

(7) Neither this section nor the repeal of section 9(8) by the Trustee Act 2000 affects the operation after the commencement of this section of any delegation effected before that commencement.

1 This section was inserted by the Trustee Act 2000 s 40(1), Sch 2 para 47 with effect from 1 February 2001.

10 CONSENTS

34.24 (1) If a disposition creating a trust of land requires the consent of more than two persons to the exercise by the trustees of any function relating to the land, the consent of any two of them to the exercise of the function is sufficient in favour of a purchaser.

(2) Subsection (1) does not apply to the exercise of a function by trustees of land held on charitable, ecclesiastical or public trusts.

(3) Where at any time a person whose consent is expressed by a disposition creating a trust of land to be required to the exercise by the trustees of any function relating to the land is not of full age—

(*a*) his consent is not, in favour of a purchaser, required to the exercise of the function, but

(*b*) the trustees shall obtain the consent of a parent who has parental responsibility for him (within the meaning of the Children Act 1989) or of a guardian of his.

11 CONSULTATION WITH BENEFICARIES

34.25 (1) The trustees of land shall in the exercise of any function relating to land subject to the trust—

(*a*) so far as practicable, consult the beneficiaries of full age and beneficially entitled to an interest in possession in the land, and

(*b*) so far as consistent with the general interest of the trust, give effect to the wishes of those beneficiaries, or (in case of dispute) of the majority (according to the value of their combined interests).

(2) Subsection (1) does not apply—

(*a*) in relation to a trust created by a disposition in so far as provision that it does not apply is made by the disposition,

(*b*) in relation to a trust created or arising under a will made before the commencement of this Act, or

(*c*) in relation to the exercise of the power mentioned in section 6(2).

(3) Subsection (1) does not apply to a trust created before the commencement of this Act by a disposition, or a trust created after that commencement by reference to such a trust, unless provision to the effect that it is to apply is made by a deed executed—

(*a*) in a case in which the trust was created by one person and he is of full capacity, by that person, or

(*b*) in a case in which the trust was created by more than one person, by such of the persons who created the trust as are alive and of full capacity.

(4) A deed executed for the purposes of subsection (3) is irrevocable.

12 THE RIGHT TO OCCUPY

34.26 (1) A beneficiary who is beneficially entitled to an interest in possession in land subject to a trust of land is entitled by reason of his interest to occupy the land at any time if at that time—

(*a*) the purposes of the trust include making the land available for his occupation (or for the occupation of beneficiaries of a class of which he is a member or of beneficiaries in general), or
(*b*) the land is held by the trustees so as to be so available.

(2) Subsection (1) does not confer on a beneficiary a right to occupy land if it is either unavailable or unsuitable for occupation by him.

(3) This section is subject to section 13.

13 EXCLUSION AND RESTRICTION OF RIGHT TO OCCUPY

34.27 (1) Where two or more beneficiaries are (or apart from this subsection would be) entitled under section 12 to occupy land, the trustees of land may exclude or restrict the entitlement of any one or more (but not all) of them.

(2) Trustees may not under subsection (1)—
(*a*) unreasonably exclude any beneficiary's entitlement to occupy land, or
(*b*) restrict any such entitlement to an unreasonable extent.

(3) The trustees of land may from time to time impose reasonable conditions on any beneficiary in relation to his occupation of land by reason of his entitlement under section 12.

(4) The matters to which trustees are to have regard in exercising the powers conferred by this section include—
(*a*) the intentions of the person or persons (if any) who created the trust,
(*b*) the purposes for which the land is held, and
(*c*) the circumstances and wishes of each of the beneficiaries who is (or apart from any previous exercise by the trustees of those powers would be) entitled to occupy the land under section 12.

(5) The conditions which may be imposed on a beneficiary under subsection (3) include, in particular, conditions requiring him—
(*a*) to pay any outgoings or expenses in respect of the land, or
(*b*) to assume any other obligation in relation to the land or to any activity which is or is proposed to be conducted there.

(6) Where the entitlement of any beneficiary to occupy land under section 12 has been excluded or restricted, the conditions which may be imposed on any other beneficiary under subsection (3) include, in particular, conditions requiring him to—
(*a*) make payments by way of compensation to the beneficiary whose entitlement has been excluded or restricted, or
(*b*) forgo any payment or other benefit to which he would otherwise be entitled under the trust so as to benefit that beneficiary.

(7) The powers conferred on trustees by this section may not be exercised—

so as prevent any person who is in occupation of land (whether or not by reason of an entitlement under section 12) from continuing to occupy the land, or
(*a*) in a manner likely to result in any such person ceasing to occupy the land,
(*b*) unless he consents or the court has given approval.

(8) The matters to which the court is to have regard in determining whether to give approval under subsection (7) include the matters mentioned in subsection (4)(*a*) to (*c*).

18 APPLICATION OF PART TO PERSONAL REPRESENTATIVES

34.28 (1) The provisions of this Part relating to trustees, other than sections 10, 11 and 14, apply to personal representatives, but with appropriate modifications and without prejudice to the functions of personal representatives for the purposes of administration.

(2) The appropriate modifications include—
(*a*) the substitution of references to persons interested in the due administration of the estate for references to beneficiaries, and
(*b*) the substitution of references to the will for references to the disposition creating the trust.

(3) Section 3(1) does not apply to personal representatives if the death occurs before the commencement of this Act.

SCHEDULE 1

PROVISIONS CONSEQUENTIAL ON SECTION 2

Minors

34.29 1—(1) Where after the commencement of this Act a person purports to convey a legal estate in land to a minor, or two or more minors, alone, the conveyance—
(*a*) is not effective to pass the legal estate, but
(*b*) operates as a declaration that the land is held in trust for the minor or minors (or if he purports to convey it to the minor or minors in trust for any persons, for those persons).

(2) Where after the commencement of this Act a person purports to convey legal estate in land to—
(*a*) a minor or two or more minors, and
(*b*) another person who is, or other persons who are, of full age,

the conveyance operates to vest the land in the other person or persons in trust for the minor or minors and the other person or persons (or if he purports it convey it to them in trust for any persons, for those persons).

(3) Where immediately before the commencement of this Act a conveyance operating (by virtue of section 27 of the Settled Land Act 1925) as an agreement to execute a settlement in favour of a minor or minors—
(*a*) the agreement ceases to have effect on the commencement of this Act, and
(*b*) the conveyance subsequently operates instead as a declaration that the land is held in trust for the minor or minors.

2 Where after the commencement of this Act a legal estate in land would, by reason of intestacy or in any other circumstances not dealt with in paragraph 1, vest in a person who is a minor if he were a person of full age, the land is held trust for the minor.

. . .

TRUSTEE ACT 2000 ss 1 to 6, 8, 9, 11 to 26, 28, 29, 31, 32, 35, 39 and Sch 1

Part I
The Duty of Care

1 THE DUTY OF CARE

34.30 (1) Whenever the duty under this subsection applies to a trustee, he must exercise such care and skill as is reasonable in the circumstances, having regard in particular—

(*a*) to any special knowledge or experience that he has or holds himself out as having, and

(*b*) if he acts as trustee in the course of a business or profession, to any special knowledge or experience that it is reasonable to expect of a person acting in the course of that kind of business or profession.

(2) In this Act the duty under subsection (1) is called "the duty of care".

2 APPLICATION OF DUTY OF CARE

34.31 Schedule 1 makes provision about when the duty of care applies to a trustee.

PART II
INVESTMENT

3 GENERAL POWER OF INVESTMENT

34.32 (1) Subject to the provisions of this Part, a trustee may make any kind of investment that he could make if he were absolutely entitled to the assets of the trust.

(2) In this Act the power under subsection (1) is called "the general power of investment".

(3) The general power of investment does not permit a trustee to make investments in land other than in loans secured on land (but see also section 8).

(4) A person invests in a loan secured on land if he has rights under any contract under which—

(*a*) one person provides another with credit, and

(*b*) the obligation of the borrower to repay is secured on land.

(5) "Credit" includes any cash loan or other financial accommodation.

(6) "Cash" includes money in any form.

4 STANDARD INVESTMENT CRITERIA

34.33 (1) In exercising any power of investment, whether arising under this Part or otherwise, a trustee must have regard to the standard investment criteria.

(2) A trustee must from time to time review the investments of the trust and consider whether, having regard to the standard investment criteria, they should be varied.

(3) The standard investment criteria, in relation to a trust, are—

(*a*) the suitability to the trust of investments of the same kind as any particular investment proposed to be made or retained and of that particular investment as an investment of that kind, and

(*b*) the need for diversification of investments of the trust, in so far as is appropriate to the circumstances of the trust.

5 ADVICE

34.34 (1) Before exercising any power of investment, whether arising under this Part or otherwise, a trustee must (unless the exception applies) obtain and consider proper advice about the way in which, having regard to the standard investment criteria, the power should be exercised.

(2) When reviewing the investments of the trust, a trustee must (unless the exception applies) obtain and consider proper advice about whether, having regard to the standard investment criteria, the investments should be varied.

(3) The exception is that a trustee need not obtain such advice if he reasonably concludes that in all the circumstances it is unnecessary or inappropriate to do so.

(4) Proper advice is the advice of a person who is reasonably believed by the trustee to be qualified to give it by his ability in and practical experience of financial and other matters relating to the proposed investment.

6 RESTRICTION OR EXCLUSION OF THIS PART ETC

34.35 (1) The general power of investment is—

(*a*) in addition to powers conferred on trustees otherwise than by this Act, but

(*b*) subject to any restriction or exclusion imposed by the trust instrument or by any enactment or any provision of subordinate legislation.

(2) For the purposes of this Act, an enactment or a provision of subordinate legislation is not to be regarded as being, or as being part of, a trust instrument.

(3) In this Act "subordinate legislation" has the same meaning as in the Interpretation Act 1978.

PART III
ACQUISITION OF LAND

8 POWER TO ACQUIRE FREEHOLD AND LEASEHOLD LAND

34.36 (1) A trustee may acquire freehold or leasehold land in the United Kingdom—

(*a*) as an investment,

(*b*) for occupation by a beneficiary, or

(*c*) for any other reason.

(2) "Freehold or leasehold land" means—
(*a*) in relation to England and Wales, a legal estate in land,
(*b*) in relation to Scotland—
   (i) the estate or interest of the proprietor of the dominium utile or, in the case of land not held on feudal tenure, the estate or interest of the owner, or
   (ii) a tenancy, and
(*c*) in relation to Northern Ireland, a legal estate in land, including land held under a fee farm grant.

(3) For the purpose of exercising his functions as a trustee, a trustee who acquires land under this section has all the powers of an absolute owner in relation to the land.

9 RESTRICTION OR EXCLUSION OF THIS PART ETC

34.37 The powers conferred by this Part are—
(*a*) in addition to powers conferred on trustees otherwise than by this Part, but
(*b*) subject to any restriction or exclusion imposed by the trust instrument or by any enactment or any provision of subordinate legislation.

PART IV
AGENTS, NOMINEES AND CUSTODIANS

AGENTS

11 POWER TO EMPLOY AGENTS

34.38 (1) Subject to the provisions of this Part, the trustees of a trust may authorise any person to exercise any or all of their delegable functions as their agent.

(2) In the case of a trust other than a charitable trust, the trustees' delegable functions consist of any function other than—
(*a*) any function relating to whether or in what way any assets of the trust should be distributed,
(*b*) any power to decide whether any fees or other payment due to be made out of the trust funds should be made out of income or capital,
(*c*) any power to appoint a person to be a trustee of the trust, or
(*d*) any power conferred by any other enactment or the trust instrument which permits the trustees to delegate any of their functions or to appoint a person to act as a nominee or custodian.

(3) In the case of a charitable trust, the trustees' delegable functions are—
(*a*) any function consisting of carrying out a decision that the trustees have taken,
(*b*) any function relating to the investment of assets subject to the trust (including, in the case of land held as an investment, managing the land and creating or disposing of an interest in the land),
(*c*) any function relating to the raising of funds for the trust otherwise than by means of profits of a trade which is an integral part of carrying out the trust's charitable purpose,
(*d*) any other function prescribed by an order made by the Secretary of State.

(4) For the purposes of subsection (3)(*c*) a trade is an integral part of carrying out a trust's charitable purpose if, whether carried on in the United Kingdom or elsewhere, the profits are applied solely to the purposes of the trust and either—

(*a*) the trade is exercised in the course of the actual carrying out of a primary purpose of the trust, or

(*b*) the work in connection with the trade is mainly carried out by beneficiaries of the trust.

(5) The power to make an order under subsection (3)(*d*) is exercisable by statutory instrument which shall be subject to annulment in pursuance of a resolution of either House of Parliament.

12 PERSONS WHO MAY ACT AS AGENTS

34.39 (1) Subject to subsection (2), the persons whom the trustees may under section 11 authorise to exercise functions as their agent include one or more of their number.

(2) The trustees may not authorise two (or more) persons to exercise the same function unless they are to exercise the function jointly.

(3) The trustees may not under section 11 authorise a beneficiary to exercise any function as their agent (even if the beneficiary is also a trustee).

(4) The trustees may under section 11 authorise a person to exercise functions as their agent even though he is also appointed to act as their nominee or custodian (whether under section 16, 17 or 18 or any other power).

13 LINKED FUNCTIONS ETC

34.40 (1) Subject to subsections (2) and (5), a person who is authorised under section 11 to exercise a function is (whatever the terms of the agency) subject to any specific duties or restrictions attached to the function.

For example, a person who is authorised under section 11 to exercise the general power of investment is subject to the duties under section 4 in relation to that power.

(2) A person who is authorised under section 11 to exercise a power which is subject to a requirement to obtain advice is not subject to the requirement if he is the kind of person from whom it would have been proper for the trustees, in compliance with the requirement, to obtain advice.

(3) Subsections (4) and (5) apply to a trust to which section 11(1) of the Trusts of Land and Appointment of Trustees Act 1996 (duties to consult beneficiaries and give effect to their wishes) applies.

(4) The trustees may not under section 11 authorise a person to exercise any of their functions on terms that prevent them from complying with section 11(1) of the 1996 Act.

(5) A person who is authorised under section 11 to exercise any function relating to land subject to the trust is not subject to section 11(1) of the 1996 Act.

14 TERMS OF AGENCY

34.41 (1) Subject to subsection (2) and sections 15(2) and 29 to 32, the trustees may authorise a person to exercise functions as their agent on such terms as to remuneration and other matters as they may determine.

(2) The trustees may not authorise a person to exercise functions as their agent on any of the terms mentioned in subsection (3) unless it is reasonably necessary for them to do so.

(3) The terms are—
(*a*) a term permitting the agent to appoint a substitute,
(*b*) a term restricting the liability of the agent or his substitute to the trustees or any beneficiary,
(*c*) a term permitting the agent to act in circumstances capable of giving rise to a conflict of interest.

15 ASSET MANAGEMENT: SPECIAL RESTRICTIONS

34.42 (1) The trustees may not authorise a person to exercise any of their asset management functions as their agent except by an agreement which is in or evidenced in writing.

(2) The trustees may not authorise a person to exercise any of their asset management functions as their agent unless—
(*a*) they have prepared a statement that gives guidance as to how the functions should be exercised ("a policy statement"), and
(*b*) the agreement under which the agent is to act includes a term to the effect that he will secure compliance with—
  (i) the policy statement, or
  (ii) if the policy statement is revised or replaced under section 22, the revised or replacement policy statement.

(3) The trustees must formulate any guidance given in the policy statement with a view to ensuring that the functions will be exercised in the best interests of the trust.

(4) The policy statement must be in or evidenced in writing.

(5) The asset management functions of trustees are their functions relating to—
(*a*) the investment of assets subject to the trust,
(*b*) the acquisition of property which is to be subject to the trust, and
(*c*) managing property which is subject to the trust and disposing of, or creating or disposing of an interest in, such property.

NOMINEES AND CUSTODIANS

16 POWER TO APPOINT NOMINEES

34.43 (1) Subject to the provisions of this Part, the trustees of a trust may—
(*a*) appoint a person to act as their nominee in relation to such of the assets of the trust as they determine (other than settled land), and
(*b*) take such steps as are necessary to secure that those assets are vested in a person so appointed.

(2) An appointment under this section must be in or evidenced in writing.

(3) This section does not apply to any trust having a custodian trustee or in relation to any assets vested in the official custodian for charities.

17 POWER TO APPOINT CUSTODIANS

34.44 (1) Subject to the provisions of this Part, the trustees of a trust may appoint a person to act as a custodian in relation to such of the assets of the trust as they may determine.

(2) For the purposes of this Act a person is a custodian in relation to assets if he undertakes the safe custody of the assets or of any documents or records concerning the assets.

(3) An appointment under this section must be in or evidenced in writing.

(4) This section does not apply to any trust having a custodian trustee or in relation to any assets vested in the official custodian for charities.

18 INVESTMENT IN BEARER SECURITIES

34.45 (1) If trustees retain or invest in securities payable to bearer, they must appoint a person to act as a custodian of the securities.

(2) Subsection (1) does not apply if the trust instrument or any enactment or provision of subordinate legislation contains provision which (however expressed) permits the trustees to retain or invest in securities payable to bearer without appointing a person to act as a custodian.

(3) An appointment under this section must be in or evidenced in writing.

(4) This section does not apply to any trust having a custodian trustee or in relation to any securities vested in the official custodian for charities.

19 PERSONS WHO MAY BE APPOINTED AS NOMINEES OR CUSTODIANS

34.46 (1) A person may not be appointed under section 16, 17 or 18 as a nominee or custodian unless one of the relevant conditions is satisfied.

(2) The relevant conditions are that—
(*a*) the person carries on a business which consists of or includes acting as a nominee or custodian,
(*b*) the person is a body corporate which is controlled by the trustees,
(*c*) the person is a body corporate recognised under section 9 of the Administration of Justice Act 1985.

(3) The question whether a body corporate is controlled by trustees is to be determined in accordance with [section 1124 of the Corporation Tax Act 2010][1].

(4) The trustees of a charitable trust which is not an exempt charity must act in accordance with any guidance given by the [Charity Commission][2] concerning the selection of a person for appointment as a nominee or custodian under section 16, 17 or 18.

(5) Subject to subsections (1) and (4), the persons whom the trustees may under section 16, 17 or 18 appoint as a nominee or custodian include—
(*a*) one of their number, if that one is a trust corporation, or
(*b*) two (or more) of their number, if they are to act as joint nominees or joint custodians.

(6) The trustees may under section 16 appoint a person to act as their nominee even though he is also—
(*a*) appointed to act as their custodian (whether under section 17 or 18 or any other power), or
(*b*) authorised to exercise functions as their agent (whether under section 11 or any other power).

(7) Likewise, the trustees may under section 17 or 18 appoint a person to act as their custodian even though he is also—
(*a*) appointed to act as their nominee (whether under section 16 or any other power), or
(*b*) authorised to exercise functions as their agent (whether under section 11 or any other power).

1 The words in square brackets were substituted by the Corporation Tax Act 2010 s 1177, Sch 1 para 319 with effect from 1 April 2010.
2 The words in square brackets were substituted by the Charities Act 2006 s 75(1), Sch 8 para 197 with effect from 27 February 2007.

20 TERMS OF APPOINTMENT OF NOMINEES AND CUSTODIANS

34.47 (1) Subject to subsection (2) and sections 29 to 32, the trustees may under section 16, 17 or 18 appoint a person to act as a nominee or custodian on such terms as to remuneration and other matters as they may determine.

(2) The trustees may not under section 16, 17 or 18 appoint a person to act as a nominee or custodian on any of the terms mentioned in subsection (3) unless it is reasonably necessary for them to do so.

(3) The terms are—
(*a*) a term permitting the nominee or custodian to appoint a substitute,
(*b*) a term restricting the liability of the nominee or custodian or his substitute to the trustees or to any beneficiary,
(*c*) a term permitting the nominee or custodian to act in circumstances capable of giving rise to a conflict of interest.

REVIEW OF AND LIABILITY FOR AGENTS, NOMINEES AND CUSTODIANS ETC

21 APPLICATION OF SECTIONS 22 AND 23

34.48 (1) Sections 22 and 23 apply in a case where trustees have, under section 11, 16, 17 or 18—
(*a*) authorised a person to exercise functions as their agent, or
(*b*) appointed a person to act as a nominee or custodian.

(2) Subject to subsection (3), sections 22 and 23 also apply in a case where trustees have, under any power conferred on them by the trust instrument or by any enactment or any provision of subordinate legislation—
(*a*) authorised a person to exercise functions as their agent, or
(*b*) appointed a person to act as a nominee or custodian.

(3) If the application of section 22 or 23 is inconsistent with the terms of the trust instrument or the enactment or provision of subordinate legislation, the section in question does not apply.

22 REVIEW OF AGENTS, NOMINEES AND CUSTODIANS ETC

34.49 (1) While the agent, nominee or custodian continues to act for the trust, the trustees—
(*a*) must keep under review the arrangements under which the agent, nominee or custodian acts and how those arrangements are being put into effect,
(*b*) if circumstances make it appropriate to do so, must consider whether there is a need to exercise any power of intervention that they have, and
(*c*) if they consider that there is a need to exercise such a power, must do so.

(2) If the agent has been authorised to exercise asset management functions, the duty under subsection (1) includes, in particular—
(*a*) a duty to consider whether there is any need to revise or replace the policy statement made for the purposes of section 15,
(*b*) if they consider that there is a need to revise or replace the policy statement, a duty to do so, and
(*c*) a duty to assess whether the policy statement (as it has effect for the time being) is being complied with.

(3) Subsections (3) and (4) of section 15 apply to the revision or replacement of a policy statement under this section as they apply to the making of a policy statement under that section.

(4) "Power of intervention" includes—
(*a*) a power to give directions to the agent, nominee or custodian,
(*b*) a power to revoke the authorisation or appointment.

23 LIABILITY FOR AGENTS, NOMINEES AND CUSTODIANS ETC

34.50 (1) A trustee is not liable for any act or default of the agent, nominee or custodian unless he has failed to comply with the duty of care applicable to him, under paragraph 3 of Schedule 1—
(*a*) when entering into the arrangements under which the person acts as agent, nominee or custodian, or
(*b*) when carrying out his duties under section 22.

(2) If a trustee has agreed a term under which the agent, nominee or custodian is permitted to appoint a substitute, the trustee is not liable for any act or default of the substitute unless he has failed to comply with the duty of care applicable to him, under paragraph 3 of Schedule 1—

(*a*) when agreeing that term, or
(*b*) when carrying out his duties under section 22 in so far as they relate to the use of the substitute.

SUPPLEMENTARY

24 EFFECT OF TRUSTEES EXCEEDING THEIR POWERS

34.51 A failure by the trustees to act within the limits of the powers conferred by this Part—
(*a*) in authorising a person to exercise a function of theirs as an agent, or
(*b*) in appointing a person to act as a nominee or custodian,
does not invalidate the authorisation or appointment.

25 SOLE TRUSTEES

34.52 (1) Subject to subsection (2), this Part applies in relation to a trust having a sole trustee as it applies in relation to other trusts (and references in this Part to trustees—except in sections 12(1) and (3) and 19(5)—are to be read accordingly).

(2) Section 18 does not impose a duty on a sole trustee if that trustee is a trust corporation.

26 RESTRICTION OR EXCLUSION OF THIS PART ETC

34.53 The powers conferred by this Part are—
(*a*) in addition to powers conferred on trustees otherwise than by this Act, but
(*b*) subject to any restriction or exclusion imposed by the trust instrument or by any enactment or any provision of subordinate legislation.

PART V
REMUNERATION

28 TRUSTEE'S ENTITLEMENT TO PAYMENT UNDER TRUST INSTRUMENT

34.54 (1) Except to the extent (if any) to which the trust instrument makes inconsistent provision, subsections (2) to (4) apply to a trustee if—
(*a*) there is a provision in the trust instrument entitling him to receive payment out of trust funds in respect of services provided by him to or on behalf of the trust, and
(*b*) the trustee is a trust corporation or is acting in a professional capacity.

(2) The trustee is to be treated as entitled under the trust instrument to receive payment in respect of services even if they are services which are capable of being provided by a lay trustee.

(3) Subsection (2) applies to a trustee of a charitable trust who is not a trust corporation only—

(*a*) if he is not a sole trustee, and
(*b*) to the extent that a majority of the other trustees have agreed that it should apply to him.

(4) Any payments to which the trustee is entitled in respect of services are to be treated as remuneration for services (and not as a gift) for the purposes of—
(*a*) section 15 of the Wills Act 1837 (gifts to an attesting witness to be void), and
(*b*) section 34(3) of the Administration of Estates Act 1925 (order in which estate to be paid out).

(5) For the purposes of this Part, a trustee acts in a professional capacity if he acts in the course of a profession or business which consists of or includes the provision of services in connection with—
(*a*) the management or administration of trusts generally or a particular kind of trust, or
(*b*) any particular aspect of the management or administration of trusts generally or a particular kind of trust,

and the services he provides to or on behalf of the trust fall within that description.

(6) For the purposes of this Part, a person acts as a lay trustee if he—
(*a*) is not a trust corporation, and
(*b*) does not act in a professional capacity.

29 REMUNERATION OF CERTAIN TRUSTEES

34.55 (1) Subject to subsection (5), a trustee who—
(*a*) is a trust corporation, but
(*b*) is not a trustee of a charitable trust,

is entitled to receive reasonable remuneration out of the trust funds for any services that the trust corporation provides to or on behalf of the trust.

(2) Subject to subsection (5), a trustee who—
(*a*) acts in a professional capacity, but
(*b*) is not a trust corporation, a trustee of a charitable trust or a sole trustee,

is entitled to receive reasonable remuneration out of the trust funds for any services that he provides to or on behalf of the trust if each other trustee has agreed in writing that he may be remunerated for the services.

(3) "Reasonable remuneration" means, in relation to the provision of services by a trustee, such remuneration as is reasonable in the circumstances for the provision of those services to or on behalf of that trust by that trustee and for the purposes of subsection (1) includes, in relation to the provision of services by a trustee who is [a deposit taker][1] and provides the services in that capacity, the [deposit taker's][1] reasonable charges for the provision of such services.

[(3A) In subsection (3), "deposit taker" means—
(*a*) a person who has permission under Part 4A of the Financial Services and Markets Act 2000 to accept deposits, or
(*b*) an EEA firm of the kind mentioned in paragraph 5(*b*) of Schedule 3 to that Act which has permission under paragraph 15 of that Schedule (as a result of qualifying for authorisation under paragraph 12(1) of that Schedule) to accept deposits.

(3B) A reference in subsection (3A) to a person or firm with permission to accept deposits does not include a person or firm with permission to do so only for the purposes of, or in the course of, carrying on another regulated activity in accordance with that permission.

(3C) Subsections (3A) and (3B) must be read with—
(*a*) section 22 of the Financial Services and Markets Act 2000,
(*b*) any relevant order under that section, and
(*c*) Schedule 2 to that Act.][2]

(4) A trustee is entitled to remuneration under this section even if the services in question are capable of being provided by a lay trustee.

(5) A trustee is not entitled to remuneration under this section if any provision about his entitlement to remuneration has been made—
(*a*) by the trust instrument, or
(*b*) by any enactment or any provision of subordinate legislation.

(6) This section applies to a trustee who has been authorised under a power conferred by Part IV or the trust instrument—
(*a*) to exercise functions as an agent of the trustees, or
(*b*) to act as a nominee or custodian,

as it applies to any other trustee.

1 The words in square brackets were substituted by the Financial Services Act 2012 s 114(1), Sch 18 para 90(1), (2) with effect from 1 April 2013.
2 Subsections (3A), (3B), (3C) were inserted by the Financial Services Act 2012 s 114(1), Sch 18 para 90(1), (3) with effect from 1 April 2013.

31 TRUSTEES' EXPENSES

34.56 (1) A trustee—
(*a*) is entitled to be reimbursed from the trust funds, or
(*b*) may pay out of the trust funds,
expenses properly incurred by him when acting on behalf of the trust.

(2) This section applies to a trustee who has been authorised under a power conferred by Part IV or any other enactment or any provision of subordinate legislation, or by the trust instrument—
(*a*) to exercise functions as an agent of the trustees, or
(*b*) to act as a nominee or custodian,
as it applies to any other trustee.

32 REMUNERATION AND EXPENSES OF AGENTS, NOMINEES AND CUSTODIANS

34.57 (1) This section applies if, under a power conferred by Part IV or any other enactment or any provision of subordinate legislation, or by the trust instrument, a person other than a trustee has been—
(*a*) authorised to exercise functions as an agent of the trustees, or
(*b*) appointed to act as a nominee or custodian.

(2) The trustees may remunerate the agent, nominee or custodian out of the trust funds for services if—

(*a*) he is engaged on terms entitling him to be remunerated for those services, and
(*b*) the amount does not exceed such remuneration as is reasonable in the circumstances for the provision of those services by him to or on behalf of that trust.

(3) The trustees may reimburse the agent, nominee or custodian out of the trust funds for any expenses properly incurred by him in exercising functions as an agent, nominee or custodian.

PART VI
MISCELLANEOUS AND SUPPLEMENTARY

35 PERSONAL REPRESENTATIVES

34.58 (1) Subject to the following provisions of this section, this Act applies in relation to a personal representative administering an estate according to the law as it applies to a trustee carrying out a trust for beneficiaries.

(2) For this purpose this Act is to be read with the appropriate modifications and in particular—
(*a*) references to the trust instrument are to be read as references to the will,
(*b*) references to a beneficiary or to beneficiaries, apart from the reference to a beneficiary in section 8(1)(*b*), are to be read as references to a person or the persons interested in the due administration of the estate, and
(*c*) the reference to a beneficiary in section 8(1)(*b*) is to be read as a reference to a person who under the will of the deceased or under the law relating to intestacy is beneficially interested in the estate.

(3) Remuneration to which a personal representative is entitled under section 28 or 29 is to be treated as an administration expense for the purposes of—
(*a*) section 34(3) of the Administration of Estates Act 1925 (order in which estate to be paid out), and
(*b*) any provision giving reasonable administration expenses priority over the preferential debts listed in Schedule 6 to the Insolvency Act 1986.

(4) Nothing in subsection (3) is to be treated as affecting the operation of the provisions mentioned in paragraphs (*a*) and (*b*) of that subsection in relation to any death occurring before the commencement of this section.

39 INTERPRETATION

34.59 (1) In this Act—
"asset" includes any right or interest;
"charitable trust" means a trust under which property is held for charitable purposes and "charitable purposes" [has the meaning given by section 11 of the Charities Act 2011][1];
"custodian trustee" has the same meaning as in the Public Trustee Act 1906;
"enactment" includes any provision of a Measure of the Church Assembly or of the General Synod of the Church of England;
"exempt charity" has the same meaning as in [the Charities Act 2011][1];
"functions" includes powers and duties;
"legal mortgage" has the same meaning as in the Law of Property Act 1925;

"personal representative" has the same meaning as in the Trustee Act 1925;
"settled land" has the same meaning as in the Settled Land Act 1925;
"trust corporation" has the same meaning as in the Trustee Act 1925;
"trust funds" means income or capital funds of the trust.

(2) In this Act the expressions listed below are defined or otherwise explained by the provisions indicated—

asset management functions	section 15(5)
custodian	section 17(2)
the duty of care	section 1(2)
the general power of investment	section 3(2)
lay trustee	section 28(6)
power of intervention	section 22(4)
the standard investment criteria	section 4(3)
subordinate legislation	section 6(3)
trustee acting in a professional capacity	section 28(5)
trust instrument	sections 6(2) and 35(2)(*a*)

1 The words in square brackets were substituted by the Charities Act 2011 s 354(1), Sch 7 para 90 with effect from 14 March 2012.

SCHEDULE 1
APPLICATION OF DUTY OF CARE

Section 2

INVESTMENT

34.60 1 The duty of care applies to a trustee—
(*a*) when exercising the general power of investment or any other power of investment, however conferred;
(*b*) when carrying out a duty to which he is subject under section 4 or 5 (duties relating to the exercise of a power of investment or to the review of investments).
Acquisition of land

2 The duty of care applies to a trustee—
(*a*) when exercising the power under section 8 to acquire land;
(*b*) when exercising any other power to acquire land, however conferred;
(*c*) when exercising any power in relation to land acquired under a power mentioned in sub-paragraph (*a*) or (*b*).

Agents, nominees and custodians

3 (1) The duty of care applies to a trustee—
(*a*) when entering into arrangements under which a person is authorised under section 11 to exercise functions as an agent,
(*b*) when entering into arrangements under which a person is appointed under section 16 to act as a nominee,

(*c*) when entering into arrangements under which a person is appointed under section 17 or 18 to act as a custodian,
(*d*) when entering into arrangements under which, under any other power, however conferred, a person is authorised to exercise functions as an agent or is appointed to act as a nominee or custodian,
(*e*) when carrying out his duties under section 22 (review of agent, nominee or custodian, etc).

(2) For the purposes of sub-paragraph (1), entering into arrangements under which a person is authorised to exercise functions or is appointed to act as a nominee or custodian includes, in particular—
(*a*) selecting the person who is to act,
(*b*) determining any terms on which he is to act, and
(*c*) if the person is being authorised to exercise asset management functions, the preparation of a policy statement under section 15.

Compounding of liabilities

4 The duty of care applies to a trustee—
(*a*) when exercising the power under section 15 of the Trustee Act 1925 to do any of the things referred to in that section,
(*b*) when exercising any corresponding power, however conferred.

Insurance

5 The duty of care applies to a trustee—
(*a*) when exercising the power under section 19 of the Trustee Act 1925 to insure property,
(*b*) when exercising any corresponding power, however conferred.

Reversionary interests, valuations and audit

6 The duty of care applies to a trustee—
(*a*) when exercising the power under section 22(1) or (3) of the Trustee Act 1925 to do any of the things referred to there,
(*b*) when exercising any corresponding power, however conferred.

Exclusion of duty of care

7 The duty of care does not apply if or in so far as it appears from the trust instrument that the duty is not meant to apply.

Appendix Part 3: Intestacy Rules

ADMINISTRATION OF ESTATES ACT 1925 SS 46, 47 AND 47A

46 SUCCESSION TO REAL AND PERSONAL ESTATE ON INTESTACY

35.1 (1) The residuary estate of an intestate shall be distributed in the manner or be held on the trusts mentioned in this section, namely:—

[(i) If the intestate leaves a [spouse or civil partner][1], then in accordance with the following Table:

[Table

(1) If the intestate leaves no issue:	the residuary estate shall be held in trust for the surviving spouse or civil partner absolutely.
(2) If the intestate leaves issue:	(A) the surviving spouse or civil partner shall take the personal chattels absolutely; (B) the residuary estate of the intestate (other than the personal chattels) shall stand charged with the payment of a fixed net sum, free of death duties and costs, to the surviving spouse or civil partner, together with simple interest on it from the date of the death at the rate provided for by subsection (1A) until paid or appropriated; and (C) subject to providing for the sum and interest referred to in paragraph (B), the residuary estate (other than the personal chattels) shall be held— (*a*) as to one half, in trust for the surviving spouse or civil partner absolutely, and (*b*) as to the other half, on the statutory trusts for the issue of the intestate.

The amount of the fixed net sum referred to in paragraph (B) of case (2) of this Table is to be determined in accordance with Schedule 1A.][2]

(ii) If the intestate leaves issue but no [spouse or civil partner][1] the residuary estate of the intestate shall be held on the statutory trusts for the issue of the intestate;

(iii) If the intestate leaves [no [spouse or civil partner][1] and][3] no issue but both parents, then ...[4] the residuary estate of the intestate shall be held in trust for the father and mother in equal shares absolutely;

(iv) If the intestate leaves [no [spouse or civil partner][1] and][3] no issue but one parent, then ...[4] the residuary estate of the intestate shall be held in trust for the surviving father or mother absolutely;

(v) If the intestate leaves no [[spouse or civil partner][1] and no issue and no][5] parent, then ...[6] the residuary estate of the intestate shall be held in trust for the following persons living at the death of the intestate, and in the following order and manner, namely:—

First, on the statutory trusts for the brothers and sisters of the whole blood of the intestate; but if no person takes an absolutely vested interest under such trusts; then

Secondly, on the statutory trusts for the brothers and sisters of the half blood of the intestate, but if no person takes an absolutely vested interest under such trusts; then

Thirdly, for the grandparents of the intestate and, if more than one survive the intestate, in equal shares; but if there is no member of this class; then

Fourthly, on the statutory trusts of the uncles and aunts of the intestate (being brothers or sisters of the whole blood of a parent of the intestate); but if no person takes an absolutely vested interest under such trusts; then

Fifthly, on the statutory trusts for the uncles and aunts of the intestate (being brothers or sisters of the half blood of a parent of the intestate);

...[6]

(vi) In default of any person taking an absolute interest under the foregoing provisions, the residuary estate of the intestate shall belong to the Crown or to the Duchy of Lancaster or to the Duke of Cornwall for the time being, as the case may be, as bona vacantia, and in lieu of any right to escheat.

The Crown or the said Duchy or the said Duke may (without prejudice to the powers reserved by section nine of the Civil List Act 1910, or any other powers), out of the whole or any part of the property devolving on them respectively, provide, in accordance with the existing practice, for dependants, whether kindred or not, of the intestate, and other persons for whom the intestate might reasonably have been expected to make provision.

[[(1A) The interest rate referred to in paragraph (B) of case (2) of the Table in subsection (1)(i) is the Bank of England rate that has effect at the end of the day on which the intestate died.][7]][8]

(2) A husband and wife shall for all purposes of distribution or division under the foregoing provisions of this section be treated as two persons.

[(2A) Where the intestate's [spouse or civil partner][1] survived the intestate but died before the end of the period of 28 days beginning with the day on which the intestate died, this section shall have effect as respects the intestate as if the [spouse or civil partner][1] had not survived the intestate.][9]

[(3) ...[10]

(4) The interest payable on the [fixed net sum][11] payable to a surviving [spouse or civil partner][1] shall be primarily payable out of income.][12]

[(5) In subsection (1A)"Bank of England rate" means—

(*a*) the rate announced by the Monetary Policy Committee of the Bank of England as the official bank rate, or

(*b*) where an order under section 19 of the Bank of England Act 1998 (reserve powers) is in force, any equivalent rate determined by the Treasury under that section.

(6) The Lord Chancellor may by order made by statutory instrument amend the definition of "Bank of England rate" in subsection (5) (but this subsection does not affect the generality of subsection (7)(*b*)).

(7) The Lord Chancellor may by order made by statutory instrument—

(*a*) amend subsection (1A) so as to substitute a different interest rate (however specified or identified) for the interest rate for the time being provided for by that subsection;

(*b*) make any amendments of, or repeals in, this section that may be consequential on or incidental to any amendment made by virtue of paragraph (*a*).

(8) A statutory instrument containing an order under subsection (6) is subject to annulment pursuant to a resolution of either House of Parliament.

(9) A statutory instrument containing an order under subsection (7) may not be made unless a draft of the instrument has been laid before and approved by a resolution of each House of Parliament.][13]

1 The words in square brackets were substituted by the Civil Partnership Act 2004 s 71, Sch 4 para 7 with effect from 5 December 2005.

2 The words in square brackets were substituted by the Inheritance and Trustees' Powers Act 2014 s 1(1), (2) with effect from 1 October 2014.

3 The words in square brackets were inserted by the Intestates' Estates Act 1952 s 1(1), (3)(*a*) with effect from 1 January 1953.

4 The words omitted were repealed by the Intestates' Estates Act 1952 s 1(1), (3)(*a*) with effect from 1 January 1953.

5 The words in square brackets were substituted by the Intestates' Estates Act 1952 s 1(1), (3)(*b*)(i) with effect from 1 January 1953.

6 The words omitted were repealed by the Intestates' Estates Act 1952 s 1(1), (3)(*b*)(ii) with effect from 1 January 1953.

7 Subsection (1A) was substituted by the Inheritance and Trustees' Powers Act 2014 s 1(1), (3) with effect from 1 October 2014.

8 Subsection (1A) was inserted by the Administration of Justice Act 1977 s 28(1)(*b*) with effect from 15 September 1977.

9 Subsection (2A) was inserted by the Law Reform (Succession) Act 1995 s 1(1), as respects an intestate dying on or after 1 January 1996.

10 Subsection (3) was repealed by the Inheritance and Trustees' Powers Act 2014 s 11, Sch 4 para 1(1), (2) with effect from 1 October 2014.

11 The words in square brackets were substituted by the Family Provisions Act 1966 s 1(2)(*b*) with effect from 1 January 1967. See notes 2 and 5.

12 Subsections (3), (4) were inserted by the Intestates' Estates Act 1952 s 1(1), (4) with effect from 1 January 1953.

13 Subsections (5) to (9) were inserted by the Inheritance and Trustees' Powers Act 2014 s 1(1), (4) with effect from 1 October 2014.

47 STATUTORY TRUSTS IN FAVOUR OF ISSUE AND OTHER CLASSES OF RELATIVES OF INTESTATE

35.2 (1) Where under this Part of this Act the residuary estate of an intestate, or any part thereof, is directed to be held on the statutory trusts for the issue of the intestate, the same shall be held upon the following trusts, namely:—

(i) In trust, in equal shares if more than one, for all or any of the children or child of the intestate, living at the death of the intestate, who attain the age of [eighteen years][1] or marry under that age [or form a civil partnership under that age][2], and for all or any of the issue living at the death of the intestate who attain the age of [eighteen years][1] or marry[, or form a civil partnership,][2] under that age of any child of the intestate who predeceases the intestate, such issue to take through all degrees, according to their stocks, in equal shares if more than one, the share which their parent would have taken if living at the death of the intestate, and so that [(subject to section 46A)][3] no issue shall take whose parent is living at the death of the intestate and so capable of taking;

(ii) The statutory power of advancement, and the statutory provisions which relate to maintenance and accumulation of surplus income, shall apply, but when an infant marries[, or forms a civil partnership,][2] such infant shall be entitled to give valid receipts for the income of the infant's share or interest;

(iii) …[4]

(iv) The personal representatives may permit any infant contingently interested to have the use and enjoyment of any personal chattels in such manner and subject to such conditions (if any) as the personal representatives may consider reasonable, and without being liable to account for any consequential loss.

(2) If the trusts in favour of the issue of the intestate fail by reason of no child or other issue attaining an absolutely vested interest—

(*a*) the residuary estate of the intestate and the income thereof and all statutory accumulations, if any, of the income thereof, or so much thereof as may not have been paid or applied under any power affecting the same, shall go, devolve and be held under the provisions of this Part of this Act as if the intestate had died without leaving issue living at the death of the intestate;

(*b*) references in this Part of this Act to the intestate "leaving no issue" shall be construed as "leaving no issue who attain an absolutely vested interest";

(*c*) references in this Part of this Act to the intestate "leaving issue" or "leaving a child or other issue" shall be construed as 'leaving issue who attain an absolutely vested interest'.

(3) Where under this Part of this Act the residuary estate of an intestate or any part thereof is directed to be held on the statutory trusts for any class of relatives of the intestate, other than issue of the intestate, the same shall be held on trusts corresponding to the statutory trusts for the issue of the intestate (other than the provision for bringing any money or property into account) as if such trusts (other than as aforesaid) were repeated with the substitution of references to the members or member of that class for references to the children or child of the intestate.

[(4) References in paragraph (i) of subsection (1) of the last foregoing section to the intestate leaving, or not leaving, a member of the class consisting of brothers or sisters of the whole blood of the intestate and issue of brothers or sisters of the whole blood of the intestate shall be construed as references to the intestate leaving, or not leaving, a member of that class who attains an absolutely vested interest.

[(4A) Subsections (2) and (4) are subject to section 46A.][5]

[(4B) Subsections (4C) and (4D) apply if a beneficiary under the statutory trusts—

(*a*) fails to attain an absolutely vested interest because the beneficiary dies without having reached 18 and without having married or formed a civil partnership, and

(*b*) dies leaving issue.

(4C) The beneficiary is to be treated for the purposes of this Part as having died immediately before the intestate.

(4D) The residuary estate (together with the income from it and any statutory accumulations of income from it) or so much of it as has not been paid or applied under a power affecting it is to devolve accordingly.][6]

(5) …[7]][8]

1 The words in square brackets were substituted by the Family Law Reform Act 1969 s 3(2) with effect from 1 January 1970.

2 The words in square brackets were inserted by the Civil Partnership Act 2004 s 71, Sch 4 para 8 with effect from 5 December 2005.

3 The words in square brackets were inserted by the Estates of Deceased Persons (Forfeiture Rule and Law of Succession) Act 2011 s 1(1), (3) with effect from 1 February 2012.

4 Paragraph (iii) was repealed by the Law Reform (Succession) Act 1995 ss 1(2)(*a*), 5, Schedule, as respects intestates dying on or after 1 January 1996.

5 Subsection (4A) was inserted by the Estates of Deceased Persons (Forfeiture Rule and Law of Succession) Act 2011 s 1(1), (4) with effect from 1 February 2012.

6 Subsections (4B), (4C), (4D) were inserted by the Estates of Deceased Persons (Forfeiture Rule and Law of Succession) Act 2011 s 3 with effect from 1 February 2012.

7 Subsection (5) was repealed by the Family Provision Act 1966 ss 9, 10, Sch 2 with effect from 1 January 1967.

8 Subsections (4), (5) were inserted by the Intestates' Estates Act 1952 s 1(1), (3)(*c*) with effect from 1 January 1953.

47A …[1]

35.3 …[1]

1 This section was inserted by the Intestates' Estates Act 1952 s 2(*b*) with effect from 1 January 1953 and repealed by the Inheritance and Trustees' Powers Act 2014 s 11, Sch 4 para 1(1), (2) with effect from 1 October 2014.

Appendix Part 4: Inheritance Tax and Capital Gains Tax

INHERITANCE TAX ACT 1984 ss 8A to 8C

8A Transfer of unused nil-rate band between spouses and civil partners[1]

36.1 (1) This section applies where—

(*a*) immediately before the death of a person (a "deceased person"), the deceased person had a spouse or civil partner ("the survivor"), and

(*b*) the deceased person had unused nil-rate band on death.

(2) A person has unused nil-rate band on death if—

$$M > VT$$

where—

M is the maximum amount that could be transferred by a chargeable transfer made (under section 4 above) on the person's death if it were to be wholly chargeable to tax at the rate of nil per cent. (assuming, if necessary, that the value of the person's estate were sufficient but otherwise having regard to the circumstances of the person); and

VT is the value actually transferred by the chargeable transfer so made (or nil if no chargeable transfer is so made).

(3) Where a claim is made under this section, the nil-rate band maximum at the time of the survivor's death is to be treated for the purposes of the charge to tax on the death of the survivor as increased by the percentage specified in subsection (4) below (but subject to subsection (5) and section 8C below).

(4) That percentage is—

$$(E \div NRBMD) \times 100$$

where—

E is the amount by which M is greater than VT in the case of the deceased person; and

NRBMD is the nil-rate band maximum at the time of the deceased person's death.

(5) If (apart from this subsection) the amount of the increase in the nil-rate band maximum at the time of the survivor's death effected by this section would exceed

the amount of that nil-rate band maximum, the amount of the increase is limited to the amount of that nil-rate band maximum.

(6) Subsection (5) above may apply either—

(*a*) because the percentage mentioned in subsection (4) above (as reduced under section 8C below where that section applies) is more than 100 because of the amount by which M is greater than VT in the case of one deceased person, or

(*b*) because this section applies in relation to the survivor by reference to the death of more than one person who had unused nil-rate band on death.

(7) In this Act "nil-rate band maximum" means the amount shown in the second column in the first row of the Table in Schedule 1 to this Act (upper limit of portion of value charged at rate of nil per cent.) and in the first column in the second row of that Table (lower limit of portion charged at next rate).]

1 This section was inserted by the Finance Act 2008 s 10, Sch 4 paras 1, 2 in relation to cases where the survivor's death occurs on or after 9 October 2007.

8B Claims under section 8A[1]

36.2 (1) A claim under section 8A above may be made—

(*a*) by the personal representatives of the survivor within the permitted period, or

(*b*) (if no claim is so made) by any other person liable to the tax chargeable on the survivor's death within such later period as an officer of Revenue and Customs may in the particular case allow.

(2) If no claim under section 8A above has been made in relation to a person (P) by reference to whose death that section applies in relation to the survivor, the claim under that section in relation to the survivor may include a claim under that section in relation to P if that does not affect the tax chargeable on the value transferred by the chargeable transfer of value made on P's death.

(3) In subsection (1)(*a*) above "the permitted period" means—

(*a*) the period of two years from the end of the month in which the survivor dies or (if it ends later) the period of three months beginning with the date on which the personal representatives first act as such, or

(*b*) such longer period as an officer of Revenue and Customs may in the particular case allow.

(4) A claim made within either of the periods mentioned in subsection (3)(*a*) above may be withdrawn no later than one month after the end of the period concerned.

1 This section was inserted by the Finance Act 2008 s 10, Sch 4 paras 1, 2 in relation to cases where the survivor's death occurs on or after 9 October 2007.

8C Section 8A and subsequent charges[1]

36.3 (1) This section applies where—

(*a*) the conditions in subsection (1)(*a*) and (*b*) of section 8A above are met, and

(*b*) after the death of the deceased person, tax is charged on an amount under any of sections 32, 32A and 126 below by reference to the rate or rates that would have been applicable to the amount if it were included in the value transferred by the chargeable transfer made (under section 4 above) on the deceased person's death.

(2) If the tax is charged before the death of the survivor, the percentage referred to in subsection (3) of section 8A above is (instead of that specified in subsection (4) of that section)—

$$((E \div NRBMD) - (TA \div NRBME)) \times 100$$

where—

E and NRBMD have the same meaning as in subsection (4) of that section;

TA is the amount on which tax is charged; and

NRBME is the nil-rate band maximum at the time of the event occasioning the charge.

(3) If this section has applied by reason of a previous event or events, the reference in subsection (2) to the fraction—

$$TA \div NRBME$$

is to the aggregate of that fraction in respect of the current event and the previous event (or each of the previous events).

(4) If the tax is charged after the death of the survivor, it is charged as if the personal nil-rate band maximum of the deceased person were appropriately reduced.

(5) In subsection (4) above—
"the personal nil-rate band maximum of the deceased person" is the nil-rate band maximum which is treated by Schedule 2 to this Act as applying in relation to the deceased person's death, increased in accordance with section 8A above where that section effected an increase in that nil-rate band maximum in the case of the deceased person (as survivor of another deceased person), and
"appropriately reduced" means reduced by the amount (if any) by which the amount on which tax was charged at the rate of nil per cent. on the death of the survivor was increased by reason of the operation of section 8A above by virtue of the position of the deceased person.

1 This section was inserted by the Finance Act 2008 s 10, Sch 4 paras 1, 2 in relation to cases where the survivor's death occurs on or after 9 October 2007.

FINANCE ACT 2008 Sch 4

SCHEDULE 4 Inheritance Tax: Transfer of Nil-rate Band etc

Section 10 Amendments of IHTA 1984

36.4 *. . . Commencement*

9(1) The amendments made by paragraphs 2, 3 and 4(4)[1] have effect in relation to cases where the survivor's death occurs on or after 9 October 2007.

(2) . . .[2]

(3) . . .

Modifications for cases where deceased person died before 25 July 1986

10(1) Section 8A of IHTA 1984 (as inserted by paragraph 2) has effect in relation to cases where the deceased person died before 25 July 1986 (and the survivor dies on or after 9 October 2007) subject as follows.

(2) Where the deceased person died on or after 1 January 1985—
(*a*) the references in subsection (2) to a chargeable transfer made under section 4 of IHTA 1984 is to a chargeable transfer made under section 4 of CTTA 1984, and
(*b*) the reference in subsection (4) to the nil-rate band maximum is to the amount shown in the second column of the first row, and the first column of the second row, of the First Table in Schedule 1 to that Act.

(3) Where the deceased person died on or after 13 March 1975 and before 1 January 1985—
(*a*) the references in subsection (2) to a chargeable transfer made under section 4 of IHTA 1984 is to a chargeable transfer made under section 22 of FA 1975, and
(*b*) the reference in subsection (4) to the nil-rate band maximum is to the amount shown in the second column of the first row, and in the first column of the second row, of the First Table in section 37 of that Act.

(4) Where the deceased person died on or after 16 April 1969 and before 13 March 1975, section 8A applies as if—
(*a*) M were the amount specified in paragraph (*a*) in Part 1 of Schedule 17 to FA 1969 at the time of the deceased person's death,
(*b*) VT were the aggregate principal value of all property comprised in the estate of the deceased person for the purposes of estate duty, and
(*c*) the reference in subsection (4) to the nil-rate band maximum were to the amount mentioned in paragraph (*a*).

(5) Where the deceased person died before 16 April 1969, section 8A applies as if—
(*a*) M were the amount specified as the higher figure in the first line, and the lower figure in the second line, in the first column of the scale in section 17 of FA 1894 at the time of the deceased person's death,
(*b*) VT were the principal value of the estate of the deceased person for the purposes of estate duty, and
(*c*) the reference in subsection (4) to the nil-rate band maximum were to the figure mentioned in paragraph (*a*).

11(1) Section 8C of IHTA 1984 (as inserted by paragraph 2) has effect in relation to cases where the deceased person died before 25 July 1986 but on or after 13 March 1975 (and the survivor dies on or after 9 October 2007) subject as follows.

(2) Where the deceased person died on or after 1 January 1985—
(*a*) the reference in subsection (1) to sections 32, 32A and 126 of IHTA 1984 includes sections 32, 32A and 126 of CTTA 1984,
(*b*) the reference in that subsection to section 4 of IHTA 1984 is to section 4 of CTTA 1984,
(*c*) the reference in subsection (2) to the nil-rate band maximum includes the amount shown in the second column of the first row, and the first column of the second row, of the First Table in Schedule 1 to that Act,
(*d*) the first reference in subsection (5) to the nil-rate band maximum is to that amount, and
(*e*) the reference in subsection (5) to Schedule 2 to IHTA 1984 includes Schedule 2 to CTTA 1984.

(3) Where the deceased person died on or after 7 April 1976 and before 1 January 1985—

(*a*) the reference in subsection (1) to sections 32, 32A and 126 of IHTA 1984 includes sections 32, 32A and 126 of CTTA 1984, section 78 of FA 1976 and paragraph 2 of Schedule 9 to FA 1975,
(*b*) the reference in that subsection to section 4 of IHTA is to section 22 of FA 1975,
(*c*) the reference in subsection (2) to the nil-rate band maximum includes the amount shown in the second column of the first row, and the first column of the second row, of the First Table in Schedule 1 to CTTA 1984 and the amount shown in the second column of the first row, and in the first column of the second row, of the First Table in section 37 of FA 1975,
(*d*) the first reference in subsection (5) to the nil-rate band maximum is to that amount, and
(*e*) the reference in subsection (5) to Schedule 2 to IHTA 1984 includes Schedule 2 to CTTA 1984, Schedule 15 to FA 1980 and section 62 of FA 1978;

but, if the event occasioning the charge occurred before 27 October 1977, the reference in subsection (4) to the personal nil-rate band maximum is to the amount shown in the second column of the first row, and in the first column of the second row, of the First Table in section 37 of FA 1975 at the time of the deceased person's death.

(4) Where the deceased person died on or after 13 March 1975 and before 7 April 1976—
(*a*) the reference in subsection (1) to sections 32, 32A and 126 of IHTA 1984 includes paragraph 1 of Schedule 5 to that Act, section 126 of CTTA 1984 and paragraph 2 of Schedule 9 to FA 1975,
(*b*) the reference in that subsection to section 4 of IHTA is to section 22 of FA 1975,
(*c*) the reference in subsection (2) to the nil-rate band maximum includes the amount shown in the second column of the first row, and the first column of the second row, of the First Table in Schedule 1 to CTTA 1984 and the amount shown in the second column of the first row, and in the first column of the second row, of the First Table in section 37 of FA 1975, and
(*d*) the reference in subsection (4) to the personal nil-rate band maximum is to the amount shown in the second column of the first row, and in the first column of the second row, of the First Table in section 37 of FA 1975 at the time of the deceased person's death.

1 I.e. The insertion of ss 8A, 8B and 8C of the Inheritance Tax Act 1984.
2 Sub-paragraph 9(2) was repealed by the Finance Act 2011 s 65, Sch 16 para 84(*d*)(i) with effect from 6 April 2011.

INHERITANCE TAX ACT 1984 ss 142, 143 and 144

142 Alteration of dispositions taking effect on death[1]

36.5 (1) Where within the period of two years after a person's death—
(*a*) any of the dispositions (whether effected by will, under the law relating to intestacy or otherwise) of the property comprised in his estate immediately before his death are varied, or
(*b*) the benefit conferred by any of those dispositions is disclaimed,

by an instrument in writing made by the persons or any of the persons who benefit or would benefit under the dispositions, this Act shall apply as if the variation had been effected by the deceased or, as the case may be, the disclaimed benefit had never been conferred.

[(2) Subsection (1) above shall not apply to a variation unless the instrument contains a statement, made by all the relevant persons, to the effect that they intend the subsection to apply to the variation.

(2A) For the purposes of subsection (2) above the relevant persons are—
(*a*) the person or persons making the instrument, and
(*b*) where the variation results in additional tax being payable, the personal representatives;

Personal representatives may decline to make a statement under subsection (2) above only if no, or no sufficient, assets are held by them in that capacity for discharging the additional tax.][2]

(3) Subsection (1) above shall not apply to a variation or disclaimer made for any consideration in money or money's worth other than consideration consisting of the making, in respect of another of the dispositions, of a variation or disclaimer to which that subsection applies.

[(3A) Subsection (1) does not apply to a variation by virtue of which any property comprised in the estate immediately before the person's death becomes property in relation to which section 23(1) applies unless it is shown that the appropriate person has been notified of the existence of the instrument of variation.

(3B) For the purposes of subsection (3A) "the appropriate person" is—
(*a*) the charity or registered club to which the property is given, or
(*b*) if the property is to be held on trust for charitable purposes or for the purposes of registered clubs, the trustees in question.][3]

(4) Where a variation to which subsection (1) above applies results in property being held in trust for a person for a period which ends not more than two years after the death, this Act shall apply as if the disposition of the property that takes effect at the end of the period had had effect from the beginning of the period; but this subsection shall not affect the application of this Act in relation to any distribution or application of property occurring before that disposition takes effect.

(5) For the purposes of subsection (1) above the property comprised in a person's estate includes any excluded property but not any property to which he is treated as entitled by virtue of section 49(1) above [or section 102 of the Finance Act 1986][4].

(6) Subsection (1) above applies whether or not the administration of the estate is complete or the property concerned has been distributed in accordance with the original dispositions.

(7) In the application of subsection (4) above to Scotland, property which is subject to a proper liferent shall be deemed to be held in trust for the liferenter.

1 Subsections (1) to (6) were derived from the Finance Act 1978 s 68(1) to (5); sub-s (7) was derived from the Finance Act 1978 s 68(4) and Finance Act 1980 s 93(3).
2 Subsections (2) and (2A) were substituted for subsection (2) by the Finance Act 2002 s 120(1) in relation to instruments made on or after 1 August 2002.
3 Subsections (3A) and (3B) were inserted by the Finance Act 2012 s 209, Sch 33 para 9 in relation to cases where the person's death occurred on or after 6 April 2012.
4 The words in square brackets were inserted by the Finance Act 1986 s 101, Sch 19 para 24, in relation to transfers of value made, and other events occurring, on or after 18 March 1986.

143 Compliance with testator's request

36.6 Where a testator expresses a wish that property bequeathed by his will should be transferred by the legatee to other persons, and the legatee transfers any of the property in accordance with that wish within the period of two years after the death of the testator, this Act shall have effect as if the property transferred had been bequeathed by the will to the transferee.

144 Distribution etc from property settled by will

36.7 (1) [Subsection (2) below applies][1] where property comprised in a person's estate immediately before his death is settled by his will and, within the period of two years after his death and before any interest in possession has subsisted in the property, there occurs—

(*a*) an event on which tax would [(apart from subsection (2) below)][1] be chargeable under any provision, other than section 64 or 79, of Chapter III of Part III of this Act, or

(*b*) an event on which tax would be so chargeable but for section 75[, 75A][2] or 76 above or paragraph 16(1) of Schedule 4 to this Act.

[(1A) Where the testator dies on or after 22nd March 2006, subsection (1) above shall have effect as if the reference to any interest in possession were a reference to any interest in possession that is—

(*a*) an immediate post-death interest, or

(*b*) a disabled person's interest.][3]

(2) Where [this subsection][4] applies by virtue of an event within paragraph (*a*) of subsection (1) above, tax shall not be charged under the provision in question on that event; and in every case in which [this subsection][4] applies in relation to an event, this Act shall have effect as if the will had provided that on the testator's death the property should be held as it is held after the event.

[(3) Subsection (4) below applies where—

(*a*) a person dies on or after 22nd March 2006,

(*b*) property comprised in the person's estate immediately before his death is settled by his will, and

(*c*) within the period of two years after his death, but before an immediate post-death interest or a disabled person's interest has subsisted in the property, there occurs an event that involves causing the property to be held on trusts that would, if they had in fact been established by the testator's will, have resulted in—

  (i) an immediate post-death interest subsisting in the property, or

  (ii) section 71A or 71D above applying to the property.

(4) Where this subsection applies by virtue of an event—

(*a*) this Act shall have effect as if the will had provided that on the testator's death the property should be held as it is held after the event, but

(*b*) tax shall not be charged on that event under any provision of Chapter 3 of Part 3 of this Act.

(5) Subsection (4) above also applies where—

(*a*) a person dies before 22nd March 2006,

(*b*) property comprised in the person's estate immediately before his death is settled by his will,

(*c*) an event occurs—
 (i) on or after 22nd March 2006, and
 (ii) within the period of two years after the testator's death,
 that involves causing the property to be held on trusts within subsection (6) below,
(*d*) no immediate post-death interest, and no disabled person's interest, subsisted in the property at any time in the period beginning with the testator's death and ending immediately before the event, and
(*e*) no other interest in possession subsisted in the property at any time in the period beginning with the testator's death and ending immediately before 22nd March 2006.

(6) Trusts are within this subsection if they would, had they in fact been established by the testator's will and had the testator died at the time of the event mentioned in subsection (5)(*c*) above, have resulted in—
(*a*) an immediate post-death interest subsisting in the property, or
(*b*) section 71A or 71D above applying to the property.][5]

1 The words in square brackets were substituted by the Finance Act 2006 s 156, Sch 20 paras 7, 27(1), (2) with effect from 22 March 2006.
2 The word in square brackets was inserted by the Finance Act 2014 s 290, Sch 37 paras 9, 16 with effect from 6 April 2014.
3 Subsection (1A) was inserted by the Finance Act 2006 s 156, Sch 20 paras 7, 27(1), (3) with effect from 22 March 2006.
4 The words in square brackets were substituted by the Finance Act 2006 s 156, Sch 20 paras 7, 27(1), (4) with effect from 22 March 2006.
5 Subsections (3) to (6) were inserted by the Finance Act 2006 s 156, Sch 20 paras 7, 27(1), (5) with effect from 22 March 2006.

INLAND REVENUE STATEMENT OF PRACTICE 10/79

Power for trustees to allow a beneficiary to occupy dwelling-house

36.8 Many wills and settlements contain a clause empowering the trustees to permit a beneficiary to occupy a dwelling-house which forms part of the trust property as they think fit. The Board do not regard the existence of such a power as excluding any interest in possession of the property.

When there is no interest in possession in the property in question, the Board do not regard the exercise of power as creating one if the effect is merely to allow non-exclusive occupation or to create a contractual tenancy for full consideration. The Board also take the view that no interest in possession arises on the creation of a lease for a term or a periodic tenancy for less than full consideration, though this will normally give rise to a charge for tax under IHTA 1984 s 65(1)(*b*) (formerly FA 1982 s 108(1)(*b*)). On the other hand if the power is drawn in terms wide enough to cover the creation of an exclusive or joint residence, albeit revocable, for a definite or indefinite period, and is exercised with the intention of providing a particular beneficiary with a permanent home, the Revenue will normally regard the exercise of the power as creating an interest in possession. And if the trustees in exercise of their powers grant a lease for life for less than full consideration, this will be regarded as creating an interest in possession in view of IHTA 1984 ss 43(3), 50(6) (formerly FA 1975 Sch 5 paras 1(3), 3(6)).

A similar view will be taken where the power is exercised over property in which another beneficiary had an interest in possession up to the time of the exercise.

INLAND REVENUE PRESS RELEASE 6 AUGUST 1975

Power to allow beneficiary to occupy house

36.9 "Commonly such a power is ancillary to a primary trust created by the will and we should not regard its presence as affecting any interest in possession existing under that trust. If there is no such interest it could perhaps be argued that the exercise of the power might create one, but in the ordinary case we should not take this view unless the trustees were empowered to, and did, grant a lease for life within the terms of FA 1975 Sch 5 para 1(3) [now Inheritance Tax Act 1984 s 43(3)]."

"If the exercise of the power reduces the value of the settled property, as it would if the trustees could and did grant a lease for a fixed term at less than a rack rent, we should in practice seek the alternative charge given by para 6(3) [repealed 1982] or 4(9) [now Inheritance Tax Act 1984 s 52(3),(4)] of the Schedule."

TAXATION OF CHARGEABLE GAINS ACT 1992 s 62

62 Death: general provisions

36.10 (1) For the purposes of this Act the assets of which a deceased person was competent to dispose—

(*a*) shall be deemed to be acquired on his death by the personal representatives or other person on whom they devolve for a consideration equal to their market value at the date of the death, but

(*b*) shall not be deemed to be disposed of by him on his death (whether or not they were the subject of a testamentary disposition).

(2) Allowable losses sustained by an individual in the year of assessment in which he dies may, so far as they cannot be deducted from chargeable gains accruing in that year, be deducted from chargeable gains accruing to the deceased in the three years of assessment preceding the year of assessment in which the death occurs, taking chargeable gains accruing in a later year before those accruing in an earlier year.

[(2A) Amounts deductible from chargeable gains for any year in accordance with subsection (2) above shall not be so deductible from any such gains so far as they are gains that are [treated as accruing by virtue of section 87 or 89(2) (read, where appropriate, with section 10A)][1].

(2B) …[2]][3]

(3) In relation to property forming part of the estate of a deceased person the personal representatives shall for the purposes of this Act be treated as being a single and continuing body of persons (distinct from the persons who may from time to time be the personal representatives), and that body shall be treated as having the deceased's residence …[4] and domicile at the date of death.

(4) On a person acquiring any asset as legatee (as defined in section 64)—

(*a*) no chargeable gain shall accrue to the personal representatives, and

(*b*) the legatee shall be treated as if the personal representatives' acquisition of the asset had been his acquisition of it.

(5) Notwithstanding section 17(1) no chargeable gain shall accrue to any person on his making a disposal by way of donatio mortis causa.

(6) Subject to subsections (7) and (8) below, where within the period of two years after a person's death any of the dispositions (whether effected by will, under the law relating to intestacy or otherwise) of the property of which he was competent to dispose are varied, or the benefit conferred by any of those dispositions is disclaimed, by an instrument in writing made by the persons or any of the persons who benefit or would benefit under the dispositions—

(*a*) the variation or disclaimer shall not constitute a disposal for the purposes of this Act, and

(*b*) this section shall apply as if the variation had been effected by the deceased or, as the case may be, the disclaimed benefit had never been conferred.

(7) Subsection (6) above does not apply to a variation [unless the instrument contains a statement by the persons making the instrument to the effect that they intend the subsection to apply to the variation][5].

(8) Subsection (6) above does not apply to a variation or disclaimer made for any consideration in money or money's worth other than consideration consisting of the making of a variation or disclaimer in respect of another of the dispositions.

(9) Subsection (6) above applies whether or not the administration of the estate is complete or the property has been distributed in accordance with the original dispositions.

(10) In this section references to assets of which a deceased person was competent to dispose are references to assets of the deceased which (otherwise than in right of a power of appointment or of the testamentary power conferred by statute to dispose of entailed interests) he could, if of full age and capacity, have disposed of by his will, assuming that all the assets were situated in England and, if he was not domiciled in the United Kingdom, that he was domiciled in England, and include references to his severable share in any assets to which, immediately before his death, he was beneficially entitled as a joint tenant.

1 The words in square brackets were substituted by the Finance Act 2008 s 8(2), Sch 2 paras 23, 29(1), (2) with effect from 6 April 2008.

2 Subsection (2B) was repealed by the Finance Act 2008 s 8(2), Sch 2 para 29(1), (3) with effect from 6 April 2008.

3 Subsections (2A), (2B) were inserted by the Finance Act 1998 s 121(3), Sch 21 paras 1, 5 with effect from 6 April 1998.

4 The words omitted were repealed by the Finance Act 2013 s 219(1), Sch 46 paras 74, 79 with effect from 6 April 2013.

5 The words in square brackets were substituted by the Finance Act 2002 s 52(1) in relation to instruments made on or after 1 August 2002.

Index

[*All references are to paragraph number*]

Abatement of legacies
generally, 10.10
introduction, 10.1
Accountants
appointment of executors, 8.23
Accrual clause
declarations, 20.8
Acquisition of land
trustees' powers
generally, 19.30
statutory provisions, 34.36–34.37
Acts of testator
revocation of wills, 4.5–4.6
Ademption
changing circumstances, 2.47–2.50
specific gifts of real property, 11.6
Ademption
declarations, 20.11
Adopted children
declarations, 20.3
statutory provisions, 33.27–33.33
Advancement
trustees' powers
generally, 19.7–19.8
statutory provisions, 34.3
Affidavit of due execution
attestation, 21.6
Age contingent gifts
generally, 16.13–16.24
inheritance tax, 22.17–22.21
Agents
trustees' powers
generally, 19.23–19.29
statutory provisions, 34.38–34.42
Agricultural property
business interests, 13.12–13.15
inheritance tax, 23.4–23.7
Alteration of will
attestation, 21.3
Anti-avoidance
inheritance tax, 22.34–22.36
Appointment of executors
accountants, and, 8.23
advice to testator, 8.2–8.4
beneficiaries, and, 8.11–8.13
Appointment of executors – *contd*
business acquaintances, and, 8.14–8.15
common appointments, 8.10
definitions, 8.1
friends, and, 8.14–8.15
public trustees, and, 8.26
solicitors, and, 8.16–8.22
trust corporations, and, 8.24–8.25
Appointment of guardians
conditionality, 9.6
consent of proposed guardian, 9.12
disclaimer, 9.12
generally, 9.4–9.8
interrelationship with trustees, 9.13
introduction, 9.1–9.3
jurisdiction of court, 9.8
other guardians, by, 9.7
precedents, 9.14
revocation, 9.9–9.11
Appropriation
trustees' powers, 19.42
Associated operations
inheritance tax, 22.36
Attestation
advice to testator, 21.2–21.3
affidavit of due execution, and, 21.6
alteration of will, and, 21.3
beneficiaries, 21.10
blind persons
special clauses, 21.7
witnesses, as, 21.9
draftsperson's duty, 21.12–21.19
formalities for wills, and, 21.1
generally, 21.1–21.7
minors, 21.8
page signatures, 21.4
persons unable to read or write, 21.7
precedents, 21.20
presumption, 21.3
procedure, 21.2
signature, 21.1
special clauses, 21.7
statutory wills and codicils, 30.28
supervision of draftsperson, 21.5
witnesses, 21.8–21.11

Bank accounts
gifts of chattels, 12.17
Beneficial share
specific gifts of real property, 11.9
Beneficiaries
appointment of executors, 8.11–8.13
attestation, 21.10
specific gifts of real property
consultation, 11.13–11.14
delegation, 11.12
Best interests
statutory wills and codicils, 30.11–30.17
Binding of wills
general considerations, 2.56–2.57
Blind persons
attestation
special clauses, 21.7
witnesses, as, 21.9
Borrowing
trustees' powers, 19.14
Burial
declaration of wishes, 7.3
expenses, 7.5
precedents, 7.9
Business acquaintances
appointment of executors, 8.14–8.15
Business interests
agricultural property relief, 13.12–13.15
business executors, 13.35–13.36
business property relief, 13.2–13.11
gift
chattels used by a business, 13.28–13.29
companies, 13.22–13.23
farming business, 13.30–13.32
generally, 13.16–13.18
limited liability partnerships, 13.27
partnerships, 13.24–13.26
sole traders, 13.19–13.21
introduction, 13.1
nil-rate band discretionary trusts, 13.3
precedents, 13.37
tax reliefs, 13.2–13.15
trustees' powers, 13.33–13.34
Business property
business interests, 13.2–13.11
inheritance tax, 23.4–23.7

Cancellation of contracts
taking instructions, and, 3.8
Capital gains tax
disabled and vulnerable beneficiaries, 18.12–18.15
minors, 17.13–17.16
statutory provisions, 36.10
Carrying on testator's business
trustees' powers, 19.40
Change in law
changing circumstances, 2.54–2.55
Changing circumstances
ademption, 2.47–2.50
change in law, 2.54–2.55
civil partnership, 2.51
divorce, 2.52
generally, 2.46
marriage, 2.51
personal circumstances, 2.53
Charges
gifts of chattels, 12.12–12.13
Charitable gifts
'charitable purpose', 14.4
'charity', 14.4
community amateur sports clubs, 14.6
discrimination, and, 14.5
forms, 14.12–14.21
inheritance tax
generally, 22.26–22.27
introduction, 14.2
mitigation, 23.20
reduced rate, 14.6–14.11
introduction, 14.1–14.2
meaning, 14.3–14.5
precedents, 14.22
purpose, 14.2
Chattels
bank accounts, 12.17
business interests, and, 13.28–13.29
collections, 12.8
debts, 12.14
gifts
bank accounts, 12.17
collections, 12.8
debts, 12.14
generally, 12.4–12.7
inheritance tax, 12.3
need, 12.1–12.2
personal chattels, 12.4–12.7
precedents, 12.16
releases, 12.14
rights of selection, 12.9–12.11
shares, 12.15–12.16
subject to charge, 12.12–12.13
personal chattels, 12.4–12.7
precedents, 12.16
releases, 12.14
rights of selection, 12.9–12.11
shares, 12.15–12.16
subject to charge, 12.12–12.13
Children
capital gains tax, 17.13–17.16
immediate post death interest, 17.10
income tax, 17.13–17.16
inheritance tax, 17.6–17.12
introduction, 17.1
precedents, 17.20

Children – *contd*
receipt clauses, 17.2
specific gifts of real property, 11.7
summary of options, 17.17–17.19
trustee powers, 17.3–17.5
vulnerable persons' trusts, 17.13–17.14
Civil partnerships
changing circumstances, 2.51
children, with
adult children, 27.4
formation of new partnership, 27.9–27.10
generally, 27.1–27.3
introduction, 24.1
minor children, 27.5–27.7
pensions, 27.8
precedents, 27.12
trusts, 27.11
drafting issues, 1.6
revocation of wills, 4.7
second civil partnerships where are children of first marriage, 29.1–29.3
Class gifts
generally, 16.25–16.27
Collections
gifts of chattels, 12.8
Conditional revocation
generally, 4.10
Codes of practice
taking instructions, and, 3.2–3.4
Codicils
generally, 24.1–24.5
precedent, 24.6
Community amateur sports clubs
charitable gifts, 14.62
Companies
business interests, 13.22–13.23
Complete wills
categories, 24.2
civil partners with children
adult children, 27.4
formation of new partnership, 27.9–27.10
generally, 27.1–27.3
minor children, 27.5–27.7
pensions, 27.8
precedents, 27.12
trusts, 27.11
civil partnerships, and, 24.1
codicils
generally, 24.1–24.5
precedent, 24.6
generally, 24.1–24.5
married couples with children
adult children, 27.4
generally, 27.1–27.3
minor children, 27.5–27.7
pensions, 27.8
Complete wills – *contd*
married couples with children – *contd*
precedents, 27.12
remarriage, 27.9–27.10
trusts, 27.11
married couples with no children
generally, 26.1
precedents, 26.2
non-dispositive clauses, 24.6
pensions, 27.8
precedents
civil partners with children, 27.1–27.12
codicils, 24.6
married couples with children, 27.1–27.12
married couples with no children, 26.1–26.2
non-dispositive clauses, 24.6
second marriages, 29.1–29.3
single persons, 25.1–25.2
unmarried couples with children, 28.1–28.2
second marriages or civil partnerships where are children of first marriage, 29.1–29.3
single persons
generally, 25.1
precedents, 25.2
trusts, 27.11
unmarried couples with children
generally, 28.1
precedents, 28.2
Complexity
drafting issues, 1.2
Conflict of laws
essential validity of wills, and, 6.12–6.17
Contentious probate claims
fraud, 2.30
generally, 2.14–2.15
improper execution, 2.16–2.18
knowledge and approval, 2.24–2.27
lack of testamentary capacity, 2.19–2.23
undue influence, 2.28–2.29
Court of Protection
statutory wills and codicils
attestation clause, 30.28
best interests, 30.11–30.17
commencement, 30.28
execution, 30.26–30.27
generally, 30.8–30.10
introduction, 30.1
jurisdiction, 30.2–30.7
precedents, 30.28
procedure, 30.18–30.25
Cremation
declaration of wishes, 7.3
expenses, 7.5

Cremation – *contd*
generally, 7.6
precedents, 7.9
Custodian appointments
trustees' powers
generally, 19.23–19.29
statutory provisions, 34.43–34.50

Debts
gifts of chattels, 12.14
Declarations
accrual clause, 20.8
ademption, 20.11
adopted children, 20.3
foreign issues, 6.23
funeral, burial and cremation, 7.1–7.9
illegitimate children, 20.3
intermediate income, 20.2
introduction, 20.1
lapse, 20.7
legitimated children, 20.3
precedents, 20.12
satisfaction, 20.9–20.10
stepchildren, 20.4
survivorship, 20.5–20.8
Deed of variation
disclaimer, 31.8–31.9
generally, 31.10–31.18
introduction, 31.1–31.7
precedents, 31.19
Delegation
trustees' powers, 19.15–19.22
Demonstrative legacies
generally, 10.2
Digital assets
current rules, 15.5–15.6
difficulty issues, 15.16
gifts, 15.13–15.15
identification, 15.7
introduction, 15.1–15.4
jurisdiction, 15.9
List, 15.12
meaning, 15.1
practical problems, 15.7–15.11
precedents, 15.17
realisation, 15.8
Directions
legacies, and, 10.8–10.9
Disabled beneficiaries
capital gains tax, 18.12–18.15
drafting considerations, 18.21–18.23
flexibility, 18.2–18.5
income tax, 18.12–18.15
inheritance tax, 18.6–18.11
introduction, 18.1
means tested benefits, 18.16–18.20
precedents, 18.24
Disabled person's interest
inheritance tax, 22.14
Disclaimer
appointment of guardians, 9.12
post-death variations, 31.8–31.9
Discretionary trusts
letters
appointment ending short term trust within two years of death, 32.8
generally, 32.5
residuary gifts, 16.28–16.29
Discrimination
charitable gifts, 14.5
Disposal of testator's body
declaration of wishes, 7.1–7.4
Dissolution of civil partnership
revocation of wills, 4.8–4.9
Distribution of residuary estate
intestacy rules, and, 2.4
Divorce
changing circumstances, 2.52
revocation of wills, 4.8–4.9
Domicile
essential validity of wills, and, 6.7–6.10
Donatio mortis causa
general considerations, 2.44
Donation of the body
declaration of wishes, 7.7–7.8
Drafting
civil partnerships, 1.6
complexity, 1.2
gender recognition, 1.7
general considerations
binding of wills, 2.56–2.57
changing circumstances, 2.46–2.55
contentious probate claims, 2.14–2.30
donatio mortis causa, 2.44
foreign issues, 2.45
inheritance provision claims, 2.31–2.43
intestacy rules, 2.2–2.7
introduction, 2.1
joint property, 2.8–2.13
Inheritance and Trustees Powers Act 2014, and, 1.9
introduction, 1.1–1.9
Perpetuities and Accumulations Act 2009, and, 1.8
Draftspersons
legacies, and, 10.14
Duty of care
trustees' powers
generally, 19.30
statutory provisions, 34.30–34.31, 34.61

Essential validity of wills
conflict of laws, 6.12–6.17
domicile, 6.7–6.10

Essential validity of wills – *contd*
EU Regulation 650/2012, 6.18–6.22
immovable property, 6.11
introduction, 6.6
movable property, 6.11
private international law of succession, 6.12–6.17
Execution
statutory wills and codicils, 30.26–30.27
Executors
appointment
accountants, and, 8.23
advice to testator, 8.2–8.4
beneficiaries, and, 8.11–8.13
business acquaintances, and, 8.14–8.15
common appointments, 8.10
definitions, 8.1
friends, and, 8.14–8.15
public trustees, and, 8.26
solicitors, and, 8.16–8.22
trust corporations, and, 8.24–8.25
business interests, and, 13.35–13.36
fees, 8.27–8.31
legacies, 8.32
meaning, 8.1
precedents, 8.33
professional charges clause, 8.33
remuneration, 8.27–8.31
role, 8.5–8.9
Executrix
meaning, 8.1
Exempt beneficiaries
inheritance tax, 23.17–23.19
Expenses
funeral wishes, 7.5

Farming business
business interests, 13.30–13.32
'Favoured' trusts
inheritance tax, 22.14
Fees
executors and trustees, and
generally, 8.27–8.31
precedents, 8.33
Foreign issues
essential validity of wills
conflict of laws, 6.12–6.17
domicile, 6.7–6.10
EU Regulation 650/2012, 6.18–6.22
immovable property, 6.11
introduction, 6.6
movable property, 6.11
private international law of succession, 6.12–6.17
formal validity of wills
international wills, 6.3–6.5
made outside England and Wales, 6.2
general considerations, 2.45
Foreign issues – *contd*
introduction, 6.1
location of declarations, 6.23
precedents, 6.24
Formal validity of wills
attestation, 21.1
international wills, 6.3–6.5
made outside England and Wales, 6.2
Fraud
contentious probate claims, 2.30
Free of tax provision
inheritance tax, 23.8
Friends
appointment of executors, 8.14–8.15
Funeral wishes
cremation, 7.6
declarations, 7.1–7.4
donation of the body, 7.7–7.8
expenses, 7.5
precedents, 7.9

Gender recognition
drafting issues, 1.7
General anti-abuse rules
inheritance tax, 22.36
General legacies
generally, 10.2
Gifts
abatement
generally, 10.10
introduction, 10.1
chattels, of
bank accounts, 12.17
collections, 12.8
debts, 12.14
generally, 12.4–12.7
inheritance tax, 12.3
need, 12.1–12.2
personal chattels, 12.4–12.7
precedents, 12.16
releases, 12.14
rights of selection, 12.9–12.11
shares, 12.15–12.16
subject to charge, 12.12–12.13
demonstrative legacies, 10.2
digital assets, and, 15.13–15.15
directions, and, 10.8–10.9
draftsperson, to, 10.14
executors and trustees, and, 8.32
general legacies, 10.2
gifts free of inheritance tax, 10.5–10.7
interest, 10.9
introduction, 10.1–10.4
nil rate band legacies, 10.13
pecuniary legacies
abatement, 10.10
generally, 10.1–10.2
interest, 10.9

Gifts – *contd*
precedents, 10.15
priority, 10.8–10.10
purpose, 10.1
real property, of
ademption, 11.6
beneficial share, 11.8
consultation to beneficiaries, 11.13–11.14
delegation to beneficiaries, 11.12
inheritance tax, 11.22–11.23
land, 11.1–11.3
minors, 11.7
mortgages, 11.4–11.5
powers of management, 11.9–11.11
precedents, 11.24
right of occupation, 11.15–11.18
right of residence by will, 11.19–11.21
trust, on, 11.7
residuary, of
age contingent gifts, 16.13–16.24
class gifts, 16.25–16.27
discretionary trusts, 16.28–16.29
introduction, 16.1–16.3
lapse, 16.25–16.27
precedents, 16.30
survivorship clauses, 16.4–16.12
'sweep all' provision, as, 16.1
transferable nil rate band, 16.5
'wait and see' provisions, 16.16
satisfaction of debts, 10.11–10.12
specific legacies
chattels, of, 12.1–12.16
generally, 10.3
real property, of, 11.1–11.24
timing, 10.8–10.10
Gifts free of inheritance tax
legacies, and, 10.5–10.7
Gifts with reservation
inheritance tax, 22.34
Grossing up
inheritance tax, and, 23.8
Guardians
appointment
conditionality, 9.6
consent of proposed guardian, 9.12
disclaimer, 9.12
generally, 9.4–9.8
interrelationship with trustees, 9.13
introduction, 9.1–9.3
jurisdiction of court, 9.8
other guardians, by, 9.7
precedents, 9.14
revocation, 9.9–9.11

Human tissue donation
declaration of wishes, 7.7–7.8

Identity of testator
opening provisions, and, 4.2–4.4
Illegitimate children
declarations, 20.3
Immediate post death interests
inheritance tax, 22.14
minors, 17.10
Immovable property
essential validity of wills, and, 6.11
Improper execution
contentious probate claims, 2.16–2.18
Incapacity
contentious probate claims, 2.19–2.23
statutory wills and codicils
attestation clause, 30.28
best interests, 30.11–30.17
commencement, 30.28
execution, 30.26–30.27
generally, 30.8–30.10
introduction, 30.1
jurisdiction, 30.2–30.7
precedents, 30.28
procedure, 30.18–30.25
Income tax
disabled and vulnerable beneficiaries, 18.12–18.15
minors, 17.13–17.16
Inheritance and Trustees Powers Act 2014
drafting issues, 1.9
Inheritance provision claims
general considerations, 2.31–2.43
Inheritance tax
age contingent gifts, 22.17–22.21
allocation, 22.28–22.30
anti-avoidance, 22.34–22.36
associated operations, 22.36
burden, 22.28–22.30
charitable gifts
generally, 22.26–22.27
introduction, 14.2
reduced rate, 14.6–14.11
death, on, 22.5–22.8
disabled and vulnerable beneficiaries, 18.6–18.11
disabled person's interest, 22.14
'favoured' trusts. 22.14
foreign aspect, 22.31–22.33
general anti-abuse rules, 22.36
gifts with reservation, 22.34
HMRC Press Release (6 August 1975), 36.9
immediate post death interests, 22.14
interest in possession, 22.13–22.14
introduction, 22.1–22.2
lifetime transfers, on, 22.9–22.11
minors, 17.6–17.12

Inheritance tax – *contd*
mitigation
agricultural property, 23.4–23.7
business property, 23.4–23.7
charitable gifts, 23.20
exempt beneficiaries, 23.17–23.19
free of tax provision, 23.8
grossing up, and, 23.8
introduction, 23.1–23.3
life interests, 23.17–23.19
nil rate band gifts, 23.14–23.16
precedents, 23.24
short term discretionary trusts, 23.21–23.23
transferable nil rate bands, 23.9–23.13
nil rate band, 22.4
outline, 22.3–22.4
potentially exempt transfers, 22.4
precedents, 22.37
pre-owned asset charge, 22.34–22.35
qualifying interests in possession, 22.13
relevant property
drafting wills, 22.16
generally, 22.13
settlements, 22.12–22.17
specific gifts of real property, 11.22–11.23
spouse exemption, 22.22
Statement of Practice 10/79, 36.8
statutory provisions, 36.1–36.7
transferable nil rate bands, 22.23–22.25
transfers of value, 22.3
transitional serial interests, 22.14
Instructions
arrangements for taking, 3.5–3.13
cancellation of contracts, and, 3.8
checklist, 3.25
codes of practice, 3.2–3.4
introduction, 3.1
IPW Code of Practice, 3.3
other matters, 3.23–3.24
protocols, 3.2–3.4
STEP Code for Will Preparation, 3.3
taking, 3.14–3.22
'Wills and Inheritance Protocol' (Law Society), 3.2
Institute of Professional Willwriters (IPW)
appointment of executors and trustees, 8.2
code of practice, 3.3
Insurance
trustees' powers
generally, 19.13
statutory provisions, 34.1
Interest
legacies, and, 10.9
Interest in possession
inheritance tax, 22.13–22.14
Intermediate income
declarations, 20.2
International wills
formal validity, 6.3–6.5
Intestacy rules
general considerations, 2.2–2.7
statutory provisions, 35.1–35.3
Investment
trustees' powers
generally, 19.9–19.12
statutory provisions, 34.32–34.35

Joint property
general considerations, 2.8–2.13
Joint wills
generally, 5.2
precedents, 5.11
Jurisdictional effect of wills
essential validity
conflict of laws, 6.12–6.17
domicile, 6.7–6.10
EU Regulation 650/2012, 6.18–6.22
immovable property, 6.11
introduction, 6.6
movable property, 6.11
private international law of succession, 6.12–6.17
formal validity
international wills, 6.3–6.5
made outside England and Wales, 6.2
general considerations, 2.45
introduction, 6.1
location of declarations, 6.23
precedents, 6.24

Knowledge and approval
contentious probate claims, 2.24–2.27

Lack of capacity
contentious probate claims, 2.19–2.23
statutory wills and codicils
attestation clause, 30.28
best interests, 30.11–30.17
commencement, 30.28
execution, 30.26–30.27
generally, 30.8–30.10
introduction, 30.1
jurisdiction, 30.2–30.7
precedents, 30.28
procedure, 30.18–30.25
Land
specific gifts of real property, 11.1–11.3
Lapse
declarations, 20.7
residuary gifts, 16.25–16.27

Law Society
'Wills and Inheritance Protocol'
appointment of executors and trustees, 8.2
appointment of guardians, 9.2
generally, 3.2
Legacies
abatement
generally, 10.10
introduction, 10.1
chattels, of
bank accounts, 12.17
collections, 12.8
debts, 12.14
generally, 12.4–12.7
inheritance tax, 12.3
need, 12.1–12.2
personal chattels, 12.4–12.7
precedents, 12.16
releases, 12.14
rights of selection, 12.9–12.11
shares, 12.15–12.16
subject to charge, 12.12–12.13
demonstrative legacies, 10.2
digital assets, and, 15.13–15.15
directions, and, 10.8–10.9
draftsperson, to, 10.14
executors and trustees, and, 8.32
general legacies, 10.2
gifts free of inheritance tax, 10.5–10.7
interest, 10.9
introduction, 10.1–10.4
nil rate band legacies, 10.13
pecuniary legacies
abatement, 10.10
generally, 10.1–10.2
interest, 10.9
precedents, 10.15
priority, 10.8–10.10
purpose, 10.1
real property, of
ademption, 11.6
beneficial share, 11.8
consultation to beneficiaries, 11.13–11.14
delegation to beneficiaries, 11.12
inheritance tax, 11.22–11.23
land, 11.1–11.3
minors, 11.7
mortgages, 11.4–11.5
powers of management, 11.9–11.11
precedents, 11.24
right of occupation, 11.15–11.18
right of residence by will, 11.19–11.21
trust, on, 11.7
residuary, of
age contingent gifts, 16.13–16.24
class gifts, 16.25–16.27
Legacies – *contd*
residuary, of – *contd*
discretionary trusts, 16.28–16.29
introduction, 16.1–16.3
lapse, 16.25–16.27
precedents, 16.30
survivorship clauses, 16.4–16.12
'sweep all' provision, as, 16.1
transferable nil rate band, 16.5
'wait and see' provisions, 16.16
satisfaction of debts, 10.11–10.12
specific legacies
chattels, of, 12.1–12.16
generally, 10.3
real property, of, 11.1–11.24
timing, 10.8–10.10
Legitimated children
declarations, 20.3
statutory provisions, 33.26
Letters
discretionary trusts
appointment ending short term trust within two years of death, 32.8
generally, 32.5
enclosing wills for completion, 32.3
introduction, 32.1–32.2
life interest trusts, 32.4
notice of severance, 32.6
promissory note, 32.7
wills for completion, 32.3
Life interest trusts
letter concerning, 32.4
Life interests
inheritance tax, 23.17–23.19
Lifetime transfers
inheritance tax, 22.9–22.11
Limited liability partnerships
business interests, 13.27
Location of declarations
foreign issues, 6.23

Maintenance
trustees' powers
generally, 19.3–19.6
statutory provisions, 34.2
Management powers
specific gifts of real property, 11.9–11.11
trustees' powers, 19.9–19.12
Marriage
changing circumstances, 2.51
revocation of wills, 4.7
Married couples with children
adult children, 27.4
generally, 27.1–27.3
minor children, 27.5–27.7
pensions, 27.8
precedents, 27.12

Married couples with children – *contd*
remarriage, 27.9–27.10
trusts, 27.11
Married couples with no children
generally, 26.1
precedents, 26.2
Means tested benefits
disabled and vulnerable beneficiaries, 18.16–18.20
Minors
attestation, 21.8
capital gains tax, 17.13–17.16
immediate post death interest, 17.10
income tax, 17.13–17.16
inheritance tax, 17.6–17.12
introduction, 17.1
precedents, 17.20
receipt clauses, 17.2
specific gifts of real property, 11.7
summary of options, 17.17–17.19
trustee powers, 17.3–17.5
vulnerable persons' trusts, 17.13–17.14
Mirror wills
generally, 5.3
Mortgages
specific gifts of real property, 11.4–11.5
Movable property
essential validity of wills, and, 6.11
Mutual wills
generally, 5.4–5.10
precedents, 5.11

Nil-rate band discretionary trusts
business interests, 13.3
Nil rate band
generally, 22.4
gifts, 23.14–23.16
legacies, 10.13
Nominee appointments
trustees' powers
generally, 19.23–19.29
statutory provisions, 34.43–34.50
Non dispositive clauses
generally, 24.1–24.5
precedents, 24.6
Notice of severance
generally, 32.6
Nullity
revocation of wills, 4.8–4.9

Opening clauses
identity of testator, 4.2–4.4
introduction, 4.1

Parental responsibility
appointment of guardians, 9.3
Partial intestacy
intestacy rules, and, 2.2–2.3
Partnerships
business interests, 13.24–13.26
Pecuniary legacies
abatement, 10.10
generally, 10.1–10.2
interest, 10.9
Pensions
married couples with children, 27.8
Perpetuities and Accumulations Act 2009
drafting issues, 1.8
statutory provisions, 34.6–34.13
Personal chattels
gifts of chattels, 12.4–12.7
Personal circumstances
changing circumstances, 2.53
Post-death variations
deed, 31.10–31.18
disclaimer, 31.8–31.9
generally, 31.1–31.7
precedents, 31.19
Potentially exempt transfers
inheritance tax, 22.4
Powers of trustees
advancement, 19.7–19.8
appropriation, 19.42
borrowing, 19.14
business interests, and, 13.33–13.34
carrying on testator's business, 19.40
custodian appointments, 19.23–19.29
delegation, 19.15–19.22
duty of care, 19.30
insurance, 19.13
introduction, 19.1–19.2
investment, 19.9–19.12
maintenance, 19.3–19.6
management, 19.9–19.12
minors, and, 17.3–17.5
miscellaneous, 19.39
nominee appointments, 19.23–19.29
precedents, 19.45
purchase of trust assets, 19.41
STEP provisions, and, 19.43–19.44
trusts of land, 19.31–19.38
Pre-owned asset charge
inheritance tax, 22.34–22.35
Principal private residence
specific gifts of real property, 11.6
Priority
legacies, and, 10.8–10.10
Private international law
essential validity of wills, and, 6.12–6.17
Professional charges clause
generally, 8.27–8.31
precedent, 8.33
Promissory note
generally, 32.7
Protocols
taking instructions, and, 3.2–3.4

Public trustees
appointment of executors, 8.26
Purchase of trust assets
trustees' powers, 19.41

Qualifying interests in possession
inheritance tax, 22.13

Real property
ademption, 11.6
beneficial share, 11.8
consultation to beneficiaries, 11.13–11.14
delegation to beneficiaries, 11.11
inheritance tax, 11.22–11.23
land, 11.1–11.3
minors, 11.7
mortgages, 11.4–11.5
powers of management, 11.9–11.11
precedents, 11.24
principal private residence, 11.6
right of occupation, 11.15–11.18
right of residence by will, 11.19–11.21
trust, on, 11.7
trustees' powers of management, 11.9–11.11
Receipt clauses
minors, 17.2
Reciprocal wills
generally, 5.3
precedents, 5.11
Releases
gifts of chattels, 12.14
Relevant property regime
drafting wills, 22.16
generally, 22.13
Remuneration
executors and trustees, and
generally, 8.27–8.31
precedents, 8.33
statutory provisions, 34.54–34.57
Residuary gifts
age contingent gifts, 16.13–16.24
class gifts, 16.25–16.27
discretionary trusts, 16.28–16.29
introduction, 16.1–16.3
lapse, 16.25–16.27
precedents, 16.30
statutory provisions, 35.2–35.3
survivorship clauses, 16.4–16.12
'sweep all' provision, as, 16.1
transferable nil rate band, 16.5
'wait and see' provisions, 16.16
Revocation
appointment of guardians, 9.9–9.10
Revocation of wills
act of testator, by, 4.5–4.6
civil partnership, by, 4.7
conditional, 4.10
Revocation of wills – *contd*
dissolution of civil partnership, and, 4.8–4.9
divorce, and, 4.8–4.9
marriage, by, 4.7
nullity, and, 4.8–4.9
precedents, 4.11
Right of occupation
specific gifts of real property, 11.15–11.18
Right of residence by will
specific gifts of real property, 11.18–11.20
Rule against perpetuities
statutory provisions, 34.6

Satisfaction
declarations, 20.9–20.10
Satisfaction of debts
legacies, and, 10.11–10.12
Second marriages
where are children of first marriage, 29.1–29.3
Settlements
inheritance tax, 22.12–22.17
Shares
gifts of chattels, 12.15–12.16
Short term discretionary trusts
inheritance tax, 23.21–23.23
Signature of wills
advice to testator, 21.2–21.3
affidavit of due execution, and, 21.6
alteration of will, and, 21.3
beneficiaries, 21.10
blind persons
special clauses, 21.7
witnesses, as, 21.9
draftsperson's duty, 21.12–21.19
formalities for wills, and, 21.1
generally, 21.1–21.7
minors, 21.8
page signatures, 21.4
persons unable to read or write, 21.7
precedents, 21.19
presumption, 21.3
procedure, 21.2
signature, 21.1
special clauses, 21.7
statutory wills and codicils, 30.28
supervision of draftsperson, 21.5
witnesses, 21.8–21.11
Single persons
generally, 25.1
precedents, 25.2
Society of Trust and Estate Practitioners (STEP)
dispositive clause
generally, 24.2–24.3
precedents, 24.6

Society of Trust and Estate Practitioners (STEP) – *contd*
trustees' powers, and, 19.43–19.44
'Will Preparation in England & Wales'
appointment of executors and trustees, 8.2
generally, 3.3
Sole traders
business interests, 13.19–13.21
Solicitors
appointment of executors, 8.16–8.22
Specific gifts
generally, 10.3
Specific gifts of real property
ademption, 11.6
beneficial share, 11.9
consultation to beneficiaries, 11.13–11.14
delegation to beneficiaries, 11.12
inheritance tax, 11.22–11.23
land, 11.1–11.3
minors, 11.7
mortgages, 11.4–11.5
powers of management, 11.9–11.11
precedents, 11.24
right of occupation, 11.15–11.18
right of residence by will, 11.19–11.21
trust, on, 11.7
Spouse exemption
inheritance tax, 22.22
Statutory trusts
statutory provisions, 35.2–35.3
Statutory wills and codicils
attestation clause, 30.28
best interests, 30.11–30.17
commencement, 30.28
execution, 30.26–30.27
generally, 30.8–30.10
introduction, 30.1
jurisdiction, 30.2–30.7
precedents, 30.28
procedure, 30.18–30.25
Stepchildren
declarations, 20.4
Succession
private international law, 6.12–6.17
statutory provisions, 35.1
Survivorship
declarations, 20.5–20.8
residuary gifts, 16.4–16.12
'Sweep all' provision
residuary gifts, 16.1

Taking instructions
arrangements, 3.5–3.13
cancellation of contracts, and, 3.8
checklist, 3.25
codes of practice, 3.2–3.4
generally, 3.14–3.22
Taking instructions – *contd*
introduction, 3.1
IPW Code of Practice, 3.3
other matters, 3.23–3.24
protocols, 3.2–3.4
STEP Code for Will Preparation, 3.3
'Wills and Inheritance Protocol' (Law Society), 3.2
Tax relief
business interests, 13.2–13.15
Testamentary capacity
contentious probate claims, 2.19–2.23
Testator's body
declaration of wishes, 7.1–7.4
Transferable nil rate band
generally, 22.23–22.25
residuary gifts, 16.5
use, 23.9–23.13
Transfers of value
inheritance tax, 22.3
Transitional serial interests
inheritance tax, 22.14
Trust corporations
appointment of executors, 8.24–8.25
Trustees
appointment
accountants, and, 8.23
advice to testator, 8.2–8.4
beneficiaries, and, 8.11–8.13
business acquaintances, and, 8.14–8.15
common appointments, 8.10
definitions, 8.1
friends, and, 8.14–8.15
public trustees, and, 8.26
solicitors, and, 8.16–8.22
trust corporations, and, 8.24–8.25
business interests, and, 13.33–13.34
fees, 8.27–8.31
legacies, 8.32
meaning, 8.1
precedents, 8.33
professional charges clause, 8.33
remuneration
generally, 8.27–8.31
statutory provisions, 34.54–34.57
role, 8.5–8.9
Trustees' powers
acquisition of land
generally, 19.30
statutory provisions, 34.36–34.37
advancement
generally, 19.7–19.8
statutory provisions, 34.3
agents
generally, 19.23–19.29
statutory provisions, 34.38–34.42
appropriation, 19.42
borrowing, 19.14

Trustees' powers – *contd*
business interests, and, 13.33–13.34
carrying on testator's business, 19.40
custodian appointments
generally, 19.23–19.29
statutory provisions, 34.43–34.50
delegation, 19.15–19.22
duty of care
generally, 19.30
statutory provisions, 34.30–34.31, 34.61
insurance
generally, 19.13
statutory provisions, 34.1
introduction, 19.1–19.2
investment
generally, 19.9–19.12
statutory provisions, 34.32–34.35
liability for agents, nominees and custodians
generally, 19.25–19.29
statutory provisions, 34.48–34.50
maintenance
generally, 19.3–19.6
statutory provisions, 34.2
management, 19.9–19.12
minors, and, 17.3–17.5
miscellaneous, 19.39
nominee appointments
generally, 19.23–19.29
statutory provisions, 34.43–34.50
precedents, 19.45
purchase of trust assets, 19.41
review of liability for agents, nominees and custodians
generally, 19.25–19.29
statutory provisions, 34.48–34.50
statutory provisions, 34.1–34.61
STEP provisions, and, 19.43–19.44
trusts of land
generally, 19.31–19.38
statutory provisions, 34.14–34.29
Trusts
married couples with children, 27.11
specific gifts of real property, 11.7
Trusts of land
generally, 19.31–19.38
statutory provisions, 34.14–34.29

Undue influence
contentious probate claims, 2.28–2.29
Unmarried couples with children
generally, 28.1
precedents, 28.2

Validity of wills
essential validity
conflict of laws, 6.12–6.17
domicile, 6.7–6.10
EU Regulation 650/2012, 6.18–6.22
immovable property, 6.11
introduction, 6.6
movable property, 6.11
private international law of succession, 6.12–6.17
formal validity
international wills, 6.3–6.5
made outside England and Wales, 6.2
general considerations, 2.45
introduction, 6.1
precedents, 6.24
Variations after death
deed, 31.10–31.18
disclaimer, 31.8–31.9
generally, 31.1–31.7
precedents, 31.19
Vulnerable beneficiaries
capital gains tax, 18.12–18.15
drafting considerations, 18.21–18.23
flexibility, 18.2–18.5
income tax, 18.12–18.15
inheritance tax, 18.6–18.11
introduction, 18.1
means tested benefits, 18.16–18.20
precedents, 18.24
Vulnerable persons' trusts
minors, 17.13–17.14

'Wait and see' provisions
residuary gifts, 16.16
'Will Preparation in England & Wales' (STEP)
appointment of executors and trustees, 8.2
taking instructions, 3.3
'Wills and Inheritance Protocol' (Law Society)
appointment of executors and trustees, 8.2
appointment of guardians, 9.2
taking instructions, 3.2
Wills in Court of Protection
best interests, 30.11–30.17
execution, 30.26–30.27
generally, 30.8–30.10
introduction, 30.1
jurisdiction, 30.2–30.7
precedents, 30.28
procedure, 30.18–30.25
Witnesses
attestation, 21.8–21.11